RUSSIA
IN REVOLUTION

Editor

RICHARD M. BRACE
Northwestern University

SNYDER, LOUIS L.—*The Imperialism Reader: Documents and Readings on Modern Expansionism*

SNYDER, LOUIS L.—*The Dynamics of Nationalism: Readings in Its Meaning and Development*

DOWNS, NORTON—*Medieval Pageant: Readings in Medieval History*

PAGE, STANLEY W.—*Russia in Revolution: Selected Readings in Russian Domestic History Since 1855*

RUSSIA

IN REVOLUTION

by

STANLEY W. PAGE

Professor of History
The City College of the
City University of New York

Selected Readings in
Russian Domestic History
Since 1855

D. VAN NOSTRAND COMPANY, INC.

PRINCETON, NEW JERSEY

TORONTO   LONDON

NEW YORK

D. VAN NOSTRAND COMPANY, INC.
120 Alexander St., Princeton, New Jersey (*Principal office*)
24 West 40 Street, New York 18, New York

D. VAN NOSTRAND COMPANY, LTD.
358, Kensington High Street, London, W.14, England

D. VAN NOSTRAND COMPANY (Canada), LTD.
25 Hollinger Road, Toronto 16, Canada

First Published January 1965
Reprinted August 1966

To my students

Preface

The purpose of this book is to provide the student of modern Russian history with meaningful insights into the characteristic conditions of Russian life since 1855, when the great reforms of Alexander II began to be instituted. The title *Russia in Revolution* is intended to suggest the constant process of change that has from that time to the present been so manifest in Russian history. That process became greatly accelerated after 1917 and more so after 1928.

I have for the most part relied on primary sources; indeed, most of the readings are by contemporaries of, or eye-witnesses to, the events described. The selections were chosen not only for their historical significance but also for their readability. I have, on the whole, attempted to do without legalistic documents, governmental proclamations, official speeches, and the like, in order to be able to reveal life as it was lived. The stress, in short, is not so much on what the government did or failed to do, but rather on the way that conditions of life led to changes and on the ways that changing conditions affected the people.

Inevitably there were space limitations. I tried to find appropriate readings to cover the periods dealt with, but I make no claim to having blanketed each one so that further reading would not be called for. As the subtitle of the book indicates, I have confined myself to domestic affairs, omitting readings pertaining to foreign affairs, diplomacy, and military campaigns. I was able only to touch in passing upon cultural and religious matters and the situation of the national minority peoples of the Imperial, and Soviet, Russian empires. I regret these omissions, but to do justice to currents in literature and music, to the story of the Church, and to the many national groups that have in one way or another shared the fate of the Russian people over the past century would have required another volume the size of this one. I have also kept clear of economic tables and statistical data because they are, usually, abhorrent to the average student of history. As a teacher I know only too well that students learn best when they enjoy their reading.

Each section is preceded by an introduction. The introductions are not intended to cover all aspects of life that might fall under the caption of a given section. They serve two purposes: to present a brief outline of the major events of a period, and to summarize the material contained in the readings. I might add that I have provided reasonably long readings, because short pieces do not give the student much feeling for an historical situation.

The translations into English are all my own. In transliterating Russian book titles or proper names I have endeavored only to make them as simple as possible for English-speaking students to read. In editing and sometimes bracketing items in the readings originally in English, my sole motive was to save space. I was not trying to improve on the author's style or change his meaning. I never altered the spelling an author used for a Russian word or proper name, even though that meant that his and my transliteration might vary. Thus the reader will find, for instance, the name Milyukov—my spelling—also rendered as Miliukov or Miliukoff. My hope is that common sense will make it clear to the reader that various spellings of a Russian name do not alter the identity of the person in question. The same rule also applies to the different spellings of English words: English as against American, archaic as against contemporary. Also, if an author used a Russian word and italicized it, I left that unchanged, although the same word may not be italicized in the writing of some other author or in my introductions. Had I attempted to standardize all the variants, I would have faced problems that would have defied solution.

The use of plurals for such Russian words as *guberniya, zemstvo,* and *volost* presented a problem, but since the non-Russian reading student would not understand the meaning of the Russian word endings, I have used the English "s" as the simplest way out of that dilemma. With regard to dates, my introductions follow the new-style calendar, but some of the authors used the old style. To avoid confusion, one need only keep in mind that Russian writers, writing before 1918, used the old style, whereas most writers dealing with the period since use the new style—that is, the modern calendar.

In omitting words or passages I employed the customary devices. But in cases where the need to save space or to eliminate superfluous material would have entailed the use of too many distracting dots, I took the liberty of adapting and abridging. I have noted that fact in each instance. However, even in such cases I have been careful to preserve intact the original ideas and language; whenever I have substituted my own words or phrases, I have so indicated by the use of brackets.

In conclusion, I want to thank Joyce Plosky. Much that is in here and much that was omitted can be attributed to her astute critical judgment.

S W P

Acknowledgments

We are grateful to the following publishers and authors for permission to use their material: from the translation of I. Turgenev's *Fathers and Sons,* by permission of The Greystone Press, New York; reprinted from *Roots of Revolution* by F. Venturi, by permission of Alfred A. Knopf, Inc. Copyright © 1960 by George Weidenfeld & Nicolson Ltd.; from "The Case of Vera Zasulich" by S. Kucherov, by permission of *The Russian Review;* from "Factory Inspection Under the 'Witte System': 1892-1903" by T. H. von Laue, by permission of *The American Slavic and East European Review* and T. H. von Laue; from "The Russian Intelligentsia of the 1890's" by A. K. Wildman, by permission of *The American Slavic and East European Review* and A. K. Wildman; from V. I. Lenin, *Collected Works,* IV, Book 2, by permission of International Publishers, New York; from the book *Workers Before and After Lenin* by Manya Gordon. Copyright, 1941, by E. P. Dutton & Co., Inc., New York. Reprinted by permission of the publishers; from A. Levin, *The Second Duma,* by permission of Yale University Press, New Haven; from H. W. Williams, *Russia of the Russians,* by permission of Sir Isaac Pitman & Sons Limited, London; from V. Chernov, *The Great Russian Revolution,* by permission of Yale University Press, New Haven; from R. Fülöp-Miller, *Rasputin, The Holy Devil,* Viking Press, New York, by permission of the author; from R. H. Bruce Lockhart, *British Agent,* G. P. Putnam's Sons, London, by permission of Peter Janson-Smith Ltd., London; from J. Pollock, "The Russian Revolution, "A Review by an Onlooker," *The Nineteenth Century and After,* by permission of *The Twentieth Century,* London; reprinted with the permission of the publisher from *The Grinding Mill* by A. Lobanov-Rostovsky. Copyright 1935 by The Macmillan Co., New York; from *New Horizons* by Olga Tchernoff, 1936, by permission of The Hutchinson Publishing Group, London; from Sophia Kossak-Szucka, *The Blaze: Reminiscences of Volhynia, 1917-1919,* by permission of George Allen & Unwin Ltd., London; from *The Way of a Transgressor,* copyright, 1936, by Negley Farson. Reprinted by permission of Harcourt, Brace & World, Inc.; from John Reed, *Ten Days That Shook the World,* by permission of Random House, Inc., New York; from A. Gordon, *Russian Civil War,* by permission of Cassell & Co., London; from "The Case of Mrs. Stan Harding," *The Nineteenth Century and After,* by permission of *The Twentieth Century,* London; from *I Write As I Please,* copyright, 1935, by Walter Duranty. Reprinted by permission of Simon and Schuster, Inc., New York; from C. E. Bechhofer, *Through Starving Russia,* by permission of Curtis Brown Ltd., London; from *I Change*

Worlds by Anna Louise Strong. Copyright 1935 by Holt, Rinehart and Winston, Inc., reprinted by permission of Holt, Rinehart and Winston, Inc., New York, and Routledge & Kegan Paul Ltd., London; from W. Reswick, *I Dreamt Revolution,* by permission of Henry Regnery Company, Chicago; from J. Stalin, *Interviews with Foreign Workers' Delegation,* by permission of International Publishers, New York; reprinted with the permission of Charles Scribner's Sons, from *These Russians,* pp. 2-5, 8-10, 12-14, 22-30, 42-56, 67-73, 75-79, 80, 85, 87-93, 95-97, 107-109, 111-113, 119-123, 125-126, 129-134, 137-138, 157, 210-213, 262-264, 358, 360-362, by William C. White. Copyright 1931 Charles Scribner's Sons, New York—renewal copyright © 1959 by Ruth White; from V. Kravchenko, *I Chose Freedom,* Charles Scribner's Sons, New York, by permission of Gerald Dickler, New York, and Robert Hale Limited, London; from C. B. Hoover, *The Economic Life of Soviet Russia,* The Macmillan Co., New York, by permission of C. B. Hoover; from *My Lives in Russia* by Markoosha Fischer, published by Harper & Brothers. Copyright, 1944, by Markoosha Fischer. Reprinted by permission of Brandt & Brandt; from *Sons* by V. A. Smirnov. Reprinted by permission of Doubleday and Company, Inc., Garden City, N.Y.; from G. Klimov, *The Terror Machine,* by permission of Faber and Faber Ltd., London, and Frederick A. Praeger, Inc., New York; to Constantin Krypton; reprinted from *Leningrad* by A. Werth, by permission of Alfred A. Knopf, Inc., New York. Copyright 1944 by Alexander Werth; from Q. Reynolds, *The Curtain Rises,* by permission of Random House, New York; from *Journey Among Warriors* by Eve Curie. Copyright 1943 by Eve Curie. Reprinted by permission of Doubleday and Company, Inc., New York, Curtis Brown, Ltd., London, and William Heinemann Ltd., London; from E. Winter, *I Saw the Russian People,* Little, Brown, Boston, by permission of Ella Winter; from *My Three Years in Moscow,* by Walter Bedell Smith. Copyright 1949 by Walter Bedell Smith. Published by J. B. Lippincott Company. By permission of J. B. Lippincott Company, Philadelphia, and William Heinemann Ltd., London, which published this book under the title of *Moscow Mission;* from F. Rounds, Jr., *A Window on Red Square,* by permission of Houghton Mifflin Company, Boston; from A. Zr., "Poems Underground," *Harper's Magazine,* by permission of A. Zr. (pseudonym); from D. Burg, "The Voice of a Dissenter, An Interview with a Graduate of Moscow University," *Harper's Magazine,* by permission of David Burg (pseudonym); from *Soviet Attitudes, Report No. 3,* by permission of American Committee for Liberation, New York; from the translation "Under the Dark Vaults of the Synagogue," *Minskaya Pravda,* by permission of Moshe Decter, Director, Jewish Minorities Research, New York; and from "In the Schools of America (Notes of a Soviet Educator)" by Z. Malkova, *The Soviet Review,* Summer, 1963, by permission of *The Soviet Review;* from Henry Tanner, "Khrushchev Ouster: Reaction in Moscow," copyright © 1964 by *The New York Times.*

Table of Contents

SECTION 3—RISE OF BOLSHEVIK POWER AMID ANARCHY

SECTION 4—NEP AND PLANNED ECONOMY

SECTION 5—WORLD WAR II AND AFTER

Section 1

Backdrop to Revolution

THE REGIMENTED PAST

"How sad our Russia is!" exclaimed Pushkin, the father of Russian literature, upon hearing Gogol read passages from his novel *Dead Souls*. All the great Russian authors since Pushkin's time—he died in 1837—have produced sensitive heroes whose lives are marked by restlessness and futility. The common folk, as they appear in the great novels, often share a kind of hangdog brutish resignation, as though some overwhelming force was pressing upon them, keeping them bent and close to the ground.

Geography, or better, topography, the infinite flatness of the great Eurasian plain coupled with the historical consequences derived from its circumstance, have done much to shape the national mood. Traveling through Russia early in the nineteenth century, Madame de Staël felt as though her speedily drawn carriage was making no progress through the monotonous land: "The country appeared to me as the image of infinite space that would take an eternity to pass through." Augustus Hare, a traveler in the 1880's, writes of the impression of "intense desolation" caused by the "vast dreary plains" south of Moscow.[1] The German, Paul Distelbarth, entrained from Moscow to Stalingrad in 1953, found an "immense spaciousness into which all details seem to become absorbed. . . . The earth itself seems not yet to have come into the possession of man. . . . Seldom does one see villages, and these appear not as vital centers of human existence . . . but they crouch low in the folds of the land as though they wished to be invisible, as though not wishing to provoke an enemy."[2] On the Asiatic side of the Urals, Distelbarth found that the immense surfaces had an hypnotic power to which it was difficult not to succumb. But even if one did not, it was "still unavoidable that things seemed different after a few days. What seemed important in a smaller framework loses all meaning in the scope of the vast. . . . One thought oneself important and sees all at once that the individual is nothing at all."[3]

[1] A. Hare, *Studies in Russia,* London, 1885, p. 428.
[2] P. Distelbarth, *Russland Heute,* Hamburg, 1954, pp. 103-104.
[3] *Ibid.,* p. 183.

I

The easy traversability of the land on which the Russian people lived subjected them to constant invasions from almost every direction since times immemorial and unrecorded. But in the fifteenth century, Ivan III, Grand Prince of Moscow (1462-1505), asserted his claim to rule all the Russian people. Ivan IV (1547-1584) called himself Tsar, that is, Caesar, destroyed the economic and political power of the large landowning boyars, and gave out grants of land to the newly risen and ever-growing military-servitor class of gentry. While the fighters garrisoned and defended the borders, unmarked by natural impediments to invaders, their fields were tended by peasants who gradually fell into perpetual bondage.

Thus, out of military needs grew the Russian State. Brought to its authoritarian peak by Peter the Great (1689-1725), this regimented pyramid of human beings extended downward from the autocrat through the aristocratic estate and serf owners. Many of the latter served as chiefs of the bureaucracy—governors of provinces, marshals of the nobility, police officials, and so on—and as officers in the army and navy. The famous travel journals of the Marquis de Custine provide a meaningful glimpse into the nature of Russian life in 1839:

[On the morning of July 10], I obtained the liberty of entering Petersburg. . . . The morning is the time for commissions and errands, and not one individual appeared to be walking on his own account. . . . Everything was dull and regular as in a barrack. Military discipline reigns throughout Russia. . . .

Now appears a cavalry officer passing at full gallop to *bear an order* to some commanding officer; then a chasseur carrying *an order* to some provincial governor, perhaps at the other extremity of the empire, whither he proceeds in a . . . little Russian chariot, without springs or stuffed seat. . . . Next are seen foot soldiers returning . . . to their quarters . . . to *receive orders* from their captain. This automaton population resembles one side of a chess-board, where a single individual causes the movements of all the pieces, but where the adversary is invisible. One neither moves nor respires here except by an imperial order; consequently everything is dull, formal, and spiritless. Silence presides over and paralyses life. Officers, coachmen, Cossacks, serfs, courtiers, all servants under the same master, blindly obey the orders which they do not understand; it is certainly the perfection of discipline; but the sight of such perfection does not gratify me; so much regularity can only be obtained by the entire absence of independence.

Among this people bereft of time and of will, we see only bodies without souls, and tremble to think that, for so vast a multitude of arms and legs, there is only one head. . . .

When Peter the Great established what is here called the *tchin,* that is to say, when he applied the military system to the general administration of the empire, he changed his nation into a regiment of mutes, of which he declared himself and his successors the hereditary colonels.[4]

Regimentation was everywhere. The towns were few and far between because serfdom and its accompaniment, a largely immobile population, deprived the activity

[4] Marquis de Custine, *The Empire of the Czar,* 3 vols., London, 1843, I, pp. 142-147.

of merchants and craftsmen of all but local importance. The urban population, such as it was, was forced to live in their towns,[5] just as the peasants were bound to their estates. The town governments, artificially constructed upon Western (German) models, were introduced by Peter the Great and modified by Catherine the Great. Both Peter and Catherine (she created 216 towns in 23 years) hoped in vain that, by designating villages as towns and providing them with burgomasters, town councils, courts, and merchant and craft guilds—along with a multitude of instructions regarding trade and industry, sanitation, schools, police organization, and so on—they would somehow convert them into citadels of a flourishing bourgeoisie as had happened in the West. Actually, the towns remained shabby clusters of log buildings with muddy and unpaved streets and an atmosphere of somnolence.

Peasant life constituted the most arduous form of regimentation. Aside from the absolute power over the peasant's person[6] which the noble held, each peasant household within a commune owed the manor lord a certain amount of dues, payable in labor or in lambs, chickens, eggs, and money. The labor obligation, *tyaglo* (tax or obligation), was reckoned by the work of a man, a woman, and a horse over a three-day period. If a household contained two *tyagla,* or labor units, one of them might work for six days, liberating other members of the household to work in towns, where money for the family purse could be earned.

Heavy obligations were imposed upon the household, not only by the master, but also by the commune, which, though democratic in its procedures (ruling as it did through an assembly of heads of households), was collectively responsible for the taxes to be paid the State. Some persons, having been granted a passport by the commune, spent years working in far-off towns. But their obligation to the commune never ceased, and the commune had the power to call them back at any time. The commune also saw to it that each person did his rightful share of communal labor. Each household, therefore, was compelled to remain a composite of numerous marital units wherein the mother-in-law tyrannized over the daughters-in-law and the entire household suffered under the iron-fisted rule of the grandfather, an elder brother, or some other member of the family who acted as the head of the house.

As mentioned before, the sole justification for this regimented, and hence static and freedom-stifling, way of life was the supposed assurance it gave that Russia was secure against invasion. Surely, the steadily growing territory of the empire—from a domain of some 150,000 square miles in 1462, to a land mass bounded by Prussia and Austria in the West and China in the East, in the reign of Nicholas I (1825-1855)— gave eloquent testimony to the success of the military state. In addition, this huge

[5] There were three kinds of towns: provincial administrative centers, district administrative centers and towns having no role in territorial administration. The total number of town dwellers, registered as burghers, merchants or, artisans, according to the taxes they paid, was less than five million in 1877.

[6] This, depending on the master, might mean the right to flog or otherwise punish a peasant, to send him into the army, to determine whom he would marry, and even to sell him to another owner.

expanse served as a damper to those in Russia who felt that serfdom was an unmitigated evil, and that absolute monarchy impeded contact with the West, intellectual activity, and progress. The failure of Napoleon's *Grande Armée* in 1812, though
not really a triumph of Russian arms, had blown up the legend of Russia's might to
proportions that were quite unrealistic in view of technological advances that were
being made in western Europe.

But in 1854-1855, the great balloon was pricked when the relatively small forces of
England, France, and Turkey (not to mention Piedmont-Sardinia) defeated the
Russian troops in the Crimea, their own back yard, so to speak. Even worse, the
defeat had been accompanied by a scandalous stench of military incompetence and
official corruption. The sacred traditions of absolute monarchy, rigid bureaucratism,
and isolation from Western progressivism were clearly in need of drastic overhauling.
Liberal sentiment, so long hushed in the name of loyalty, now became extremely
vociferous in its demands for reform.

"The public feeling and aspirations," writes a contemporary observer, "were not
strong enough to conquer the traditional respect for the Imperial Will and create an
open opposition to the autocratic power, but they were strong enough to do great
things by aiding the Government, if the Emperor [Alexander II] voluntarily undertook a series of radical reforms." [7]

INADEQUATE REFORMS AND MARTYRS OF REVOLUTION

Early in 1856, in the conclusion of his Manifesto announcing the terms of the
Paris Peace Treaty that ended the Crimean War, Alexander II declared that "internal welfare" would be established and "truth and kindness" would reign in Russian courts, and he spoke of a newly developing "aspiration for enlightenment,"
allowing all to "enjoy the results of honest labor under . . . laws equally just for
all. . . ." Asked by an alarmed conservative, Count Zakrevsky, Governor-General
of Moscow, what that statement meant, Alexander said that he did not intend to
abolish serfdom by mere decree. However, he made it clear that he desired an early
emancipation of the serfs, while leaving it to the nobles to decide the manner in
which it should be done.

Even though it took almost five years and considerable prodding by the Tsar before the nobles' committees had performed their task, emancipation, nevertheless,
swept upon the Russian people like a tidal wave, to suddenly overturn the habits
of centuries and the conceptions regarding the legal, economic, and social status
of almost 48 million peasants. Somewhat less than half of them had been the virtual
slaves of landed nobles; the remainder, the serfs of the crown or State, enjoyed
greater personal freedom and suffered less in terms of service obligations. About

[7] D. M. Wallace, *Russia*, London, 1881, p. 448.

one million had served as household help or skilled artisans in and around the manor houses.

Almost all concerned, peasants as well as nobles, were bewildered by the problems of adjusting to the new way of life. The people of the towns, soon to become much more lively because of rapidly growing commercial and industrial activity, were likewise unprepared for the great change.

Following upon the proclamation of the Emancipation Edict on March 3, 1861, the Statutes of Emancipation, an enormous book of instructions, written in dry legalistic language, was distributed to every village by way of the local officials. It was meant to serve as a guide for determining what land was to be allotted to the peasants and for figuring the amounts of money due the noble in return for giving up land and the peasants' worth to him in terms of their labor in the fields (*barshchina*) or the money dues or tribute in kind (*obrok*) they had been obliged to give him. A two-year period was set for the solution of the complex problems that were sure to arise; the State or crown serfs were not freed until 1866. An effort was made to render the Statutes flexible by setting down stipulations intended to suit the general state of affairs in each of the many sections of the empire. However, no such rule of thumb could apply successfully since arrangements between lords and serfs varied from estate to estate and even from one peasant household to the next. Special arbitrators were appointed for each district to mediate between peasants and nobles and to meet at district and *guberniya* congresses for the purpose of threshing out the infinite number of knotty problems.

Since the new laws were naturally weighted in favor of the nobles, the peasants, being largely illiterate, were doubly distrustful. It is not hard to imagine the anxious state of mind that prevailed in the countryside during the transition from serfdom to emancipation.

The ardently progressive and humanitarian sentiment that flourished among the intelligentsia following the Crimean debacle received encouragement from the Tsar in the form of relaxed censorship rules. Alexander wanted the enlightened elements to enjoy relative freedom of expression so that they might help him in ridding the land of its slave-based property, class, and social relationships. The Zemstvo, a body of representatives elected on the district and *guberniya* levels, was introduced in most of European Russia in 1865. It replaced the rule of the local estate owners and the authority of the district and *guberniya* marshals of the nobility. A similar body, the Duma, appeared in towns and cities after 1870 in order to aid in administering the growingly complex urban life that was beginning to stir with commercial and industrial activity. The Zemstvos and Dumas conducted their affairs along distinctly Western parliamentary and democratic lines.

Even more important, because they did so much to liberate the spirit of the

lower classes from a long-inculcated sense of personal unworthiness, were the en-
actments of a veritable flood of reform measures dealing with crime and punishment, the establishment of a Western-style system of courts along with honest
judges and justices of the peace, and much-needed improvements in the hitherto
barbarous conditions of military service.

Liberalization in the sphere of education was also introduced. In 1859, the first
secondary schools, or gymnasia, for women were established. To the university
faculties in 1863 was restored the privilege, generally within the limits of the statute
of 1804, to run their institutions free from government supervision. In 1864, the
gymnasia were opened to young people of all classes and faiths. In the field of
primary education, it was left to the Zemstvos to add systematized public schools
to the meager and dubiously valuable educational facilities hitherto provided by the
Church or by progressive-minded individuals. Educational progress was curtailed
when an assassination attempt on the Tsar's life in 1866 brought the reactionary
Dmitry Tolstoy, High-Procurator of the Holy Synod, into the post of Minister of
Education. Striving in every way to stifle freedom of thought, his main success was
in loading the curriculum of the gymnasium adolescents with exercises in classical
languages and in mathematics. So fearful was Tolstoy of the spread of ideas that
he and his associates even tried to keep persons having higher education out of
the army where they might influence the lower classes in an "unhealthy" manner.

Whatever credit is due Alexander II for liberating the serfs and introducing many
reforms, it must be recognized that the Tsar-Emancipator was not a social scientist
or a community planner but an old-fashioned Russian autocrat with a touch of the
enlightened monarch. He was fully committed to the ways of bureaucracy and
firmly attached to the land-owning aristocracy. Had the emancipation been undertaken with the purpose, however long-range, of bringing economic, social, and
cultural benefits to the masses, it might well have led to significant improvements
in their dark and misery-laden lives. But such a purpose was not in the Emperor's
mind. Just as the good Lord said: "Let there be light," so Alexander, in effect, said:
"Let there be freedom." But the people themselves were never consulted about the
impending reforms.

The Tsar, as indicated by the Edict of Emancipation, was particularly concerned
with giving "the fatherland's well deserved recognition" to the "highminded nobility" for its "zealous and unselfish efforts on behalf of the common good." Where
the soil was rich, the nobles retained far too much of it, and were overcompensated
for whatever they gave up. The peasants were expected to pay them one-fifth of
the assessed value of the land directly, the remainder to be collected by the government in 49 annual installments intended to cover the $6\frac{1}{2}$ per cent interest-paying
bonds with which the government had reimbursed the landlords. Where the land

was poor, so that losing it meant little, the noble was generously compensated for the loss of dues formerly drawn from serfs who had earned money by working away from the village.

In one way or another, the peasants became burdened with impossible taxes. No provisions were made to educate the peasants for living under the new conditions, and the spontaneous progress that free people make, simply by moving about and making contact with others and by exercising the right to engage in individual enterprise, was largely prevented by the emancipation law which stipulated that the peasants remain legally bound to the commune. This was done mainly because the government wanted the peasants to be collectively responsible for paying off their indebtedness.

For administering village life, a new institution called the *volost* was established by law in the larger villages. The authority of the *volost* extended to neighboring smaller villages, and its officials were peasants elected by their fellows. So the blind led the blind, as the communal strait jacket, and the strait jacket of economic and legal disabilities, confined the peasants to their world of backwardness and ever-increasing poverty. Drunkenness frequently became the peasant's sole escape.

More and more peasants, driven by need, sought work in urban factories and were treated almost as though they were still serfs in the pre-emancipation commune. Indeed, these peasant-workers, returning each summer to their villages to farm the land, brought the communal spirit with them to the cities. Many lived in small co-operative groups, eating together and sharing expenses. The factory owners fed the workmen and paid them the lowest possible wages, sometimes keeping them waiting days for their pay. If they protested, they could be charged with striking and be sent to Siberia. At times, in case of a lockout, the factory owner accused the workers of revolutionism, and then soldiers would compel them to return to their workshops.

All told, the emancipation, coupled with the horrors resulting from incipient industrialization, had made the lot of the people unbearable. Among the youthful and idealistic intelligentsia, drawn from the various classes of a society now become socially mobile, bitterness rose against a regime and a social order so tied to its traditions of *noblesse oblige* and bureaucratic procedures that it was unable to fulfill its duty to the people. Although the adherents of Western-type liberalism (who had manifested themselves in Russia for decades prior to the emancipation and had helped it into being) were desirous of limiting the autocrat's powers, on the whole they thought in terms of progress within the existing social order. With such attitudes of fine talk and half measures, the young radicals lost all patience. Advocates of drastic change—the so-called Nihilists—in the early 1860's contented themselves largely by demonstrating their total contempt for the existing order and the past it rested upon. They did this through their rebellious manner of behavior and through the publication of literary tracts, most notably represented by Pisarev's *Annihilation of Aesthetics* and Chernyshevsky's *What Is to Be Done?*

The movement, however, soon gave way to sects of revolutionists who were determined to destroy the society they thought so rotten. It is noteworthy that already in their initial efforts at conspiratorial activity the revolutionists of post-emancipation Russia, trapped as they were between mass ignorance and bureaucratic persecution, began to formulate the patterns of theory and practice that were one way or another to be utilized by extremist socialists through 1917. It is clear from the case of Vera Zasulich, dealt with in this section, that by 1878 the martyrdom of the revolutionists had won them support among middle- and upper-class liberals, the persons they most despised.

POBEDONOSTSEV AND PLEHVE, GUARDIANS OF AUTOCRACY

From the point of view of the Russian government, the reforms of Alexander II had proved disappointing. Police and censorship controls had been relaxed in the period 1855-1875, and yet the educated elements had repaid the "kindness" by biting the hand that had loosened the leash. The youthful killers might be discounted as mad dogs, or "possessed ones," as Dostoevsky labeled them. But what about the socially "respectable" liberals who surely would not have dirtied their hands to fashion bombs? Did they not, despite their relatively moderate proposals for limiting the monarch's power and for other reforms, also lust for the blood of officialdom? Did they not boldly applaud the brutal acts of the young men and women assassins?

The main fault of the reforms was their inadequacy. But to Alexander III (1881-1894) and to his successor, Nicholas II (1894-1917), the reforms had erred in permitting too much freedom. Behind the attempts of Alexander III and Nicholas II to revivify the axiomatic absolutism of the Romanovs was the mastermind of Konstantin Pobedonostsev, the childhood teacher and closest associate of Alexander III and in the reign of both Tsars, the High-Procurator of the Holy Synod, that is, minister in charge of Church affairs. To Pobedonostsev, the various aspects of civil liberties—freedom of worship, freedom of thought and expression, the right to vote or to be elected—were all signs that the "poison of democracy" was at work. Pobedonostsev accurately perceived the ways in which Western democracy weakened a State's authority. Each religion was a self-contained body of laws. Therefore, unless it was the State-controlled religion, it would inevitably come into conflict with the dictates of the State. The masses under democracy were not in his opinion really free in their thinking, but subject to the influence of a handful of politicians and newspaper editors. The politicians and editors, needing on their side to cater to the ignorant majority, often sponsored unwise policies.

In short, any attempt at broadening the base of power or of increasing the number of channels through which ideas might reach the masses was harmful and would lead only to democracy and hence to the decay and destruction of the Russian State and its people. Thus was absolute autocracy justified. Until October, 1905, when Pobedonostsev resigned from active service, it was the principal aim of the Russian State to stifle all manifestations of popular thought and activity that went counter to the slogan "Orthodoxy, Autocracy, Nationalism (*Narodnost*)," [8] the trinity of words that stood for unquestioning subservience to the State.

This same doctrine had been enunciated by Nicholas I (1825-1855). From it his son Alexander II had found it necessary to deviate for the sake of progress. If the doctrine was obsolescent by 1855, it was even more so in the subsequent decades. The growing mobility of Russian society, the increase of travel and communications, the concentration of laborers in factories and cities, and the spreading of literacy had made for the relatively easy flow of ideas. The process whereby the Tsar had traditionally transmitted his wishes to a benighted populace through a small and all powerful land-owning bureaucracy was no longer effective. In the place of the ukase, instantly put into effect, grew the devious methods of the police-state apparatus, so characteristic of absolutism in the modern world.

The problem of maintaining the status quo of privilege and of curbing revolutionary activities now fell largely to police-minded officials. They and their underlings were drawn from the most corrupted and sadistic elements of society, for such were the types required to devise and execute the schemes designed to delude and terrorize the majority. This dirty business, requiring an utter lack of ethical considerations on the part of those who conducted it, was made even more cynical by pretensions of official honorability.

The "respectable" members of society wanted no part of this work. So long as they were able to pursue their pleasures without interference from the rabble, the upper classes had no interest in the "lower depths." So the poor, the dissident, and the pariahs (Jews, Poles, sectarians, and so on) were quite at the mercy of the venal brutes who remained so completely unmolested in their operations that they could easily manage to cheat their masters as well as those over whom they held the whip. They could torture people merely by carrying out the letter of the law, but they could also derive immense profit by accepting bribes for ignoring the law. Corruption, once sanctioned, soon became the normal way of life in the daily process of administration. This had its good sides, for many whose lives would have been unbearable were able to survive through bribery. The Russian police tyranny reached its apogee during the tenure of V. K. von Plehve as Minister of the Interior, 1902-1904.

Unrest fomented through persecutions and police agents, and then efficiently

---

[8] Nationalism, or *Narodnost,* referred to the ethnic pre-eminence of Great Russians in the empire.

crushed, proved Plehve's personal indispensability to the Tsar. Persecutions of defenseless groups had the additional merit, Plehve believed, of channeling the smoldering bitterness of the masses against the nonconformists. In the pogroms, sanctioned if not incited by the officials, the participants, by the rules of the game, might murder, rape, and loot the Jews. Thus "bread and circuses" were provided at little cost to the State.

Universal misery, however, could not be resolved by distractions. Peasant unrest, terrorist assassinations, and industrial strikes continued at an alarming rate. Arrests, beatings, and banishments to Siberia of thousands of martyrs only brought more martyrs to the fore. Plevhe's last *coup* (so it is said) was his deliberate effort to provoke the Japanese to start a war with Russia in the belief that a "small victorious war" would divert the people from thoughts of revolution.

Plehve, police agent *par excellence,* knew but one sin—that of permitting the wrath of the underfed to get out of control and cause discomfort to those whose wish it was to remain above the battle. Plehve did not live to see the end of the "small victorious war." In August, 1904, amid universal approval of the regime-haters, a university student, E. S. Sazonov, flung the bomb that ended his career.

THE GROWTH OF INDUSTRY

However rigidly the pharoah-like regime of Alexander III attempted to avoid moving its gaze forward, there was no forestalling the inevitable march toward capitalism and large-scale industrialization. Industry, appearing later in Russia than in Europe's other great nations, made rapid progress after 1880. The government of Alexander III tried desperately to prop up a dying agrarian elite, fearing the potentially constitutional and Western orientation of an industrial bourgeoisie. Still, it was aware of the connection between military and industrial power. The railway building boom, begun in the 1870's, was heartily sponsored by the regime for strategic reasons. Out of railway building grew rapid advances in metallurgy and coal mining. The government, and the Ministry of Finance, particularly, favored such industrial expansion. Foreign investments were encouraged and capital was brought into Russia by large exports, paid for through low peasant wages that produced a gold reserve, and through borrowing abroad—mainly from France. A good credit rating was established by prompt interest payments, made possible by means of taxes levied upon the lower classes. Protective tariffs, which kept the prices of industrial products high, and subsidization in the form of low tax rates for industrialists, further combined to load the major burdens of the rapid industrialization upon the backs of the poorest. In the 1880's and 1890's profits flowed into the coffers of the *nouveaux riches* and of foreign investors. The peasants and workers, meanwhile, spent far too much of their sweat-stained money in the taverns and wine shops.

Needless to say, Russia, with her vast store of unexploited resources, was a horn of plenty for investors, foreign or native. And the late start gave Russian industry the advantage of skipping the small-scale stages of industrialization and of moving directly toward large concentrations of production, personnel, and capital.

Thanks to Bunge, the first Minister of Finance in the reign of Alexander III, Russia's industrial revolution was initially accompanied by extremely progressive-minded labor legislation, including an elaborate program of factory inspection. However, in the tenure of Witte, appointed Finance Minister in 1892, humane considerations gave way to policies of *laissez-faire*. To Witte, nothing was more important for Russia than her industrial development, and he strove to subordinate all other factors in Russian society to that end. Witte's reorganization of 1894, according to Professor T. H. von Laue,

greatly altered the complexion of the factory inspectorate. Originally designed for the protection of the workers, it was now made a state agency for the promotion of industrialization. [The inspectors] now had the troublesome task of harmonizing the divergent interests of capital and labor. . . . As an agency designed to promote peace at the factory, the inspectorate was too frail . . . an instrument. The best energies of the factory inspectors were sapped by the subtle contradictions in their tasks. They could not entirely shake off the obligation . . . of feeling themselves the protectors of the workers in their free bargaining with their employers. They were apt to bring constant pressure upon their superiors to initiate more social legislation. On the other hand, they were also to promote industrial efficiency and production. They were defending the *status quo* at the factory in the name of legality. And finally, they were to prevent the subversion of the workers' loyalty when they themselves too often had no faith in the existing conditions at the factory. All these unresolved problems weakened their authority. . . . In addition, the management remained either woefully uninformed of the law and careless even when they were aware of its provisions; enforcement, as already stated, remained lax. . . . A still deeper ignorance prevailed among the workers, whose peasant sense of justice was naturally at odds with the predominantly liberal and Western conceptions of the Industrial Code. What particularly were they to make of the government's . . . abstention from any interference in dispute over wages and work hours? [These] key issues [were left] to the free play of economic and social forces which were bound to humiliate the peasants-come-to-the-factory.

And [finally,] unrest in the factories was not only the result of [labor] conditions; it stemmed from the elemental resentment of peasants forced into an alien environment by the poverty of their village. Of this more comprehensive aspect the factory inspectors and their superiors were only dimly aware, and in the contemporary social legislation they could find no answer whatever.[9]

Witte was not antilabor, but his insistence that nothing should retard production heightened the bitterness between labor and capital that, in turn, led to a growing

[9] T. H. von Laue, "Factory Inspection Under the 'Witte System': 1892-1903," *The American Slavic and East European Review*, October, 1960, pp. 347-362.

number of strikes. However, because the troops and the police suppressed them, these strikes, thanks to the indoctrination of the workers by socialistic groups, began to acquire the flavor of antigovernmental demonstrations. This feature led to conflict between Witte's Ministry of Finance and the powerful Ministry of the Interior. The latter, primarily concerned with preventing revolutionism, tended to favor governmental intervention on behalf of the laborers, through the efforts of police agents that were sent into factories to divert the friendly sentiments of the workers away from socialist agitators toward their beneficent Tsar. That program, originated by Moscow Secret Police Chief, Sergei Zubatov in 1902, got out of hand, evoking so much enthusiasm that it finally led to the goriest clash of all between labor and government: the Petersburg massacre of "Bloody Sunday," January 22, 1905.

THE INTELLECTUALS AND THE REVOLUTION

Russia, as part of the European economic area, was also fast becoming an intellectual marketplace in which the ideological and philosophical currency of the West was exchanged. The anachronistic attempt on the part of the State to lace the modern-minded intellectuals of all stripes, the men of commerce and industry, the fervent nationalists of this or that minority group, into a strait jacket of Holy Russian conformity could have but one result. It drove most of the thinking elements of the country into a position of dissidence. At the same time, as previously suggested, the lower classes—peasants and industrial workers—were no longer insulated from the currents of progressive thought. The harder the government pressed down upon an ever-swelling mound of discontent, the more powerful grew the pressure from below.

Among the techniques of revolutionism, the practice of assassinations was prominent, as the many attempts made upon high officials and the person of the emperor himself would indicate. The sustained popularity of this technique caused many army officers, students, and members of the national minority groups to be brought to trial. But to this rather haphazard manner of political warfare was added a variety of long-range programs formulated by the intellectuals.

Ever since the earlier part of the nineteenth century, intellectual giants had been appearing on the Russian scene in the persons of such poets, novelists, and writers of ideological tracts as Pushkin, Chaadayev, Turgenev, Belinsky, Herzen, and Chernyshevsky. Increasing contact with western Europe after the Crimean War, new career opportunities provided by the economic development, and the reforms that accompanied the emancipation of the serfs greatly augmented the numbers of intellectuals.

Differing from the "superfluous men" of the earlier period—so labeled because there was no worthwhile place for them in a bureaucratic slave state—these later

figures were drawn into the main streams of Russian life as lawyers, writers, physicians, engineers, agronomists, and statisticians, and as professors and students of
universities and gymnasia. With their predecessors and with one another they
shared a profound, almost guilt-ridden, awareness of the plight of the working
people on the land or in industry. Willing, as so many of them were, to help
ameliorate the evils besetting their society, they were given too little opportunity
to play a part in shaping its destiny.

Their frustration gave rise to feverish activity in the form of illegal pamphleteer-
ing and the establishment of circles of agitation in exile or underground. The followers of the terrorist People's Will, the *Narodovoltsi,* had been apprehended or
been driven abroad by the State Security Police, or *Okhrana,* after the assassination
of Alexander II. But the memory of their martyrdom remained alive to stir the
student youth in their love for the people. The Populist, or *Narodnik,* idea of
socialism based on the peasantry remained a vital doctrine and was, around 1900, to
blossom forth as a political group, called the Socialist Revolutionary Party. But because of the ever-increasing flow of peasants into industry, the Populist movement
had found it expedient to include in its program various elements of anticapitalist
Marxism. Although the revived Populism generally stood for progress through
peaceable agitation, the Socialist Revolutionary Party retained in its midst a secret
Battle Committee, committed to the task of disorganizing the government through
acts of terrorism.

Marxism, as an organized Russian movement, got its start in the League for the
Liberation of Labor, founded in 1883 in Geneva by George Plekhanov, a former
Populist. Although they concentrated their agitation among the urban working
classes in the 1890's and thereafter, the Russian Marxists had, nevertheless, to reckon
with the facts that their would-be disciples were barely removed from their peasant
condition and were largely illiterate. The Marxists, moreover, were operating within
the same system of police surveillance as were the Socialist Revolutionaries, their
arch contenders for the souls of Russia. So, as the Populists accepted certain Marxist
tenets, the Marxists, principally the faction that came to center about Lenin, saw
the need for adopting a *Narodnik*-type program that would include peasant as well
as proletarian participation in the drive for revolution, to be directed by a party based
on conspiratorial principles and made up solely of hard-core devotees to the revolutionary cause.

The Marxist, or Social Democratic Party, came into effective being in 1903 and
immediately split into Leninists, or Bolsheviks, and anti-Leninists, or Mensheviks.
The latter, led by Julius Martov, regarded the urban proletariat alone as the stand-
ard-bearers of a socialist revolution. Seeing no possibility of an early establishment
of socialism in Russia, they thought it necessary to work along with bourgeois-
liberal elements, permitting the latter to dominate the postrevolutionary democratic

process, thereby allowing capitalism to prepare the way for the extension of industry and the proletarization of Russia. This faction envisaged a loosely linked party organization designed, like the Social Democratic parties of central and western Europe, for functioning in a relatively free political arena.

The liberal intelligentsia, like the Mensheviks, tended to identify themselves and their aims with their counterparts in France, Germany, and England, but their situation was unhappily different. They had no intention of overthrowing the Tsar but sought only to limit his power through a constitution. However, lacking the freedom of assembly, they were forced into quasi-revolutionary activity. Among the politically oriented intelligentsia were the men of the Zemstvos and the city Dumas, who, by 1904, had organized themselves into a League for Liberation. Working for the Zemstvos were various professional persons—agronomists, statisticians, and so forth—who sought to influence public opinion toward reforms through working in the Zemstvos or by writing for periodicals or journals. This group was dubbed the "Third Element" (of administrative influence in Russian life), that being a scornful reference to the fact that they were neither state officials nor landlords; in other words, they were upstarts.

The Zemstvo Act of 1890 sought to curtail the activities of the Zemstvo liberals and the professionals by packing the Zemstvos with landowner delegates and by giving each provincial governor the power to veto all Zemstvo decisions. That act was preceded the previous year by a law placing a noble, the so-called *Zemsky Nachalnik,* or Land Captain, at the head of each *volost.* These laws had the effect, among others, of seriously hampering the persons best equipped to deal with rural problems so that unnecessary sufferings were caused by the disastrous famines of 1891-1892—the worst to that date in Russia's history. In the famines of 1901-1902, bureaucratically caused hardships were again quite evident.

Along with the "Third Element," other professional persons, such as teachers, doctors, lawyers, engineers, writers, and journalists, began in 1904 to organize professional unions in order to evade the prohibition of political meetings. In May, 1905, all the professional unions combined to form a Union of Unions, which, in October of that year, joined forces with the Zemstvo constitutionalists to form the Constitutional Democratic or Kadet Party, under the leadership of the historian Paul Milyukov.

Notable, if only for its enormous latter-day influence in India, was the teaching of Leo Tolstoy, who tried to convince the liberals that their best hope for change lay in the Christian credo of noncooperation, coupled with nonviolence. Wrote Tolstoy in his "Letter to the Liberals" [10] of 1896:

And what can government do . . . with a man who is not willing publicly to lie with uplifted hand, or who is not willing to send his children to an establishment which he

[10] L. N. Tolstoy, *Essays, Letters, Miscellanies,* New York, 1902, p. 387.

considers bad, or who is not willing to learn to kill people, or is not willing to take part in idolatry, . . . in coronations, deputations, and addresses, or who says and writes what he thinks and feels? By prosecuting such a man, government secures for him general sympathy, making him a martyr. . . .

And it is only necessary for all those good, enlightened, and honest people, whose strength is now wasted in revolutionary, socialistic, or liberal activity . . . to begin to act thus, and a nucleus of . . . enlightened, and moral people would form around them . . . , and to this nucleus the ever wavering crowd of average people would at once gravi- tate, and public opinion—the only power which subdues governments—would become evident, demanding freedom of speech, freedom of conscience, justice, and humanity. And as soon as public opinion was formulated . . . all those inhuman organizations—the "state of siege," the secret police, the censor, . . . the Holy Synod, and the rest . . . would disappear of themselves.

A Village Reacts to
the Statutes of Emancipation*

May, 1861

. . . The Governor of Novgorod had appointed me to the post of government representative at the district congresses of communes.[1] . . . I arrived in Isakovo two months after the proclamation of the emancipation manifesto and was much amazed to find the landlords rather apathetic with respect to a matter so important to them as the emancipation of the serfs. . . . The peasants were . . . in a tense frame of mind, mainly because they had no idea at all what awaited them either in the immediate or in the somewhat distant future. The published peasant statutes had been read to them— they had perhaps even read them themselves; but they could make no sense out of them.

Earlier, passing through Demyansk District . . . I had heard of many misunderstandings that had risen between the land-

lords and their former serfs. I do not know whether the statements of my informants were fair, . . . but I was told that all of the disagreements grew out of the stubbornness of the landlords, solidly opposed to the reforms, and that the flogging rods usually decided the issues to the disadvantage of the peasants who were forced to listen in silence not really knowing what was true and what was not.

Prior to my arrival at Isakovo the *obrok* peasants [required to pay money dues to the landlord] had been refusing to perform their field labor because of what they had understood the statutes to say. After much futile discussion the district leader of the nobility was called in, as was the police inspector, whose arrival frightened the peasants. However, the officials employed no harsh measures. They briefly explained to the peasants what their error was; that although the amount of their labor had been reduced, some labor was still required of them. It must be said that even before the arrival of the authorities . . . the peasants had invariably remained respectful and although protesting vigorously, always added such phrases as:—"not wishing to blame

* Source: S. I. Nosovich, Krest'yanskaya reforma v Novgorodskoy Gubernii; zapiski S. I. Nosovicha 1861-1863gg. (Peasant Reform in Novgorod Province; Notes of S. I. Nosovich, 1861-1863), St. Petersburg, 1899, pp. 16-24.

[1] That is, district mediator between landlords and peasants.

your grace," or "we, little mother, were always devoted to you, but the people tell us that we no longer are obliged to do the work."

There were other disagreements. *Tyaglo*[2]-exempt peasants did not want to fulfill their *barshchina* [labor owed the landlord] requirements. Others did not want to weave . . . and sometimes refused to do any kind of work. The woman's *barshchina* . . . had been set at two days a week . . . but many women did not care to do the work in the middle days of the week, regarding those days as inconvenient. Whatever the explanation for all the confusion in our village . . . , the main thing that can be deduced is that nobody on our estate, besides mother and sister, could understand the new arrangement.

Upon my arrival I asked all of the heads of [peasant] households to convene in the church on the first Sunday so that a thanksgiving service might be held to celebrate the emancipation. . . . I also wanted to explain to them the principal aspects of the peasant statutes. Before the prayers the priest delivered a very poor speech in which he greeted me as their master and chief. As a matter of fact the peasants did . . . address me as chief of the communal arbitrators; some even congratulated me upon my rank, saying that the tsar had made me elder over the district. Upon completion of the service I went out to the church square. There, surrounded by a crowd of peasants and women, I expounded upon [the great change] wrought by the grace of the tsar. I mention in passing that the tsar's prestige was unusually high in the eyes of the common folk of our parts. When the manifesto was read to the peasants, many of them said with feeling: "See, the little father looks after all of us." I tried to build upon this prestige in the hope that the peasants, seeing how the tsar . . . cared for them, would in their turn . . . respect the provisions of the statutes. At the same time I constantly suggested that they trust the persons whose task it was to carry out the regulations of the statutes with fairness and conscience.

I spoke to them of the major judicial, administrative and economic changes that were to come. The last interested them the most, being more comprehensible to them, and when I was on the subject of the land or of their obligations, their attention doubled and they pressed closer about me. I explained to them what their present obligations to the landlords were. . . . I assigned the *barshchina* peasants equal shares of work and read them the list drawn up to indicate to each by name his day of labor. Then I gave this list to our steward, whom I instructed daily to mark off the workers. I asked him to be most careful and not cause me or himself unpleasantness. I did not think the fulfilment of *obrok* payments a matter altogether fair to the peasants, but I could not touch upon that . . . in order not to undermine the influence and importance of the district marshal of the nobility who had categorically expressed himself to the peasants on that score. . . . In conclusion I explained to the peasants that they would be free hired workers commencing with the coming year; that I intended to deal fairly with them and give them land as specified by the statutes. I said I would place them all on an *obrok* basis in order to figure their payment and would equate six *desyatins*[3] of land to nine silver rubles per peasant. Several times the peasants asked me how large a *desyatin* was and how the cost of inferior land would be reckoned. . . . [Many] peasants told me that they had little faith in what the masters told them, that the priests too were [interpreting the laws] in favor of the masters and that in many parts of our region the laws were being interpreted in a manner different from that explained to them by their masters.

I asked them about their personal views . . . and realized how greatly their hopes had been disappointed. All of them expressed the most communistic conceptions . . . and had expected that all the land ". . . would be divided among the peasants." . . . I was able to see at this time that in their communal affairs the peasants were guided mainly by principles of expediency rather than of justice. So, for instance, the rich *muzhik*, who did not need grain,

---

[2] See page 3.

[3] A *desyatin* equals 2.7 acres.

did not want to give it to the poor out of his stores. Moreover, in the communes there were loudmouths who took control over the . . . average peasant and often induced him to act more along the lines of personal gain than of common interest. . . .

. . . I already mentioned that the peasants were exclusively interested in the economic aspects of the reforms and regarded administrative arrangements as secondary. They listen willingly enough to my explanations about the volosts[4] and communal sharing, about the *volost* elder, the peasant court and the communal mediators. But I must sadly confess that the peasants are quite indifferent toward the juridical side of the statutes. Personal rights, the legal definition of property, their rising to the status of fully privileged citizens—all these are of absolutely no interest to them. I explained to them at length the advantage of a man, who, for instance, could take himself a wife, whenever and wherever he chose, without having to ask the landlord's permission. But many said that this would be bad, because a peasant girl would not marry a poor fellow, who, however, could not do without a housewife —as a worker, that is. They said it was better the old way, when the master forced them to marry, thinking of his own economic interests—and the increase of taxable persons—as well as of the welfare of his peasant who needed a household worker.

I argued that in such a case my own position, even as a master, was not better than theirs, and that no girl wanted to marry me so that it would be better if someone forced one of them to marry me. The peasants fully understood my joke, laughed and recognized the unfairness of their attitude. Strange, sad . . . how low the level of the people's morals is. They see in a woman nothing more than a footstool and a toiler. Yes, even the women see themselves in this light. . . .

And so our peasants are quite indifferent to all that does not bear directly upon their material welfare. True, I have so far dealt only with such villages in which the peasants were not oppressed by their masters, were generally satisfied, and could, therefore, feel no great discomfort in having no

civil and human rights *de jure*. All peasants calculate only whether there will be an addition to their present *obrok*,[5] and if that is not substantial they are almost indifferent to the forthcoming reform. They even distrust the *volost* and their *volost* and communal chiefs—the way they view all authorities. The purchase of property with the aid of loans by the government not only does not interest them but angers them. The forty-nine years in which they are to repay [the government] seems to them like an eternity. . . .

[With regard to the masters] many understand the practical value of the reforms for the future, but the first two or three difficult years will compel them to oppose the new order of things as being damaging to themselves. In my opinion, serfdom was a most difficult situation for the masters themselves. Naturally, I do not mean the monstrous landlords who didn't care, but was it possible for a sensitive man not to feel a twinge in the heart, seeing the poverty of his peasants, their illness, their crudeness of morals and of understanding? Each of us had willy-nilly to relate himself to all the misfortunes of his peasants, and the peasant on his part, did this too and within himself always blamed the master. Many masters, before this time on good terms with their serfs, have been hurt by minor unpleasantnesses directed toward them recently by the peasants. They attribute such actions to hostilities growing out of the past. I say this is a punishment brought upon respectable people for centuries of serfdom which warped the Russian person. I feel more sorry for the peasant who now trusts no one but distinguishes between the good master and the bad. I have not yet mentioned how difficult it was . . . to take care of one's peasants, to concern oneself with all their needs, to distinguish the feigning from the real, to be fair but not weak, in general, not to be an uncontrolled despot as one had the right to be and whom the peasant was accustomed to accepting, but on the other hand always to perceive oneself in contradiction to one's beliefs and desires. Yes, difficult times are coming to an end for us, and if a new epoch

<hr/>

[4] See page 7.

[5] See page 5.

equally difficult is beginning, this is so only with respect to economic conditions. . . .

I have had talks with many manorial serfs. . . . They regard themselves as wronged in comparison with the peasants. All of them expected that the landlords would have to settle them on land; many still persist in their delusion. Some of the manorials want to have land not for themselves but for their children. They want to partake in the communal sharing of the commune fields so that they can lease out the land for added income. . . . They expect to continue working in their customary capacities but want the land to serve as a real estate fund to secure the future of their children. They think more about this now than formerly, since they want their children to become

literate and they worry about their education and the like. The manorials should be settled on state lands and be given some aid in paying the cost. Many manorials have lately become smarter about marriage. Some feel they made mistakes in that respect, seeing that the whole brood of children will be their full responsibility after exactly two years. . . . Previously the landlord, one way or another, provided for each growing child. The marriage of manorials required no foresight and nowhere were there as many children as in the manor. The old manorials are worried about their future and are constantly—by word as by deed—trying to win over their former masters . . . , fearfully envisioning themselves thrown out on the street in two years.

The New Local Self-Government*

The Zemstvo is a kind of local administration which supplements the action of the rural communes, and takes cognizance of those higher public wants which individual communes cannot possibly satisfy. Its principal duties are to keep the roads and bridges in repair, to provide means of conveyance for the rural police and other officials, to elect the justices of peace, to look after primary education and sanitary affairs, to watch the state of the crops and take measures against famine, and in short to undertake, within clearly-defined limits, whatever seems likely to increase the [popular] well-being. In form the institution is parliamentary; it consists of an assembly of deputies which meets at least once a year, and of a permanent executive bureau elected by the assembly from among its members. Once every three years the deputies are elected in certain fixed proportions by the landed proprietors, the rural communes, and the municipal corporations. Every province (*guberniya*) and

* SOURCE: D. M. Wallace, *Russia*, London, 1881, pp. 214-227. (Adapted and abridged.)

each of the districts (*uyezdi*) into which the province is subdivided has such an assembly and such a bureau.

In Novgorod I [attended] a District Assembly. I found forty men seated round a long table. Before the president—the Marshal of Noblesse for the district—stood a small hand-bell, which he rang at the commencement of the proceedings and when he wished to obtain silence. To the right and left of the president sat the members of the executive bureau (*uprava*), armed with piles of documents, from which they read long extracts, till the majority of the audience took to yawning and [some] went to sleep. At the close of each of these reports the president rang his bell—presumably [to awaken] the sleepers—and inquired whether any one had remarks. Not unfrequently a discussion ensued. When [a] difference of opinion appeared, a vote was taken.

[The] assembly was composed partly of nobles and partly of peasants—the latter decidedly in the majority—and no trace of antagonism seemed to exist between the two.

Proprietors and their [former] serfs evidently met [here] on a footing of equality. The discussions were always carried on by the nobles, but more than [once] peasant members spoke, and their remarks were listened to with attention. [There] was too much unanimity, indicating that [most] members did not take a very deep interest in the [proceedings].

This assembly was held in September. [In] December the Assembly for the Province met, and [in general] resembled closely the District Assembly. [Its] members were chosen, not by the primary electors, but by the assemblies of the ten Districts which compose the Province, and it took cognizance merely of matters which concerned more than one district. The peasant deputies were very few in number [because] the District Assemblies choose their most active members to represent them in the Provincial Assemblies and consequently [choose] landed proprietors. [The] peasants make no objection, for attendance at the Provincial Assemblies [costs money] and payment to the deputies is prohibited by law.

[What are the] elements composing this assembly? [Most] are commonplace men, who have spent part of their youth as officers in the army, or officials in the civil administration, and have since retired to their estates, where they [earn] a modest [living]. Some add to their agricultural revenues by acting as justices of the peace. All these men belong to what may be called the party of progress, which anxiously supports all proposals recognized as "liberal," and especially all measures likely to improve the condition of the peasantry.

The Zemstvo of Novgorod had at that time the reputation of being one of the most enlightened and energetic, and in the assembly of 1870 the proceedings were conducted in a business-like way. The reports were carefully considered, and each article of the annual budget was submitted to minute scrutiny. In several of the provinces which I afterwards visited I found that affairs were conducted [differently]: quorums were formed with extreme difficulty, and the proceedings were treated as mere for-

malities and dispatched as speedily as possible. The character of the assembly depends of course on the amount of interest taken in local public affairs.

The [Zemstvo] law, published in January, 1864, produced inordinate expectations. At that time a large section of the Russian educated classes assumed that the excellence of an institution must always be in proportion to its "liberal" and democratic character. The question as to how far it might be appropriate to the existing conditions and to the character of the people, and as to whether it might not, though admirable in itself, be too expensive for the work to be performed, was little thought of. Any organization which rested on "the elective principle," and provided an arena for free public discussion, was sure to be well received, and these conditions were fulfilled by the Zemstvo.

The expectations excited were of various kinds. People who thought more of political than economic progress saw in the new institutions the basis of boundless popular liberty. [Every] district would have its elective assembly, in which the peasant would be on a level with the richest landed proprietors. People who were accustomed to think of social rather than political progress expected that the Zemstvo would soon provide the country with good roads, safe bridges, numerous village schools, and well-appointed hospitals. Agriculture would be improved, trade and industry developed, and the condition of the peasantry ameliorated. The listless apathy of provincial life and the hereditary indifference to local public affairs were now, it was thought, about to be dispelled; and in view of this change patriotic mothers took their children to the assemblies in order to accustom them from their early years to take an interest in the public welfare.

[These great] expectations have not been realized. The Government had no intention of conferring on the new institutions any political significance, and very soon showed that it would not allow the assemblies to exert even a moral pressure by means of petitions and political agitation. As soon as the Zemstvo of St. Petersburg gave evidence of a desire to play a political part, the assembly was at once closed by Imperial command.

Even within its [legally defined] sphere, the Zemstvo has not accomplished what was expected of it. The country has not been covered with a network of [good] roads, and the bridges are [none too] safe; there are still few village schools and infirmaries. Little or nothing has been done for the development of trade or manufactures; and the villages remain [as before]. Meanwhile the local rates have been rising [rapidly]; and many people [view] the Zemstvo [as] a worthless institution which has increased the taxation without conferring corresponding benefit on the country.

The Zemstvo has, however, done much. [It] is very little tainted with [corruption]. [It] has greatly improved the condition of the hospitals, asylums, etc., and it has done much [to found] village schools and a few seminaries for the preparation of schoolmasters. [The] Zemstvo has created a more equitable system of rating [compelling] landed proprietors and owners of houses to bear their share of the public burdens. Last, and not least, it has created a system of mutual fire insurance for the villagers—a most valuable institution since [most] peasants live in wooden houses.[6]

[Nevertheless], the Zemstvo no longer enjoys public confidence, and already shows symptoms of exhaustion. [The] best authorities [generally agree] regarding the cause. The Government, they say, conceived in a moment of enthusiasm the project of conferring local self government on the people, but [later] became frightened. The assemblies were obliged to accept as presidents the marshals of noblesse. The publicity which was at first granted to the assemblies was afterwards diminished by giving to the governors of provinces the right to prevent the publication of the minutes and other documents. These restrictions, it is said, have rendered all free, vigorous action impossible.

The Zemstvo, it is true [did awaken a] large portion of the nobles to the necessity of improving the administration, and the popular interest in public affairs was much greater than at any former period. Hence there was at first a period of enthusiasm, during which great preparations were made for future activity, and not a little was actually effected. The institution had all the charm of novelty, and the members felt that the eyes of the public were upon them. For a time all went well. But when the novelty had passed and the public turned its attention to other matters, the spasmodic energy evaporated, and many of the most active members looked about for more lucrative employment. Such employment was easily found, for at that time there was an unusual demand for able educated men. Several branches of the civil service were being reorganized, and railways, banks, and joint-stock companies were being rapidly multiplied. With these the Zemstvo had great difficulty in competing. It could not, like the Imperial service, offer pensions, decorations,

---

[6] In 1868 the combined revenues of the Zemstvos of thirty provinces . . . was expended as follows:

	Roubles	Per Cent
1. Houses for the police and other members of the Imperial administration	669,719	= 4.6
2. Quarters for the troops	118,080	= 0.8
3. Means of conveyance for the police and other officials	2,485,973	= 17.0
4. Special administration for peasant affairs	2,160,258	= 14.9
5. Justice of peace courts	1,925,388	= 13.2
6. Roads and bridges	1,906,777	= 13.1
7. Sanitary affairs (physicians, hospitals, etc.)	1,204,162	= 8.3
8. Popular education	738,859	= 5.1
9. Payment of debt and sundries	562,991	= 3.8
10. Working expenses of Zemstvo administration	2,797,360	= 19.2
	14,569,567	100.0

and prospects of promotion, nor could it pay such large salaries as the commercial and industrial enterprises. In consequence, the quality of the executive bureaus deteriorated at the same time as the public interest in the institution diminished.

It is right to point out this fact, because it has had some influence in producing that languor from which the Zemstvo is at present suffering. It is not, however, the chief cause. The languor has appeared among the deputies and the public quite as much as in the executive committees. The chief cause lies in the fact that very few people feel keenly the want of those things which the Zemstvo is intended to supply. Take, for instance, a matter of first necessity. That good roads are necessary for the development of the national resources is a principle well known to every [educated] Russian. But very few of the enlightened deputies who occasionally voice the principle feel the necessity of having good roads in their own district in the same sense as they feel the necessity of having opportunities for card-playing. The one is a theoretical, the other a practical, want. When the landed proprietors learn to keep accounts accurately, and discover that a certain amount of money spent on roads will be more than compensated for by the diminution in the cost of transport, then, and not till then, will the road committees become vigorous institutions. The same remark may be applied to all the other branches of the local self-government.

In order to illustrate the essentially impractical character of the institution, I describe an incident which I once witnessed in a District Assembly. When the subject of primary schools came [up], an influential member proposed that an obligatory system of education should be at once introduced throughout the whole District. Strange to say, the motion was very nearly carried, though all the members present knew—or [should] have known—that the actual number of schools would have to be multiplied twentyfold, and that the local rates were already very heavy. To preserve his reputation for liberalism, the honorable member further proposed that, though the system should be obligatory, no fines, punishments, or other means of compulsion should be employed. How a system could be obligatory without using some means of compulsion, he did not condescend to explain. To get out of this difficulty one of his supporters suggested that peasants who did not send their children to school should be excluded from serving as office-bearers in the communes; but this proposition merely created a laugh, for many deputies knew that the peasants would regard this supposed punishment as a valuable privilege. And whilst this discussion about the necessity of introducing an ideal system of obligatory education was being carried on, the street before the windows of the room was covered with a stratum of mud two feet in depth!

Corporal Punishment and Army Life*

Already [around 1855 it was recognized that] corporal punishment degraded rather

* SOURCE: L. Dobrov, *Otkrovennoye slovo o vazhneishikh sobitiakh nashei vnutrennei zhizni za . . . 1855-1880* (A Frank Discussion of the Most Important Events in Our Internal Affairs . . . 1855-1880), St. Petersburg, 1880, pp. 49-57.

than improved the human personality because it damaged a person's self-esteem. But until the lawmakers ruled it out entirely, a lessening number of categories remained subject to corporal punishment. So, in 1855 church wardens became exempt; in 1861 exemption was extended to women of fifty, to those attending educational institutions, to midwives, hospital supervisors and children in rural schools. Somewhat earlier the shameful means of preventing the escape of convicts were abolished. In 1858 . . . permanent chains were removed from prisoners [and] the shaving of half the head . . . was abolished. Finally [in] 1863 came the tsar's decree completely outlawing corporal punishment. . . .

The rule was extended to soldiers, "so that the morale of the lower ranks might be raised." . . . At the same time the branding . . . of . . . criminals was abolished. For a fuller awareness of the great importance of this law, it is enough to remind oneself of the poorly developed sense of dignity that characterized our simple folk . . . , the ones most frequently subject to corporal punishment. Soon after the decree of 1863, many cases occurred wherein some of those sentenced to prison terms . . . tearfully fell to their knees and pleaded with the President of the St. Petersburg Criminal Court to punish them with the rod but deliver them from imprisonment. If this happened in St. Petersburg, it must surely have happened elsewhere.

A sense of dignity was lacking not only among the plain folk . . . [but also] among our student youth. The rod was so universally used . . . that it would seldom have entered the head of one so punished to feel ashamed. In fact, many gloried in not crying out when being flogged. There appeared a special type of schoolboy champion, and he was viewed with envy by his weaker brethren who were unable to bear the birch whippings with equanimity. . . .

Even after the legal abolition of corporal punishment, . . . those who raise our youth continued to have strong doubts about the value of replacing the . . . whippings . . . by other punitive means. There were quite a few pedagogues who decidedly favored . . . what they called "rapid learning" and even wrote serious articles on the subject. . . . Even at that time, fortunately, their opinions received the appraisal they deserved. From 1861 on corporal punishment began to disappear from the . . . schools [and] . . . in the gymnasium rules issued

in 1864, corporal punishment was not even mentioned among the [permissible] means of punishment. . . .

Turning to the improvement of the life of the soldiers, we recall . . . what dramatic scenes accompanied the induction of recruits amid [those] close to them. . . . The soldier's dear ones bemoaned not only [his going away] but also the martyrdom which would be his for twenty-five years; the heavy toil of military drill, . . . always cleaning himself and always being devoured by insects, besides . . . the many forms of corporal punishment. They cried harder over a recruit . . . than they did over a corpse. . . . The soldier's lot was so awful that it was indeed one of the forms of punishment for troublesome persons of the lowest classes. Even the law recognized the "sending into the army" as a legitimate form of punishment for "persons of bad behavior." The former life of the soldier was actually worse than exile to a labor camp, if only because of the length of the term of service.

[Soon after 1855 there was] some improvement. . . . In 1856 the right to short furloughs was extended, independently of the prolonged furlough which formerly had been the soldier's sole period of relief from the long term of service. In 1858 . . . garrison service for the lower ranks was eased [by a law] forbidding the ordering of sentries to guard objects of little importance. With respect to the improvement of the soldier's status it was necessary also to change the commonly-held notion that military service was a means of punishing criminals. The law of 1861 abolished the practice of condemning to military service all persons not exempt from corporal punishment [that is, the lowest classes] who had committed crimes and misdemeanors.

Russians had the highest respect for the courage of their defender—the soldier, but in ordinary life the latter did not enjoy a good reputation. Which of us does not recall the days when the crime rate in a locality, the number of thefts, particularly, was directly related to the troops stationed there? . . . Two decades have passed, and we find that transferring soldiers to a given locality means the lessening of its crime rate. All Bessarabians remember . . . that the transfer of troops to Kishinev [1876-1878] enhanced the safety of that city, making it possible . . . to walk on remote streets, even at night, without being attacked.

This notable improvement of morals in the lower ranks is due mainly to the law forbidding the sending of criminals into the army. Formerly there had been persons entering the lower ranks of the service who, unlike most members of the lowest classes, had a higher opinion not only of their soldierly calling but also of their personal dignity. As long as their work was equated with a form of criminal punishment, then, inevitably, their close association with their convict comrades-in-arms was bound to demoralize them. . . .

The lawmakers' concern with raising the moral level of the soldier and of developing in him a feeling of social honorableness continued and within two years corporal punishment was abolished. By the decree of April, 1863, . . . running the gauntlet of rods and whips was abolished. Flogging remained, but only as a temporary measure—until guardhouses were built—and then the maximum number of strokes was set at two hundred. . . .

Later, in 1863 and in 1865, there followed the . . . statutes on . . . military discipline and disciplinary penalties. The statutes, necessitated by the abolition of corporal punishment, have a very special significance in the improvement of soldier life. By limiting the concept of discipline to legally established rules unconditionally observed, the lawmakers intended to introduce the principles of humaneness into the sphere of relations between officer and soldier. . . .

In striving to raise soldier morale, the lawmakers did not overlook the need to improve his material situation. . . . A series of measures were enacted that removed the formerly easy ways of misusing monetary amounts set aside for food for the lower ranks, of which only part was spent for that purpose.

Who does not know how bad and insufficient the soldier's food was? It consisted of overly diluted tea, buckwheat gruel, of bread, often baked of damp meal —all . . . because the money to be spent on food, melted away . . . as it passed from hand to hand. The establishment of business committees in the [various] troop units has made such actions impossible, and . . . now every kopek assigned for food goes where it should go. Thanks to the principle of self-administration in unit provisioning, the food of the soldier . . . leaves nothing to be desired.

Besides the improvement in feeding, the gradual shortening of the term of service inevitably encouraged the soldier toward a more energetic and more sensible fulfillment of his duties, in that it removed sluggishness in learning the arts of war. . . . That is proved by the fact that he successfully completes a more complicated course of instruction in the shorter term than he did in the pre-reform era when barracks drilling was the major object of instruction, while other aspects of training—among them target shooting and literacy—were considered of lesser importance.

One can say that dress parades became secondary after 1867 and the greatest attention began to be given to the soldiers' learning the essences of the arts of war. That was the year when special education for the lower ranks was instituted. Since special [military] education presupposed some general education, it was necessary to extend literacy to the soldiers. . . .

But certainly the most important act in the improvement of military conditions, and therefore having broad social significance, was the manifesto of January, 1874—the introduction of universal military duty. The influx into the army of educated and intellectually influential persons serves as the best school for the lower ranks. That influx also aids the improvement of the soldier's personality . . . and helps to raise his spiritual level.

Universal conscription benefits society in still another way. The short term of service, the annual draft of soldiers from all classes, the counter-flow of discharged men into civilian life—that is, the quick transformation of civilians to soldiers and vice-versa— heighten the sense of civic duty. So people take with them into the service a practical civic education, and that above all teaches a person to be serious about his obligations. The participation of all classes in military service has the further advantage of diluting, and thus weakening, the spirit of that caste which develops in the special military clique, that class of persons which does so much to inhibit social progress.

The New Justices of the Peace*

The impression created by the first acts of the justices of the peace, [instituted in the spring of 1866 in St. Petersburg and Moscow], was immense and staggering. . . . The very first months of their activity wrought a real transformation in the existing relationships and ideas. To convince oneself how little exaggeration there is in those words, one had to see the astonishment of people, who having previously taken the law into their own hands now had to submit to the sentences of the judge. One had to see the amazement, yes the amazement, the forcefully suppressed irritation, with which those gentlemen, having discharged servants just because they didn't like them, and owing them a half years' pay, listened to the sentences; or workers, who had simply walked out of their jobs before the expiration of their written contracts just because of a rise in prices; or drunkards, having never heard that wallowing and cursing in the streets was not allowed; or husbands, who had no awareness that there was any wrong in beating their wives half to death; or gentlemen riding in their sleighs, who would not even bother to notice a child running out upon the road in front of them. In all such cases it took a superhuman endeavor to make people of all persuasions and classes understand that they had been called before the judge, not in jest, but so that sentence should be passed and carried out in its entirety. This was a true transformation in thinking and it was moreover effected very swiftly as the brief utterances of the judges were energetically enforced. The persons concerned were quite shocked. They could not believe their senses when they discovered that the patronage of a police official did not free them from their obligation to pay the wages they owed, or that friendly drinking bouts with the chief of the police department did not give them the right to beat workers or even the clerks in the police department. The amazement, however, quickly changed to other feelings and large numbers of people rushed to the courts to expose to the light of day all of those long suppressed desires for justice, all the disputes which within human memory had been settled no other way than through the right of the fist, or at very best through patience and forgetting.

* SOURCE: G. A. Dzhanshiev, *Epokha Velikikh' Reform'* (The Epoch of Great Reforms), St. Petersburg, 1905, pp. 459-461.

Introduction of the Jury*

At the time of the reforms the introduction of the jury awakened among the educated classes a great amount of sentimental enthusiasm. The institution had the reputation of being "liberal." This was sufficient to excite most exaggerated expectations as

* SOURCE: D. M. Wallace, *Russia*, London, 1881, pp. 568-572. (Adapted and abridged.)

to its beneficent influence. Ten years of experience have [cooled] this enthusiasm. It is now held by many that the Russian people is not yet ripe for such an institution. One jury, for instance, is said to have returned a verdict of "*not* guilty with extenuating circumstances"; and another, being unable to come to a decision, is reported to have cast lots before [a holy figure], and to have given a verdict in accordance with the result! Juries often give a verdict of "not guilty" when the accused makes a full confession.

In England the Bench is allowed great latitude in fixing the amount of punishment. The jury can therefore confine themselves to the question of fact and leave to the judge the appreciation of extenuating circumstances. In Russia the law fixes minutely the punishment for each category of crimes, and leaves almost no latitude to the judge. The jury know that if they give a verdict of guilty, the prisoner will inevitably be punished according to the Code. Now the Code, borrowed [largely] from foreign legislation, is founded on conceptions very different from those of the Russian people, and in many cases it attaches severe punishment to acts which, in the opinions of the Russian people, are merely peccadilloes, or are positively justifiable. Even where the Code is in harmony with the popular morality, there are many exceptional cases.

Suppose, for instance—as actually happened—that a fire breaks out in a village, and that the Village Elder, driven out of patience by the laziness of some of his young fellow villagers, oversteps the limits of his authority as defined by law, and accompanies his reproaches with a few blows. Surely such a man is not guilty of a very heinous crime—certainly not in the opinion of the peasantry—and yet if he be prosecuted and convicted he falls into the jaws of

an article which condemns to transportation for a long term of years.

In such cases what are the jury to do? They know that the judge must condemn the prisoner according to the Code. There remains, therefore, but one [way] out—a verdict of acquittal; and Russian juries generally adopt this alternative. Thus the jury, in those very cases in which it is most severely condemned, provides a corrective for the injustice of criminal legislation. Occasionally, it is true, they go a little too far in this direction and arrogate to themselves a right of pardon, but [such] cases are rare. I know of only one. The prisoner had been proved guilty of a serious crime, but it happened to be the eve of a great religious festival, and the jury thought that in [acquitting him] they would be acting as good Christians!

The legislation has tried to prevent this practice by concealing as far as possible from the jury the punishment that awaits the accused if he be condemned. It forbids the counsel for the prisoner to inform the jury what punishment is prescribed for the crime in question. This device has sometimes a directly opposite effect. Fearing that [the punishment] may be out of all proportion to the crime, the jury sometimes acquit a criminal whom they would condemn if they knew what punishment would be inflicted. And when a jury are, as it were, entrapped, and find that the punishment is more severe than they supposed, they can take their revenge in the succeeding cases. [In one case a] jury convicted a prisoner of an offense which they regarded as trivial, but which entailed seven years of penal servitude. So [shocked] were the jurymen by this unexpected consequence of their verdict, that they obstinately acquitted, in the face of the most convincing evidence, all the other prisoners brought before them.

Consequences of the Emancipation*

The present money-dues and taxes [of the peasants] are often more burdensome than the labor-dues [of serfdom]. If the serfs had many ill-defined obligations, such as carting the master's grain to market, preparing his firewood, supplying him with eggs, chickens, home-made linen, they [also] had many ill-defined privileges. They grazed their cattle on the manor-land; they received firewood and occasionally logs for repairing their huts; sometimes the proprietor lent them or gave them a cow or a horse when they had been visited by the cattle-plague or the horse-stealer; and in times of famine they could look to their master for support. All this has [ended]. Their burdens and their privileges have been swept away and been replaced by unelastic legal relations. They have now to pay the market-price for every stick of firewood, for every log, and for every rood of land on which to graze their cattle. The demand to pay is encountered at every step. If a cow dies or a horse is stolen, the owner can no longer go to the proprietor [and get] a present, or a loan without interest, but must apply to the village usurer at a twenty or thirty per cent rate of interest. Sometimes the peasant has to pay without getting any return, [as] when his cattle stray into the proprietor's fields—[a common] accident in a country where walls and hedges are almost unknown. Formerly he escaped with a scolding, but now he [pays] a fine. Thinking of all this, he is quite sincere when, on being asked whether his new position is better than the old, he replies, "How shall I say? It is both better and worse!"

Why has the abolition of serfage not yet had those beneficent consequences which even moderate men predicted? [In] my opinion the result [is] one of various causes. The peasantry [suffer because of] drunkenness and improvidence. If the

* SOURCE: *Ibid.,* pp. 536-555. (Adapted and abridged.)

Orthodox Church could make the peasantry refrain from drink and could instill a few simple moral principles, it would certainly [help]. But [the] parish clergy are unfit for such a task, and the few who [aspire] in that direction rarely acquire a preceptible moral influence over their parishioners. Perhaps more is to be expected from the schoolmaster than from the priest, but it will be long before education can produce even a partial moral regeneration. Its first influence is often in [the] opposite direction. When only [few] peasants in the village can read and write they are very apt to employ their knowledge for dishonest purposes; [so] it occasionally happens that the man who has the most education is the greatest scoundrel in the Mir. This is sometimes used as an argument by the opponents of popular education, but in reality it is a reason for disseminating primary instruction as rapidly as possible. When the majority of the peasantry will be [literate] they will present a less inviting field for swindling.

[Under] the Emancipation Law [the] Communes received almost complete autonomy, and the landed proprietors were carefully excluded from the administration and jurisdiction of the *Volost*. This has produced a vast system of peasant self-government, [so] carefully protected from the influence of the other social classes that even the proprietor whose estate lies in the middle of the *Volost* has no right to meddle in *Volost* affairs. The more laborious and well-to-do peasants do all in their power to escape election as office-bearers, and leave the administration in the hands of the less respectable members. In the ordinary course of affairs there is little evidence of administration of any kind, and in cases of public disaster, such as a fire or the cattle-plague, the authorities seem to be apathetic and powerless. Not unfrequently a *Volost* Elder trades with the money he collects as dues or taxes; and sometimes, when he becomes insolvent, the peasants have to pay their taxes and dues a second time. The *Volost* Court, [with peasant judges who apply the law of custom], is very often accessible to the influence of *vodka* and other kinds of bribery, so that in many districts it has fallen into utter discredit, and the peasants say that any one who becomes a judge "takes a sin on his soul." The Village Assemblies, too, have become worse than they were in the days of serfage. At that time the Heads of Households—who, it must be remembered, have alone a voice in the decisions—were few in number, laborious and well-to-do, and they kept the lazy, unruly members under strict control; now that the large families have been broken up, and almost every adult peasant is Head of a Household, the Communal affairs are often decided by a noisy majority; and almost any Communal decision may be obtained by "treating the Mir"—that is, by supplying a certain amount of *vodka*. Often I have heard old peasants remark, "There is no order now; the people have been spoiled; it was better in the time of the masters."

[Some believe] that the material progress of the peasantry is prevented chiefly, not by the mere abuses of the Communal administration, but by the essential principles of the Communal institutions. Serfage, say those who adopt this view, has been abolished only in name. Formerly the peasant was the serf of the proprietor; now he is the serf of the Commune. He is still attached to the land, and cannot leave his home even for a short period without receiving from the Commune a formal permission, for which he has often to pay a most exorbitant sum. When he has found profitable employment in the towns, or in some other part of the country, the Commune may at any moment, and on [any] pretext, order him to return home; and if he does not obey, he is brought back like a convict. He receives a share of the Communal land, but he has no inducement to improve it, for he knows that the Commune may at any time make a re-distribution of the land, and that in this way the labor he has expended on his share will be lost to him.

Those who write and talk on the matter almost always overlook the important fact that the Commune has not everywhere the same nature and functions. In the Black-Earth Zone, where the annual dues are less than the normal rent of the land, to belong to a Commune is a privilege; in the Northern Agricultural Zone, on the contrary, where the dues exceed the normal rent, to belong to a Commune is a burden. [Admitting] that in the northern regions the Commune has really taken the place of the serf-proprietors, and holds its members in semi-serfage; it must be added that the Commune is not to blame. As it is held responsible for all dues and taxes, and these exceed the value of the benefits which it has to confer, it is obliged to retain its members by force, whether they desire to possess land or not. In short, the Commune in this part of the country has been transformed into a tax-gatherer, and it is obliged to use stringent measures, for the taxes are heavy. What is called the Communal tyranny, therefore, must be laid, not to the Commune, a mere instrument in the hands of the financial administration, but to the Emancipation Law, which compelled the serfs of this region to purchase their liberty under the disguise of paying for the land which was conferred on them without their consent. In the Black-Earth Zone, where the dues do not exceed the normal rent, and where the Commune has more the character of a voluntary association, we have few or no complaints of Communal tyranny. Here any member who wishes to absent himself can easily transfer his share of the land and of the burdens to some one of his neighbors who require more land than they actually possess. He may even, if he wishes, leave the Commune altogether, and inscribe himself as burgher in one of the towns; for the other members willingly consent to pay his dues in return for the share of land which he abandons. [So], many of the accusations made against the Commune ought to be made against the system of dues established by the Government. However burdensome a tax may be, the tax-collector cannot reasonably be blamed for doing his duty, especially if he has been made a tax-collector against his will.

The direct taxes, in the wider sense of the term, which the peasants have to pay are of two kinds—taxes properly so called, and yearly dues paid for the land. The taxes properly so called may be divided into three categories—Imperial, Local, and Communal. Of these, the first is fixed by the State, the second by the Zemstvo, and the third by the Commune. All three combined amount to a heavy burden for [most] peasant families.

The land-dues cannot properly be called taxes, for the peasant receives in return for them the usufruct of a certain quantity of land; but they have something of the nature of taxes, for they were not fixed by voluntary contract, but were imposed upon the peasantry, together with the land, without their consent. In some parts of the country, as I have already explained, this "imposition" is a privilege; in others it is a burden. In the former—that is to say, in those localities where the normal rent exceeds the dues [as in the south]—the peasant may liberate himself from the dues by giving up the land; in the latter—that is to say, where the dues exceed the normal rent [in the north] —he cannot liberate himself in this way, for neither the Commune nor any of the individual members would voluntarily accept his land on such conditions. We may therefore fairly regard as taxation the part of the dues which remains after we have subtracted the normal rent of the land. If, now, this part of the dues be added to the taxes properly so called, it forms a sum too heavy to be borne by peasants who live by agriculture alone. So long as it has to be paid yearly these peasants have no possibility of improving their condition. Nay, more, their condition is becoming worse. Statistics show that the number of cattle in these regions is decreasing, and that means less manure and less abundant harvests.

In the time of serfage the peasant families, as I have already remarked, were generally very large. They remained undivided, partly from the influence of patriarchal conceptions, but chiefly because the proprietors, perceiving the economic advantage of large families, prevented them from breaking up into independent units. As soon as the proprietor's authority was removed the process of disintegration began and spread rapidly. Every one wished to be independent, and [soon] nearly every able-bodied married peasant had a house of his own. The influence of this on Communal self-government I have already pointed out; its influence on the economic position of the peasantry was still more injurious. The building and keeping up of two or three houses instead of one entailed [much] extra expenditure. It must be remembered, too, that many a disaster which may be successfully resisted by a large family inevitably ruins a small one. But this is not the worst. To understand fully the injurious influence of this breaking up of families, we must consider the fact in conjunction with the Emancipation Law.

The Emancipation Law did not confer on the peasants as much land as they require, and consequently the peasant who has merely his legal portion has neither enough of work nor enough of revenue. If the family were large this difficulty would be easily overcome. One member, with the help of his wife and sisters-in-law, and with the additional assistance of a hired laborer during the harvest-time, might cultivate the whole of the family land, whilst the other members sought occupation elsewhere, and earned money to pay the taxes and meet the necessary outlay. When each able-bodied man is head of an independent household this form of domestic economy is impossible. Each head of a household is obliged either to remain at home or to intrust the cultivation of his land to his wife. In the former case he has a great deal of idle time on his hands, unless he can rent land at a moderate price in the immediate vicinity, and in the latter case the harvests are pretty sure to be meager, for a woman can rarely cultivate as well as a man, even when she has no domestic duties. In many localities the necessity of obtaining arable land in the immediate vicinity of the villages compels the peasants to pay "rack-rents."

The Spirit of Nihilism*

"I begin to agree with my uncle," remarked Arkady; "you certainly have a poor opinion of Russians."

"As though that mattered! The only good point in a Russian is his having the lowest possible opinion of himself. What does matter is that two and two make four, and the rest is all foolery."

"And is nature foolery?" said Arkady, looking pensively at the bright-coloured fields in . . . the beautiful soft light of the sun. . . .

"Nature, too, is foolery in the sense you understand it. Nature's not a temple, but a workshop, and man's the workman in it."

At that instant, the long drawn notes of a violoncello floated out . . . from the house. Some one was playing Schubert's *Expectation*. . . .

"What's that?" cried Bazarov in amazement.

"It's my father." . . .

"And how old is your father?"

"Forty-four."

Bazarov suddenly burst into a roar of laughter. . . .

"Upon my word, a man of forty-four, a *paterfamilias* in this out-of-the-way district, playing on the violoncello!" . . .

"You don't know my father well enough," said Arkady.

"Your father's a nice chap," said Bazarov, "but he's behind the times; his day is done. . . . The day before yesterday I saw him reading Pushkin. . . . Explain to him, please, that that's no earthly use. He's not a boy, you know; it's time to throw up that rubbish. And what an idea to be a romantic at this time of day! Give him something sensible to read."

"What ought I to give him?" asked Arkady.

"Oh, I think Büchner's *Stoff und Kraft* to begin with."

"I think so too," observed Arkady approvingly, "*Stoff und Kraft* is written in popular language. . . ."

"So it seems," Nikolai Petrovitch said the same day after dinner to his brother . . . "you and I are behind the times, our day's over. Well, well. Perhaps Bazarov is right; but one thing, I confess, makes me feel sore; I did so hope, precisely now, to get on to such close, intimate terms with Arkady, and it turns out I'm left behind, and he has gone forward, and we can't understand one another."

"How has he gone forward? And in what way is he so superior to us already?" cried Pavel Petrovitch impatiently. "It's that high and mighty nihilist, who's knocked all that into his head. . . . I'm convinced, for all his tadpoles, he's not got very far even in medicine."

"No, brother, . . . Bazarov is clever, and knows his subject."

"And his conceit's . . . revolting," Pavel Petrovitch broke in again.

"Yes," observed Nikolai Petrovitch, "he is conceited. But there's no doing without that, it seems; only that's what I did not take into account. I thought I was doing everything to keep up with the times; I have started a model farm; I have done well by the peasants, so that I am called a "Red Radical" all over the province; I read, I study, I try in every way to keep abreast with the requirements of the day—and they say my day's over. And, brother, I begin to think that it is."

"Why so?"

"I'll tell you why. This morning I was sitting reading Pushkin. . . . All of a sudden Arkady came up to me, and, without speaking, . . . as if I were a baby, took the book away from me, and laid another before me—a German book. . . ."

* SOURCE: I. Turgenev, *Fathers and Sons*, New York, Greystone Press, n.d., pp. 29-35.

"Upon my word! What book did he give you?"

"This one here."

And Nikolai Petrovitch pulled the famous treatise of Büchner . . . out of his . . . pocket. . . .

*   *   *

The conversation turned on one of the neighbouring land owners. "Rotten aristocratic snob," observed Bazarov indifferently. He had met him in Petersburg.

"Allow me to ask you," began Pavel Petrovitch, and his lips were trembling, "according to your ideas, have the words 'rotten' and 'aristocrat' the same meaning?"

"I said 'aristocratic snob,'" replied Bazarov, lazily swallowing a sip of tea.

"Precisely so; but I imagine you have the same opinion of aristocrats as of aristocratic snobs. I think it my duty to inform you that I do not share that opinion. I venture to assert that every one knows me for a man of liberal ideas and devoted to progress; but, exactly for that reason, I respect aristocrats —real aristocrats. . . . Personal character, sir—that is the chief thing; a man's . . . character must be firm as a rock, since everything is built on it. I am very well aware, for instance, that you . . . consider my habits, my dress, my refinements, in fact, ridiculous; but all that proceeds from a sense of self-respect, from a sense of duty. . . . I live in the country, in the wilds, but I will not lower myself. I respect the dignity of man in myself."

"Let me ask you, Pavel Petrovitch," commented Bazarov; "you respect yourself, and sit with your hands folded; what sort of benefit does that do to the *bien public*? If you didn't respect yourself, you'd do just the same."

Pavel Petrovitch turned white. "That's a different question. It's absolutely unnecessary for me to explain to you now why I sit with folded hands, as you . . . express yourself. I wish only to tell you that aristocracy is a principle, and in our days none but immoral or silly people can live without principles. . . ."

Nikolai Petrovitch nodded his head. "Aristocracy, Liberalism, progress, prin-

ciples," Bazarov was saying meanwhile; "if you think of it, what a lot of foreign . . . and useless words! To a Russian they're good for nothing."

"What is good for something according to you? If we listen to you, we shall find ourselves outside humanity, outside its laws. . . ."

"I've told you already, uncle, that we don't accept any authorities," put in Arkady.

"We act by virtue of what we recognise as beneficial," observed Bazarov. "At the present time, negation is the most beneficial of all—and we deny——"

"Everything?"

"Everything!"

"What, not only art and poetry . . . but even . . . horrible to say . . ."

"Everything," repeated Bazarov, with indescribable composure. . . .

"Allow me, though," began Nikolai Petrovitch. "You deny everything; or, speaking more precisely, you destroy everything. . . . But one must construct too, you know."

"That's not our business now. . . . The ground wants clearing first." . . .

"No, no!" cried Pavel Petrovitch, with sudden energy. "I'm not willing to believe that you, young men, know the Russian people really, that you are the representatives of their requirements, their efforts! No; the Russian people is not what you imagine it. Tradition it holds sacred; it is a patriarchal people; it cannot live without faith . . ."

"I'm not going to dispute that," Bazarov interrupted. "I'm even ready to agree that in that you're right."

"But if I am right . . ."

"And, all the same, that proves nothing." . . .

"How does it prove nothing?" muttered Pavel Petrovitch, astounded. "You must be going against the people then?"

"And what if we are?" shouted Bazarov. "The people imagine that, when it thunders, the prophet Ilya's riding across the sky in his chariot. . . . Are we to agree with them? Besides, the people's Russian; but am I not Russian, too?"

"No, you are not Russian, after all you have just been saying! . . ."

"My grandfather ploughed the land," answered Bazarov with haughty pride. "Ask any one of your peasants which of us—you or me—he'd more readily acknowledge as a fellow-countryman. You don't even know how to talk to them."

"While you talk to him and despise him at the same time."

"Well, suppose he deserves contempt. You find fault with my attitude, but how do you know that I have got it by chance, that it's not a product of that very national spirit, in the name of which you wage war on it?"

"What an idea! Much use in nihilists!"

"Whether they're of use or not, is not for us to decide. Why, even you suppose you're not a useless person."

"Gentlemen, gentlemen, no personalities, please!" cried Nikolai Petrovitch, getting up.

Pavel Petrovitch smiled, and laying his hand on his brother's shoulder, forced him to sit down again.

"Don't be uneasy," he said; "I shall not forget myself, just through that sense of dignity which is made fun of so mercilessly by our friend . . . the doctor. Let me ask," he resumed, turning again to Bazarov; "you suppose, possibly, that your doctrine is a novelty? That is quite a mistake. The materialism you advocate has been more than once in vogue already, and has always proved insufficient . . ."

"A foreign word again!" broke in Bazarov. He was beginning to feel vicious. . . . "In the first place, we advocate nothing; that's not our way."

"What do you do, then?"

"I'll tell you what we do. Not long ago we used to say that our officials took bribes, that we had no roads, no commerce, no real justice . . ."

"Oh, I see, you are reformers—that's what that's called, I fancy. I too should agree to many of your reforms, but . . ."

"Then we suspected that talk, . . . and nothing but talk, about our social diseases, was not worth while, that it all led to nothing but superficiality and pedantry; we saw that our leading men, so-called advanced people and reformers, are no good; that we . . . talk rubbish about art, . . . parliamentarism, trial by jury, and the deuce knows what all; while, all the while, it's a question of getting bread to eat, while we're stifling under the grossest superstition, while all our enterprises come to grief, simply because there aren't honest men enough to carry them on, while the very emancipation our Government's busy upon will hardly come to any good, because peasants are glad to rob even themselves to get drunk at the gin-shop."

"Yes," interposed Pavel Petrovitch, "yes; you were convinced of all this, and decided not to undertake anything seriously, yourselves."

"We decided not to undertake anything," repeated Bazarov grimly. He suddenly felt vexed with himself for having, without reason, been so expansive before this gentleman.

"But to confine yourselves to abuse?"

"To confine ourselves to abuse."

"And that is called nihilism?"

"And that's called nihilism," Bazarov repeated . . . this time with peculiar rudeness. . . .

Revolutionism of Despair*

This youthful and revolutionary lack of scruples was the kernel around which were

* SOURCE: F. Venturi, *Roots of Revolution*, New York, Knopf, 1960, pp. 334-347. (Adapted and abridged.)

crystallized the political ideas that inspired Ishutin and his group. Expectation of a peasant revolution in the near future—within five years, they usually said—was at the very centre of their beliefs. They were in fact merely altering the time predicted by their immediate predecessors of *Land and Freedom* and *Young Russia*. As the revolution was to be "economic" and radical, anything that stood in its way was considered to be harmful to the cause. Thus emancipation in 1861 was only one of the steps aimed at "delaying the revolution in Russia."

This violent opposition to reforms inevitably coincided with the opinions of the most reactionary nobles who had always opposed the emancipation and continued to criticize it. Ishutin's group debated whether revolutionaries had the right to make use of this reactionary state of mind against the "liberator Tsar." Certainly they were opposed to any constitution and liberal concessions. [They desired] to keep intact the collective principle in the life of the Russian peasant and were prepared to destroy any obstacle which stood in the way of its development on Socialist lines. Hence liberalism was the worst enemy of "popular principle." Ishutin's terrorism was a compound of revolutionary Machiavellism and extreme Populism. The killing of the Tsar was to be the shock which would incite a social revolution or compel the government to make substantial concessions to the peasants. The idea of assassination [which arose after earlier appeals to the Tsar and attempts to incite the peasants had failed] was both an act of extreme lack of confidence in the State and a confession that the revolutionaries were too immature to replace it with an organization of their own.

Around a small group of young men inspired by these ideas grew a revolutionary organization, made up of about ten students who were extremely poor. Some were of peasant stock, but most were the sons of country priests whose way of life bordered on that of the [peasants]. They came mainly from the Volga [region], and were students at universities, seminaries and agricultural academies.

Between 1865 and 1866 a secret society was built up which called itself *Organization*. It was to be an extremely select group. Three members were to stay in Moscow to organize the centre and a library; all the others were to disperse in the various provinces and find work as schoolmasters, clerks, etc. Each was to try to build up a library and organize revolutionary activities designed to collect students and above all seminarists. They were then to act on instructions from the centre, forming cooperatives and preaching Socialism among the workers. Their goal was revolution.

But though this *Organization* might [accomplish] propaganda and agitation, it [could] not achieve the group's other aim —terrorism. Within *Organization* there [rose a] still more secret cell which took the name of *Hell*. This consisted of a "commune" of students; i.e., a number of students who lived together in common.

We first hear of this small group of tried revolutionaries at the beginning of 1864. The cell was to remain secret even within *Organization* itself. Its members were to keep secret watch on *Organization*, and invisibly guide it. They were also to enter other secret societies to direct and control them. Any member of *Hell* who made a mistake was to pay for it with his life.

Its goal was terrorism aimed at those members of the government and landowning classes who were particularly hated by the people. Its supreme end was the assassination of the Emperor. The potential assassins were to draw lots to determine who should make the attempt, and the man chosen was to cut himself off from his colleagues and adopt a way of life quite at variance with that of a revolutionary. He was to get drunk, find friends in doubtful circles, and even denounce people to the police. On the day of the assassination he was to use chemicals for disfiguring his face, so as to avoid being recognized, and to have in his pocket a manifesto explaining his reasons for what he was doing. As soon as he had carried out his attempt, he was to poison himself, and in his place another member of *Hell* would continue the work. Even after the outbreak of the revolution, *Hell* was to continue its activities, secretly directing the political forces engaged in the fight and suppressing superfluous or dangerous leaders. Said Ishutin:

"A member of *Hell* must live under a false name and break all family ties; he must not marry; he must give up his friends. He must live with one single aim. For his country he must give up all personal satisfaction and must feel hatred."

The assassination was attempted because a man was found who [believed] that action was needed immediately. "A pale and tired face, hair flowing to his shoulders, [careless] of his clothes." Such was Karakozov between 1863 and 1864, as remembered later by a professor at Kazan University. He came from a family of nobles, small half-ruined landowners, with about fifty peasants.

In 1864 Karakozov went to Moscow to study, but a year later he was dismissed from the university for not paying his taxes. He tried to work as a clerk for a noble, but this left him only with a profound hatred of the aristocracy. He always spoke with scorn of the meetings held between landlord and peasants after the emancipation for the purpose of deciding the size of the land to be given to the latter. Like many others, he too began his activities by devoting himself to education and propaganda. [In] March [1866] he went to St. Petersburg, where, because he had no passport, he was compelled to live in hotels and hired rooms and constantly change his residence. He had brought a revolver with him. He then wrote a manifesto which he left where he thought the workmen would find it:

Brothers, I have long [wondered] why my beloved simple Russian people has to suffer so much! Why next to the peasant and the labourer in his factory are people who do nothing—idle nobles, a horde of officials and other wealthy people, all living in shining houses? They live on the shoulders of the simple people; they suck the peasants' blood. The man responsible is the Tsar. It is the Tsars who through centuries have built up the organization of the State and the army; they who have [given] the land to the nobles. [The Tsar] is the people's worst enemy. So I have decided to destroy the evil Tsar, and to die for my beloved people. Then we will have real freedom; land will no longer belong to the idlers but to the *artels* and to societies of the workers themselves; capital too will belong to the *artels* and the workers.

On 4th April 1866 while the Tsar was about to get into his carriage Karakozov fired at him—and missed; he was [caught] by the police and volunteers among the crowd. To them he shouted, "Fools, I've done this for you." He was led to the Emperor, who asked him if he was a Pole. He answered: "Pure Russian." When asked why he had fired, he replied, "Look at the freedom you gave the peasants!"

The shooting made an enormous impression. It put an end to the few remaining traces of collaboration between the Emperor and the liberal intelligentsia in the direction of reforms.

*V Narod*¹ in 1868 *

Neshdanof was . . . writing to his friend. . . .

"My dear Vladimir: I have been in a large mill with Marianne for a fortnight.

* Source: I. Turgenev, *Virgin Soil*, New York, Henry Holt, 1877, pp. 235-238, 252-253. (Translated from the French, with the author's sanction, by T. S. Perry.)

¹ To the People.

. . . We are waiting for the proper time to act. . . . Judging from what is going on, the moment is not near. . . . I am very, very sad. . . .

". . . Marianne is . . . very earnest. . . . She has plunged wholly into this work, she believes in it—and I!

"But to leave love, and personal feelings, and all such things.

"For a fortnight I have been living [among] the people, and it would be hard to imagine a duller occupation. . . . It is my fault. . . . I am not a Slavophil; I am not one of those who get strength from the people; I never use them for my own ailments. I want rather to act upon them; but how?

"How should we proceed? . . . When I am with them I can only listen and observe, but if I try to speak it won't go at all. I remind myself of a bad actor playing too hard a part. . . . It's worth less than nothing. I'm disgusted with these old clothes that I've put on, with this whole masquerade. . . .

"They say we should begin by studying the language of the people [and learn] their ways. . . . That is false. . . . Have faith, believe in what you say, and speak as you please.

"I . . . [heard] a sort of sermon delivered by a *Raskolnik*[2] prophet. Heaven knows what a jumble of biblical phrases . . . popular expressions . . . using the same words over and over again, like a grouse . . . calling its mate. 'The spirit has seized me, the spirit has seized me'—. . . .

"His hearers did not understand a single word, but what veneration, what enthusiasm, and they followed him.

"But . . . when I begin to speak, I'm like a criminal who is begging their pardon. . . . Marianne . . . has faith. She's at work as soon as its daylight. . . . She is delighted that her hands are becoming red and hard, and she is always awaiting the moment of climbing the scaffold if it should be necessary. . . .

"Oh, how I curse . . . my delicate senses . . . all this heritage from an aristocratic father! What right had he to [beget me] with organs out of harmony with the sphere in which I was fated to live? . . . To beget a man of taste and hurl him into the mire! Create a democrat, a friend of the people, who is sickened by the mere smell of vodka! . . .

[2] Sectarian. Russian religious sects and their often fanatical adherents, grew out of the split from the established Orthodox Church of large numbers of schismatics (Raskolniks) embittered by reforms introduced in the seventeenth century. See pp. 56-57.

". . . Paul, a workman, in the factory . . . has a friend, Elisarius . . . clearheaded, . . . honest as day. . . . As soon as we talk together, there [is] a wall between us; he looks at me as if he were saying, 'No, no.'

"There was [another, more violent fellow]: 'Now, don't talk so much, sir,' he said, 'just one word—do you want, yes or no, to give us all the land you own?' 'Come, come,' I answered, 'what makes you think that I'm a proprietor?' (I remember saying 'God bless you' to myself.) 'But if you belong to the people,' he answered, 'what's the good of all this stuff you're talking? Leave me alone, please.'

"I have noticed one thing: those who like to listen and take the pamphlets without being urged . . . are simple creatures. . . . Or else you come across some fine talker, some fellow with a scrap of education, whose whole learning consists in using continually one and the same word, his favorite word. One of them annoyed me terribly. . . ."

*　　*　　*

This is the way it happened. . . . Neshdanof suddenly became . . . excited. . . . He began to call out and stop the passing peasants. . . .

"Hulloh!" he shouted, "are you asleep? Get up! The hour has come. Down with taxation; down with the proprietors!"

Some of the peasants stared at him with surprise, others . . . thought he was drunk. One . . . when he reached home, said he had met a Frenchman lisping [some] jargon. . . .

Neshdanof was . . . able to understand how ridiculous his conduct was; but . . . he worked himself up into such a state that he lost the power to distinguish [the] reasonable from [the] absurd. . . .

Neshdanof saw eight peasants . . . near the road. . . . He sprang . . . from [the carriage] and for five minutes [made a wild speech].

The words, "Liberty! Forward! Shoulder to shoulder!" . . . [could be heard].

The peasants . . . stared at [him] and seemed to listen . . . attentively; but probably . . . did not understand . . . much, for when at last he . . . ran back with a parting cry of "Liberty!" one of . . . the cleverest . . . said, "How severe he is!" and another added, "He must be one of the leaders." To which the clever peasant replied, "Certainly, or else he wouldn't be rasping his throat in that way. We must look out for our money; they'll be taking it out of us."

Neshdanof . . . said to himself, "Good God, what . . . nonsense! But after all no one knows exactly how to arouse the people. . . ."

Revolutionary Martyrdom and Liberal Sympathy*

On January 24, 1878, Vera . . . Zasulich, 28, . . . appeared in the reception room of General . . . Trepov, Governor of . . . St. Petersburg, allegedly . . . to present a petition. . . . When Trepov approached . . . , she fired a shot, wounding him. . . . Arrested, Zasulich declared that she fired at Trepov because he had given the order to flog a political prisoner, Bogolubov, for rude behavior.

. . . On July 13, 1877, General Trepov [passed through] the prison yard. . . . Bogolubov failed to doff his headgear. . . . Trepov . . . ordered that twenty-five rod strokes be administered. . . .

Zasulich was tried on March 31, 1878. The counsel for the defense, P. A. Alexandrov, asked the court to summon as witnesses several persons who were . . . in [the] prison when Bogolubov was whipped. The court rejected his demand. However, . . . the Code of Criminal Procedure provided that a defendant had the right to summon witnesses at his own expense. . . . Zasulich's counsel made use of this provision. . . .

[According to] E. Naryshkin-Kurakin: "The appearance of [the] young political prisoners created quite a stir. They had been brought into the courtroom from the Peter and Paul Fortress. . . . Their pale faces, their voices trembling with tears and indignation, the details of their depositions —all these statements made me lower my eyes in shame. Then the strong . . . voice

of the defense attorney, Alexandrov, rang out. . . . He mercilessly disclosed the whole despotism of government power."

The counsel based his plea on the tremendous impression produced on [Zasulich] by the unlawful order . . . to whip Bogolubov, which she got from newspaper accounts. To expand on this impression Alexandrov turned to a description of the defendant's former life. . . .

It is easy to imagine how Zasulich passed the best years of her life . . . in the . . . Peter and Paul fortress. [She suffered] complete isolation. . . . No human being, except the warden who brought her meals. . . . Instead of . . . love, . . . only the consciousness that behind the wall, to the right and to the left, were fellow . . . victims. . . .

Indeed, during these years . . . , Zasulich . . . created in her soul one sympathy—a selfless love for everyone who, like herself, [lived the life] of a political suspect. . . .

Then after describing Zasulich's unhappy life in banishment under police supervision, the counsel reverted to the punishment of Bogolubov:

Fifteen years after the abolition of corporal punishment, a political prisoner was subjected to [such] ignominious punishment. . . . The short newspaper accounts [made] an overwhelming impression on Zasulich. A man to whom, by birth . . . and education, the rod was alien; a man who . . . understood all its . . . disgraceful significance. . . ." "What ter-

* SOURCE: S. Kucherov, "The Case of Vera Zasulich," *The Russian Review*, April, 1952, pp. 86-96.

rible torture," thought Zasulich, "what . . . profanation of . . . an intellectual. . . ."

Alexandrov gave a dramatic description of the whipping as Zasulich had mentally reconstructed it. . . . When he said the words: "Everything stood still in the anxious expectation of a moan, and this moan was heard; it was not a moan of physical pain— it was the . . . moan of [an] humiliated, . . . man . . ." passionate applause and bravos shook the hall, . . . overcrowded by a select audience. Alexandrov went on to picture Zasulich's feelings when she learned all the shocking details of the affair.

The fateful question confronted her: "Who will stand up for the . . . honor of a defenseless political convict? . . . Who will stand up for the . . . other wretches? . . . Zasulich expected intercession on the part of the press. . . . But, mindful of the restrictions, the press remained silent. Zasulich also expected help from public opinion. However, public opinion did not crawl out of the seclusion of private study rooms . . . and conversations among friends. She expected, finally, a word of justice . . . but justice remained silent. . . . "If I commit a crime," Zasulich thought, "the silenced question about Bogolubov's punishment will arise; my crime will provoke a public trial, and Russia, in the person of her people's representatives, the jury, will be compelled to pronounce a verdict not on me alone . . . and in the sight of Europe . . . which likes to call us a barbarian state, in which the attribute of the government is the knout. . . ." It was irrelevant to her goal whether the shot directed against a certain person would cause any harm. Zasulich did not want to [hurt or kill] Trepov. . . .

Gentlemen of the jury! It is not for the first time that a woman appears before [this] court. . . . Women who have [killed] their seducers, have appeared here. These women [were] acquitted. These sentences were . . . divine justice, which [weighs] not only the external side of an action, but also its inner meaning—the real guilt of the accused. These women did . . . summary justice, they . . . avenged themselves. But for the first time there appears here a woman who had no personal interest in her crime, a woman [fight-

ing] for an idea, for . . . a man who was for her no more than a companion in distress. If these reasons for crime prove lighter on the scale of public justice, . . . then let your . . . justice take place!

The jurors did not deliberate very long. When they reentered the court hall, their foreman . . . started to read. . . . But when he pronounced "Not guilty . . ." he was unable to continue. "One who was not present," Koni writes, "could not imagine . . . the burst of sound. . . . Sobbing, . . . applause, stamping of feet, shouts of 'Bravo! Good boys! Vera, Verochka, Verochka!'—all this merged into a continuous noise, scream, and howl. . . . In the upper rows, . . . occupied by a lower-class public, people embraced one another; but even in the seats behind the bench [reserved for dignitaries] zealous applause was heard. . . . Somebody was especially active in the demonstration of his approval, just beside my ear. I turned my head. . . . Count Barantsov, an old, stout man, red in the face, violently clapped his hands. When our eyes met, he stopped, disconcerted, but as soon as I looked away, he started . . . again."

As Naryshkin-Kurakin puts it: "The judges, jury, dignitaries, and officials grown grey in the service, all the spectators— [were] carried away by the mood. . . .

Alexandrov was carried on the shoulders of the crowd from the court to his house. [The next day . . . Zasulich was sought by the police and would have been arrested if found. But she had fled abroad.]

. . . The trial . . . had an important consequence: a further limitation of the competence of the jury. [Most] cases of violence against officials were exempted from jury [trial] by the law of May 9, 1878. The most important of these crimes were transferred to the courts-martial by a measure of August 9, 1878. The only political trial which the government took the chance of entrusting to the jury had ended with a defeat for the government. . . . The trial revealed the deep dissatisfaction of the people with the government and its methods. The great majority of the intelligentsia and even a part of the bureaucracy approved the verdict. It was felt that the verdict . . . was a public expression of indignation against administrative violence.

. . . The reactionaries, on the other hand, [were shocked]. Prince V. P. Meshchersky wrote . . . :

The . . . acquittal [was] a nightmare. . . . Nobody could understand how such an impudent triumph of faction could take place in the courtroom of an autocratic empire. [It] showed, alas, . . . the . . . mood of contemporary society. I can say without exaggeration that there were very few of us in St. Peters-

burg at that time who were extremely shocked by this fearful act of violence against justice. We were an insignificant minority, and [in] the highest circles of the hierarchy, including the Senate and the State Council, the . . . acquittal . . . was accepted by . . . almost everyone with sympathy. I remember how persons who later, under Alexander III, spoke of this acquittal with loud indignation, had quite forgotten that in 1878 they had joined those dignitaries who had dared to shout "bravo" when they heard about the acquittal of Vera Zasulich, and lifted their glasses to the victory of justice. . . .

Autobiography of a Tsar-Killer*

From the deposition of Yu. N. Bogdanovich, September 22, 1882; found in the government files (Bogdanovich was implicated in the assassination of Alexander II in March, 1881):

Upon completion of a course in the Pskov land surveyor-assessor classes I entered service in the Velikiye Luki district land surveying office . . . in 1869. In 1871 I was subjected to my first house raid . . . [and] all my . . . books were seized. . . . Judging by the confiscation of the books, among which was not a single forbidden or uncensored one, one can assume that [the raid] was aimed at stopping my pursuit of knowledge in my spare time. This assumption makes sense [since] my closest friends were not my co-workers, but former gymnasium comrades with whom I had very much in common both in years and in spiritual makeup.

[Because] of the raid the governor deprived me of my summer assignments, . . . my main source of earnings. Partly as a result of that, but also because I wished to

continue my education, I quit my job and moved to St. Petersburg. I audited public lectures at the Medico-Surgical Academy and participated in various *kruzhki*[1] of self-education. In 1873, at the time of the famous Samara famine, I, in order to learn about this kind of thing from actual experience and also to acquaint myself directly with the life of the people, went to Saratov and made my way to . . . the starving localities. . . . This trip had an important meaning in my life. . . . I decided . . . to give up my personal career and devote myself to the people's cause. In order to come into closer contact with the simple folk—not for political agitation, but to learn about their life and remodel my own (my previous Russian experience had given me no understanding of their problems)—I went from Samara to the estate of my elder brother, Nicholas. There, in the course of a year, I mastered the blacksmith's trade and was able to open a shop. Shops founded by my brother . . . had the usual purposes of business enterprises, but . . . [he allowed me] to bring in with me students of my acquaintance who also wanted to learn the blacksmith's trade. . . .

In 1875 . . . I went to Moscow to attend a congress of the representatives of *kruzhki* of various orientations and of [various non-

* SOURCE: *Iz narodovol'cheskikh avtobiograficheskikh dokumentov* (From the Autobiographical Documents of the Members of the People's Will), *Krasni Arkhiv,* 1927, XX, pp. 205-231.

[1] Circles. See page 47.

affiliated] individuals. The congress was the first attempt to unify the mounting numbers of narodnik *krulzhki*[2] and individuals. But this purpose succeeded only partly. No general program was worked out. The only decision adopted was to join forces in settling in several central guberniyas where we were to involve ourselves in all forms of popular life, in order—a year later—to be able to present experienced answers to the questions posed at the congress of 1875. To that end, I, for my part, opened a blacksmith and locksmith shop, which I was soon obliged to abandon because the police got hold of [an incriminating document about me]. I was threatened with being arrested and being drawn into the case of the 193.[3] From that time on I decided not to live under my own name.

The above-mentioned preliminary work led to a congress in Petersburg in 1876. There the foundation of a social-revolutionary party was laid down. It was called the Narodnik Party. The theoretical part of its program remains unchanged to the present day [1882]. It made three basic demands: —political freedom, meaning that the right and duty of each person should be subject only to the law; popular representation, as the only basis for really achieving such freedom; and a solution of the agrarian problem in the sense of allowing the customary peasant law to prevail. In that law are included all the essentials of Russian socialism as it exists in practice.

The practical tasks of the party were laid down as follows:—the party must not try to stir up a revolution since that grows out of the total conditions of life, and calling it forth artificially makes success highly doubtful. Each party member should make use of the existing rights and institutions of the

people; (that is, village and *volost* assemblies and courts, the right to representation in zemstvos, schools, co-operatives and artels, etc.) and must raise these institutions to their true significance. Thereby he would evoke in the people and in society the awareness of their common interests, defend the people from oppression by all the social parasites, and try at the same time to bring the people to awareness of their own worth and of their own rights, etc.

As a member of the party I acted according to that program in the course of 1877, '78 and '79 in the Samara and Saratov groups. . . . There came a succession of . . . decrees, increasing the practice of political denunciation. The last possibility of legal activity vanished. . . . At the Lipetsk congress[4] . . . the whole party accepted the program of political struggle.

In 1879 I went . . . to St. Petersburg to take part in the activity of the then organized *Zemlya i Volya,*[5] but arrived on the eve of the assassination [attempt] of Solov'ev[6] and as a result of investigations . . . I had to depart for the provinces. In 1880 I again came to St. Petersburg and received an invitation from the Executive Committee[7] to take part in [the assassination of Alexander II]. . . . I was arrested in March 1882. . . . I have nothing more to say on the subject. . . .

[2] Populist circles.
[3] A famous trial involving revolutionaries charged with spreading revolutionary propaganda. It took place in the period October, 1877, to January, 1878.
[4] A meeting of revolutionists in June, 1879, at Lipetsk, near Voronezh. The delegates decided that terrorism was the only way of struggle left them and that Alexander II must be killed to avenge those executed by the State.
[5] Land and Freedom: the party of the radical narodniks founded in 1877. In 1879 it split into two factions on the issue of terrorism. The group favoring terrorism called itself *Narodnaya Volya*—the People's Will.
[6] In April, 1879, Alexander Solov'ev fired five shots at Alexander II in front of the Winter Palace. All of them missed.
[7] Executive Committee of the newly formed People's Will.

Turgenev's Tribute to Perovskaya*

Sofya Perovskaya, daughter of a highly placed government official, died on the scaffold in April, 1881, for masterminding the successful assassination of Alexander II the previous month.

The Threshold

I see a great edifice. In front a portal opens wide. Beyond the portal I see a gloomy haze. Before the high threshold stands a girl . . . a Russian girl. Freezing winds blow from out of that impenetrable gloom and from the depths of the edifice comes a slow hollow voice:

"Oh, you, who wish to cross this threshold, do you know what awaits you?"

"I know," the girl replies.

"Cold, hunger, hatred, mockery, scorn, injury, sickness, even death."

"I know."

* SOURCE: N. Asheshov, *Sofya Perovskaya, Materiali dlya Biografii i Kharakteristiki* (Sofya Perovskaya, Materials for a Biography and Characteristics), Petrograd, 1921, p. 141.

"Alienation, complete isolation."

"I know. I am ready. I shall bear all the sufferings, all the blows."

"Not only from enemies, but even from relatives, friends?"

"Yes—even from them."

"Good. Are you ready for sacrifice?"

"Yes."

"For anonymous sacrifice? You will die, and no one will even know how to honor your memory."

"I need neither thanks nor pity. I need no name."

"Are you ready to commit crimes?"

The girl nodded her head.

"Do you know," the voice finally said, "that you may dissuade yourself of what you now believe, that you may come to understand that you have deceived yourself and have given your young life in vain?"

"I know that too. I still want to enter."

"Enter!"

The girl crossed the threshold and a heavy curtain fell over the entrance.

"Fool!" Said someone from behind it.

"Saint!" Came the answer from somewhere.

Terrorism and Reaction*

The aim of the *narodovoltsi* [the assassination of Alexander II] had been achieved, but they gained nothing thereby for the country. Having departed from the principle of the narodniki "all for the people—through the people" their heroic struggle led them into a dead end. At best they could gain a victory over separate highly placed

* SOURCE: L. Barrive, *Obshchestvennoye dvizheniye v tsarstvovaniye Aleksandra Vtorogo* (The Social Movement during the Reign of Alexander the Second), Moscow, 1911, p. 154.

governmental persons, but they were not able, with their insignificant strength, to change the political order, nor even to have a serious influence upon such a change.

True, the prestige of *Narodnaya Volya* apparently rose in the eyes of the general public, and even the government of Alexander III thought about entering into discussions with the terroristic party with respect to the coronation and was seemingly prepared to make certain concessions. But the course of internal policy changed in no way because of that pressure. On the contrary—from the first days of the new reign there was no doubt about the course of the government's policy. Characteristic of that was the session of the Council of State of March 8, 1881, presided over by Alexander III. The matter at hand was Loris-Melikov's "constitutional" project. The youthful monarch clearly enunciated his hostility toward anything that bore even a shadow of popular representation and expressed his liveliest approval for the words of K. P. Pobedonostsev, High-Procurator of the Holy Synod. The latter, foaming at the mouth, lashed out at educational attempts of a public character and also came down upon the reforms of the previous tsar, calling upon the government to take decisive action.

In Pobedonostsev's opinion, the zemstvos, the municipal and legal institutions and the press were merely chatter chambers in which were "broadcast anti-governmental ideas, sowing the seeds of dissatisfaction among peaceable and honest people, arousing passions, and stirring the people to the most lamentable illegalities." . . .

"The ruler," Pobedonostsev said, in concluding his speech, "must, in such horrible times, think not about instituting new chatter chambers in which new corrupting speeches will be made, but about taking action. . . . It is necessary to act!"

All actions of the regime of Alexander III. . . . were permeated with the point of view of Pobedonostsev and it was one of the most inspired systems of universal repression in all spheres of social activity.

The Tsar-Persecutor*

[Alexander III] was the ardent champion of the three Slavophil principles of Autocracy, Eastern Orthodoxy and Nationality—" one king, one faith, one law." His watchword became "Russia for the Russians." To carry out this policy, however, time was required. Should war break out, and an enemy gain foot on Russian soil, a revolution might ensue. It was therefore essential that there should be peace, and if Alexander III gained so much credit for keeping the peace of Russia abroad, it was only at the cost of a deliberate attempt to root out of the Empire proper every non-Russian element, and at the same time reduce the homogeneous nation thus produced to a more absolute state of subjection to the will of one man than it had [perhaps] ever known before.

Alexander II had no more devoted subjects than the Finns. They were his best soldiers. While St. Petersburg and other [cities swarmed] with conspirators, Finland remained loyal. "When," says Stepniak, "the

revolutionary propaganda in the army was initiated, it was enough for those conducting it to hear that a certain officer was a born Finn to give up as hopeless the task of converting him."

[Alexander III] loved the Finns, but they must come into the general fold all the same. The contrast between them and the dark Empire of which they formed so bright a fringe was too great. Their free press must take its orders from the [Petersburg] censor. Their Post Office must resign itself to violation of the secrecy of private correspondence. [Finnish stamps were abolished.] Russian must be used as the medium of teaching. Many of the privileges of the Parliament, including legislative initiative, were rescinded. At first the Finns tried to win over Alexander III by their devoted attentions during his annual trips to their country. "Now," says Stepniak, "we hear of all the people running away wherever he appeared. No bouquets, no loyal speeches, nothing but cold isolation."

If Germany cast covetous eyes on the Baltic Provinces, the Tsar would at least deprive

* SOURCE: C. Lowe, *Alexander III of Russia*, New York, Macmillan, 1895, pp. 178-234. (Adapted and abridged.)

Germany of one of the motives for her territorial cupidity by stripping them of their Teutonic character. At the same time if these provinces underwent a radical process of Russification, they would have less craving for assimilation to [Germany]. It was decreed that German was henceforth to be treated as a foreign language and Russian was to replace it. German was at first restricted, then abolished in all educational establishments. A ukase was issued prohibiting all foreigners from inheriting, acquiring, or in any way possessing real property in the western provinces of the Empire outside the ports and the cities. The measure was chiefly aimed at the Germans, whose success as merchants and manufacturers in Poland and elsewhere had excited [Russian] jealousy. In consequence of this decree many German factories were closed, and the persons employed in them returned to Germany, as the only means of acquiring a right to possess property in Russia was to accept Russian nationality.

Poland had to go through the same process. [By decree, numerous persons of Polish extraction were suddenly deprived of their landed estates] thereby reducing many families to beggary. The Polish language was replaced by the Russian for all official purposes.

As the main pillar of despotism is ever ignorance, the Tsar [sought] to withhold from his subjects all illumination of their minds. "Education," wrote an authority, "was restricted to a degree that decimated the universities, reduced the number of schools, sent thousands of young Russians abroad."

An object of even greater hatred than [education] was the Press, which he gagged and persecuted. The most characteristic symbol of [Alexander III's] despotic power was the blacking brush with which he daubed out every article in a foreign journal that might kindle a gleam of intelligence in his subjects. This bondage of the Press was [a major obstacle] to the practical carrying out of reforms and utility of *zemstvos* and municipal councils [and] was also [a] reason why government officials, and even the Tsar

himself, were so ill-informed about what was going on.

[According to an authority who knows Russia]: "The governors and other lieutenants of the Tsar take a keen pleasure in showing what a vast amount of license is compatible with loyalty. Officials of highest political rank acknowledge no law but their own caprices. No epoch or country has ever yet offered such a spectacle of systematic demoralisation."

A propos of the famine [1890-1891] which drove about twenty [million] to the doors of death, M. Dournovo, Minister of the Interior, summoned to St. Petersburg the Governors of all the famine-stricken provinces to [discuss] means of relief. As a matter of course, they saw the Minister before their reports were shown to the Tsar. The [reports] were found too gloomy to be presented to his Majesty. They were modified, and the famine was represented as being almost over when it was entering upon its severest phase.

*   *   *

Whatever the doctored showing of Russian budgets, from the year of [Alexander III's] accession the Imperial revenue [increased] at an incredible rate, "utterly disproportioned to the paying powers of the poverty-stricken population. The peasants are still continually flogged to make them pay up their exorbitant taxes, their live stock, furniture, fowls and huts are sold by auction, and thousands are turned adrift yearly to beg or steal."

*   *   *

Alexander III had not been [long] upon the throne before [serious] anti-Semitic riots broke out in various parts of [the Empire]. What [caused] these outbreaks? Was it fury with the Jews, on account of their supposed connection with the [assassination of Alexander II]? It was to a great extent this conviction (well or ill founded) that acted as a spark to the combustible piles of popular feeling against the Jew. Within six weeks of the crime of March 13, "the Jewish quarter of Elisabethgrad was sacked. Soon after came the terrible fires and looting at Kief.

It was said that between April, 1881, and June, 1882, "no fewer than 225,000 Jewish families fled from Russia." At Easter, 1882, the town of Balt, in Podolia, was the scene of another anti-Semitic outbreak. When asked why they thus indulged their hatred of the Jews, the rioters replied: "They say that our little father, the Tsar, wishes it"; or, "If the Tsar did not wish us to murder the Jews he would have long since issued a ukase to that effect."

Rightly or wrongly, Alexander III, with the vast majority of his subjects, "regarded the Jews as social parasites." Their usurious habits, it was argued, made them the bane of the peasantry, they refused to amalgamate with the Slavs, they made bad soldiers, they shirked manual and agricultural labour; they exploited vice; they cheated in trade; they banded themselves with the Nihilists, and, indeed, formed the brain-power of [the revolution]; they evaded the laws, made to regulate their existence in Russia; and, above all things, they had overleaped the limits of the vast "Ghetto," or "Pale of Settlement," an area nearly eight times the size of England and Wales in which they had been assigned a home. The "May Laws" of 1882 forbade the Jews "henceforth to settle outside the Pale, the only exception being those Jewish colonies that have existed before, and whose inhabitants are [farmers]." A second edict suspended all the Jewish mortgages and leases on landed property, and also their powers of attorney for managing estates; while a third forbade them to carry on business on Sundays and Christian holidays. As some one said of the May Laws, "it was as if all the Jews of Russia were to [be] piled on top of each other, like grass hoppers in a ditch." "When microbes have to be destroyed," said Prince Metchersky, "we do not pause to inquire how microbes like the process."

I have not the space [to describe] the dreadful miseries [resulting] from the expulsion from Russia of *all* foreign Jews; of the hunting of all Russian [Jews], like herds of escaped cattle, back into the pen of the "Pale," where death or desertion of their country stared them in the face; of incidents like the terrible passover "purification," of Holy Moscow under the Grand Duke Sergius, brother of the Tsar. I think that if Alexander III ever becomes known to history by any particular title, like his father, who became the "Tsar Emancipator," that title is likely to be the "Tsar Persecutor."

In 1888, in reply to the representations of the Evangelical Alliance concerning the persecution of the Protestants in the Baltic Provinces, M. Pobedonostseff had the effrontery to write:

"The Russian Government is convinced that nowhere in Europe do all religions enjoy such liberty as in Russia." [The nature of this liberty] was well shown in [the] treatment of the Stundists, [a sect that grew out of the work of German missionaries in Russia around 1860]. They are what the early Puritans and the Methodists were to England. The monstrous fabric of Russian Orthodoxy, with its debasing image worship and sacerdotalism, was put away. "Ceremonies are mummeries," said the Stundist leaders. "God is love, and what He asks of us is love for each other." [By 1880] the new creed [numbered] 300,000. [Said a police superintendent of the Stundists:] "The Stundists are distinguished by their standard of morality; and in [their] villages crime has disappeared. Owing to their sobriety, their economical condition is incomparably better than that of the Orthodox population. Almost all Stundists can read and write. Their family life is exemplary, and their relations with each other are [truly] Christian."

Take the testimony from Orthodox Russian journals: "The insults and injustice which they suffer evoke their compassion. [They feed] the hungry, and [clothe] the naked."

The [hostility of] the [Orthodox] hierarchy [toward] these simple folk may be judged from the leaflet circulated among the faithful, and believed to be the composition of the Archbishop of Kief:

Boom, ye Church thunders,
Flash forth ye curses of the Councils!
Crush with eternal anathemas
The outcast race of Stundists!

The Stundist strikes at our dogmas,
Scoffs at our traditions,
Loathes our holy icons,
The heretic, the damned Stundist. . . .

Such, then, was the spirit which the Church managed to infuse into the Government. In 1878, the persecution began. The infected districts were raided by the police, who closed meeting-houses, confiscated Bibles and hymn-books, [and threw] the leaders into prison. "We must sorrowfully confess," wrote a rural dean in 1881, "that, notwithstanding the earnest attempts made by the Church to wean these schismatics from their errors, *notwithstanding the gentle pressure of the worldly powers,* they continue in their stiff-necked course." Alexander III [was] determined to root out the accursed sect. All through the winters of 1882 and 1883 it was common to see in the village auctions [Stundists'] bedding, clothes, and furniture being sold to liquidate scandalous fines. Soon there was hardly a wretched gang of prisoners on the way to Siberia or Transcaucasia that lacked a Stundist preacher.

The Persecutor Persecuted*

Alexander III persecuted millions of his subjects, [but] many of these subjects in turn persecuted him. The coronation period formed but a lull in the fierce warfare between the terrorists and the Tsar. It had been preceded in April [1881] by another mass trial at St. Petersburg, which showed that the Nihilist organization [had] members in the higher ranks of the army. Towards the end of [1883] the Tsar was [shocked] by the audacious murder of Colonel Soudeikin, chief of the secret police, [who was lured into a private home and beaten to death with iron bars]. About the same time the Nihilists issued a manifesto contrasting the peaceful life led by the Tsar during his visits to Denmark, with the incessant anxieties of which he was the victim while immured in his palace-prison at Gatchina, and declaring that he would never enjoy peace in his own country until he had granted a Constitution to his long-suffering people.

[In October] 1884, there was another mass trial of Nihilists at St. Petersburg. Among the fourteen Nihilists [on] trial for "high treason" were six officers, one of them a Lieutenant-Colonel Aschenbrenner [who]

had banded the officers of his regiment into a revolutionary group, and bound them over to the payment of regular money contributions for the promotion of its aims.

Among this group of revolutionaries was the wife of a physician, Vera Filipoff. She sought to gain over the [army] officers by offering to surrender her beautiful person to their will in return for a written undertaking on their part to restrain their men from firing on the people in the event of a rising. Such a document made every officer who succumbed to her charms—and the number was a large one—the instrument of her self-sacrificing purpose.

In 1885 the police again succeeded in frustrating several plots against the Tsar. When searching a house at Kharkoff [for] a printing press and dynamite, a police inspector was shot dead by a student. But worse than all, Warsaw had been discovered to be the seat of a most serious conspiracy, headed by a justice of the peace.

In the following year (1886) the Tsar was a good deal on the wing, and Europe was presented with the curious spectacle of a monarch hurrying from end to end of his Empire through a lane of troops to protect him from the bombs, and mines and other machinations of his own subjects. Every bridge, every level-crossing of the railway

* SOURCE: *Ibid.,* pp. 234-259. (Adapted and abridged.)

lines by which he journeyed was guarded by well-tried sentries. The Imperial train itself was always divided into several sections, so as to make it impossible for the public to guess which portion carried the Tsar.

And then, how did he live—at Gatchina? [1] Let the following description show:

The park surrounding the castle is surrounded by a strong wall. The forest adjoining the park is also enclosed. These enclosures have been constructed within the last five years at enormous cost. The roads leading to Gatchina are constantly patrolled. Persons not in the service of the Court cannot enter a train or alight at the Gatchina station.

Round the wall of the park [stand] sentries at distances of twenty-five metres, who are changed every hour. Entry into the park and castle is not permitted even to the servants or to the *employés* of the Imperial Cabinet without a special card, the colour of which is changed every week. All persons residing in the Castle are forbidden to lock their doors by day or night. [The] General Inspector of the Imperial residences and [the] Chief of the Police [may] make investigation in the apartments of the castle whenever they think proper.

[An eminent scientist] was specially employed to search for wires or other indications of electric batteries in the apartments, corridors, and outlying buildings of the palace.

On March 13, 1887, the anniversary of his father's murder, the Emperor, [having] at-

tended the commemoration service [in St. Petersburg], was informed that [the] police had arrested six young men, who had posted themselves to [kill] the Emperor on his way back from church. Three carried bombs made to look like books.

Shortly after, the Tsar received a letter from the Executive Committee informing him that it had decreed his death, and that fifty persons had been entrusted with [his] execution. [Among the fifteen] arrested in connection with the plot of March 13 [were] three women and nine university students, mostly Poles and Cossacks. On learning that several of those implicated were teachers and students who did not belong to the class of nobles, the Tsar wrote upon the report, "Education to be abolished!" [2]

In the following year the [Imperial] train [was] completely wrecked. The Tsar had a miraculous escape, [as did] the Empress. His little daughter threw her hands about his neck, and exclaimed, amid sobs: "Oh, papa dear! Now they'll come and murder us all!"

After this the Emperor grew more moody than ever before. He lost his confidence in the ability and the devotion of his Ministers. He avoided even more systematically than before all public ceremonies and amusements. The officers grumbled that he was so seldom to be seen at a review, the aristocracy were dissatisfied that he should avail himself of every slight pretext to stop the annual balls at the Palace.

---

[1] Alexander III took to residing in that palace-fortress, located about 25 miles outside of St. Petersburg, entirely for reasons of security. Hence he was ironically dubbed "prisoner of Gatchina."

[2] The acknowledged ringleader of the plot of March 13, 1887, and the principal defendant in the trial that followed, was the 21-year-old Alexander Ulyanov, whose brother Vladimir (Lenin) was then 17. Alexander was sentenced to death by hanging.

Profits and the People*

Russia's financial situation at first glance reveals a happy and even brilliant appear-

* SOURCE: A. A. Issaieff, *Zur Politik des Russischen Finanzministerium seit Mitte der Achtziger Jahre* (The Policy of the Russian Ministry of Finance since the mid 1880's), Stuttgart, 1898, pp. 1-33.

ance. Comparing 1885 with the present we observe extraordinary progress; an increase of income and expenses in all areas of activity. . . . Tax income has increased by 81 million rubles [88%], railway income by 197 millions [almost 1,000%]. Income from commerce and industry has increased by almost 17 million rubles, tax collection from incomes of capital investments has increased by 221.9% and income from alcohol consumption by 67 million rubles [28.6%]; etc.

Certain [divisions of the government] reveal especially rapid expansion. . . . Expenses of the Ministry of Communications increased . . . 328%, . . . the Ministry of War . . . 13.94% [the Ministry of Finance —25.03%, the Ministry of the Interior—20.07%]; etc.

The Ministry of Finance does not fail to inform us of the advances in Russian industry. . . . The production of factories in millions of rubles went from 1,214 in 1880 to 1,656 in 1890. Vast plants have appeared . . . in recent years, among them steam powered grain mills, brandy distilleries, beet sugar factories and iron foundries. . . . In 1886 the total production of iron ore was less than 33 million poods;[1] in 1894 the figure was 82 million. . . . The Don Basin produced 33 million poods of hard coal in 1889 as compared with 236 million in 1894.

The development in stock exchange trade and the rate of exchange of the shares testify further to the growth of industry. Toward the end of 1895 the stocks of 109 different enterprises, having a par value of 468 million rubles, but a rate of exchange value of over a billion, circulated on the St. Petersburg Exchange. This clearly reveals the enormous increase of profits.

*   *   *

But . . . other infinitely weightier facts reveal Russian life in a different light and prove the great and often pitiful poverty of the people. The statistical data of the Zemstvos show that in many guberniyas one-fourth to one-third of the village population live in huts about four and a half square meters in floor space and no more than two and a quarter meters high. In such a room there often live an entire family of peasants as well as animals. In many guberniyas, even among those in the Black Earth region, one-fourth to one-third [and often more] of the peasant holdings are worked without horses. But enough of Zemstvo sta-

[1] One pood equals 36 pounds.

tistics. Let us turn to government publications. [There it is shown] that 6½% of the population of European Russia has no employment. . . . The average daily wage of the field laborer in the summer, the best season, in the Black Earth region comes to 27-36 kopeks [about 12-17 cents in United States money of the period]. In southwest Russia the daily wage is 40-60 kopeks. In Lithuania and White Russia the average wage is 35-40 kopeks. Everywhere the decline of the handicrafts is apparent. From information compiled about domestic industry by the Ministry of Agriculture we see that an annual income of 50 rubles for a domestic worker is considered quite good. . . . The woodworkers of Tambov and the potters and mat-makers of Kostroma *Guberniya* earn less than 40 rubles. . . . The marble workers and nailsmiths of Perm *Guberniya* earn 26-27 rubles if they are lucky and the potters earn only 17 rubles.

Let us add to these data the figures on tax arrears which have grown to serious dimensions in recent years. According to the reports of the State Control Board [arrears grew from] 50 million rubles in 1885 to 142½ million by 1896. . . . The situation seems even worse when figures from separate guberniyas are examined. . . . In Voronezh . . . , arrears amounted to 164% of the direct payments, . . . to 355% in Kazan . . . , to 492% in Orenburg.

*   *   *

The conditions of consumption also show that the actual welfare of the masses is not advancing. Let us consider the consumption of alcohol, which for all of European Russia, has dropped from 2.8 to 2.32 liters per capita [in the period 1885-1894]. Great numbers of unemployed keep industrial wages at a low level. According to the figures for 1894—a year of good harvests— a weaver earned an average of 10-16 rubles a month. . . . Other industrial workers earned considerably less.

Aside from the condition of the peasants, handworkers, and factory workers . . . , the economic position of the middle and great landowners has also worsened as marked by their great indebtedness. In

1887 the debts to the Nobles' Bank alone came to [69] million rubles. That figure has risen to 667.2 million. . . .

Optimists maintain that the death rate . . . has fallen significantly since only 33-34 deaths per thousand occur each year. But if we recall the not too distant past . . . , we see that the death rate was lower. From 1801 to [1820] the death rate was [about 26.5 per thousand] despite the many wars Russia was then engaged in. . . . From 1831 to 1840 it was 33.6; yet there was famine in 1833 and a cholera epidemic in the years 1830-1831.

How does one resolve the contradictions? How is it to be explained that our financial position is presently so marvelous, but that undeniable facts nevertheless reveal a marked decline in popular welfare, an increase in the indebtedness of the state and the people . . . ? One must ask whether the Ministry of Finance—and precisely that ministry administers the main lines of economic policy—has failed to take measures designed to raise the popular welfare, or, if it has actually done all it could, why its efforts have been fruitless? [The author goes on to discuss the principal measures by which the Ministry of Finances has striven to improve Russian economic life in the decade since 1885.]

I shall now turn to the liquor policy. It was said for many years that a state monopoly on liquor sales would do much good. Since 1894 that project has gone into effect in the four eastern guberniyas—Perm, Samara, Orenburg and Ufa . . . and will eventually extend throughout the empire.

The government has given itself a very complicated task: the state income is to be increased by excluding private citizens from the liquor trade and alcoholism is thereby supposed to diminish. That, the government believes, will be the result if only for the reason that the tavern's replacement by the liquor store will deprive the peasant of the opportunity . . . to trade his clothing and household items for drink. Let us see what the experiment in the eastern guberniyas has accomplished, according to reports in *Vestnik Finansov* [Financial Herald].

The correspondent from Orenburg notes the population's approval of the present quality of the liquor. The monopoly liquor, no longer adulterated with fusel oil, does not go to the head the way the previous liquor did. Liquor consumption has therefore become a more orderly affair: "Observations of the city folk on holiday occasions and of the village population during the annual fair reveal a significant lessening of drunkenness in its overt forms. The limiting of the hours per day when spirits could be bought and the replacement of the former tavern owners by new persons was bound to result in a visible lessening of drunkenness." [The same correspondent also speaks of an increase in state income in various districts despite the lessening sales. A correspondent from a district of Samara *Guberniya* also hails the change as beneficial for the same reasons cited by the first correspondent.]

This information would be encouraging if the correspondents did not at the same time give us less comforting information. "It is true," writes the man from Orenburg, "that drinking in the streets as an evil outcome of the liquor reform has aroused much discontentment." To prevent drinking and disorderly behavior on the streets a police post has been set up in Orenburg in the vicinity of the official liquor shop. The number of drunks picked up in the streets has increased. . . . The purchase of liquor has diminished by almost 220,000 liters, but, the correspondent reminds us, the figures must be viewed with caution if one considers the bootlegging of liquor from outside the guberniya's borders. A correspondent from Chelyabinsk complains about the unfortunate influence of restaurants. Since there are no more taverns many workers visit restaurants. The temperance committees complain . . . , wondering whether one should not diminish the number of restaurants. In Slatust the fight against the restaurants has already commenced. The city government taxed the restaurant owners so heavily . . . that at present there is not a single restaurant in Slatust. It would seem that this would surely eliminate drunkenness. But, the report continues: "Because the habit is centuries old one cannot dream of eliminating it in an abrupt manner—and so street drinking has appeared. In the villages, peasants gather for drinking bouts in the home of one of their comrades, but in the cities, the streets and parks are preferred, and in Slatust the surrounding hills have become the hangout. The disorder, in any case, requires energetic measures on the part of the police."

The Students and the Revolution*

The nurturing bed of Russian intelligentsia ideas and values in the 1890's was the *kruzhok* [study circle]. . . . In these *kruzhki* literature was . . . discussed, . . . theses . . . debated, and sooner or later *kruzhki* became [centers for] conspiratorial [activity]. . . . *Kruzhki* . . . existed . . . in the capitals, in the provinces, . . . in the university, among professional groups, . . . anywhere individuals found some . . . tie of . . . occupation, or interest. . . . They were the hearth of militant oppositional sentiment and the smithy for one's . . . "understanding of life." . . . In barely furnished . . . student quarters *kruzhki* took the form of . . . all night debates over . . . strong tea. . . .

The student days of Chernov, Martov, Maklakov, Posse, and Struve bridged the famine of 1891, and their memoirs . . . picture . . . the strivings . . . of the rising generation. Most of the memoirists date the awakening of their political consciousness to their gymnasium days and their feelings of rebellion against authority and of . . . love for the people even to childhood. Chernov [at] twelve was moved to tears by Nekrasov's poetry extolling the people and copied revolutionary poems . . . from illegal literature. . . . Often influences came . . . through *intelligenty* parents. Martov's father . . . , though a bureaucrat, cherished a cult of Herzen, and as a boy Martov revelled in *My Past and Thoughts*. Acquaintances [visiting] his father spoke with venom of the reactionary press, of Pobe-

donoscev, and [praised revolutionists on trial]. The impressionable youth [heard] of daring exploits in behalf of justice, . . . of fearless courage. . . . Sometimes a . . . youth was infused with radical doctrines through a tutor who [was] an expelled student or an exiled revolutionary. . . . [So] . . . the revolutionary cast of mind [was] implanted . . . at an . . . early age. A number of the memoirists belonged to radical *kruzhki* already in their gymnasium days. . . .

Often older *intelligenty* [sponsored] gymnasium *kruzhki* and supervised their reading. . . . Now and then gymnasium *kruzhki* were "contacted" by revolutionaries or older university students and requested to participate in "demonstrations." Martov recalls his *kruzhok* participat[ing] in the funeral procession of Shelgunov (1891). Thousands of students, representatives of "society," and even workers, walked behind the casket . . . under the careful eye of a police escort. The impulsive youths wished to show their colors and denounce the autocracy openly . . . and were restrained only by the orders of "those who organized the demonstration." . . . When these youths reached the university, they were already well initiated into the sacred literature, knew all the . . . exploits of the *narodovolcy*[1] by heart, and were charged with an expectancy of something grandiose. The emotions of the radical youth upon entering the university are . . . expressed by Martov: "Vague feelings disturbed me and . . . I could not determine . . . what I expected from this holy of holies. . . . The task of

* SOURCE: A. K. Wildman, "The Russian Intelligentsia of the 1890's," *The American Slavic and East European Review,* April, 1960, pp. 157-166.

[1] Members of the terrorist People's Will.

pursuing scientific truth was combined in my imagination with a militant fraternity of youth, hostile to the 'social order.' " . . .

The government had long since noticed that the gymnasium and the university [spawned] radicalism, and decided to reform these institutions. . . . The introduction of the classical gymnasium . . . in the 1870's was designed for this purpose and began to bear its fruit in the 1880's. History, literature, and science were excluded . . . as dangerous subjects. . . . The whole curriculum consisted of Latin, Greek Mathematics, and religious instruction. The theory was that . . . pupils . . . , busy [with] translations and . . . grammar . . . , would [have no time] for . . . dangerous ideas. The new policy had . . . the opposite effect. . . . The harsh . . . discipline and the . . . dry . . . subject matter . . . fostered . . . rebellion. . . . Especially the more intelligent students studied only for exams, and otherwise [satisfied] their intellectual curiosity in circles of their comrades for "self-education." . . . Those memoirists who have no recollection of radical political *kruzhki* nevertheless mention *kruzhki* for the investigation of natural science, history, or literature. . . . Maklakov studied chemistry in such a *kruzhok;* Miljukov, history and literature. Maklakov tells of a student who, having . . . literary talent, neglected his regular studies to develop it. Having an unusually facile mind, he [passed] his final examinations brilliantly [despite] poor marks during the semester. [He was] nevertheless failed with the explanation that "in the gymnasium you are to study what is taught here, and not to occupy yourself with outside subjects only to 'do brilliantly' on examinations." Any evidence of occupation with outside interests . . . aroused suspicion that the student was politically unreliable. The gibe circulated . . . that if a student carelessly left a button on his uniform unfastened the authorities immediately branded him as an "assassin of the Tsar." . . . All the memoirs [recalled] senseless . . . disciplinary measures. Martov . . . was repeatedly humiliated before his classmates by . . . anti-Semitic instructors. [Thus] without . . . radical influences from the outside, an . . . attitude of rebellion against all authority and everything official was instilled in the youth in the gymnasium. The regimen . . . was submitted to only because it was the gateway to the university, where, it was assured, everything would be different.

However, most of the students who reached the . . . university . . . were soon bitterly disappointed with their formal studies. After wandering from one lecturer to another . . . , they soon became bored with the instruction, and, true to their gymnasium habits, resorted to the proven method of "self-education" in *kruzhki,* seldom attending lectures and devouring the instructed material from specially prepared *syllabi* in a few sleepless nights before examinations. . . . The statute of 1884 attempted to impose the same regimen on the university which had successfully been introduced into the gymnasium. The students now wore uniforms, [and] organizations were forbidden. . . . The students were constantly spied upon, their activities reported, and often their quarters broken into . . . by university police who searched for compromising literature. In Moscow the inspector Brizgalov trained his own battalion of loyal students who reported on their fellows, guarded distinguished persons from humiliations by the radical students, and staged demonstrations of . . . patriotism. These students . . . received special privileges, such as cancellation of their fees.

These strictures bred in the students a . . . spirit of protest . . . which soon manifested itself in chronic disorders and demonstrations. As usual, the government . . . broke them up with Cossack troops, mass arrests, and exclusions. [That brought] the studentry to a boiling point. The suppression of one demonstration simply evoked [a] larger one, and often they spread from one institution to another. The . . . disorders of 1886 led to the closing of five universities.

. . . The critical turning point was the famine of 1891. Students became infected with the enthusiasm of "society" and went in droves to the people as volunteers in staffing the canteens or as doctors' assistants during the epidemics. Many became disgusted by the ineptness and delays of the government. The question was raised squarely of how such a catastrophe could overtake Russia. The radical ideologies offered a ready-made answer and provided an outlet for their indignation. . . . A definite change in attitude [arose] among the students. The majority no longer reacted against mixing "politics" with student demonstrations. . . . [The student groups tended] to spread, to form central organizations, and to unite with other universities:

The organized studentry was acknowledged as a . . . component part of the revolutionary intelligentsia . . . the natural *avant-garde* of the nation-wide . . . movement. . . . The students were summoned to go to the aid of the starving, to enter units for struggle with epidemics, to enter . . . Sunday schools [these were *not* for religious instruction, but for giving workers a basic education, often used by radicals for propaganda purposes] in workers quarters, with the basic aim to strengthen ties with the working masses and subsequently to make use of these ties . . . for the revolution.

A central bureau was set up in Moscow to restrain from "isolated, scattered outbreaks" and upon occasion to "set the whole studentry in motion at once. . . ." Because of its policy of biding its time for a concerted revolutionary outbreak, the Union Council often found itself in the curious position of restraining their fellow students who were inclined to "demonstrate" at every opportunity. . . . Demonstrations over purely academic matters were regarded as a waste of time by the leadership and likely to bring about premature repressions . . . by the authorities.

Purely academic disorders continue to take place on a considerable scale. The government again provokes a radicalization of the studentry by senseless repressions. The climax comes with the introduction of new "temporary rules" in 1899 which revived an institution from the era of Nicholas I of sending students involved in disorders into the army. The . . . moderate protest of Kievan students [became a] test case and 183 students were sent into the army. [That started] demonstrations on a large scale, climaxing in the massive demonstration by St. Petersburg students and the sympathizing public . . . on March 4th, 1901. Its brutal repression through beatings and exiles led to [further] radicalization of the studentry, making it an important component force in the revolution of 1905.

Lenin on Liberal Activity (1901)*

Famine
Again famine! Not only the ruin of the peasantry has been taking place in the last ten years, but their positive extinction. . . .

Since famine has become an habitual phenomenon in our country, it would be natural to expect that the government would try to entrench itself in the policy it has been conducting in regard to the distribution of food. While in 1891-1892 the government was caught unawares, and was at first

* SOURCE: V. I. Lenin, *Collected Works,* 1929 IV, Book 2, pp. 13-51.

thrown into consternation, now . . . it is rich in experience and knows quite well [what to do]. In our July issue . . . of *Iskra* we wrote:

. . . misfortune is hovering over the country, and the government is once again preparing to play the . . . heartless rôle of taking the bread from the starving people, and of punishing every one who in the opinion of the officials has no "authority" to render aid to the starving.

The government . . . rapidly . . . [made] its preparations. [That] is illustrated by the

Elizavetgrad affair. Prince Obolensky, the governor of the Kherson province, immediately declared war against all who dared to write or speak about the famine in Elizavetgrad, appeal for public aid for the famine-stricken, organise private circles and invite private persons to organise this aid. The Zemstvo doctors wrote to the newspapers stating that famine raged in the county, that the people were disease-stricken and dying, and that the "bread" they were eating was positively beyond belief, and could not be called bread at all. The provincial governor enters into a controversy with these doctors, and officially denies that there is famine. Any one at all acquainted with the conditions under which our press has to work, any one who will . . . recall the . . . persecution to which even moderate organs and . . . authors have been subjected . . . , will understand the significance of this "controversy" between the provincial governor and mere Zemstvo doctors, who are not even in the government service! It was simply a gag, an obvious . . . declaration that the government will not tolerate the truth being told. . . . But what is a mere declaration? . . . The Russian government [never restricts] itself to mere declarations when the opportunities exist to "make a display of authority." And Prince Obolensky hastened to make a display of authority, personally appeared at the scene of war—war against the famine-stricken and against those who, though not on the payroll of any department, desire to render *real* aid to the famine-stricken, and *prohibited* a number of private persons (including Madame Uspenskaya), who had come into the famine-stricken area, *from opening food kitchens*. Like Julius Cæsar, Prince Obolensky came, saw and conquered. And the telegraph immediately informed all the reading public in Russia of this victory. One thing, at least, is astonishing, and that is that . . . this brazen challenge to all Russians who have retained . . . a shred of decency . . . met with no resistance whatever on the part of those who, one may say, were most interested in this matter. Very many persons in the Kherson province . . . knew . . . what is behind this silence

about the famine, and the fight against famine relief, but no one has published a single statement on this . . . case . . . or even a simple . . . protest against the monstrous order prohibiting the setting up of food kitchens.

. . . Apparently the administrators, who are conducting war against the famine-stricken, consider the most important "enemy" . . . to be private relief circles, private food kitchens, etc. With a frankness deserving of full recognition Mr. Sipyagin[1] explains why private philanthropy has . . . disturbed the slumbers of the Ministry of the Interior:

Commencing from the bad harvest of 1891 and 1892, and during all subsequent calamities of a similar kind [says the circular], it has [often] been found that certain philanthropists, while rendering material aid to the inhabitants of the affected districts, strive to rouse . . . dissatisfaction with the existing order . . . and stimulate . . . unjustified demands upon the government. At the same time the failure to meet the distress to the full, and the inevitable . . . disturbances of industry that arise from that, create very favourable ground for anti-government agitation which is . . . taken advantage of by politically unreliable persons . . . under the cloak of helping their neighbour. Usually, [with] the first news of a serious shortage of grain . . . , persons with not irreproachable political pasts stream into the affected districts . . . , [make] contact with representatives of charitable organisations in the capital who have come into the district, and who, through ignorance, engage these persons as helpers, and [thus] create serious troubles to the interests of good order. . . .

The Russian government is becoming hard pressed in the land of Russia. There was a time when only the students were kept under special guard . . . ; contact with them on the part of persons with not irreproachable pasts was regarded as a great offence. . . . In those very recent times, there was no other [group] that in the eyes of the government, represented "an extremely favourable soil for anti-govern-

[1] Minister of Interior, 1899-1902.

ment agitation." But since the middle of the nineties . . . government communications have pointed to another and [much] more numerous class . . . as requiring special surveillance—the factory workers. The growth of the labour movement compelled the government to establish a whole system of institutions to maintain surveillance over this new rebellious element. Among the districts [closed to] residence for politically doubtful persons were included, in addition to the capitals, and university cities, factory centres and settlements, counties and whole provinces. Two-thirds of European Russia was placed under special protection against unreliables, and the remaining third is becoming so crowded with "persons with not irreproachable political pasts" that even the most remote province is becoming restless.

The Third Element

The term "third element" or "third persons" was employed . . . by the vice-governor of Samara, Kondoidi, in his speech at the opening of the Samara Provincial Zemstvo Assembly in 1900. He used this term to designate persons "belonging neither to the administration nor to the representatives of the estates." The increase in the numbers and influence of such persons serving in the Zemstvo as doctors, technicians, statisticians, agronomists, pedagogues, etc., has long ago attracted the attention of our reactionaries, who have also described these hated "third persons" as the "Zemstvo bureaucracy."

Generally speaking . . . our reactionaries (including . . . the higher bureaucracy) reveal a fine political instinct. They are so well-trained in fighting against oppositions, . . . popular "revolts," religious sects, . . . and revolutionists that they . . . understand far better than naïve simpletons . . . that the autocracy can never reconcile itself to . . . independent convictions and pride in real knowledge *of any kind whatsoever.* . . .

Indeed, if men in public office are to be judged, not by the positions they hold in the service, but by their knowledge and merits, will it not logically . . . lead to the creation of freedom of public opinion and public control, which would judge this knowledge and these merits? Will it not undermine the privileges of the estates and ranks upon which alone the Russian autocracy rests? Listen to the argument Kondoidi advances to justify his displeasure: "Representatives of the estates, sometimes without proper reason, hearken to the words of intellectuals, notwithstanding the fact that the latter are merely salaried servants of the administration, merely because they talk about science or quote . . . from newspapers or magazines." *What!* Mere "salaried servants" teach "representatives of the estates!" . . . It can be said that in Russia there are two governing "classes": 1. The administration, and 2. The representatives of the estates. There is no room for a third element in a monarchy resting on the estates. And if disobedient economic development more and more undermines the foundations of the estates by the very growth of capitalism, and gives rise to the need for "intellectuals," the number of which is continuously increasing, then it must be expected that the third element will strive to push out the framework that hems it in.

"The dreams of those belonging neither to the administration nor to the representatives of the estates in the Zemstvo," said Mr. Kondoidi "are fantastic, but if used as a basis for political tendencies, may become harmful." . . .

We shall now relate the attempt of another administrator, the chief of one of the central provinces, to advance a different argument for being displeased with the third element. According to [him] the activities of the Zemstvo in [his] province "are year by year departing from the principles upon which the regulations governing Zemstvo institutions are based." According to these regulations, the local inhabitants are empowered to manage affairs dealing with local needs and requirements. Owing to the indifference which the majority of landowners display towards the right granted them, "the Zemstvo Assemblies have become *a mere formality,* and affairs are conducted by the administration in a manner that leaves much to be desired." This "in many administrations has led to the growth of large staffs and to the practice of inviting to the Zemstvo the service of *experts*—statisticians, agronomists, . . . sanitary inspectors, etc.—who, conscious of their *educational* and sometimes their *intellectual superiority* over the members of the Zemstvo, have begun to display *increasing independence,* which, in particular, is achieved by convening all kinds of *assemblies* and by setting . . . committees in the administrations of the province. As a result, the whole of the Zemstvo administration has fallen into the hands of persons *who have nothing in common with the local population.*" Although, "among these persons there is a large number of well-intentioned persons, worthy of . . . respect, nevertheless, they cannot regard their service as anything else than a means of livelihood, and they are interested in local needs . . . only to the extent that their personal welfare depends upon it." In the opinion of the chief of the province, "in Zemstvo affairs, *the hired man cannot take the place of the employer.*" . . . The real master of everything is the property-owner—proclaims the representative of the camp from which praises are constantly heard of Russia and its strong and . . . independent government which is above all the classes and which, thank God, is free from the domination of the selfish interests and parliamentary corruption that prevail in Western countries. And since the property-owner is the master, he must be master also of medical, statistical and educational "affairs." . . . [Thus the provincial chief openly recognizes] the political predominance of the propertied classes. What is still more curious, he does not hesitate to admit that these "experts" are conscious of their educational and sometimes intellectual superiority over the members of the Zemstvo. Of course, what other measures can be taken against intellectual superiority than measures of severity? . . .

Recently, our reactionary press had presented to it an excellent opportunity for raising the demand for these measures of severity. The refusal of the intellectuals to permit themselves to be abused like ordinary hired men, . . . instead of being treated like citizens fulfilling definite public functions, has [occasionally] led to conflicts between the bureaucrats of the administration and the doctors—in consequence of which they used to resign in a body—with the technicians, etc. Recently, the conflicts between the administrations, and the statisticians have assumed a positively epidemic character.

. . . The lengths to which the suspicious provincial authorities went can be judged from the following:

S. M. Bleklov, manager of the Taurida bureau, in his *Report on the Investigation of the Dnieprovsk County During May and June, 1901* . . . , relates that work in this county was carried on under . . . unprecedented conditions. Notwithstanding the fact that the provincial governor had given his consent to their undertaking these duties, that they were furnished with the necessary documents, and . . . were entitled to the assistance of the local authorities, the investigators *were surrounded with extreme suspicion* on the part of the county police who *followed on their heels* and expressed their distrust of them *in the rudest manner,* so much so that, as a peasant related, a . . . constable followed in the wake of the statisticians and questioned the peasantry as to whether "the statisticians were not carrying on propaganda . . . against the state. . . ." The statisticians "encountered various . . . difficulties which . . . hindered their work, [and] outraged *their . . . personal dignity.* Frequently the statisticians found themselves, as it were, *in the position of persons charged with a crime.* . . . The moral depression which they . . . suffered can therefore be very well understood.

Not a bad contribution to the history of agrarian statistical conflicts, and the description of the surveillance which is maintained over the "third element," is it?

No wonder the reactionary press rushed in to attack the "rebels." The [*Moscow News* in September published an angry] article, entitled "The Strike of the Zemstvo Statisticians," . . . and [another] entitled "The Third Element," [in October]. "The third element is raising its head too high," [says the latter] article. It is resorting to "systematic opposition and strikes," in order to resist the attempts to introduce "necessary discipline in the service." The blame . . . rests upon the Zemstvo Liberals who have demoralized the employees.

Pamphleteers and Peasants in 1902*

The first great portent of the broad peasant movement were the peasant risings in Poltava and Kharkov Guberniyas in 1902. Tens of thousands of peasants were involved in the movement, but only a thousand or so were brought to court for partaking in the mass disorders. A . . . large peasant movement also took place in Voronezh and Saratov Guberniyas. Unrest also took place the same year in the villages of Chernigov *Guberniya.* . . .

The governor of Chernigov received the following notice from the police department:

"As can be ascertained from the report of D. P., the spread of the revolution among the rural populace . . . in most cases happens in the following manner: In one or another region there appear unknown young people, who, passing through in railroad trains and in carriages, or on horseback along country roads, or on foot through the villages, scatter the revolutionary books and pamphlets about, . . . or hand them to peasants, asking that they read them or give them to others to read. Often these books are secretly left on the property and in the buildings of the peasant farmsteads. . . . In the market places and bazaars they are placed in peasant carts, and are thus carried by the peasants themselves to the most remote places. The books and pamphlets are eagerly read by the rural populace and . . . are passed on without any thought of evil from one person to the next. In some cases public readings of them have been delivered to whole crowds of peasants. When the peasants learn the contents of the literature, rumors spread among them about imminent partition of the proprietor's lands and relations with the local landowners become more or less strained. Soon thereafter the district police, alarmed by the news of excitement among the peasants, arrive upon the scene. . . . The literature is of course gathered up,—far from all of it,—and . . . interrogation takes place. This usually has no results since the revolutionists guilty of distributing it remain undiscovered and . . . have merely transferred their activity to another locality. It is easy enough to see that in a struggle with that sort of propaganda, administrative investigation and confiscation of . . . pamphlets can have no success and that all endeavors must be directed toward uncovering and arresting the agitators and distributors of underground literature. . . . To this end the local gendarmerie is . . . inadequate in view of their small numbers and the vastness of the regions they must watch over. It would seem then to be necessary to take measures to alert the peasants themselves to seize the agitators and hand them over to the authorities and thus nip the evil in the bud."

* SOURCE: I. G. Drozdov, *Agrarniye Volneniya v Chernigovskoy Gubernii v Gody Pervoy Revolyutsii* (Agrarian Disturbances in Chernigov Province in the Years of the First Revolution), Moscow-Leningrad, 1925, pp. 11-12.

Plehve's Scapegoats*

Minister of the Interior, M. von Plehve, is to-day, at the head of the greatest state in the world, nothing else but the greatest police spy in the world. His politics are stamped with all the characteristics of a police origin, police in the Machiavellian sense—*i.e.,* crime in the service of order. His unbelievable falseness is the thing about which all complain. "Every word that he speaks is a lie," is the assertion which one oftenest hears about him. He persuades the Czar that revolution is at hand, and keeps him in continual, nerve-killing anxiety by means of threatening letters, proclamations, and so forth, which he causes to be smuggled into the Emperor's pockets. He actually provokes disorders, in order to strengthen his position. He is continually discovering conspiracies and handling the supposed members in the most fearful way in order to prove his indispensability. The whole store of police tricks has been pillaged by Plehve in order to bring his system to a state of perfection. In particular the Jews and the Poles must suffer in order to contribute to the indispensability of Plehve. Not a soul in Russia doubts that the Kishinef massacres were the direct result of his commands.

In Warsaw the windows of the members of a committee which had collected money for a Polish hospital corps were stoned by students. Immediately was sent the telegraphic order to investigate the thing most thoroughly, and if those who were the sufferers had not refused all assistance to the police another couple of dozen would-be rioters would have been sent to Siberia, in order that the existence of a Polish revolution might be proved. A Russian editor, whose paper had been suppressed because of the publication of a revolutionary poem, [was told], according to a Russian nobleman, that if he should simply declare to

[Plehve] that the poem had been smuggled into the paper by Jews, he would immediately obtain permission to publish his paper again! From a conservative aristocrat in the service of the state, I received in all seriousness the information that only Plehve, in league with Alexeyev,[1] had conjured up the war by holding off the Japanese, simply because in this way he would become so much the more indispensable.

The government [tells] foreigners that to permit the Jews to settle beyond the pale[2] would mean the ruin of all Russia. [However, a] memorial in regard to the Jews, written in 1884 and published by the ministry of the interior—*The Jewish Question in Russia*—shows by statistics that the prosperity of the peasantry in the governments within the pale is incomparably higher than in the territory from which the Jews are excluded. The arrears of revenue in districts in which there are no Jews are three times as great as in the pale. The usurers who advance money to the peasants at from three hundred to two thousand per cent. are without exception Christians. The assertion that the Jews tempt the people to drunkenness stands morally upon about the same level as the statement that the Jews are never found engaged in agriculture. The latter statement is true, but only because the Jews are not allowed to live in the open country. The government has now monopolized the

---

* SOURCE: H. Ganz, *The Land of Riddles,* New York, 1904, pp. 154-256. (Adapted and abridged.) The author was a Viennese journalist.

[1] In the summer of 1903, the Tsar appointed Admiral Alexeyev, a proponent of Russian expansionism, to the post of Regent for the Far East. His headquarters were at Port Arthur.

[2] The Jewish pale of settlement, outside of which Jews were not permitted to reside, was a belt of territory running through Lithuania, Poland, Belo-Russia, the Ukraine, and Bessarabia. For the most part, it coincided with the domains that Catherine II had taken from Turkey and Poland in the period 1768-1795. Catherine had instituted the restricted zone to prevent the Jewish merchants that had fallen under Russian rule from competing with those of Russia proper.

retail sale of spirits, thus driving out of the business thousands of Jewish tavern-keepers. This measure, however severe, is viewed with satisfaction by intelligent Jews as tending to improve the morals of the Jewish masses.

All these are only idle excuses in justification of the policy of extermination of the Jews, which policy has in reality a quite different cause. Three conditions have already been cited, any one of which is alone sufficient to place the Jews in an especially bad situation.

The first is the great influence which the rich Russian usurers possess with the authorities. The Jew exacts usury when he can but in comparison with his Russian colleague he keeps within modest limits, being indeed compelled to do so by his circumstances. He necessarily prefers to keep the debtor solvent rather than to drive him out of house and home, which he, the Jew, moreover, cannot buy in. The Russian usurer, on the other hand, is accustomed to show no mercy, because he calmly seizes the land of his victim. For a great part of the Russian usurers belong to the guild of village usurers. These people influence the under authorities with bribes, while the millionaire usurers of Moscow and St. Petersburg, who likewise would have to fear the milder methods of their Jewish competitors, are powerful enough to influence senators and ministers.

The second and more powerful cause is the spirit of Pobydonostzev, the fanatic of uniformity. A prisoner who endangered the spirit of blind obedience by a tendency to dispute orders could not be tolerated in a prison. As little can the great Russian prison state endure men who might lead the prisoner to think whether he must be absolutely a prisoner. Of such thoughts, however, the Jews, who are subject to special taxation, are suspected above all others. Their criminality is certainly of the smallest; they are the most punctilious of tax-payers, and the best-conducted citizens in the world. But, perhaps because of their Talmudic-dialectic occupation, perhaps also because they have little cause to be enthusiastic over the ruling order, they are inexorably subtle critics of

all existing things, and so could easily upset the simple minds of the Russian lower classes. That is the chief reason why they are surrounded by a cordon of plagues. Quite without Jewish criticism the Russian peasant, [lashed by hunger], begins to grumble; and although his unruly sentiments express themselves chiefly in the specifically Russian form of the organization of religious sects, nevertheless each new sectarian shows a new desertion from Pobydonostzev's ideal of a Russian subject. Upon the organization of sects, however, the Jews have of course no direct influence whatever.

The third cause of the persecution of the Jews is to be found in the Satanic brain of Plehve, who wishes to furnish to the Czar an indication that without the Jews there would be no opposition whatever in Russia. For this purpose he not only has the Jews entered more strictly on the police-registers, if they are guilty of any political offence, such as being present in a forbidden assemblage, but he also directly provokes them, in order to drive them into the ranks of the revolutionaries and thereby to compromise the latter.

The final cause of the persecution of the Jews is the certain income which legislation against the Jews means for every unscrupulous official. Most of the laws passed against the Jews are quite impossible of execution, or are executed only in a very imperfect way, thanks to the corruptibility of the Russian officials. The bureaucracy, not willing to renounce its income from bribes and extortions, prevents all legislative decrees in favor of the Jews.

The worst thing that has happened to the Jews is not an occasional "pogrom" in which defenceless people are slain and plundered by command of the authorities. The worst is the restriction to particular zones and to particular callings. That is a deliberate policy of destruction and extirpation. Even if the misery of the ghetto has, thanks to the strict abstemiousness of the Jews, failed as yet to kill them, nevertheless the moral result is frightful. Even the iron family morality of the Jews is shaken in the western governments. A deplorable percentage of prostitutes is made up of Jewesses.

Whoever can tries to free himself from the ghetto. Legislation has left some small gates open, and through these the struggling Jews squeeze themselves. The authorities try of course to prevent too many of them from settling in cities which it is desired to keep as free from Jews as possible. But the Jews try again and again to evade the prohibitions and to settle where there is a possibility of a means of livelihood. Such cities are, for example, St. Petersburg and Moscow. A non-resident Jewess is not allowed to study in these places, but may live there as a prostitute. An innocent young girl wished to have herself registered as a prostitute, so that she might attend the university.

A well-known Orientalist, a man of seventy years, had business to execute in Moscow which he did not succeed in finishing before night. No hotel would have taken him in; and he could not endanger any of his friends, for if in the frequent nocturnal rangings of the police in Jewish dwellings a Jewish guest without a passport should be taken, the host would lose his right of residence. In his difficulty the old man asked a railroad official how he could pass the icy-cold night. The man told him of the only place where a man is permitted to take a room and spend the night without a passport—a brothel. Accordingly, this man of seventy was obliged to pass the night in a room with a drunken prostitute, and sat until morning in a chair, praying.

Whoever works as assistant to a dentist, and has obtained a certificate, may open an office for himself. The only requirement for this is that it shall be well fitted up and that nobody shall sleep in it. This facilitation is granted because of the fact that in Russia there is a great lack of dentists. The Jews meet tricks of the authorities with tricks of their own. They pay for a dentist's certificate, fit up an office, and then go into trade in bed-feathers or calico. The police official who wishes to prove whether the dentist's profession is really practised has some ruble notes slipped into his hand. Very recently the Jews have found a means to

become known as Christians without baptism. Good-natured priests, who receive nothing at all for a baptism but a large price for a written declaration that X. Y. is an orthodox Christian, draw up such declarations. The unbaptized Hebrew comes as an orthodox Christian to Great Russia and carries on business, while the helpful priest receives a little income from him.

In general, the Jew must be able to pay; in that case life is not hard for him in Russia. But woe to the poor wretch who cannot pay at every step!

The Sectarians

The significance of sects in Russian life is best shown by some figures. In 1860 about ten million Raskolniks (non-conformists) were counted; to-day they number thirty million. These non-conformists not only do not belong to the orthodox church, but stand in hostility to the state, which identifies itself with the orthodox church. The sects answer much better to the religious needs of the Russian people than the state church, just as they already comprise what is morally the best part of the nation.

They are to be distinguished at present— sects with priests ("Popovtzy") and sects without priests ("Bezpopovtzy"). [Among the] sects without priests are the Danielites, the Khlysty, [and] the Skoptzy. With the Danielites voluntary death by fire is considered meritorious. The Khlysty have direct revelations from heaven. They are flagellants, dance in rings until they are exhausted, and then sink all together in a general orgy. The Skoptzy castrate themselves. All these sects are accused of child murder. They are said to wish to send children unspotted to heaven. The persecution of these sects by the government is easy to understand. Spiritual epidemics must be fought as much as physical disease.

The persecution of the rationalistic sects is quite unjustifiable. They do not deserve the name of sects at all, for in other countries similar ones form simply free political, ethical, or philosophical societies. Certainly they can only benefit the communities in which they exist by their strict morality.

Tolstoi has already made the [infamous] banishment of the Doukhobors known to all the world, and has thereby raised large contributions for their settlement in Canada. The Shaloputy and the Malevents have a really ideal character, free from the narrowness and superstition of the church, without ritual, industrious, [and] peaceful. They live together in free-love marriages, without constraint of church or state, neither lie nor swear, and do good even to their ene-mies. The Stundists are similarly virtuous communists.

Why is all this [persecution]? Pobydonostzev's system permits no falling away from the official church. The police state tolerates no suspicious morality. The crime of the [sectarians] consists in wishing [to live] in the spirit of Christ, and in being disaffected towards that diabolical machine the Russian state. For this they are persecuted in the name of Christ and of the state.

A Lawyer on Corruption (1904)*

I was introduced to one of the foremost lawyers of St. Petersburg.

"One circumstance makes it uncommonly difficult here to obtain justice," began the lawyer. "I refer to the strained relations between the bench and the bar. Here the judge is more hostile to counsel than in other countries, and often is inclined to make them feel his power. In [criminal] cases the defendant may easily pay the penalty of the animosity which the judge feels towards his counsel."

"What is the cause of this?"

"It has only too human a cause. It is not unheard of for a busy lawyer of reputation and good connections to earn thirty or forty thousand rubles a year, or more. Compare with that the wretched salaries of the judges, imagine the over-burden of work of the bench and the lack of public appreciation, and you will comprehend why our judges do not look at the world in general through rose-colored glasses, and particularly at the prosperous lawyer."

"You say lack of public appreciation. Is the position of judge not an honorable one?"

"On the whole, no official in Russia is much respected. At the most he is feared. The most lucrative positions, however, are those of the administrative department and the police. In these branches are to be

* SOURCE: *Ibid.*, pp. 182-194. (Adapted and abridged.)

found the most rapid and brilliant careers, and therefore the sons of great families, in so far as they become officials, prefer them. The judge must work hard, and has small thanks."

"Does not this evil have a moral effect on the impartial administration of justice also?"

"You mean, in plain speech, are not our judges to be bought? Well, I must say that the majority of them are superior to bribery. To be frank, there is professional ambition enough; and the effort to please superiors is almost a matter of course, since the independence of the judges, which had brought us extraordinary improvement in the candidates for the office, has been set aside again."

"Your judges are not, then, independent and irremovable?"

"What are you thinking of—under our present régime? We do not wish independent judges. A minister of justice like Muraviev, who certainly constitutes the supreme type of all that is meant by the expression, 'A man of no honor,' is the strongest hindrance to justice. Therefore, a monetary acknowledgment to the whole senate is expected for each satisfactory judgment. Seven judges were promoted out of turn by Muraviev on consideration of the kind support which they gave to the Ryaboushinskys, the Moscow millionaires, against the Bank of Kharkov."

"But you said," I objected, "that the

judges are not open to bribery. Yet they performed an illegitimate service to millionaires."

"Certainly I said the judges are not open to bribery; but I did not say that of the minister of justice."

"You mean, then, that he was paid for the judgment given in the interest of the millionaires?"

"Your astonishment only betrays the foreigner. Only the little debts of the honorable minister were paid off—good Heavens!"

"It is incomprehensible."

"On the other hand, the judge has everything to fear when he is not compliant. Do you suppose that a comedy of justice like that of Kishinef can be played with independent judges? And yet there are always heroes to be found who fear no measures, but administer justice according to their convictions. That is the astonishing thing, not the opposite, under a Muraviev-Plehve régime."

"Was it better, then, formerly?"

"It was, and would have become better still if our authorities had remained true to their mission of uplifting the altogether immoral people instead of corrupting them still further. In the system of Pobydonostzev, politics take the place of morality. Premiums are set upon all sorts of unwise actions, if only they seem to lead to the levelling of the masses, who are to be kept unthinking."

"You say the people are immoral?"

"They lack—above all things, the sense of justice. No one here has rights. No one thinks he has. The natural state of things is that everything is forbidden. A privilege is a favor to which no one has any claim. To win a lawsuit is a matter of luck, not the result of a definite state of justice. One has no right to gain his cause simply because he is in the right. You were to-day in the Hermitage. At a certain door, before which stood a servant, you asked whether people were permitted to enter. The answer was not 'yes' or 'no,' but 'Admittance is commanded,' or 'Admittance is not commanded.' This spirit extends to the smallest things. If you should to-day suffer heavy loss by robbery or burglary, what should you do?"

"I should report the matter, of course."

"You say of course, because you feel the duty of personally upholding law and order. When the same thing happens to me, a Russian, I must first conquer my natural tendency, and then after a long struggle I, too, will report the matter, because—well, because I, as a lawyer and a representative of justice, am no longer a naïve Russian, but am infused with the usual ideas of justice. The normal Russian [rarely] reports a case to the police, because he absolutely lacks the conviction of the necessity of justice. When he says of anybody that he is a clever rascal, his emphasis is laid on the word clever, which expresses unlimited appreciation."

"That must make general intercourse exceedingly difficult."

"Certainly. To live in Russia means to use a thousand arts in keeping one's head above water. One never has a sure ground of law under his feet."

*   *   *

"And can your press do nothing to better this general corruption?"

"We have a saying, 'It is hard to dig with a broken shovel.' Talented people like ourselves soon learned from abroad the little art of corrupting the press. With a fettered press like ours, this is less difficult here than in other countries, where a paper respecting public opinion might under some circumstances be unreservedly outspoken. Moreover, you must always keep one thing in mind: a press may exert tremendous power by publishing a man's worthlessness, until he is made powerless in society; but since here notorious sharpers are readily accepted in the highest ranks of society, and even grand-dukes do not escape the suspicion of corruption, it does no one any harm to be reported as having dexterously spirited away a few hundred thousands."

"You say even grand-dukes?"

"—Are not safe from suspicion. I can personally testify that not one of them takes a ruble himself. But the persons who live by obtaining concessions for joint-stock companies, etc., know how to represent that they need considerable sums for the purpose of influencing the highest persons."

"And intelligent business men believe that?"

"Believe it? No one would understand the opposite. Imagine a scene in my office. A business man comes to me with a case. He inquires my fee. I say five hundred rubles. He asks what will be the expenses. I say a few rubles for stamp duties, etc. Then he becomes more definite. He means the *charges.* 'There are none,' I answer. The man of business rises, disappointed. 'Ah! so you have no influential connections?' Outside the legal profession, which still lives on the tradition of the time of its independence, every one is open to bribery; and every one reckons with the fact."

"And no one is angry at open injustice?"

"What is injustice? Despotism of the great. We have been used to that for thousands of years and accept it like the caprices of fortune. The peasant makes no distinction between a hail-storm which ruins his crop and an authority who oppresses or injures him. There is no way of resisting either; for when one curses God, He sends greater misfortune; and when one disputes with the authorities, one is absolutely lost. 'Duck, little brother; everything passes'; that is the final conclusion of our wisdom. We are educated to it by inhuman despots and by an official service of thieves and debauchees. We lack, too, the sharply defined idea of ownership, in which the sense of justice, considered psychologically, has its root. You know that here the peasants own their own land only to an extremely small extent. The individual is merged and lost in the 'mir' (village community), where the trustee, the 'zemski nachnalnik,' the village elder, and liquor rule. This *obshtchina,* communism, is the strongest fortress of reaction. No ray of enlightenment penetrates it. At the utmost, misery and ever-returning hunger produce finally a condition of despair in which the peasant is capable of anything except an action which might advance him in civilization. In the census of 1898 there were found villages where no one had any idea what paper is, and peasants who did not

know the name of the Emperor. The 'mir,' moreover, is in its nature opposed to private ownership, and every discussion between the member of the village communism and the property-holder is artfully prevented by the scattering about of compulsory peasants. For property-owners are at present for the most part Liberal. The régime, however, stands or falls with the isolation of the peasantry from Liberal influences. For the peasant is not unintelligent by nature, and, if he is not prevented, he learns very quickly."

"That is also, then, one of the causes of the ill-treatment of the Jews?"

"It is *the* cause. Sectarians and Jews are the only people who have a moral code of their own, and, therefore, know how to distinguish justice from injustice. They are also the only ones who criticise the actions of the authorities. Therefore, it was a matter of self-preservation for the autocracy to isolate the Jews and make them harmless. Do not suppose that any anti-Semitic feeling is prevalent among us. The autocrats are trying artfully to implant it. . . . But the effect does not go deep, thanks to the same circumstance which makes the progress of civilization difficult; the peasant cannot read, and does not in the least believe the priest. The massacres of Kishinef were directly commanded. Every man was killed by order of the Czar. No anti-Semitism exists among the people. Whatever anti-Semitism there is is sown by the government for the purpose of isolating the peasants in order that 'the urchins may grow up stupid.' "

"Ought not the Jews to take that into account and not meddle with politics?"

"I see no reason why the Jews should become accomplices of this soul-killing régime. They will be oppressed whether meek or unruly. Moreover, the Jews have never received so much sympathy from us as since they began to place themselves on the defensive and to make common cause with our Radicals. Thanks to [Plehve's] machinations, all the intelligent opinion among us has become favorable to the Jews. They are our brothers; they suffer with us and for us."

I closed my interview, as in all cases, with the question, "What hope is there for the future?" and received the [usual] answer: "Everything depends upon how this war ends. If God helps us and we lose the war, improvement is possible; for then . . . the chronic bankruptcy of the nation, can no longer be concealed.

Police as Union Organizers*

In 1902 Zubatov[1] was at the top of the official ladder and resolved to establish friendly relations between labor and the monarchy. With that objective in mind he set himself to remove all the radical elements from the labor ranks, at the same time encouraging the workers to fight for their economic interests. Zubatov had no difficulty in persuading a few of the imprisoned revolutionists and several Moscow professors to join in his project. The university men began a series of lectures among the workers on mutual aid, consumers' societies, labor exchanges, the housing crisis, and the long working day. Workers' aid societies were organized in Moscow, St. Petersburg, Kharkov and other cities, and became the foundation of the Zubatov idea. Supported everywhere by the gendarmerie these organs of "police socialism" developed with extraordinary rapidity. Encouraged by the success of their initial effort Zubatov and his agents ventured a step further. Not only did they encourage the workers to demand reforms but actually began to direct the economic struggle of the wage earners against their employers.

In this sphere the Zubatovites were very successful in Moscow where the chief himself was in command, and also in Odessa and in the west. Bent on stealing the thunder of the revolutionists the Zubatov forces did not limit their activities to propaganda, the management of strikes and the organization of factory committees. They began to organize mass demonstrations. One of these took place in Moscow on March 3, 1902, and enlisted 50,000 workers who placed a wreath on the monument of Alexander II in commemoration of the abolition of serfdom.

Alarmed by the proportions of the demonstration and stirred by the opposition of the industrialists who in a memorandum to Finance Minister Witte protested against the "anti-capitalistic" activities of the Zubatov organizations, the government gave orders against the repetition of similar demonstrations and for the suppression of the Zubatov societies.

The workers' aid societies were officially liquidated and Zubatov was transferred to St. Petersburg. However it soon became evident that it was much easier to handle Zubatov than the workers. Labor had tasted fraternization and liked it. The workers refused to relinquish their new privileges and continued to hold meetings.

Again Zubatov perceived the need of conciliation rather than repression. After a weeding out of the radical elements the St. Petersburg Aid Society was reorganized as the "Society of the Russian Factory and Mill Workers." To make sure of the right leadership Zubatov appointed as director of the new society the priest Gapon who was a trusted member of the secret police. Every effort was made to keep the workers out of politics. Dances, musicales and discussions on legitimate subjects were arranged for them. How long, under normal conditions, the gendarmerie would have succeeded in keeping the society within the prescribed sphere of interest is difficult to say. The unpopular war with Japan changed the character of the organization and turned the tide more definitely against the autocracy. Because of the general unrest among the

* SOURCE: Manya Gordon, *Workers Before and After Lenin,* New York, Dutton, 1941, pp. 30-34. (Adapted and abridged.)

[1] Sergei Zubatov, chief of the Moscow secret police.

workers there was a rapid influx into the society which soon had a membership of 8,000.

The result of this persistent effort of the secret police to win the wage earners away from the influence of the very few revolutionists and to establish an alliance between the workers and the monarchy is historically both interesting and instructive. Numerically the underground revolutionary organizations were trivial. They were not in the least responsible for the agitation among the workers, which was inspired by the war and the general condition of the country, but the monarchy and the industrialists remained insensible to the situation. Father Gapon on the other hand was greatly affected by the awakening in the labor ranks and was completely carried away by the unsettled atmosphere. Instead of leading the workers he was being led by them.

Gapon did not sever his connection with the police department, but under the influence of the wage earners his lectures assumed a political slant. Toward the end of 1904, at the Putilov Works, four workers of the Gapon organization were dismissed for subversive propaganda. Gapon and other members of the society took up their defence and as a result of their efforts a strike was declared. The demands of the strikers, which were drawn up by the priest and his associates, included an eight-hour day, the question of wages to be left to joint committees representing labor and the management; organization of a permanent committee of members of the administration and freely elected employees; a 55 per cent in-

crease in the pay of women, and 43 per cent in the wage of unskilled male workers. The employers refused to meet these terms and strikes were called in other industries. Within three days the ranks of the strikers embraced 140,000 workers and Gapon's organization became the centre of this teeming mass. Under the spell of the aroused and at the same time pliable mood of the strikers, the priest and his associates harangued and lectured unceasingly. The employers remained unperturbed and unwilling to make any concessions, insisting that acceptance of the terms of the strikers would be "followed by the complete collapse of Russian industry."

Having failed in his negotiations with the industrialists Father Gapon conceived the idea of taking the matter directly to the Czar. This proposition was received by the workers with great enthusiasm. The strikes grew with amazing rapidity and the hopes of the strikers were concentrated on the priest. They hung upon his every word, confident that he was leading them in the right direction. Yet they saw Gapon merely as a mediator and guide. Their real faith was in the Czar. At that moment their trust in the benevolence of Nicholas II had mounted to the point of frenzy.

[On Sunday, January 22, 1905, the workers, their wives, children and parents, marched behind Gapon, who bore a petition which he hoped to be able to place in the hands of the Czar at two o'clock in the square before the Winter Palace. So began "Bloody Sunday."]

Section 2

Twilight of the Romanovs

REVOLUTION OF 1905

T HE revolutionary movement had been amply inspired in the preceding decades by the government's indifference to the sufferings of the poor on the land and in the cities and by the persecution of the non-Russian peoples and the liberal and radical intelligentsia. However different the goals of the various opposition elements by the turn of the century, there existed a vast body of sentiment that was united on the general principle that one way or another the plaints of the vast majority should be heeded. Adding fuel to all the separate flames was the universal hatred for the war with Japan that was sacrificing the young men on battlefields and waters so distant that it could not be justified in terms of national defense. The political aims of the war were likewise without meaning to the general public.

Further impetus was given the revolutionary movement by the weakness manifested by the government late in 1904, when, after the assassination of Plehve, it relaxed the regulations with regard to press censorship and public meetings of the liberal opposition and even permitted demands for constitutionalism to be stated openly. A similar weakness was also apparent when, in March, 1905, shortly after the assassination of the Tsar's uncle, who was Governor General of Moscow, Nicholas II called upon the Minister of the Interior, Alexander Bulygin, to draw up a project for a consultative assembly of "the worthiest men" to be elected by the people for the purpose of aiding him in the drafting of legislation. These slight concessions were in no way intended to lead to a restriction of the autocrat's power and were designed mainly to appease the liberals. With regard to the people at large, whether in or out of uniform, whether Russian or non-Russian, the Tsar felt no need to make compromises. Bureaucratic brutality went on unimpeded.

The indifference of the regime to the plight of the striking St. Petersburg factory workers led to the politically disastrous massacre of hundreds of workers, their wives, and children in the January (Bloody Sunday) demonstrations before the Winter Palace of the Tsar. Growing peasant bitterness brought armed mass attacks upon private estates, some 2,000 of which were sacked and burned in the course of the year. Soldiers and sailors, maltreated as ever, responded with mutinies. Strikes and demonstrations multiplied, workers being joined by teachers, students, and even by professional people. In Poland, the Baltic Provinces, Finland, and the Caucasus, antigovernmental flare-ups became the order of the day.

In the meantime, the government's strong right arm—the front line army—was engaged in a life-and-death struggle 6,000 miles away from European Russia. Still failing to appreciate the extent of the popular fury, the Tsar, in August, heightened it further by announcing that Bulygin's consultative Duma of the "worthiest men" [1] was soon to be elected. The right wing of the zemstvo liberals (but not the left wing) accepted this concession. The socialists, who led the workers, regarded it as a slap across the face. So came the grand October climax of the Revolution of 1905. A railway strike on October 21 paralyzed the government's forces and was followed by a nine-day general strike, history's first, that began on the twenty-sixth.

Having no choice, the Tsar proclaimed, in the Manifesto of October 30, his intention to convoke a representative assembly, or Duma, to be elected by universal manhood suffrage. For a few weeks thereafter, the Soviet (Council) of Workers' Deputies that had risen in St. Petersburg to direct the strike movement seemed all-powerful. But soon the revolution was on the defensive. The revolution-minded elements rejected the continuation of a monarchical regime, however limited, and broke ranks with the liberals. After peace had been made with Japan in September, the army began returning from Manchuria to give the regime the armed strength it had lacked. At the same time a propaganda and pogrom machine, organized early in the year, was put into motion by the Union of the True Russian People. The so-called Black Hundreds, headed by the most reactionary elements of the upper classes and composed of all manner of thugs and self-seekers, roamed the land to beat and murder all those who would upset the autocracy and despoil Holy Russia. The St. Petersburg Soviet was forcibly dissolved on December 16, and a last-ditch protest rising of Moscow workers, beginning December 21, was quickly suppressed. From late in 1905 through 1906, punitive military expeditions were sent throughout the empire to drown the revolution in the blood of workers, intellectuals, and national minority peoples. The Jews, as usual, bore the brunt of the barbaric vengeance.

THE ERA OF STOLYPIN

Constitutional government in Russia began with the convocation of the First Duma in May, 1906.[2] That body and its successor, the Second Duma, were rendered

---

[1] The council of the "worthiest" was to have included nobles, wealthy members of the bourgeoisie, and peasants. Property qualifications in the towns would have excluded much of the intelligentsia and all the workers.

[2] While the Tsar was reading his speech of greeting to the newly elected Dumas delegates—mostly workmen and peasants—who thronged the Georgevsky throne room of the Winter Palace, Stolypin, looking nervously about, expressed the fear that one of the "M.P.'s" might have a bomb on his person. See V. N. Kokovtsov, *Iz Moego Proshlago, Paris,* 1933, I, pp. 173-174.

ineffectual as legislatures, because they were respected neither by the Tsar nor by the preponderant majority of the democratically elected deputies. The Third Duma (1907-1912) and the Fourth, the latter's activity having been abruptly curtailed after the outbreak of war in 1914, managed to function as parliaments, however unrepresentative and restricted. The Gordian knot of mutual and unremitting hostility between the Duma and the Tsar's government was slashed by P. A. Stolypin, Prime Minister from 1906, when he replaced Goremykin, until his assassination in 1911.

Stolypin, having successfully employed police agent tactics to create a pretext for dissolving the "rebellious" Second Duma in June, 1907, proceeded arbitrarily to alter the democratic electoral laws in such a way as to assure that conservative deputies would predominate in the next Duma. Thus he converted the Duma into a body willing to work along with the Tsar's ministers. At the same time, delegations of all significant political movements were given the opportunity to express their views. In the Duma sat the representatives of the extreme right—the monarchists, the clergy, and the nationalists; the Octobrists, who represented the rising capitalists and the less reactionary landowners; the Constitutional Democrats (Kadets), representing mainly professional persons; and national minority parties and the various socialist factions. Of all these, it was the Kadets who were primarily interested in maintaining parliamentary forms on the English model. The press, although badgered by administrative restrictions, remained a force able to influence public opinion.

Stolypin regarded it as essential that the government itself sponsor reform measures rather than allow all progressive initiative to come from the Left. Although notorious for the stern measures he used against activists from the socialist and national minority camps, Stolypin realized that mere suppression was not enough to quell the spirit of revolution. Hostility to the government, he believed, was best assuaged by laws that would improve the conditions of life, particularly of the long-suffering peasantry. Also, in a country moving rapidly from a feudal toward a capitalistic way of life, he understood the need for reform in the spheres of court and police procedures and in education and industry.

In striving to act as a constitutional reformer, Stolypin was faced with immense difficulties. The Tsar, not responsible to the Duma, had wide freedom of policy action. The Duma, moreover, even the "respectable" and law-abiding majority, was split between status-quo-minded landowners, clerics, and bureaucrats, on the one hand, and the business and liberal groups on the other. The men of commerce and industry desired a controlling voice with respect to governmental expenditures, and the liberals objected to government brutalities against revolutionaries and repressive acts directed against national minority groups. The majority of the people, being inadequately represented in the legislature, remained resentful and were often made more so by the insufficiency of the reform measures and their inefficient manner of execution.

Basically, Stolypin had three aims: (1) He strove, through a series of measures introduced in 1906 and in 1910, to remove the peasant from his commune-bound status and radical social orientation and transform him into a conservative-minded private farmer. He further provided for new land tracts to be purchased by the peasants with the aid of state loans and promoted the resettlement of peasants from overcrowded regions of European Russia into Western Siberia. (2) He attempted to bring about an alliance between the landowning nobles and the *nouveaux riches* of the business and industrial classes, as had been achieved in Prussia, so that the government would have stability at the top. This plan met with little success. (3) He sought to avoid all tensions in foreign affairs, since he reckoned that "twenty years of quiet" [3] would be required to reform Russia. That accounts for his attempt at ameliorating somewhat the situation of the Jews, whose persecution had brought Russia's government such bad publicity in western Europe and the United States. With revolutionaries he was ruthless, and the military tribunals set up throughout the land sent hundreds to the gallows.

Since his policies met with considerable opposition in and out of the Duma, he acted as a virtual dictator. He often resorted to emergency article 87 of the constitution to adjourn the Duma and legislate by decree, and he sometimes even used his great authority to force concessions from the Tsar. The revolutionaries naturally regarded him as an unmitigated tyrant. The seventh attempt on his life, made while he was attending a gala opera performance in Kiev, was successful. Nevertheless, his successors, who continued his policies, seemed well on their way toward achieving his aims when war broke out. It is conceivable that had he enjoyed his "twenty years of quiet": his policies, designed to raise the living standards of the broad masses, would have obviated the revolution that grew out of the war.

WORLD WAR I

At the war's outbreak in August, 1914, the government received an unmerited measure of patriotic support. Except for the Bolshevik Party—its Duma delegates spoke out against participation in the "imperialist war," and were soon arrested, tried, and found guilty of subversion—liberals, moderate socialists, trade unions, even most of the national minority peoples (all usually in opposition) rallied behind the Tsar in the so-called Sacred Union.

Blockaded and little industrialized, Russia, in the first year of the war, yielded vast stretches of territory, including all of Russian Poland, to the efficient and powerful German forces. Granting that the cards were stacked against Russia in the military-industrial sense, the Tsar's regime fought its worst battles on the public opinion front and rapidly antagonized both upper and lower classes. Poles, Jews,

---

[3] Stolypin meant an absence of war and revolution. Lenin, however, mockingly referred to Stolypin's "quiet" as "the quiet of the grave."

and the industrial workers suffered from the usual restrictions and persecutions. Minority groups, in general, were subjected to brutality while serving in the army. Patriotic efforts on the part of Zemstvos and city Dumas were hampered by bureaucrats. General disgust with the conduct of the administration led even deputies of the conservative parties in the Duma, hitherto suspicious of Kadet "radicalism," to join forces in a Progressive Bloc, organized during the summer of 1915 by Kadet leader Paul Milyukov. The Bloc hoped to exert enough pressure to compel the Tsar to appoint a ministry of capable men who could work in harmony, "enjoy the confidence of the country," and be able to organize the active co-operation of all citizens.

Scandals involving shortages of military supplies at the front and consequently astronomical numbers of casualties had shocked the people. Further undermining their morale were stories of their leader, the Tsar, dominated by an hysterical wife, alleged to be pro-German. She in turn heeded the counsel of Grigory Rasputin, self-appointed emissary from heaven and also rumored to be in the pay of German agents. It was common knowledge in the capitals that the free-living Rasputin passed upon all important official appointments and that these could be had, regardless of a candidate's merit, through bribes in the form of money or through the favors of beautiful women, or, simpler yet, by joining the *starets* (elder) in night-long drunken brawls in the cabarets of St. Petersburg.

Few honest or capable men could stand the climate of stupidity and corruption that soon prevailed in all the departments of government. But to criticize the existing state of affairs—that is, to complain about Rasputin—meant to court instant dismissal. And so, by late 1916, Russia was, in effect, a rudderless ship. A fog-like gloom descended upon the populace. The patriotic murder of Rasputin in December, 1916, by the Tsar's nephew, Prince Yusupov, came much too late to do any good.

Rubbing further against the already tense nerves of the people were the urban food shortages and the fuel crisis in the factories. The latter particularly affected the Petrograd industrial region which, before the blockade, had depended for its coal supplies upon imports from Britain. But coal production in Russia also fell, and the result was the closing down of numerous plants. The food crisis was the product of a variety of factors. Petrograd, Moscow, and other centers had become swollen with refugees, but the usable railway cars and locomotives had dropped to one-third their prewar number by 1917 and were much less able to transport food. To check the widespread drunkenness, the sale of liquor had been prohibited. The peasants were thereby deprived of, what Kerensky terms, their "last and very weighty reason" for carting grain to urban markets. Manufactured goods were not available and "all the peasant could get in exchange for his grain, butter and meat was the depreciating ruble." [3]

[3] A. Kerensky, *The Crucifixion of Liberty*, New York, 1934, pp. 202-203.

By the winter of 1916 there were food shortages even in the army, and the city workers, whose real wages had fallen, found it ever more difficult to supply their families' needs. Those who had the means could get what they needed from the growing swarms of speculators. By early 1917, long lines of working-class women, babies in their arms, stood outside bakeshops, frequently waiting in vain while the supply of bread ran out. In March, 1917, the bread shortage in Petrograd led to riots that marked the beginning of the revolution.

Bloody Sunday and the Tsar*

The following is from the notations of A. S. Ermolov, Minister of Agriculture and Government Properties in the period of the political "springtime" of 1904-1905, with respect to his conversations with Nicholas II on the subject of Bloody Sunday:

After my most respectful report of January 17, 1905, the emperor asked me about the true state of affairs. To this I gave my honest opinion . . . as follows:

"Russia is at present going through the most serious period in her history and it is impossible to foresee the consequences. Your Majesty is the autocratic tsar of the Russian land, but if the autocracy is to remain firm it must rest on a solid base. . . . But events move swiftly and one must anticipate every possibility. If the bloodshed on the streets of St. Petersburg was supposed to stop the workers movement, it not only did not do this, but possibly had the reverse effect. The agitation has not stopped but has only assumed different forms; it may express itself in a series of assassinations, which, for all we know, are already being prepared. . . . From these . . . , even you are not safe, whatever security measures you may take. . . . We are all convinced of your personal bravery, but your life belongs to Russia, and you must think of what would happen to

the State and the throne if an assassination attempt were to succeed."

Tsar: "I don't fear death, I trust in God, but I know that I have no right to risk my life."

"Yes, you have no right to risk it . . . , but you must also consider upon what principles the autocratic rule must base itself. It cannot base itself on troops alone. On the 9th of January the troops carried out the grim task assigned them; they fired on the defenseless crowd. The excitement produced in Petersburg has now spread to most of the cities of Russia and it is everywhere necessary to suppress it with the force of arms. So far this has been successful. The soldiers have done their duty. But one must consider firstly what would happen if the disorders move from the cities to the villages, and the peasants rise. . . . With what forces and what soldiers would one then suppress that new *Pugachevshchina*,[1] raging through the whole country? Secondly, can one be sure that the soldiers now obeying their officers and firing on the people will do it again if the occasion rises, especially now that they have heard the curses heaped on them by their victims?"

Tsar: "I understand that a government's position is impossible if it rests on soldiers alone."

"Yes, Your Majesty, but you must make it clear to yourself, upon what your rule is

[1] A great peasant rebellion like the one led by Pugachev in 1773-1774.

based. You can base yourself only on the people, but for that, it is necessary that the people have faith in you and continue to view you as their protector. Consider for a moment what occurred on January 9. Masses of workers from all quarters of Petersburg came to the court of Your Majesty not with evil intentions, not to overthrow the throne, not with political demands; all such demands contained in their petitions were based upon the teachings of revolutionary leaders. The great majority of the workers knew nothing about those demands or did not understand them. They came to their tsar in order to bring to the throne the most respectful expressions of their essential needs, in order to lay before you all their bitterness, all the hardship of their situation. The representatives of those masses had first turned to your ministers, but none of them was admitted, none was heard, although at that very time a conference of factory owners was held and their opinions were listened to and taken into account. The crowd came to you, confused by their leaders and believing that you would admit them, that you would appear and listen to their appeals. I won't speak of what happened next. . . . Perhaps it was necessary for the maintenance of order. . . . But the truth is that among the defenseless crowd there were hundreds of victims who did not even understand why they were being killed. Your Majesty, I think that if you had a real government you could have been forewarned. I do not know whether it would have been possible for Your Majesty to go out before that crowd, but I do believe that its declarations should have been looked at in advance. Your Majesty could have announced your willingness

to admit a deputation of workers, to look over and approve of their legal wishes, excluding all those which could not have come from the workers, like the absurd demand for separation of Church and State and similar expressions [of revolutionists' influence]. Unfortunately such precautionary measures were not taken and terrible things happened. But . . . one way or another you must turn to the people with your word as tsar. The people must hear from you personally of your profound sympathy with respect to the tragic occurrence and must hear the expression of Your Majesty's will to review and approve of the just and legal demands of the workers. Needed most of all is an expression of sympathy for the innocent victims of the catastrophe. Among the fallen masses were not only ringleaders and revolutionaries, but women and children, who just happened to be on the site of the events. Your Majesty must come to their assistance. Even if the guilty deserved their fate, their families and children were innocent victims. . . . In Petersburg various ladies and sisters of mercy are making collections for the sufferers. I know that they have approached members of the Council of State. If they come to me, I shall feel obliged to give as much as I can without asking where the money is going; whether it is really to be used for the victims of the catastrophe or whether it will be used for further agitation. . . . Only if you also help, Your Majesty, will the people separate you from responsibility for the events of January 9."

Tsar: "I have already decided to turn to the people with an appeal. . . . I propose to see a deputation of workers . . . , and I intend to aid the victims of the catastrophe."

The Peasants in 1905

A secret report of April 7, 1905, from the Governor of Tver Guberniya to the Minister of the Interior:[1]

[1] SOURCE: M. N. Pokrovsky (ed.), *1905, Materiali i Dokumenti* (1905, Materials and Documents), Moscow-Leningrad, 1925, pp. 82-84.

In completing form No. 3522 requested on March 21, I have the honor to inform Your Excellency that there are no indications that general dissatisfaction with existing conditions have been uncovered among the peasants of Tver *Guberniya*. Also one sees no peasant risings as in most places. However, turning to the specific questions raised in your form, I consider it necessary to add, that (1) with regard to the matter of the unwillingness of rural communes to draw up their accounts of taxes due, there are indications that in certain localities . . . the peasants, as rumored, intend to evade their legal obligations. Among the peasants of Iverov, Gnezdov . . . volosts, of Staritsa District, the story goes around that one does not have to pay one's dues. The peasants of V . . . *Volost* . . . stubbornly refuse to pay any kind of taxes, and the peasants of several villages of L . . . , F . . . , D . . . and C . . . volosts . . . are saying that they will soon stop paying. (2) With regard to the violation of the property rights of owners one must say that large-scale wood filching has been going on all over the *guberniya* for a long time, and that such stealing has no relation to the present conditions. Among such violations of owners' rights there [is the] stealing of wood in the forests of Zhivoy and Tsvetov, dating from the time of the abolition of serfdom and carried on by the peasants of R . . . *Volost* . . . ; the former estate of the landlord Orlov, consisting of seven villages. These thefts went on from year to year thanks to the initial absence of supervision and punishment, and then the peasants, because of what they considered an unfair division of the land, proceeded to rob the woods, considering themselves justified despite the judgments of the courts. At present the majority of the villages of the above-mentioned estate have made peace with the owners of the woodlands on the basis of new arrangements with respect to the partitioning of the land. . . . [The report lists many more instances of forest robbing.] From the above it is obvious . . . that the reason for the filchings in the indicated forests and the acutely tense feelings of the peasants toward the forest guards rises out of the fact that four or five years ago the government office of agriculture and State lands took away from peasant use, and enclosed, many publicly rented fields, long under lease of peasants who had raised the fields to a fine condition after many years of labor. Then these areas were turned over to the protection of the forest guards. This

ruined the peasants and placed them in unbearable straits since they needed the land badly. Besides that, the peasants of the villages of M . . . and T . . . volosts . . . , under the influence of recent events,[2] are openly saying that since they have insufficient land of their own they intend to use that of the landlords. . . . (3) There are rumors of division of land to be taken away from private owners, but only in certain districts. . . . (4) It should be mentioned that in certain villages of Korchev and Kalyazin districts the peasants, basing themselves upon incorrect interpretations of newspaper accounts of His Majesty's manifesto of August 11, 1904,[3] have since that date avoided making tax payments and their refusal to pay has led to [further] rebelliousness and complications.

At my disposal are . . . indications that workers returning from factories in the chief cities and persons sent from factories and workshops to their places of registry [in the communes] act as disturbing elements among the peasants. In most cases the [rurally] rooted peasant shows distrust toward those outsiders. They believe that the factory people are in a better material condition than they and regard strikes and disorders in the factories as signs that the city workers, "having no real needs, are frying in their fat" [getting angry for no reason]. In any case . . . the workers' movement in the cities is getting no sympathy from the peasants. Equally small is the influence of agitators, trying to involve the people in the antigovernment struggle on questions of constitutions and political rights. These matters on the whole interest the peasants little. . . . On the other hand matters pertaining to land and taxes . . . bring them to life. They interest themselves in news of the war. The peasants have begun to read the papers whenever convenient and while believing all that is printed in the legal publications they are closely acquainted with all questions found in papers of various political views. They are mainly concerned with articles and discussions appearing many times

[2] Violent seizures of land by peasants during 1905.
[3] The proclamation of the Bulygin Duma; see page 64. The exact date was August 6.

in the daily press on the subject of the economic condition of the peasants and, of course, interpret all news from the point of view that suits them. One must admit that the influence of the papers on the peasantry is at present very great and that the papers' present tone of passion, of disquiet with respect to all issues, regardless of their political position, helps to excite the people. . . . Despite the aforementioned circumstances and the generally heightened feelings of all classes of people, produced by the war and the internal complications in the government's functioning, I still don't expect, at least not in the near future, any serious peasant disorders in Tver *Guberniya*. Disorders might break out in isolated villages and communes that need land or in those that have long had strained relations with the neighboring landowners . . . , but I don't think that they will reach the stage of actual civil disobedience.

However, I cannot omit mention of one factor; namely, that the maintenance of order in local regions depends largely upon whether new mobilizations will take place in the *guberniya*. The drafting of the reserves from the lower classes took much strength and means of support from the people, and a new mobilization, especially during the working season, could hardly be accomplished. Although one notes the feeling of patriotic pride among the peasants, compelling them to understand the government's wish to continue the war, in truth the present war is not popular among the peasants since it is carried on far from Russia, and is fought for the benefit of profiteers . . . and not really for Russian interests.

GOVERNOR PRINCE URUSOV

A police department report to S. Yu. Vitte, Chairman of the Council of Ministers, dealing with peasant violence against landlords in 1905; submitted in November, 1905:[4]

On the night of February 6, peasants of the villages S . . . and Kh . . . of Dmitriev

[4] SOURCE: *Krasni Arkhiv*, No. 9, 1925, pp. 70-102.

District of Kursk *Guberniya* undertook mass pillaging on the estate of the merchant Popov, who had bad relations with the peasants. In the course of these events, armed resistance was rendered the police officials. On the night of February 15 the estate of the merchant Chernichin was destroyed and since then the movement spread with astonishing swiftness and proceeded according to an obviously pre-arranged plan. It works as follows:—in each village, come evening, the peasants harness their horses and await the signal given them by looters who set fire to piles of straw. Then the whole village, yelling, screaming and firing guns, hurls itself upon the nearest estate. At the same time as the attack upon Chernichin's estate took place, arson was committed on the properties of Baron Meyendorf. . . . On February 18 the peasants fell upon the farm of proprietress Meyer, seizing grain and valuable possessions. . . .

These . . . violent acts . . . attracted the attention of surrounding settlements, and in the neighboring District of Sevsk in Orel *Guberniya* it was already known on February 19 that fifteen estates and farms had been looted within several days in Dmitriev District. In Sevsk District these seeds of information fell upon excellent soil since the local peasantry had significantly less land and were generally worse off economically than the peasants of Kursk *Guberniya*.

On February 19 in Sevsk District a pogrom took place against the estate of Pogreb in the village of V . . . ; then on February 20 the . . . farm belonging to Polinev was raided and fire was set to hay, straw and farm stores. . . .

The arriving troops were not immediately able to restore order since the movement of infantry on carts was very slow. . . . This gave the . . . peasants the opportunity to raid still more estates on February 22 and to move into Khinel where the fields and the brandy distillery of Tereshchenko are located. At a given signal a huge mob, aided by local peasants, began to batter and burn the distillery. All the buildings of the plant were destroyed and the grain and spirits robbed.

. . . In Voronezh *Guberniya* the disorders were centered in Biryuchensky District, where the peasants have less land as compared with other localities of the *Guberniya,* and grew out of the reverberations of the Kursk disorders when rumors were circulated to the effect that the tsar had asked the peasants to come to his aid in taking the land from the nobles. . . .

In Saratov *Guberniya* the most serious disorders arose at the end of May . . . and took the form of mass cropping and burning of landlords' fields by night and in broad daylight, and in attacks upon police officers. . . .

At the end of June and in July the revolutionary movement in the rural areas of Lifland and Kurlyand Guberniyas began to grow and by the end of July had assumed a positively threatening character. Speeches were made calling for the use of force, for a general strike and for arming the people. Roaming bands of desperadoes were . . . compelled to join forces with the peasant bands . . . who gave them arms of which they apparently had a plentiful supply. . . .

In August the peasants of village B . . . , of the Roslavl District of Smolensk *Guberniya,* violently seized the lands of the neighboring landlord Evstaf'ev, believing the stories of the elders who told them that the land was theirs of old by the right of donation.

A secret report to the Governor of Vladimir by zemsky nachalnik *[land captain] of Kovrov District, November 17, 1905:*[5]

Very many workers in the Kovrov railroad workshops and in the Treumov, Remizov and other factories are drawn from the peasants of my region, and these workers in most cases take advantage of the proximity of their homes to go there from work to spend the night.

In the city of Kovrov a nest of trouble-makers has been stirring and they include people of various classes and professions. They cover themselves by functioning as local *zemstvo* officials, working on agricultural committees and economic councils and serving on the committee for public temperance. This group has grown significantly and persistently carries on its evil work. They distribute pamphlets by Henry George, revolutionary leaflets and proclamations; they circulate appeals of an edition of *Donskaya Rech'* [*Voice of the Don,* a newspaper], carrying the French 18th century declaration of the rights of man and the citizen, and distribute large quantities of harmfully oriented newspapers to the peasants free of charge. They make tours of the villages and conduct secret discussions with . . . ruinous effects upon the population. Many workers among the peasants (I assume that they are paid by the agitators), promising all kinds of future gains, recruit their fellow villagers, who, as is known, are extremely ready to trust the tale-bearers and know-it-alls of their own villages. In daily mass meetings in the workshops even visiting orators lecture on all manner of subjects. It is rumored that some of the workmen are armed and evenings the youth walk about boldly singing revolutionary songs, and the townsfolk [of Kovrov], fearing unpleasantness, try to avoid leaving their homes at such times. In these meetings both the workers and the peasants of my region take part. Seeing that they get away with their illegal activity these people act insolently and teach this to the peasants.

All pronouncements of the Moscow Peasant Union[6] appear in the villages in the form of proclamations which call for changing the old ways . . . yes, even of banishing the chiefs, the clerks and the land captains from the *volost* assembly. . . .

[5] SOURCE: M. N. Pokrovsky (ed.), *1905, Materiali i Dokumenti* (1905, Materials and Documents), Moscow-Leningrad, 1925, pp. 66-67.

[6] The Peasant Union was roughly the rural equivalent of the Soviet of Workers' Deputies that appeared in St. Petersburg in October, 1905. The Union's purpose was to co-ordinate the action of the Russian peasants. Rising out of a Peasant Congress held in Moscow in May, 1905, it was founded on August 13 by peasant delegates sent to Moscow from 22 provinces.

A declaration of June 9, 1905:[7]

We, the undersigned peasants of Tver *Guberniya,* Novtorozhky District, village of Ryleev, consisting of 124 persons and 57 household heads, gathered today in the number of 53 household heads for a discussion of our vital problems. In the course of our meeting we unanimously agreed to demand the following from the government:

That the person of the peasant, yes, of the people as a whole, be inviolable.

That the people be given freedom of conscience, speech, press, assembly, unions and strikes.

The courts must be equalized with reference of peasants to all other classes.

Peasants, yes, all persons suffering for their [religious] persuasions must at once be pardoned and released.

For peasant education . . . grade schools must be introduced that teach various trades such as . . . shoemaking, tailoring, etc., along with baking, horticulture . . . and market-gardening. The learning in such schools must be free, and we desire . . . the right of equality with all other classes to advance without limitations and discrimination to the highest levels of knowledge.

All government organs without exception must be under control of popular representatives, elected by the people themselves under their own system without any educational qualifications. Those elected should also require no property and educational standards but need only to be literate and of legal age. For [the electors] being old enough should suffice.

The *zemsky nachalnik* [land captain] and the separate peasant status must be abolished and in general the peasant should be free from the guardianship of the [*volost*] bureaucracy. A local rural unit should be introduced in its place.

The land should be available to the plowers; each peasant should receive an adequate amount of land from the village, and the government must provide material aid for its cultivation. . . .

[7] SOURCE: *Ibid.,* pp. 85-86.

The *obrozhni* tax[8] and all indirect taxes must be abolished and replaced with taxes that will be suitable.

The conditions in the factory-workshop industry must be corrected in the interests of the workers.

The evil-bringing . . . war should become a matter of discussion by an immediate government-convoked popular assembly. That way it would soon become evident whether the war should be continued or whether peace should be made.

Do not think that our needs can be satisfied by half measures. We have become so demoralized, so in need of land, and ruined under your wardship that the measures we ask can bring us help only after several years. Therefore, it must be clear to you that we are driven to extremes by large-scale conditions of misery and by a dismal life. Either you give us all we have asked for or you can shoot us all and live on, obtaining all your wants, whims and luxuries. But to us life is actually a hundred times more burdensome than death, and therefore we dare to face it. We are interested in the question of how you would go about killing us. Our children and our brothers are under your orders [in the army] but they promised that they would not kill us, for they understand that having killed us, they, having returned [from service] into our position, would be subject to suffering like ours and would risk being killed by their brothers and children in turn. . . .

NIL SMIRNOV
Elder of the village of Ryleev

Secret report of the Governor of Kazan to the police department, October 7, 1905:[9]

A landlord of the village of Burakov, Spassk District, Yu. V. Trubnikov, on Octo-

[8] *Obrok* was the tax paid by peasants who, although working in towns, were still expected to pay off the obligation incurred for the allotment they had received at the time of the emancipation.

[9] SOURCE: M. N. Pokrovsky, *1905, Materiali i Dokumenti* (1905, Materials and Documents), Moscow-Leningrad, 1925, pp. 464-466.

ber 4 reported to the local police officer that the peasants of his village refused to perform the farm work on his estate. Through the village elder they sent him a written notice threatening to till his land for their own use and to take wood from his forest land.

I am informing the police department of that report and enclose a copy of the notice of the peasants of Burakov. An official has been despatched to the scene to investigate conditions and take appropriate measures. I will be directly informed about the results of those measures.

The petition of the villagers to the landlord Yu. V. Trubnikov:

Much respected gracious master, Yuri Vladimirovich. We ask you, please, for God's sake, to pity us. . . . Don't let rebellion rise within us and cause yourself troubles. We have gone through such anxious times—things are so bad that we are beside ourselves. Yuri Vladimirovich, listen, please, for this is the truth. The lands that you give us [to work] are so insufficient that we cannot make a living. You chain us like a boat to the shore. The time has come to break loose. Give us 165 desyatins. We will be able to manage and you won't be badly off. Then we will do our work as usual.

If you do not give us the land that we ask for, then we won't get it. But we won't do the harvesting. So be it, we are lost without land and will go where God leads us. We have no land, no meadows, no wood. What is there to do? Things are bad!

Yuri Vladimirovich, the half of the land you give us and the 105 [desyatins] that is yours, 210 in all; we will divide it among ourselves and let the authorities know that we will plow it ourselves and pay for it after the harvest.

And still another thing, Yuri Vladimirovich. We have no fuel, no straw, no wood and can buy it nowhere. Give us at least some shrubbery either for money or for our labor. If you give us no wood then we will take bushes and cut them on account and will let outsiders and the authorities assess them. Whatever the shrubbery is worth we will pay. Yuri Vladimirovich,—live and let live—it is best that way. . . . Let us know whether you will or will not give us what we ask.

Secret report of the Kazan Governor of October 11, 1905, to the police department:

With respect to the dispute . . . between the peasants . . . and the landowner Yu. V. Trubnikov . . . , I now have the following report.

The district police chief arrived in Burakov on October 5 and ordered the peasants to congregate in the church. He called upon the Elder to discuss the matter of land with Trubnikov, the latter agreeing to enter upon the discussion. Upon questioning by the police chief the peasants explained that they had no intention of acting arbitrarily. The declaration had the purpose of getting Trubnikov to discuss matters with them in person since he always refused to do that. He had his employees conduct the negotiations and they often distorted the nature of the case in their representations. The true wishes of the peasants were not brought to the attention of the landlord.

In the course of discussions, Trubnikov agreed to the peasants' taking wood for fuel, but added that he could not give them as much as 165 desyatins. But he agreed to give them the entire 210 desyatins if they would pay him rent for it in money. The peasants asked for time to think it over and the discussions ended peaceably.

GOVERNOR KHOMUTOV

Agitation in the Army*

One propagandist got into a barrack in Warsaw through the aid of workers who lived nearby. The workers around the barrack served as spies prepared to signal the soldiers about the actions of their chiefs.

Suddenly the signal came that Cossacks were on the way. . . . That was at the beginning of 1905. The soldiers, realizing that there would be a search, placed the propagandist by a wall and using loose bricks that were at hand built a whole wall up to the ceiling. This was done in minutes, all taking a hand. He was not discovered by the Cossacks and the police officials. . . .

In Warsaw I myself was exposed to a very typical search. On the streets of Warsaw a patrol was set up and passersby who seemed suspect were searched by the soldiers. The soldier who was searching me looked at the leaflets and said . . . , "Oh,—these are yours," and placing them in his jacket let me go my way. . . . This meant that the soldier was no longer afraid of an agitational leaflet. And the government was fully aware of the situation. It understood that if it kept a soldier from Tambov *Guberniya* in or near his native region he would not carry out the tsarist orders. Therefore soldiers from Tambov were sent to Poland.

The government understood that if it kept Poles in Poland or Latvians in Latvia, that when a punitive expedition came to a village and when a soldier was supposed to shoot his parents . . . he might refuse to do so and might fall under the influence of his native village. So the system was adopted [of sending soldiers to places remote from their homes]. . . .

. . . It was a regiment of Poles that crushed the Moscow rising of 1905. I remember they called me to St. Petersburg and asked that I appear before a meeting of troops at which there were many Poles. The party asked me to speak in Polish and to give them the picture of what the tsarist soldiery was doing in Poland. They were conducting a reign of terror. They shot people in the streets whenever there was a demonstration. They were robbing, raping and having a good time. At the meeting I painted the whole picture and out of the ranks one of the soldiers yelled in Polish: "So, and we're paying them back in Moscow." These were the . . . ignorant . . . tools in the hands of the tsar. In Moscow they revenged themselves on revolutionaries for what tsarism was doing in Poland, and Russian and Latvian soldiers were at the same time setting things right in Poland. Polish soldiers killed Russians, Russians killed Latvians, Latvians killed Tatars, Tatars killed Estonians and tsarism was the victor.

We revolutionaries had to . . . deal with this problem. A congress, in which representatives of all nationalities participated, adopted a resolution to exchange their revolutionaries. In Petersburg, for instance, if there were Polish soldiers, it would be necessary to send them ten Polish revolutionaries to deliver propaganda. Estonian units were in the Ukraine—therefore send revolutionaries into the Ukraine who could give them the propaganda in their own language, tell them what was happening in their native villages and so organize the soldiers. Only then was it achieved that in certain units the soldiers began to become aware of the way they were being used by the tsar.

* Source: F. Ya. Kon, V. A. Pleskov, F. N. Chuzhak (eds.), *V Tsarskoy Kazarme, Soldati i Matrosi v pervoy revolyutsii (1905)* (In the Barracks of the Tsar; Soldiers and Sailors in the First Revolution, 1905), Moscow, 1929, pp. 7-12.

Revolt in the Navy*

The writer of the material below spent more than two months among the interned sailors of the Potemkin in Rumania, deliberately gathering information from them about their historic experience.

Regimental life, in general, is nothing less than a replica of the entire political and social order of the country. So the conditions of life on the Potemkin were exactly like those in the entire fleet. Everywhere there are the same shortcomings, the same evils. On the part of the officers, mostly the older ones, there is always the same senseless bestiality, the same failure to understand the more human needs of the sailors. . . .

Antagonism and distrust between officers and soldiers exists in all armies but is especially notable in the Russian. . . . The following will illustrate the degree to which sailors distrusted their commanders. At the end of May or early in June [1905] the commander of the Potemkin ordered that a pamphlet be given to the sailors explaining precautionary measures to be taken against cholera. . . . The circulation of the pamphlet was perfectly natural in view of the fear of the possibility of cholera. But the sailors, familiar only with brutality on the part of their commanding staff, wondered about the true motive for this action. The officers wanted to convince the sailors that cholera was inevitable. Why? Because the officers deliberately intended to make the crew sick with rotten food in order to weaken its energies and eliminate the chances of struggle on the part of the sailors.

The Russian officer class, and the navy's

* SOURCE: A. P. Berezovsky, *Odinadstat' Dnei Na "Potemkine"* (Eleven Days on the Potemkin), 1907, pp. 7-17. Place of publication not given.

above all, was drawn from the nobility. In Russian military academies there predominated the dregs of the upper classes, so to speak. All of the elements most devoted to human causes were drawn to the revolutionary movement in their very tender years. The honest, . . . talented youth . . . fills the . . . jails and inundates the intellectual professions while the least capable and most servile persons enter upon bureaucratic or military careers. No wonder that the military . . . in Russia contains incomparably more incompetence and ignorance than that of any other country. . . . Officers consider their profession a mere means of subsistence to which they try to devote as little energy as possible and from which they try to extract the greatest possible gains. This causes the type of relations between officers and sailors that lead to catastrophes. . . .

Once at Kronstadt an officer encountered a recruit and asked, "Do you know me?" "Yes, your excellency." "What's my name?" The sailor failed to answer. "You don't know my name?" "No, your excellency." "In that case, let me introduce myself," said the officer and struck the sailor twice in the face. . . .

Admiral Chukhin issued an order for the Sevastopol sailors placing them lower than dogs. Order number 184 of April . . . 1905, forbade the sailors "under threat of jail sentence" to walk on two boulevards, two parkways and one street. Several days later a group of wounded sailors, returning from Port Arthur, was walking on one of those boulevards. . . . An officer cried out gruffly to them, "How dare you walk here? Don't you know that this boulevard is forbidden to the lower ranks?"

One of the more daring sailors explained: "Do you mean, your excellency, that we can't walk on our native soil for which we shed our blood?"

"You still open your mouth, scoundrel!"

And several resounding blows let the recently returned "sailor heroes" feel all the charm of the thankful native land.

* * *

. . . The revolt on the Prince Potemkin was not an accidental and unexpected act; it was partly a premature explosion of a . . . daring . . . plan for a general rising which was to involve the entire . . . Black Sea Fleet. Having seized the naval bases the Russian revolution would have captured an impregnable base for future conquests. By bombarding the coast and organizing troop landings it would have been able to support the entire South and thence reach out to the remaining parts of the great domain. Upon an arranged signal—two rockets, fired one after the other, from the deck of the battleship Catherine II—the sailors partaking in the conspiracy were to arrest or kill their officers and take command of all ships "in the name of the people." As is known, the unfortunate incident of the putrid food produced a premature revolt on the Potemkin and ruined the entire plan. . . .

The question rises, would the general rising have succeeded, if the Potemkin incident had not occurred . . . ?

When one knows how near success was at certain moments, despite the fact that only one ship was at the disposal of the rebel sailors, it appears almost certain that the general rising would have succeeded. The fact, for instance, that the absence of the signals compelled the sailors to halt the bombardment of Odessa, thereby losing the entire fruits of the bombardment, shows the role that accident played in the whole affair. The attempted rising of the Black Sea Fleet, aside from its effect on the further course of the Russian revolution, has another significant aspect historically speaking. From the purely military and technical point of view . . . the idea of the rising of the fleet as a start for a general military revolution was a very brilliant one. This was so not only because the sailors, thanks to their special selection, are the most receptive of all the armed forces to socialist propaganda, but mainly because the fleet in revolt can hold out and defend itself much longer than any other part of the fighting forces. Let us assume that the entire fleet had risen. It is hard to imagine what means the government would have used to suppress it. If it was easy for the Potemkin to supply itself with provisions even in such fortified cities like Odessa, then it would have been even easier for the entire fleet [which] would have dominated the entire coast. . . . A victorious rising in the entire fleet would have made for a situation unprecedented in the history of civil wars. Russian absolutism with all of its armies would have been helpless in the struggle with a handful of people. The rulers of Russia would have found themselves in the same absurd position as was the Rumanian government when it learned that the Potemkin had appeared at Constantsa [for internment]; it gave orders for a whole garrison to be mobilized including even the cavalry corps. The officers wondered ironically what role the horses would play in a war against a battleship.

A University Becomes a Fort*

On the 11th and 12th of October, 1905, Kharkov went through its "days of the

* SOURCE: V. P. Bezeskul', "Dni barrikad' v Kharkove v oktyabre 1905 g." (Days of the Barricades in Kharkov in October, 1905), *Golos Minuvshago* (Moscow), Nos. 7-8 (July-August, 1917), 335-350.

barricades." On the streets near the university, students aided by sympathizers, erected barricades that converted the university into a kind of military fort and manned them. At the time I was dean of the historical-philological faculty and I was obliged to take part in the discussions of the university presidium with the civil and military authorities, in order to prevent the bloodshed which it seemed threatened the inevitable destruction of the university and in order to lead the students safely out of their siege. I then wrote down what I witnessed on those memorable days. . . .

I won't go into detail about the reasons which led to the barricades. They lay partly in the previous conditions of university life, partly outside the university. I say "in previous conditions" since not long before the described events there was a change of rules which Kharkov University accepted quite literally. By the decree of August 27, 1905 some academic autonomy was given the universities. The elective principle was reestablished with respect to the university administration—the rector, the deans and the secretaries of the faculties; the staff of the university governing board was revamped and the former system [as of the statute of 1884] was changed. A system of suspicion, censorship and repression was replaced by a system of faith in the students. Inspections, with their "observations" so exasperating and insulting, in particular when conducted by petty officials, were practically removed. The students were allowed to have meetings, to have organizations supported by dues, to elect chiefs, etc. The council and administration of the university tried to make its influence felt by moral means. It sought by way of discussions with student representatives, and by acting through these representatives, to forestall the destruction of order, to mollify the excitement. In the course of time this succeeded.

But stimuli to excitement continued from outside the university. Society was at the time in a state of intense political agitation, and the students were even more so. There were strikes, meetings, conferences, and since the freedom to hold such assemblages was lacking, it was precisely the university which became the place where a crowd could be gathered most speedily. As early as February, 1905 the council of Kharkov University "specifically stated, that the normal course of academic life was impossible without the universal political freedom of

the Russian people." In the session of September 29, within two weeks of the barricades, the council unanimously "declared anew, that autonomy of a university in a society, deprived of its freedom of speech, press, assembly and person, by necessity serves as the place where society expresses the elementary awareness of its rights, just as a destructive whirlwind flows to the place of lowest pressure. The council is doing and will do all in its power to support the normal course of academic life, but the forces outside are more powerful and it is impossible to oppose that pressure. The council cannot and does not have the right to take upon itself the responsibility for the results of outside forces rising from the course of an historical process. The prevention of a catastrophe is possible only in the event that the Russian citizen is guaranteed the sacred rights of a human being, inviolability of the person, freedom of speech, press and assembly." In fulfillment of the council's resolution the rector sent a telegram to the Minister of Education.

At the beginning of September an assembly of all the students resolved that the university must take part in the political struggle, that it must serve as a place of political education, and that therefore meetings would be arranged in which students and outsiders would participate. True, to that resolution a statement was added providing that such meetings must not interfere with academic activities. The representatives of the students promised, moreover, not to let it come to a "catastrophic meeting," i.e., to a meeting of the type that would provoke disorders and lead to shutting down the university. Nevertheless one could anticipate meetings with various complications, interference with activities and the like. But barricades! This was wholly unexpected and not only by us the professors. . . . More than once I asked the students how this could have happened? And they replied that they themselves did not understand how the decision had arisen among them to build barricades and to turn the university into a fort. . . .

So we succeeded in our task—the prevention of bloodshed. I can not imagine what would have happened if the university had been subjected to military attack and the lecture halls covered with blood. How could we have gone into them and delivered our lectures? . . .

Within a week after the first day of the barricades we read the Manifesto of October 17. . . . Three of my students came to me . . . enraptured—drunk with the constitu- tion, with the advent of the era of political freedom. They were apparently surprised that I could not share their optimism. In that moment it was strange for them to hear that actual political freedom is not ac- quired so fast, that this was only a begin- ning, that ahead lay much experimentation —that a long tortuous process still im- pended.

A British Newsman Views
the Revolution's Climax*

The Turning Point

On September 25 . . . 300 representatives of the zemstvos . . . [met] at Moscow to consider their attitude towards the promised Duma, which was regarded as a concession to their previous representations during the year. They recognized that the Duma of the August manifesto would not be either a representative or legislative assembly, but regarding it as a possible rallying-point for the general movement towards freedom, they agreed to obtain as many seats as pos- sible, so as to form a united group of ad- vanced opinion.

They further drew up a political pro- gramme . . . , including the formation of a National Legislative Assembly; . . . equal rights for all citizens, including peasants; . . . inviolability of person and home and freedom of conscience, speech, press, . . . and association.

* * *

On October 21, the workmen . . . de- livered their first telling blow, . . . a gen- eral railway strike. . . . [It disorganized] trade . . . and [prevented] the Govern- ment from [rushing] troops to any par- ticular point of disturbance. . . .

The objects of the strikers, [expressed]

by a deputation [to Witte] on October 24, [were that the] "claims of the working men . . . be settled by laws constituted by the will of the people. . . . [That could be done only by the proclamation of] political guarantees for freedom and the convocation of a Constituent Assembly, elected by direct, universal and secret suffrage." . . .

. . . Witte's reply was . . . characteristic —"A Constituent Assembly is . . . impos- sible. Universal suffrage would . . . only [benefit the rich] because [their money] could influence all the voting. . . . There is not in the entire world a single cultivated man who is in favor of universal suffrage."

. . . On October 26 the Central Strike Committee—or Council [Soviet] of Labour Delegates, . . . in St. Petersburg, declared a general strike throughout Russia. About a million workers came out.

This . . . second workmen's blow . . . shook Tsardom from top to bottom.

Four days [later] the . . . Manifesto of October 30 [promised] personal freedom and a constitution. . . .

This Manifesto was greeted by an out- burst of joy . . . [but] the [Soviet] rightly refused to trust the tsar without guarantees, and . . . continued [to demand] political amnesty and the convocation of a Con- stituent Assembly. They also demanded the restoration of . . . liberties to Finland, and the dismissal of Trepoff.[1] When anti-Jewish

* SOURCE: H. W. Nevinson, *The Dawn in Russia*, London and New York, Harper and Brothers, 1906, pp. 16-21. The author was a special correspondent for the *Daily Chronicle*.

[1] Governor-General of St. Petersburg.

riots broke out at Kieff, Warsaw and . . . Odessa, they . . . justly maintained that the "Black Hundred" or "Hooligans" of the massacre and pillage were encouraged by the police and priests . . . to make [it seem] that the Russian people were opposed to political liberties.

The panic of the government continued. They could not measure the strength of this new force among the [workers] or of this new instrument, the general strike. They were uncertain also about the army. . . . Pobiedonostzeff, . . . the embodiment of an obstinate tyranny . . . resigned. On November 4th [a limited] amnesty was proclaimed for political offenders. . . .

On the same day a manifesto restored the old liberties of Finland. . . .

On November 9 Trepoff [resigned] and Durnovo, since infamous for his brutality, took office. . . .

[Soon] the Government began to recover courage. . . . The change was quite apparent in a manifesto of November 12th, declaring the present situation unsuitable for the introduction of reforms, which would only be possible when the country was pacified.

Next day a ukase proclaimed martial law in Poland, and excluded that country from the manifesto, on the pretence that the Poles were plotting against the integrity of the Russian Empire by establishing a separate nation of their own.

The [Soviet] . . . on November 14 [de-clared] another general strike in sympathy with Poland. . . . Witte . . . retaliated by posting an appeal . . . conceived in his most unctuous and fatherly style. . . .

"Brothers! Workmen! Go back to your work. . . . Have pity on your wives and children. . . . The Tsar has appointed a Ministry of Commerce and Industry [to] establish just relations between masters and men. Only give us time, and I will do all that is possible for you. Pay attention to the advice of a man who loves you and wishes you well."

This appeal was immediately followed (November 17) by a manifesto to the peasants, reducing their payments for the use of land by one-half after January, 1906, and abolishing it altogether after January, 1907. . . .

Three days later . . . the [Soviet] declared the strike at an end. This second general strike was felt to have been a failure. People and funds were still exhausted by the first. . . . Few of the great factories came out; the object of the strike was too remote from the workman's daily life. . . .

Nevertheless, the [Soviet] remained the most powerful body of men in the Empire and their order [ending] the strike called . . . upon the working classes to continue the revolutionary propaganda in the army, and to organize themselves . . . "for the final encounter between all Russia and the bloody monarchy now dragging out its last few days."

The Birth of the Soviet*

On October 20 movement ceased on the Moscow-Archangel, Moscow-Kursk, Moscow-Nizhni Novgorod railway lines and on the Ryazan-Ural line (between Moscow and Ryazan).

* SOURCE: G. Khrustalev-Nosar, "Istoriya Soveta Rabochikh Deputatov" (History of the Soviet of Workers' Deputies). *Istoriya Soveta Rabochikh Deputatov g. S.-Peterburga*, 1906, pp. 57-61. The author was the first President of the St. Petersburg Soviet.

On October 21 the Moscow-Kiev-Voronezh line went on strike. . . .

On October 23 strikes stopped the Syzran-Vyazemsk, the Kharkov-Nikolaevsk, the Kursk-Kharkov-Sevastopol lines and both Ekaterinsk roads.

On October 25 the Petersburg tie-up began, except for the Finland line which struck on the 27th.

On October 27 the Transcaucasian, the

Central Asian, the Moscow-Brest . . . and the Siberian lines resorted to strikes.

Within ten days strikes had seized the entire network of Russian railways, extending over 40,000 kilometers and employing 750,000 clerks and workers. Out of Moscow, as the center, the strike flame sent its rays spreading to the periphery. The railway strike predetermined the general strike.

The strike movement traveled on steel rails and shut down factories, plants,—all of life in the industrial centers. On October 27 work ceased in all workshops and factories and on all the trolley and horse cars . . . of Moscow, Kharkov and Revel. On October 28 life died in all the commercial and manufacturing establishments of Smolensk, Kozlov, Ekaterinoslav, Minsk and Lodz. . . .

The telegraph agency forgot its clumsy, colorless language and spoke in the style of military reality. The Petersburg agency telegraphs on October 28: "Ekaterinoslav. City in darkness. Stores are closed. Streets are deserted. Occasional military patrols pass by. The railway station is closed. Some telegraph lines have been cut." . . .

The cutting of railway communications destroyed the economic organism of the country at all junctures. The railway strike even hit the exporters. With the cessation of postal communications, bills of lading for freight, sent by sea, could not be delivered to the purchasers. In the meantime, ships with grain, sent from Petersburg, Livadia, Windau, . . . for destination to foreign ports, remained unloaded for lack of itinerary documents. All costs for demurrage of boats or for failure to fulfill contracts fell upon the exporters. The exporters appealed to the government.

Panic seized the stock exchange. . . . "On October 24 the exchange was lifeless [reported the journal *Rus*]. There was no business, neither buyers nor sellers being present." The stock exchange appeals to the government. . . .

The Petersburg proletariat channelled all its forces into a general strike. The matter of a political strike in concrete form is placed by the workers, meeting on October 21 at the Military-Medicine Academy. From the 22nd on, at meetings devoted to instructions from the center, all the speeches were directed toward the political strike. There were also opponents of the strike. They referred to the negative allusion to the idea made by German Social Democracy or spoke of the limited approval given the idea of a general strike by the Amsterdam Socialist Congress.

The inevitability of the general strike was [eventually] felt by all. . . .

On October 27, on the Schlisselburg road, work ceased in the Alexandrov locomotive factory, in the Neva shipbuilding plant, in . . . the Emperor cardboard factory, [etc.]. The strike wave tried to hurl itself onto the right bank of the Neva—into the Torton and Vargunin factories. An administrative measure blocked boat passage across the Neva. Then the [workers on] the Schlisselburg road signaled the right bank comrades to stop work. The Torton and Vargunin workers struck. On October 27 workers by the thousands, meeting at the Technological Institute, adopted a resolution calling for the entire Petersburg proletariat to join in a general political strike.

On October 26 the Obukhov plant, both the Rechkin plants, the Gelbov and the Pinch plants, the Putilov factory, [etc.] went on strike. On the [same date] after 2:00 P.M. work ceased on the horsecar lines, with the exception of the Neva line. . . . On the 26th activities ceased in many gymnasia and [other secondary schools]. And on October 26 the first session of the Soviet of Workers' Deputies took place in one of the auditoriums of the [Technological] Institute.

The strike revolution gave birth to the Soviet.

With the cessation of work in each plant there rose the question of clarifying the situation with regard to other plants. The common tactic demanded general information. To that end, in various factories, as, for instance, in the Obukhov factory, special Elders were elected on October 27. The Obukhov Elders, going into the city on October 28 for reconnaissance purposes, came upon the first session of the Soviet. A mass of workers spontaneously pressed for the creation of an all-city apparatus to serve the factory-workshop strikes. . . .

On October 26, the Petersburg group of the Social Democrats had given its agitators the directive to agitate for elections to the workers' Soviet and the assignment of those elected to the Technological Institute.

A November Session of
the St. Petersburg Soviet*

Admission was by ticket only. . . . On the first night that I went, the big chamber . . . was crowded with [workers].

Many women were there. . . . Most were evidently journalists, doctors, or students, from the intellectual middle classes, which in Russia produces the woman revolutionist. . . . For Russian women enjoy . . . equality and comradeship with men, whether in martyrdom or in triumph, such as [in] no other nation. . . .

The workmen were delegates from the . . . trades of the capital and . . . the provinces—railway men, . . . iron workers, . . . and others. About five hundred . . . had been chosen, and each . . . represented about five hundred other workers. But round the long green table . . . sat [those] whom the delegates had appointed as their executive committee. [About twenty-five] were there—men of a rather intellectual type among workers. . . . That Strike Committee . . . had won fame in a month. . . . A handful of unarmed . . . men . . . had shaken the [world's] strongest . . . despotism.

. . . Their president, the compositor Khroustoloff—or Nosar, . . . his real name, was a man of about thirty-five, . . . worn with excitement and sleeplessness. . . . Yet he controlled an excited and inexperienced meeting with temper and ease. . . . There was no time for sleep or other human needs, but [facing] Khroustoloff and . . . all those men lay the prison or the grave, and in them there is always time enough.

* SOURCE: H. W. Nevinson, *The Dawn in Russia,* London and New York, Harper and Brothers, 1906, pp. 26-33.

. . . The meeting was [discussing] the eight-hours' day. One of the executive read out the reports [on hours of labor in] all the factories represented by delegates. . . . In some . . . the masters had conceded an eight-hours' day after the first strike. In others, they had come down to nine [or] ten. Most had . . . refused a reduction. These reports, though monotonous and many, were listened to with the silence that characterizes a Russian meeting.

. . . Ages of dumb suffering have given these people [infinite] patience . . . and a public meeting is so new to them that they find . . . pleasure in speeches which our free-born electors would howl down in . . . minutes. Any meeting of British trade-unionists would have polished off the Strike Committee's business in an hour, but when I [left] past two [A.M.] . . . discussion was still [lively] . . . , and there were [many important] subjects still to be settled. The Committee . . . sat almost continuously night and day.

As soon as all the reports were read, the executive gathered up their papers and adjourned . . . to consider their decision. During their absence, the other delegates broke up into groups according to trades, [to discuss] their own affairs. Standing on a chair, a man would shout, "Weavers, this way, please!" "Engineers, here!" or "Railway-men, this way!" and the various workers clustered round. . . . All spirits still were high with success and the confidence of victory. At last, as the executive remained over an hour in conference, a . . . young workman with a voice like the Last Trumpet, raised the Russian "Marseillaise," and in a moment the room was resounding to the hymn of freedom. Russian words . . . have been set to the old French tune. . . .

[Then] the workmen turned to national songs. . . . All had one burden—the hatred of tyrants, the love of freedom, the willingness to die for its sake. To us, such phrases . . . bear an unreal . . . sound, for it is many centuries since England enjoyed a real tyranny. . . . But in Russia both tyranny and revolt are genuine . . . and at any moment a man or woman may be called upon to prove how far the love of freedom will really take them on the road to death.

A few days before this . . . meeting, I had been at an assembly of the educated classes to protest against capital punishment. One speaker—a professor . . . was worn and twisted by long years [in Siberia]. He was the worst speaker present, but it was he who received the deep thunder of applause. Another had, with Russian melancholy, devoted his life to compiling an immense history of assassination by the State. Before he began to speak, he announced that he was going to read the list of those who had been executed for their love of freedom since the time of Nicholas I. Instantly the whole great audience rose . . . and [stood] in silence. . . . It was as when a regiment drinks : . . to fallen comrades. . . .

The executive returned from their consultation. . . . President Khroustoloff announced that in the opinion of the executive, a fresh general strike on the eight-hour question would at present be a mistake. The eight-hour day was an ideal to be kept before them; they must allow no master who had once granted it to go back on his word; they must urge the others forward . . . and . . . meanwhile organize and combine till they could confront both capitalism and autocracy with assurance. . . . Then the delegates of the [opposition] had their turn. [They pointed] to the evident intention of Witte's Government to thwart the workmen's advance. They pointed . . . to the [recent] renewal of police persecution and to the encouragement given to masters who declared a lock-out. They urged that it was best to fight before the common enemy regained his full power, and that the general strike . . . was still the [worker's] only weapon. It was all true. Yet the recent strike had almost failed. . . . A second failure within a fortnight would show the Government that freedom's only weapon was not so dangerous after all. In the end the executive had its way [by] three hundred votes against twenty. . . .

Freedom at that moment was just hanging in the balance. . . . Already things were [less] hopeful . . . , and many good revolutionists spoke [grimly] of the future. . . . [Self-] proclaimed Liberals [of] three weeks before, now began . . . to hesitate and look round. In subdued whispers commerce sighed for [Trepoff's return] and the ancient security of a merchant's goods. They pretended terror of peasant outbreaks, and the violence of "Black Hundred" mobs, organized by the police just to show the dangers of reform. But it was reform itself that they dreaded, and [they feared] Socialism [more] than . . . tyranny.

Day by day the police were becoming active again. . . .

Nevinson in Moscow, December, 1905 *

On . . . December 9 . . . I arrived in Moscow. . . . Trailing in disorder through dirt and mud . . . came a loose string of soldiers. . . . A few cavalry came first . . . , then a few straggling infantry . . .

* SOURCE: *Ibid.,* pp. 97-128.

covered with filth, their uniforms torn and patched . . . faces yellow, [and] thin. . . . Behind the infantry [came] a rambling line of [carts carrying] muffled . . . forms, their heads or arms . . . bound up with dirty and blood-stained bandages.

These were the soldiers returning from the war. . . . At last they had completed the 5,000 or 6,000 miles of their journey from the starving East, across the frozen lake, through the long Siberian plains. . . . And this was how they were received. Certainly the Moscow municipality had intended to arrange some sort of festivities at the station. They had intended to give little presents to the men—something in the shape of chocolates and cigarettes that comfort the hearts of heroes. . . . The papers had announced that the army from the Far East would begin to arrive on the Sunday. The paternal Government took care that they should arrive on the Saturday. . . . So little interest was taken in the whole thing that the evening papers continued to announce that the army would begin to arrive on the morrow. The market people and cabdrivers stopped for a moment to look at them before hurrying on through the snow, and no further notice . . . was taken of the defenders of the country.

So they drifted . . . down the dirty streets and disappeared. On reaching the barracks, the Reservists among them were discharged, and the crowds of beggars who, with threats and curses, violently demanded the milk of human kindness at every corner, were increased by many tattered figures. They limped about in traces of departed uniforms, and as they passed, people said, "A soldier from the war." One night I saw two or three of them seated on a curbstone beside a fire. . . . One was swaying gently . . . , continually repeating, "At home and alive! at home and alive!" The others took no notice, but stared like imbeciles into the flames.

Some were drafted back by rail to their villages, and the terror of comfortable people was that they would there spread the tale of mismanagement, corruption and misery till all the peasants would rise in fury and sweep upon the cities in ravenous . . . hordes. Sometimes a dim rumor reached us from the Far East of a distracted army, mutinous and starving; maddened with hardship; . . . longing for home, but unable to crowd into the worn out trains that crept along those thousands of miles of single line, choked with stores and blocked by continual accidents and strikes. If they should all come home—all the 500,000 or 600,000 . . . at once? The comfortable citizens—and even in Moscow there were such people—shuddered in their furs and thanked Heaven for that narrow road.

On the other hand, a big manufacturer told me he was delighted to see the army returning. "For now," he said, "the Reservists on garrison duty here will be dismissed, and we can always trust the line to obey their officers and shoot in defence of law and order." At the time I hoped he was over-sanguine.

*   *   *

Nearly every night meetings were held for the new unions . . . springing up on every side. . . . Moscow, . . . built in concentric circles round the Kremlin, . . . had been divided off into wedges, or "rays," as they were called, and each ray sent so many delegates to the central committee—corresponding to the [Soviet] of Labour Delegates in St. Petersburg—which . . . had to decide the moment for strikes. . . .

First came the great Railway Union, which controlled the powerful instrument of the railway strikes, and had its headquarters in Moscow because the city is the obvious centre of all Russian railways. Perhaps next in size, . . . came the . . . [30,-000] Floor Polishers—a class of workers unknown in England, because we are not clean enough to have parquetted floors. . . . There were other large unions [including] a very strong printers' union called "The Society of the Printed Word," said to be the oldest in Russia. . . . The Union of Bathmen and Bathwomen, a very large class of labour in Russia, is also old, and in those weeks they came to the very satisfactory decision of declaring a boycott against the editor of [the] reactionary . . . *Moscow News*. . . . No [member] of the union would wash the editor of the *Moscow News* at any price.

*   *   *

The University was closed. Her seven thousand students were scattered. . . . For the most part they swelled the army of the Social Democrats. . . . They were also collecting arms. . . .

[While] I was in Moscow, Professor Miliukoff brought out his new paper called *Life.* . . . He began with a long . . . appeal for the unity of Progressive parties against . . . Absolutism. "Let us all combine," he cried, "into a bloc. . . . When Absolutism is overthrown, there will be time enough to discuss the divergent lines of our own programmes." . . . The advice was obviously sensible. Its only fault was that it was . . . too sensible for times of high exhilaration, when the position of the moderate man is always painful and usually neglected. Neither workmen nor Social Democrats cared in the least for a Liberal alliance.

*   *   *

St. Nicholas' Day of December 19 had long been awaited with expectation, both of triumph and fear. It was the Tsar's christening day. . . . It had been rumoured . . . that the work of the great Manifesto would then be completed—that the Tsar himself would come to Moscow, . . . issue the charter of a free Constitution, and, like a generous father, distribute the Crown lands among the peasants. . . . But the mood of concession had passed away. It was a time of reaction now, the imprisonment of labour leaders, the arrest of editors, . . . the incitement to murder.

. . . The day before the festival, the . . . Black Hundred . . . had [called for] the final extermination of all Jews and foreigners in the city. . . . So the Jews and many . . . foreigners fortified their houses and hid themselves. . . . In the evening . . . all was gloom . . . and fear. . . . A . . . drunken soldier, who had [boasted] of his revolutionary convictions, was surrounded by a little knot of loyalists, beguiled down a side court, and quietly slaughtered. . . . [A shouting mob had beaten] a student senseless. . . . His body [had been dragged] into . . . a cellar. Through . . . the shutter you could see it lying there, [oozing] blood, while a girl student . . . knelt [beside him] and cried aloud. At the sound of her crying,

the mob yelled with exultation, and fought for a place at the shutter.

Morning came, intensely cold. . . . The priesthood had [requested] a special ceremony of prayer on account of Russia's troubles. . . . The prayer meeting was fixed for the . . . Red Square. . . . By ten o'clock the sacred banners from all the great shrines of Moscow began to assemble. . . .

[A vast] number of people . . . swarmed [about]. . . . All were bowing and crossing themselves or kneeling in the snow. . . . Many peasants had come in from the country. . . . But the greater part were simply the poor of Moscow—the pious, the patriotic, the criminal poor—all . . . the natural enemies of change. They went from shrine to shrine, [and] filled the cathedrals till it was impossible to stir inside.

. . . By eleven . . . , the holy banners . . . began to move slowly and with difficulty towards the gate into the Red Square. . . .

Small bodies of Cossacks, and of infantry with fixed bayonets, were stationed along the route or accompanied the procession. . . . When at last the glittering banners had staggered by, there came a group of priests in robes stiff with gold and many-coloured embroideries. . . .

Last of all, supported by an extra strong detachment of Cossacks, came the banners of the most sacred shrine in Moscow, accompanying the picture of the Iberian Virgin herself. . . . As she passed . . . the crowds on each side bowed . . . like corn when the wind blows.

. . . The procession . . . gathered on the round stone platform where Ivan the Cruel used to enjoy the executions. . . . The service of special prayer was . . . performed, . . . the clocks struck twelve and . . . the religious part of the day came to an end. The banners went back into the Kremlin; the Iberian Virgin was carried in a four-wheeler to her shrine; the bishops and archimandrites drove away to lunch in huge coaches drawn by four black horses. . . .

Then the moment came which all had awaited. . . . Now . . . was the time for slaughter and enrichment. A fervid orator sprang [on to] the stone platform, and [appealing] to heaven and the Tsar, [lashed] the crowd to . . . fury. Other patriots [gave out] photographs of the Tsar with his baby-boy upon his knee. The people . . . began to rush up and down, like caged wolves just before feeding-time. Then raising the Russian hymn, the orator . . . set off to march up the whole length of the square. The crowd swarmed after him. . . .

They were going to slaughter the Jews and . . . the students, and purify the city. . . . [Arriving] in front of the Government House, . . . they stopped to make speeches, calling again upon heaven and the Tsar, and urging . . . vengeance upon all revolutionaries and other enemies of the country.

The Governor-General appeared . . . upon the balcony. . . . He [told] the crowd how delighted he was to see so many . . . still on the Tsar's side, . . . promising to [wire] the Tsar [that he] could rely upon the . . . loyalty and . . . courage of ancient Moscow.

. . . Just at that moment, before the cheers could even begin, some one . . . near me [cried], "The students are coming! The students! . . ." Terror swept over the crowd, . . . and plunging, falling, . . . the people rushed down any street and hid round any corner. . . . I have seen many fine panics . . . but [nothing] so ludicrous as that stampede of bloody-minded patriots. For nothing . . . had happened, and when at last the terrified loyalists took heart to look behind them, they saw the square peaceful, silent, and almost empty. One by one they crept back into courage. They even tried to rekindle their patriotic zeal and resume their murderous aspect. But it was no good. The Governor-General had gone indoors to dispatch his telegram in praise of their courage. That unhappy run had spoilt the whole massacre, and gradually the orators ceased to rage, and every one went home for dinner.

The End of the Moscow Rising, December, 1905 *

In many battles there comes a moment when little . . . appears to be changed, and yet you suddenly realize that all is over. . . . Such a moment came on Xmas [morning]. . . . The barricades were still standing, the Sodovaya was still covered with such a network of wire about four feet from the ground that one had to walk under it bent double, and no horse could have moved. The guns had not come perceptibly nearer, and in the center of town I had seen an officer . . . deprived of his sword by . . . men with revolvers, who threatened to strip him naked. . . . There were rumours of . . . attacks . . . on prisons, on barracks . . . yet . . . I . . . realized . . . that the tide had turned. . . . [I wanted] to photograph the barricades before they disappeared. . . . I began taking [pictures] and

* SOURCE: Ibid., pp. 169-177.

had just secured a fine construction of doors, benches, barrels, railings, shop signs, and trees, when I [was] surrounded by [revolutionists who demanded the film]. . . . The incident . . . proved how impossible it was to know where the revolutionists were stationed, or in what force. There was nothing to distinguish them from . . . others. . . . I think I could have picked out the leaders . . . by their pale and intellectual faces. . . . But the possession of a [gun] was the only admissible evidence, and that required search. [To] the soldiers [that] was sufficient evidence for death, and . . . anyone caught with a revolver . . . had no further chance. . . . That morning, for instance, an English officer . . . saw five men suddenly come upon a strong picket. . . . Summoned to halt . . . , they walked quietly on. One after the other they were shot down, 'till only one was left, and he also walked on, taking no notice. Then he was shot, and there was an end of the five. No doubt the more usual form of courage would have been to rush upon the picket and die fighting. But they may have been out of cartridges, and in any case it would be hard to surpass their example in passive bravery.

In expectation of sudden death like theirs, all the students, both men and girls, had stitched . . . labels inside . . . their coats, so that, [if] killed, their parents might possibly hear the news. . . . Most of the revolutionists had done the same, but the dead were piled up and carted into the country for burial with such . . . carelessness, that I doubt if the precaution was of . . . much avail. And, indeed, it was not the revolutionist who suffered most during the days of combat, but the sightseers and the . . . passers-by.

. . . The crisis, as I had felt in the morning, was really over. When I passed through the middle of the city again . . . the crowds were still running . . . in panic round the theatre square, men and women were still falling unexpectedly in the streets . . . and the ambulance yards were continually [filling]. But the life [had] dropped out of the rising. People were talking with terror of a great peasant invasion, hundreds of thousands strong, that was already marching to deliver their Little Mother Moscow, and hew us all to pieces. With better reason they said that Mischenko, the hero of the Japanese war, was coming as military governor with 7,000 Cossacks. Hour by hour the citizens were agitated by new alarms, and the cautious began to think enough had been done for freedom, and to remember that something, after all, was due to the sacred stove of home. . . . On Tuesday, for the first time I heard revolutionists beginning to describe the whole movement as a dress rehearsal and to congratulate themselves upon [their] excellent practice in street fighting. . . .

Pogrom in Odessa, November, 1905 *

When I reached Odessa [in January, 1906] . . . only about eleven weeks had passed since she celebrated her festival of liberty. . . . Youths paraded . . . , aged professors embraced . . . , and women, as on . . . Easter Day, felt hurt if they were not kissed . . . all because the Tsar had issued a manifesto. . . .

Two days later they buried freedom, and whilst I was there the Government was still . . . stamping the bloody earth to lay her ghost. . . . Every [Government] promise had been falsified, and every hope deceived. No meetings were allowed except to legal hooligans. No papers could appear, except the Government organ of violence. Even the paper of the Constitutional Democrats had been . . . suppressed. The friends of liberty choked the prisons, and as I went

down the streets I saw their white faces peering between the bars.

Trepoff began it [with] an order from St. Petersburg urging the Governor-General Neidhart to allow a demonstration of the loyalist Black Hundred on November 1. Infuriated by religious conviction and the lust for [loot], the Black Hundred exhibited an enthusiastic loyalty, unchecked by the police, who directed their movements. . . . For three days the city lay at the mercy of law and order. . . . In the middle of the town, shops that had been the richest had the shutters up in January, their windows . . . broken, their stores all gone. . . . In the . . . Jewish districts whole rows of houses stood desolate. . . . People pointed out windows, three storeys high, from which babies, girls and women had been pitched sheer upon the stoney pavement below. . . . Clubs were the weapons chiefly used

* Source: *Ibid.,* pp. 215-219.

by the champions of Christ and the Tsar [but] butcher knives were found even more convenient for killing children. . . . In that three days' massacre nearly all who suffered were Jews, and out of a population of about 600,000 in Odessa, the Jews are estimated at [about] 300,000, so that the game for the Christian sportsmen lay thick upon the ground.

The Jews of Odessa are said by their Christian neighbours . . . to [be] particularly unpleasant. They are accused of . . . selfishness, greediness, and indifference to suffering, even to their own. I cannot say . . . whether that is so. I only know that they . . . are an amazing people. Their Christian neighbours, as in Kieff and all centres of Jewish persecution, chalk a conspicuous cross on their shutters in dangerous times, or stick a . . . saint's portrait over the door. . . . No Jew would do any such thing—not for dear life. . . . Christians say he could not conceal himself, even if he wished—his look, his dwelling, his passport, the police, all would betray him. And no doubt that is true, though, if I were a Jew, I would cover my house with crosses from ground to roof in the hope of saving any one I cared for from being flung out of my top window. But, even if such hope were vain, that is no reason why a Jew should cover his outside shutters and the lintel of

his door with Hebrew inscriptions or Hebrew information about his Kosher goods. . . . Yet on ruin after ruin I saw these inscriptions written; and, . . . more remarkable, I saw the surviving owners repainting these inscriptions as they patched up the wreckage of their homes.

They are not, perhaps, exactly the race I should call chosen, but certainly they are a peculiar people. I saw . . . one aged [Jew] who had been counted a prosperous man, but in the massacre had lost wife, family, ducats, and all. When . . . the days of the mourning passed, he borrowed a few cigarettes to sell. Next week he had a stall, and when I saw him he was hoping to open a tobacconist shop where before he sold secondhand clothes and saw his family murdered. It seems impossible that all the Christians in Russia, backed . . . by the open support of the army, police, and Church, can ever succeed in exterminating such a race.

But for the time their misery was extreme. They had crowded for refuge into courts which ran far back from the ordinary streets. . . . There I found them living in stinking . . . rooms or cellars, and often I had to grow accustomed to the darkness before I could discern exactly how many families were accommodated in the corners.

Forces of Counterrevolution:
A Social-Democrat's Analysis*

On February 18, 1905, along with the rescript on calling selected people from the upper classes for preliminary work on statutory proposals,[1] there was issued a manifesto, calling upon the entire bureaucratic apparatus, and all dark forces of the land,

* SOURCE: L. ___g, "Momenti Kontr'-revolyutsii" (Moments of Counter-revolution), *Itogi i Perspektivi, Sbornik Statei,* Moscow, 1906, pp. 45-49.

[1] This refers to the Bulygin project. See page 63.

to a battle by word and deed against the "rebels."

What classes responded to that call to a struggle against the revolution? . . . There were three separate groups . . . , belonging to distinct social classes. In the first we see those elements directly concerned with guarding the old regime. Secondly, there are the elements who participate in the movement because they are bought or pressured by the administration, and finally there are the ignorant ones who do not yet know what their general interests are, who appear under an enemy banner in defense of their foes against their friends.

In the first group the large landowners predominate. . . . They comprise the heart and soul of the reactionary party [and] are in fact the ruling class of Russia. [Among] our officials of the five highest ranks [there were 14 *chins* or ranks in the bureaucratic hierarchy], the greatest majority are large landowners having more than 5,000 desyatins of land. . . . All of these landowners —their excellencies—ministers, governors, having thus far [held] Russia . . . in a tight rein, are at present worried both about their fat paychecks and the fate of their large estates; should the revolution be victorious. It is not surprising, therefore, that as early as the spring of 1905 a declaration was drawn up by twenty-two leaders of the nobility, stating that it was necessary to fight against "the joint forces who supported the west European theory of a constitutionally based government." It is further not surprising that at the head of the Black Hundred movement in Kursk, Tula, Moscow and other guberniyas we see the names of the illustrious Russian nobility, [such as] Prince Shcherbatov, . . . Prince Kasatkin-Rostovsky, Count Dorrer, and Count Bobrinsky. "Why have we been convened here?" asked the chairman at the meeting of the Black Hundreds at Kursk. He was the petty contractor and merchant Sushkov—the very same who, together with the police and the hooligans, massacred the students in the October 19th pogroms against Jews and intelligentsia. Said Sushkov: "The initiative must be taken by the true Russian boyars headed by the guberniya's leader of the nobility (Count Dorrer). A deputation from this congress has asked General Panteleev to permit the party of order to arm itself in the event of the need to wipe out the intelligentsia, which is lawlessly shooting at the Russian people."

Furthermore, it is not difficult to understand the counter-revolutionary sympathy of our higher clergy. Besides their natural tendency to oppose any change in the social or-

der, . . . they know that monastic land, along with that of nobles and State land, is slated to be given to the peasants in all programs of the revolutionary and even of the moderate parties. . . . In this same group . . . are the small-numbered, but influential, journalists who have sold their pens in return for writing pro-government statements. This group also includes the professors whose road to the lecture platform has not been by way of laboratory and library, but through the ante-room of a ministry or some kind of special influence. . . .

In the second group we must first mention the proletariat which in western Europe and also in America always represents "military forces" selling their fists to any buyer. Such were the thugs . . . who . . . sold themselves for monarchist demonstrations in France, getting one franc if the demonstration was peaceable and three francs if it involved clashes with the police. . . . With us all this is done in a much more barbaric manner and for less pay. In Pskov one is hired to beat up children for fifty kopeks.

But besides these . . . , one must take note of whole categories of professions, whose fate is entirely in the hands of the police. The small shopkeeper, the inn-keeper, the contractor and the like, can exist only with the permission of the police. At any moment, an order concerning rotten food, or the non-observance of official regulations and sanitary laws, . . . can put an end to their livelihood. . . . There are professions which by customary law, not by written law, are completely under police jurisdiction. There are the secret brothels, the gambling dens, the thieves' hideouts, the buyers of stolen goods, etc. Over persons involved in such matters, the police hold the key to existence or non-existence.

When such elements are told, "Beat!" they do so no less obediently than any policeman or fireman. "We are people without a will of our own. We would not do these things of our free will." So spoke an old fireman who took part in the child beatings in Pskov.

The third and broadest group of elements to defend the old regime are those who side with autocracy because of ignorance. Here we are dealing first of all with the psychology of old peasant Russia and in particular with the naive faith in the peasant-loving tsar, whom only the hated nobles prevent from making the peasants happy with land and all other benefits to be derived from it. Because of his natural tie to the insulated commune, the peasant has had to bear the twofold yoke of exploitation by the landowner and the police state. Separated from the whole world by the double walls of illiteracy and lack of means of communication, he has had to carry on a lonely, hopeless struggle against the landowner-police state. Seeing no help anywhere, and in order . . . not to fall into despair, the muzhik began to dream that there was somewhere, somehow a force, strong and just, that saw his suffering and would finally come to his aid. So, like a flower in a swamp, there grew in his childish soul a faith in the tsar—the defender of the peasant. . . . This belief has been widely exploited by our reactionaries because, thanks to it [there is a great] hostility in peasant circles toward the intelligentsia fighting the tsarist autocracy. The muzhik, after all, views the intellectual as an aristocrat and all will remember what deep roots were left among the peasants by the legend about Alexander II's death, broadcast by the reactionaries, to the effect that the landlords probably killed him because he liberated the peasants from serfdom.

It was the same thought process by which the ignorant formed the idea, popular at the time of the cholera revolts, when they tried to explain the epidemic to themselves by blaming it on the activities of the medical personnel. Along the Volga and the Don the legend circulated stressing the following idea: "These landlords see that the peasants are reproducing rapidly and that the land is getting eroded. They see this and fear that the tsar will once more take land from them and give it to the peasants. So they decided to let death loose upon the land, to kill peasants thinking that the tsar would then have no need to take land from them. . . ."

With the rapid growth of Russian cities, each year new waves of peasants flowed into them from the land. This population even in the cities retain their traditional village views for a long time, and for even a longer time retain both their hostile attitudes toward the intelligentsia and their old muzhik faith in the tsar. A characteristic lingering of these feelings distinguishes those groups who become petty bourgeoisie, storekeepers, tailors, shoemakers, artisans, inn-keepers, and the like. Thus they are good material for the reactionary party. Moreover, to this tradition which maintains the reactionary attitude, they add a hatred for all that is new. This is natural to the petty bourgeoisie and rises out of the fact that due to the competition of large-scale industry and new-type trading their very existence as a small bourgeoisie is threatened. From this point of view the small bourgeoisie joins with the elements described in our first group—the group vitally interested in preserving the old regime. On the other hand, the small bourgeoisie is to a certain extent also interested in the development of democracy and to that extent they view the defenders of the old regime with suspicion. However, because of the low standards of education prevailing in our country, they willingly join the cries of: "Beat the students, beat the intelligentsia" and especially the cry of "beat the Yids!" because that way they may in any case hope to do away with their competition.

Stolypin and the "Rebellious" Duma*

Stolypin [enunciated the government's] legislative program for the duma. The en-

* SOURCE: A. Levin, *The Second Duma*, New Haven, Yale University Press, 1940, pp. 115-122. (Adapted and abridged.)

actment of so vast a reform program, the premier explained, depended directly on the condition of the finances of the state. Therefore, he regarded the examination of the budget as a very important matter, and invited the duma to undertake that task as soon as possible. He promised that in the future the tax burden would be more equitably distributed, and that, insofar as possible, the administration would refrain from placing additional levies on the poorer elements. In concluding, he expressed the belief that the enactment of reforms would pacify and revive the country, and to that end he was ready to place at the disposal of the duma all of the government's resources and experience.

Stolypin's statement was greeted with a vigorous applause on the right and a deep silence in the rest of the hall. Although this declaration of intentions was a distinct advance toward liberalism, especially since the administration now offered to consider the proposals of the opposition, it had several defects. In the first place, the government was still allowed the final word in all legislative matters, and there was no hint of a concession to the demand for a duma ministry. Then, the government had emphatically declared that it would brook no opposition to its agrarian program. [Besides, there] was still too much of the bureaucratic, patriarchal spirit in the address to evoke sympathetic response from any part of the opposition.

The chairman of the council of ministers was followed immediately by the Social-Democratic spokesman, I. G. Tsereteli. In the opinion of the youthful Menshevik leader, Stolypin spoke for "feudal" Russia, and clearly demonstrated the connection between the government and large landowners.

He accused the government of interfering in the capital-labor struggle; of abetting and organizing lockouts; of persecuting the press and political organizations; of terrorizing two-thirds of the population [through its] uncontrolled satraps. He further accused the administration of organizing pogroms. This government, he asserted, could not pacify the masses, but only exasperate them, [making] an explosion inevitable.

In the elections, he continued, the people had expressed its will, but only by the organization and unification of the people could official tyranny be ended. For only the

organized people could force the executive power to resign and guarantee the realization of a real constitution. The duma, assembled for legislative work, would analyze the government's bills which took from the people the few gains it had made, and would point out the abyss between it and the administration. The duma would arouse the population for the struggle in order to win both land and freedom. Since the government would bow only before force, he called on the duma to wield that power which would help it to subordinate the executive authority to the legislative.

First the silent reception of Stolypin's near-conciliatory declaration, then the Social-Democratic reply; here was a cold welcome for the government, from the most representative body [in] Russian [history]. But the Kadets had never meant their opposition to go as far as the Marxists pushed it, and they hastened to define their position and forestall further harsh utterances. Prince Dolgorukov (Kadet), supported by the *Narodniki*, the Kolo,[1] and the Moslems, urged that criticism be postponed until particular measures should be discussed. And he proposed the simple Kadet formula: "Having heard the statement of the chairman of the council of ministers on the introduction of bills, the duma passes to the regular order."

The Social-Democrats prolonged the assault begun by Tsereteli. The Lett, Ozol, condemned the government for its sins against labor: For isolating the worker from the rest of the population, for suppressing trade unions and the labor press, for its punitive expeditions which fell with especial fury on strikers, for its neglect of the unemployed. Aleksinskii jeered at rightist orators who had called themselves representatives of the people; those rich landowners and high church dignitaries who would enslave Russia for they feared her people. The peasant, the worker, and soldier might expect nothing from the government which represented these elements, and would have to struggle against it for every gain. That was the single truth which the Social-Democrats had come to the duma to propagate.

Through the daily press Stolypin must

---

[1] The Polish delegation in the Duma.

have been well posted on what to expect in the duma, and could prepare a reply accordingly. At any rate, before the end of the session he appeared on the tribune for a second time, with an olive branch, and defiance for the revolutionaries. He had not intended to speak again, he began, but the course of the debate forced him to do so. He wished first to state that the government would always act strictly within the law. Then, he would like to find grounds for common work and a common language with the duma; but he was certain that it could never be that of hatred or malice. In order to make the administration's position perfectly clear he affirmed that the duma had no legal right to express non-confidence in the government which, of course, did not mean that this government, entrusted with power at a moment of great reform, would try to escape responsibility.

He reiterated his contention that the part of the duma which desired to work, to enlighten the people, and solve the land problem would be able to declare its views even though they were opposed to those of the government. Even more, the government would welcome any revelation of maladministration. And he lightly excused past irregularities on grounds of human fallibility at a time when legal norms were not yet fully defined.

But, he declared, the government would regard differently attacks made for the purpose of arousing the population in order to facilitate the preparation for an open attack. And he closed with a peroration which rang as a challenge in the ears of revolutionaries to the last days of the Old Régime: "These attacks count on paralyzing the will and thoughts of the government. They all come down to two words: 'hands up.' To these two words, sirs, the government can reply: 'You will not frighten us.'"

The session closed with the adoption of the Kadet formula.

The government was as yet conciliatory. Stolypin's addresses were reassuring to those who had feared immediate dissolution. Yet the premier had displayed disturbing characteristics of the old bureaucratic type. He would co-operate with the duma, but basically on his own terms. He would allow very little tampering with his all-important agrarian reform and he evolved a constitutional theory which was the very negation of the idea of a parliamentary ministry. A vote of non-confidence by the duma meant nothing, for he was responsible to the tsar alone. Then, his emphatic defense of repression and his vigorous assault on the revolutionaries made him appear more anti-revolutionary than pro-reform. The skepticism of the liberals increased and Stolypin attracted only the conservatives and reactionaries.

The Electoral Law of 1907*

The electoral law of 1907 was so constructed that the duma would have an assured predominance of landlords and big commercial-factory bourgeoisie. The landlords chose one elector per 213 persons; industrialists, merchants and homeowners one per 1,000; peasants—one per 60,000; the petty bourgeoisie of the cities, one per 15,000; workers—one per 125,000. Elections were by

* SOURCE: G. Barandov, *Stolypinskaya Reaktsiya* (The Stolypin Reaction), Moscow, 1938, pp. 7-8.

class—separate for landlords, bourgeoisie, peasants, workers. . . .

The workers elected proxies, the proxies chose electors. The peasants elected representatives to the *volost* assemblies. These representatives selected proxies who chose electors. This multi-level election process was designed to keep revolutionary-minded workers and peasants out of the duma.

Even more restricting were the regulations concerning the workers of the national minority groups. If in European Russia there was one deputy for 279,000 persons, in Siberia there was one deputy for 1,000,000. Completely deprived of voting rights were the regions of Akmolinsk, Zakaspisk, Samarkand, Semipalatinsk, Semirechyansk, Syr Darya, Turgaisk, Uralsk, Fergansk, Yakutsk. Deprived of voting rights were also all nomadic peoples and those who did not know the Russian language. The tsarist law deprived women of the right to vote. Youths under twenty-five could not vote. Students, regardless of age, had no vote. Also deprived were field hands and the poor. Only peasants who owned a house could vote. All those serving in the tsar's army were also deprived of voting rights.

So, only 15% of the adult population could take part in the elections to the duma. At that, the landlords, having 36,000 voters (1/500 of all the voters), chose 2,644 electors, or 51.3% of all the electors [who voted for duma deputies].

As a result of this system the deputies of the Third Duma, according to class division, was as follows:

		Per Cent
Hereditary nobles . . .	192	(44)
Clergy	47	(11)
Merchants and notable citizens	54	(12.5)
Peasants	99	(23)
Others	45	(9.5)

Stolypin on the Settlement of Siberia*

Siberia is rich in everything save people and can attain a flourishing economic and cultural life only if vigorous working people flow in from Russia. . . . [The rigid patterns of life, the] robber economy of the aborigines, the . . . primitive economy of the Nomads as well as the local labor markets will have to adjust to the new conditions brought about by the arrival of the new immigrants.

The re-settlement problem, therefore, deserves . . . constant aid on the part of the government.

In the 300 years [since Russia first expanded into Siberia] only four and a half million Russians accumulated there. But in the last fifteen years [1897-1912] three million were suddenly added, and of these over 1,500,000 came within three years (1907-1909). However, in the feverish exodus across the Urals and in the mass settlement in new places . . . not everything was properly arranged. . . .

The conditions of transportation have im-

* SOURCE: P. A. Stolypin and A. W. Kriwoschein, *Die Kolonisation Sibiriens,* . . . (The Colonization of Siberia), 1912, pp. 1-95. Place of publication not given.

proved in the past years. The speed of re-settlement trains has been accelerated; definite travel plans have been instituted. On the Siberian Railway new re-settler cars of the passenger type have been introduced. In the past four years the number of stations for the settlers on the routes of the re-settlement movement have been doubled. There are now a hundred of them. In addition, the military administration places certain military equipment, such as kitchen and laundry cars, at the disposal of the settlers whenever they are available.

The health conditions of the transportation . . . are bearable. . . . Since 1908— when cholera broke out in European Russia —there has thus far been no cholera epidemic among the settlers in transit. . . . During our journey the cholera barracks in many Siberian cities were full of sick people, but in the railway cars and on the settler stations there were none sick with cholera. This was the case despite the fact that. . . the settlers, worn out by the long journey, were most likely to be susceptible to disease. . . .

In the re-settlement movement of the current year [1910] there has been, along with the decrease in the number of settlers, a definite rise in the level of living standards.

This is proven . . . by the very large quantity of household furnishings that the settlers brought with them. The number of railway cars carrying goods of the settlers was larger in 1910 than the numbers of cars carrying persons. . . . The relative wealth of the settlers [of 1910] has also been noted by several district committees of the railroads and in Chelyabinsk. This could be due to the . . . eased conditions for the liquidation of communal shares of land and the possibility of raising money for these shares in the Peasant Bank. But it may also have dawned upon the peasants that it is better to have cash when entering upon emigration and to postpone it if one does not have it. A basic feature of this year's movement is the evident decline in percentage of those going ahead "on their own." They no longer represent half the re-settlers, as was the case in the past years, but constitute less than a third. Two-thirds of the migrants went to lands specifically assigned to them.

A sad feature this year is the increase of the returners from Siberia,—14,000 families more than last year. Part of this is explained by the same general cause that has also led to the decrease of the re-settlement movement; i.e., the crop failure in Siberia coupled with the good harvest in European Russia. Temporarily the flow of peasants to the lands beyond the Urals is decreasing and a stream of migrants from the Urals is in progress. Predominating among the returners are the persons who went, as it is called, "on their own"—those, that is, who despite all their efforts and pleadings, failed to get a piece of land in Siberia. This indicates that the recently instituted and not fully successful system of organized re-settlement has also had an unfortunate effect upon the process of re-settlement.

The basis of this system was the following: In the best districts of Western Siberia, in the Altai [Mountains region], and in the steppe-lands of Kirgizia, the land parcels have since 1907 been inadequate for the migrants. There have not even been enough for a tenth of them. So, in order to prevent too great a number of customers coming in to

meet certain disappointment, it was decided to limit the movement of buyers and to bring it into accord with the amount of land available. To select the customers, local aid was solicited. The zemstvos and the agricultural commissions[1] were given the assignment to establish a closer link between the migration beyond the Urals and the agricultural organizations of European Russia. That made it necessary . . . to determine each year in advance the number of purchasers to be allotted to the respective guberniyas and also the place of settlement for each prospective migrant. . . .

Each year the re-settlement authority, having consulted with delegates from such regions, designated the Siberian district in which parcels were to be allotted and how many per capita one might allot to each *guberniya* of European Russia. Then there was executed on the spot [in European Russia] the division of the specified number of parcels among the various counties within a *guberniya*. Thus each county of European Russia was authorized to dispose of a strictly limited number of settlers' portions in certain regions of Siberia. Groups of buyers were then listed for settlement in Siberia but only those were included who had been selected by the agricultural authority or the *zemstvo*. What seemed to be a carefully thought out system had no positive results. All the conditions which made the Altai or Kirgiz steppe the favorite regions for settlers remained unchanged. Given almost the same outlay of money and an equal size of parcel, one might receive a splendid piece of land in Altai or a miserable plot in the *taiga*[2] in the northern part of Irkutsk *Guberniya*. Naturally there were more persons favoring the Altai. But the local agricultural authorities, for the most part, offered them land in some entirely different region. So the buyers stayed home, or, having agreed to travel to Irkutsk *Guberniya,* got off the train, on the way, in Tomsk *Guberniya*. Or, having

---

[1] The district and provincial agricultural commissions were established in 1906 to aid in the Stolypin-initiated process of enabling peasants to withdraw their land from the communes and become privately-operating farmers.

[2] Forest land.

viewed the land parcel hung upon them, they refused to take it and returned empty-handed. Or, some, having scoffed at all authorities and ordinances, suddenly picked up and took their families [to Siberia] at their own risk and without information. They paid dearly.

* * *

Even in localities where the economic conditions for settlement are favorable, the general conditions of Siberian life are raw. Upon visiting the populated parcels one feels that the newcomers must live in worry "for bread alone" in an exhausting struggle with nature. These settlements that are for the most part lost in the *taiga* or in the steppe are made up of people having no blood ties and no common pasts, but have just found themselves together and must now exist under the circumstances they all share. They struggle to make a bare living. Often they have not even a church. There is no city nearby, no annual fair. Not all can endure this. The rougher hewn ones, such as the Latvians and the sectarians, manage it better. Re-settlers from the central Russian guberniyas, who have been raised under different circumstances, especially women, cannot for a long time get accustomed to the wildness of their new conditions of life.

* * *

An important matter . . . is the government's aiding the settlers with food on occasion of crop failures. The settler . . . has no stores on hand for the time of need. One crop failure . . . in the first years of settlement is a terrible misfortune. It is even harder to retain a feeling of confidence in

the new land from which one expected better results, but which produced less than the old. Often an accidental crop failure in the early years is the sole, but so understandable reason, for abandoning the parcel and fleeing back to the homeland; and so the welfare of the settler's family is forever ruined. Timely assistance, which goes beyond the normal limits of settler loans, is particularly important in this respect. But the organization of credit for aiding in hard times and also for sowing the fields is not even instituted in Siberia; not even in the established settlements.

* * *

. . . From 1896 to 1909, . . . about 3,000,000 went to Siberia and about 300,000 returned. . . . [and] 300,000 returners, even when distributed over a fifteen year period, [cast] a dark shadow upon the migration. But . . . one must not forget the 2,500,000 who successfully managed the re-settlement. Also, . . . with respect to the returners, one must keep in mind that the vast majority merely stopped off in Siberia but never set up farms. Almost two thirds of the returners were migrants "on their own," who went with their families without previously having provided themselves with land. They found no land and, having suffered disaster, were forced to return. It is clear that these failures are not merely due to the carelessness of those "on their own," but also due to certain irregularities in the arrangement of the re-settlement system. Still, this returning movement . . . is not the return of persons who actually established an economic basis for life and were then ruined. All of which proves that conditions in Siberia are in general fully favorable for settlement.

Lenin on Stolypin's Agrarian Policy*

In order to understand the causes of the *failure* of the government's so-called "Stoly-

* SOURCE: V. I. Lenin, *Selected Works*, IV, Moscow-Leningrad, 1935, pp. 226-241

pin" agrarian policy, which the . . . Duma is invited once more to approve by sanctioning the budget (and which undoubtedly will be approved by the landlords' parties in the

Duma), I shall dwell . . . on the *two* principal . . . *trump cards* of our "new" agrarian policy: First, on the re-settlement of the peasants, and, secondly, on the notorious *homesteads.*

As regards re-settlement, . . . 1905 . . . forced [the landlords] to "open" the safety valve a little, and instead of hampering migration as they had done before . . . to try to *pack off* as many *restless* peasants as possible to Siberia.

Did [the government] achieve . . . any improvement in the peasants' conditions in Russia and Siberia? Just the opposite.

. . . In the . . . memorandum of the Minister of Finance on the Finance Bill for 1913 we find the usual official . . . praises of the "successes" of the government's policy.

The settlers, we are told, transform the vacant regions into "civilised localities," the settlers are growing rich, improving their farms . . . and so forth. . . .

The only pity is that the . . . memorandum *completely* ignored the statistics of returned settlers!! A strange and significant silence!

. . . Yes, [gentlemen], by 1908, the migration wave reached high water mark: 665,000 settlers in one year. But later the wave began *rapidly to recede,* and reached 189,000 in 1911. Is it not clear that the highly praised government "settlement" of the migrants has turned out to be *bluff?* . . .

And the statistics of the number of returned settlers—so prudently ignored by the Minister of Finance . . . reveal a *monstrous* increase in the number of returned settlers . . . —*up to 60 per cent in 1911.* This . . . reveals the desperate suffering . . . of the peasants who sold everything at home . . . to go to Siberia, and who are now forced to come back . . . utterly . . . pauperized.

. . . I shall quote another opinion, that of an official, who for twenty-seven years— *twenty-seven years,* gentlemen!—served in the Forestry Department in Siberia, an official who has studied the conditions of migration. . . .

This official is State Councillor *A. I. Komarov,* who . . . could not but acknowledge that the notorious journey of Stolypin and Krivoshein, the Prime Minister and the

Minister of Agriculture and Land Settlement respectively, to Siberia in 1910 was a "buffoonery tour"—such is literally the expression used by a State Councillor. . . . This official *resigned the service,* he could not tolerate the deception of all Russia that was being practiced by means of such "buffoonery tours," and he published a special pamphlet [describing] the thefts and embezzlement of government funds, the utter absurdity, brutality and wastefulness of our re-settlement policy.

This pamphlet is entitled *The Truth About Re-settlement* and was published in St. Petersburg in the present year, 1913, price sixty kopeks—not dear, considering the wealth of revealing material it contains. . . . The official, Komarov, had to *lie low* as long as he was in the service, he had to write his letters of exposure to the newspapers under an *assumed name,* and the authorities tried to *"catch"* the correspondent. . . .

. . . Komarov is not a revolutionary. . . . He himself tells us about his loyal hostility to the theories of both the Social-Democrats and the Socialist-Revolutionaries. No, he is an ordinary, very loyal . . . official, who would be quite satisfied with elementary . . . honesty. . . .

The following are [his] conclusions: "Utter unpreparedness of the General Re-settlement Board for carrying on the work on a large scale . . . absolute lack of planning in the work and bad quality of the work . . . allotment of plots with soil unsuitable for agriculture, where there is no water at all, or no *drinking water."* (p. 137.)

When the tide of migration rose, the officials were caught napping: "They divided up the state forest lands . . . into tiny plots . . . took the first thing they set their eyes on, as long as they could find place for, get rid of, those *scores of emaciated people with tired faces* who were hanging around the re-settlement base and standing for hours in the ante-chamber of the Re-settlement Board." (p. 11.) . . .

"Many hundreds of thousands," he says about those . . . destitute returned settlers, "return as elements of a type . . . such as in the future revolution, if such takes place, is destined to play a terrible role. . . . These

men are a menace to any political system." (p. 74.) . . .

Let us pass on to the question of the homesteads. . . .

We are informed [by the Minister of Finance] that by 1912 over one and a half million households had . . . abandoned the village commune; that over a million of these . . . have been established as homesteads.

Not a single truthful word has been uttered *anywhere* in the government reports about the real state of the homesteads!!

We know . . . that there are *homestead peasants* of two altogether different categories. The government, by confusing these categories, by giving data of a general kind, is only deceiving the people.

One category of homestead peasants, an insignificant minority, are the well-to-do peasants, the kulaks, who even before the new land settlement schemes were introduced lived very well. Such peasants, by leaving the . . . commune and buying up the allotments of the poor, are undoubtedly enriching themselves at other people's expense, still further ruining . . . the masses. . . .

Another category of homestead peasants predominates . . . to an overwhelming degree, viz., the . . . destitute peasants, who went to the homesteads out of sheer need, for they had nowhere else to go. . . . Starving and toiling on their beggarly farms, they clutch at the last straw for the sake of the re-settlement grant, for . . . the settlement loan. On these farms they suffer untold hardships; they sell all their grain . . . to pay . . . the bank; . . . they live like beggars; they are *driven* from the homesteads for *non-payment of instalments* and . . . finally [become] homeless tramps. . . .

. . . [They are] living in dugouts, herding together with their cattle, starving, with sick and ragged children.

. . . The government does its utmost to conceal this truth about the homesteads. Independent, detached observers of peasant life are prosecuted and deported from the villages. Peasants writing to the newspapers come up against tyranny. . . .

A handful of rich homestead peasants are represented as masses of thriving peasants! The official lie about the kulaks is represented as the truth about the countryside!

Anti-Semitism of the "Black Hundreds" *

An article in Russkaya Pravda (*Russian Truth*), *an Astrakhan newspaper, March 9, 1910:*

The duma's committee on interpellations has decided to interpellate the Minister of the Interior [P. A. Stolypin] about his unlawful order of May 22, 1907 to governors, giving the Jews a right which does not lawfully belong to them.

. . . Stolypin's circular arbitrarily permits

* SOURCE: A. Chernovsky (ed.), *Soyuz Russkogo Narodo, po materialam chrezvychainoy sledstvennoy kommissii vremmenogo pravitel'stva 1917* (The Union of the Russian people [the "Black Hundreds"], from the Materials of the Special Investigating Committee of the Provisional Government of 1917), Moscow-Leningrad, 1929, pp. 313-315.

[the many] Yids[1] who, during the time of the revolution, dispersed themselves (beyond their zones of settlement) throughout all of Russia, to remain in the places seized by them, if in such places they had already established "domicile,"—that is, if they had as much as a table, a broken stool, some stinking straw to sleep on and a tub to wash in. In short, he has fed Russia to these Yids.

The supreme council of the Union of the Russian People ordered the membership to complain to the Senate about this unlawful act and that was duly done by Count E. I. Konovintsyn [one of the founders of the supreme council]. The act of Stolypin was

[1] This is the gutter equivalent to the Russian word *Zhid*, as used in the original. The proper Russian word for Jew is *yevrei*.

unlawful. But since the Senate is subordinate to the Minister of Justice who in turn is subordinate to the Chairman of the Council of Ministers, i.e., Stolypin, . . . Stolypin was able to quash the issue raised by the Union. Now it has been raised again—this time by the duma. So, both the Senate and the duma committee on interpellations admit the unlawfulness of Stolypin's action. We know that this article will not please the local censor, and so, to avoid an attempt to confiscate this number of the paper entirely, we should like to warn him that the above-stated information about the unlawfulness of Stolypin's act is not a lie and was taken in full out of the non-confiscated No. 43 of the *Russkoye Znamya* [Russian Banner] of this year, and that, if despite our admonition, this number of *Russkaya Pravda* should be confiscated, we will be obliged to raise the special issue of the unlawfulness of the censor of Astrakhan.

Letter of N. N. Tikhanovich to the Governor of Astrakhan, March 29, 1909:

Your Excellency:

According to information of the Committee of the "Astrakhan People's Monarchist Party" the following new shocking trick of the Astrakhan Yids is being played.

In the Astrakhan male gymnasium there are approximately 560 students. Among them, according to the 5% norm, there should be only 28 Yids. However, . . . the gymnasium has 57 Yids,—more than 10%. . . . There are even 10 Yids in the gymnasium dormitory. An especially large number of these have been accepted this year.

Upon questioning by the Committee it became clear that the parents of the Yids accepted beyond the norms call themselves Karaites. Undoubtedly we have here a case of a new fraud on the part of the Yids.

Up to now all Astrakhan Yids were ordinary Yids, and suddenly, almost half of them (to judge by the gymnasium enrollment) have turned into Karaites. If the most extreme measures are not taken at once to expose this new Yiddish trick, it is possible that soon all the Yids of Astrakhan will

have become Karaites and the high schools of Astrakhan will have turned into Kheders [Hebrew schools].

There are about 10,000 Karaite Jews in Russia. . . . They have their own synagogues and don't accept the Yiddish Talmud [teaching]. They are hostile toward the Talmudist Yids. Since Karaites have full civil rights, so, undoubtedly, it is marked in their passports that they are Karaites in order that they should not be confused with the usual Yids. Besides that, the so-called "Karaite spiritual administration" . . . keeps an exact listing of all Karaites. There are two Karaite spiritual administrations in Russia, —one in Evpatoria (Tavrida *Guberniya*), the second in Trok (Vilna *Guberniya*). So it is always easy to determine the truth— whether [a person is a] Karaite or an ordinary Yid.

I appeal to Your Excellency to order an immediate probe of the passports of Yids who call themselves Karaites.

Letter of N. N. Tikhanovich to the Governor of Astrakhan, November 30, 1909:

The committee of the People's Monarchist Party calls your attention to the fact that the manager of a local theatrical group who signs himself "Efim Mikhailovich Dolin," is none other than the Yid, Kagan.

The committee asks Your Excellency to order a probe into whether the Yid, Kagan, has the right of residence in Astrakhan, and, if not, then to send the Yid, Kagan, out of Astrakhan and call him to account for giving himself a name and a patronymic . . . by which he deceives people and commits a fraud, since the Yids have no Efims or Mikhails.

Telegram of N. N. Tikhanovich to P. A. Stolypin, March 18, 1910:

Your Excellency:

Again hundreds of Russian workers are being ousted from their jobs by Jews of this and other areas. This great assemblage of persons made idle by these Yids asks you to take measures, finally, for the protection of the . . . Russian worker. The present situation would be impossible and unbearable in any country. The native Russian population, the real owners of our land, are systematically squeezed out by the marauding foreigners, but the government does nothing. . . .

Then, when as a result of governmental negligence, the Russian people are driven

[to fight against their oppressors in their own way] they are jailed or sent into exile as pogromists. This meeting of Russian workers asks you either to remove the Jews from the jobs, or to give out money or food to Russian workers and their families who are condemned to starvation [by the Jews]. The Jew must not be allowed to benefit at the expense of the Russian who is dying of hunger.

The Nature of Press Censorship*

The newspapers in the capitals maintain a fairly tolerable existence in spite of occasional fines and the constant prosecution of responsible editors. There is a very wide range of subjects now in regard to which free discussion is entirely permissible, and the fact that the whole extent of Imperial Policy is publicly discussed in the Duma makes it impossible to carry restrictions on the metropolitan Press to an extreme. The case of the provincial Press is infinitely worse. In the small . . . towns where the officials have little to do, everybody knows everybody, and there are all kinds of petty intrigues and personal accounts to settle, journalists are wholly at the mercy of governors and other officials armed with discretionary powers. The treatment of the provincial Press supplies an inexhaustible fund of curious anecdotes. One day, in 1906, the *Viatsky Krai*,[1] in Viatka, failed to appear, because the governor had expelled from the town every member of the staff. A newspaper in Kherson was fined for publishing a telegram of the official Telegraph Agency reporting a speech of Sir Francis Younghusband's on Tibetan affairs. A governor of Tambov . . . drew up a list of newspapers under three heads, "desirable," "undesirable," and "absolutely intolerable," and closed public libraries and dismissed elementary school teachers who subscribed to

organs of the latter two categories. Printing works are frequently closed so as to prevent the publication of a newspaper. The only printing works in the town of Kozlov, for instance, were closed three times so as to make it impossible to publish a little paper called the *Kozlovskaia Gazeta*.[2] To evade such measures several papers intended for the town of Kaluga were printed in Moscow, which is only a few hours distant. The Administration constantly prohibits reference to certain facts in the Press. It has been forbidden, for instance, at various times and in various places, to refer to the dissolution of the Duma, to the funeral of the Speaker of the First Duma, Muromtsev, and the funeral of Tolstoy, to the fanatical monk Iliodor, or to the notorious *agent provocateur*, Azev. All these subjects might be regarded as political, but reference has also been frequently prohibited to events of an entirely non-political character. The papers of one town were forbidden to refer to a woman who had thrown sulphuric acid in the face of a priest, other papers were forbidden to touch on the behaviour of the teachers in the local high school, while the papers of a town in the . . . Caucasus were not permitted to mention the bad acting of an artiste with whom the local police chief was on friendly terms. Papers are occasionally fined for printing reports of Panslavist meetings, for misprints, and even for publishing shorthand reports of debates in the

* SOURCE: H. W. Williams, *Russia of the Russians*, London, Pitman & Sons, 1915, pp. 104-106.
[1] The Viatka Region.

[2] The Kozlov Journal.

Duma. . . . The editor of a paper named *Yug*[3] declared he was ill, whereupon the local governor suspended his paper on the ground that a sick man could not edit a newspaper. Many provincial editors have been so harassed by the authorities that they have in despair offered to submit their papers to a preventive censorship. A paper called the *Yuzhnia Viedomosti*,[4] published in the Crimea, was confiscated seventy times.

. . . In spite of the abuses . . . the Russian Press, especially in the provinces, is steadily developing [in number and quality]. . . . There is a fairly wide neutral sphere which lies outside the range of the

[3] The South.
[4] The Southern News.

most acrimonious political dispute. . . . There are governors and governors, and, if in one town, the chief of police persecutes the editor of the Opposition journal, in another town he plays cards with him. And many editors have grown wise . . . and have learned to avoid . . . pitfalls. Journalists suffer far more from administrative penalties than they did in the days of preventive censorship. But over against this must be set the fact that there are far more newspapers than there were, and that the number of journalists has greatly increased. And in spite of all restrictions the Press is now actually in a position to express, however imperfectly, to guide, and to educate public opinion.

Labor Conditions*

. . . In prerevolutionary Russia the right of the entrepreneur in his factory was identified with that of "the master in his own house." . . . The Russian bourgeoisie insisted that relations between capital and labor in Russia were "patriarchal," and did not require regulation . . . from outside the factory.

The absolutism of the Tsar in the state and of the entrepreneur in the factory harmonized perfectly, supplemented each other. The appearance on factory territory of anything like a "labor union" or even of "concerted action" was regarded as "rebellion," just as in the civil arena the . . . collective submission of a petition was regarded as a crime against the state. . . .

On the eve of the twentieth century Russia knew no liberty of strike or coalition. . . . The employers were often forbidden . . . to make concessions to the workers under "illegal" pressure of the strike. The

* SOURCE: V. Chernov, *The Great Russian Revolution*, New Haven, Yale University Press, 1936, pp. 128-132. Victor Chernov, founder and leader of the Socialist Revolutionary Party, became Minister of Agriculture of the Provisional Government in May, 1917.

political police . . . attacked Witte's very moderate projects tending to legalize to some degree labor organizations and strikes. . . .

It was only . . . in 1903 that Russian legislation created the first legal channel through which the workers could submit their needs to the employer: the "factory elders." But it did this in so pitiful a form that the workers often boycotted the elections and contemptuously called this "law on factory elders" the "law on factory doorkeepers." The Revolution of 1905, during the government's helplessness and the owners' confusion, laid the first foundations of a factory constitution, with elective factory committees and an embryonic system of collective agreements. But counterrevolution came. The workers' organization declined. Militant associations of capital grew up (by 1907 there were 120) forbidding their members to shorten the working day, to allow the workers' deputies to interfere in regulating the hiring, discharge, and payment of the workers, or above all to agree in direct or camouflaged form to pay for time lost in strike. . . . The conquests of the revolutionary period were gradually eliminated.

This was furthered through systematic destruction of labor organizations by the police.

Organized lockouts began to be applied more frequently against strikes. . . . The working day reverted to the prerevolutionary norm of 10-10½ hours. "A ray of the new dawn seemed to break for our workers, but not for long. The more enlightened workers have been discharged. Everything is as before," reads a typical report from a working class district.

Just before the World War there was a new advance in the labor movement. In 1911 the workers lost 51% of their strikes, . . . in 1913 only 31 per cent. The number of strikes, which varied in 1909-11 between 300 and 400, with total participation as low as 46,000 in 1910, again exceeded 2,000 with 725,000 to 860,000 participants annually. This advance and its achievements had not succeeded in modernizing the structure of the Russian factory when they were cut short by the World War. The further evolution of the factory was simple. At first the government cherished a grandiose bureaucratic Utopia: organizing all war industry as a state monopoly, serving all the needs of defense without the aid of private or civil initiative. The methods of this organization were at times . . . peculiar. Rodzianko tells how he once encountered a crowd of people on their way to the county seat, under armed convoy as if prisoners. He learned that this was a . . . "mobilizing" [of] trained shoemakers to stitch boots for the army! Only in May, 1915, when the front was without clothing, shoes, or ammunition, did the bankruptcy of bureaucratic procedure force the government to have recourse to the organized effort of private industry. Its voluntary mobilization was tardily begun through the War Industries Committees, which aimed to adapt Russian industry to the needs of national defense, to abolish competition and to secure the most sensible allotment of military orders. The government's failure to cope with this task and its appeal to private capital tremendously raised the confidence of the Russian bourgeoisie. "The commercial and industrial class of the twentieth century," declared Professor V. Storozhev in *News of the Moscow War Industries Committee,* "is no longer a purse from which the state may take as much as it likes, repaying with occasional titles, orders, or the granting of hereditary nobility. In the great European War the commercial and industrial class acts as a real force, for which both the bureaucratic privileges of the old and the democratic tasks of the new period must make way."

However, the entrepreneurs had no serious quarrel with the "bureaucratic privileges of the old"; these were only family tiffs. It was the "democratic tasks of the new period" that suffered from their alliance. First, workers subject to military conscription were attached to plants working for national defense. In case of strike they were menaced by dispatch to the front. Secondly, through Article 87, i.e., by emergency decree, the labor laws were repealed, and the employment of women and children immediately expanded, together with overtime. Thirdly, the servile labor of prisoners of war was offered to manufacturers in great quantity. Finally, enrolment of "yellow" labor, Chinese and Korean, was widely practiced. Not content with this, the Right press strenuously prepared public opinion for the universal militarization of the industrial workers. The factory was to become a barracks under absolute military discipline; the factory administration was to obtain the full powers of army officers over the workers. Special wartime laws already in force threatened the workers with forced labor for ceasing work. The militarization of war industry implied a still greater threat: flogging had already been introduced at the front!

Underneath, the workers were stirring. A certain safety valve was provided by the factory elections of delegates to the Workers' Group connected with the War Industries Committee. [The group] appealed to the employers, pointing out the measures adopted in all warring countries to attach the workers to the cause of national defence. . . . The Workers' Group appealed to the . . . manufacturers to break with the traditions of factory feudalism. The group attempted to secure . . . for the Russian workers: recognition of the right of coalition, creation of arbitration boards to settle conflicts between capital and labor, and resistance to "militarization" of the factories. It suffered a complete defeat. . . . Meanwhile, the government shut down the unions of printers and metal workers, sole survivals of an embryonic and camouflaged trade-union movement. The bill for arbitration boards, drafted by the Workers' Group, was rejected by the Minister of Commerce . . .

pending decision of the general question of legalizing unions. Attempts of the Workers' Group to mediate in conflicts at the Lessner plant and the "Naval" plant in Nikolayev were rejected by the factory administrations. It was also completely unable to prevent dispatch of strikers to the front after conflicts at the Nobel machine plant and the Admiralty shipyard. This explains the adoption by the Workers' Group of more radical tactics.

The Power Behind the Throne*

Rasputin's Power

Rasputin gave the strongest proof of his influence when he succeeded in depriving of his command the commander-in-chief, Nikolai Nikolaevich. The Grand Duke, in whose house Grigori had at first been welcomed with open arms, soon recognized that this "repulsive muzhik" would endanger his position, and afterwards tried by all means in his power to turn the Emperor against Rasputin. Rasputin, aware of this, began to hate the Grand Duke fanatically, especially after Nikolai Nikolaevich, at the beginning of the war, replied to a telegram in which Grigori had announced his arrival at the front with the words: "You come, and I will have you hanged." After this Grigori took every opportunity of inciting the Empress and the Emperor against the Grand Duke.

With the great defeats of the summer of 1915 the starets[1] succeeded in implanting in the Empress the conviction that the Tsar must himself assume the supreme command. Although all the ministers expressed themselves against this plan, and although Nikolai himself long hesitated to humiliate his uncle by degrading him in this way, Grigori

finally succeeded in having the Grand Duke removed from his post as generalissimo and transferred to the Caucasian front.

For a long time the advice of the "Friend" had been asked in every important appointment. Soon no one could hope for a ministerial post unless he had previously submitted to an examination by Rasputin. For example, when a new Chief of the Police was to be appointed, Rasputin sent for the person in question, looked him in the eyes for a few minutes, and the examination was at an end. In this way he raised to dignity and office a large number of corrupt and incompetent men. Most remarkable was the incident of Rasputin's expedition to "examine the soul" of a prospective minister. The Emperor decided first to entrust the "Friend" with the mission of obtaining further particulars about the candidate.

Rasputin at once proceeded to Nizhni-Novgorod and appeared one day in the office of the unsuspecting Governor.

"Here I am," he said simply. "Papa has sent me to examine *your* soul, as we are thinking of making *you* Minister of the Interior."

At these words from the peasant in his clumsy boots and dirty sheepskin, fat Khvostov, Governor of Nizhni-Novgorod, burst into laughter. Grigori Efimovich was much offended. Before he left the town, he turned up again and called out in a threat-

* SOURCE: R. Fülöp-Miller, *Rasputin, The Holy Devil*, New York, Viking Press, 1928, pp. 165-207. (Adapted and abridged.)

[1] Elder; conveying the idea of patriarchal dignity.

ening tone: "I have dealt with *you* all right. I've wired a report to Tsarskoe Selo." [2]

At first the Governor again laughed heartily; but soon apprehension crept over him. He sent for the postmaster and ordered him to produce Grigori Efimovich's telegram.

"Anna Vryubova,[3] Tsarskoe Selo," it ran: "Tell Mama that the grace of the Lord is in Khvostov, but that for the time being there is still something lacking."

The Governor [realized that what] the peasant had said was true. He might have been a minister! After this Khvostov made every effort to meet [Rasputin] as often as possible, and he treated [him] with courtesy and devotion. But some years had to pass before he had a chance of becoming intimate with Rasputin. It was at a drinking party. On meeting the Tsar soon after this Rasputin said that he had had an opportunity of examining Khvostov's soul afresh, and found that it had improved. A few days later the fat Governor at last became Minister of the Interior.

Police Reports on Rasputin

"14th October. Rasputin came home drunk at 1 A.M., insulted the concierge's wife."

"6th November. Rasputin [came home drunk]. As he went up to his flat he inquired if there were any visitors for him. On hearing that there were two ladies he asked: 'Are they pretty! Very pretty? That's good. I need pretty ones.' "

"12th December. Rasputin came back with Varvarova at 9.50 A.M.; he must have spent the night with her."

"18th January. Rasputin came home [drunk] at 7.30 A.M. with two men and a woman. He sang songs on the public street."

"26th May. Rasputin came home in the motor-car of the merchant Mandel with the prostitute Gregubova. He kissed Gregubova passionately. After she had gone he sent for Katia, the seamstress, who lives in the same house, but she was not at home."

[2] Residence of the royal family near St. Petersburg.
[3] Confidante of the Empress.

Father Grigori Receives

The best time to find Rasputin was about ten o'clock in the morning. However boisterous the previous night, he was nearly always in his flat about ten o'clock, awaiting the daily call from Tsarskoe Selo. Petitioners and visitors [were often] so numerous that many had to wait on the staircase. On holidays the whole street was often full of people. Cars and carriages stood everywhere. The poorer flocked in long queues.

Rasputin exercised great influence on the supreme dignitaries of Church and State. People told each other that Rasputin's sovereignty over Russia was more far-reaching than that of the Tsar himself, since only Rasputin was able to enforce his will. Many people gave him the title of "Tsar above the Tsars." He was also regarded as a holy man [who] could foresee the future and heal the sick. People said that Rasputin, like Christ, had performed miracles. Not only peasants [but also] wide circles in St. Petersburg society [regarded him] as the newly arisen Lord.

*   *   *

[It was known] that Rasputin was prepared to carry out various transactions, arrange releases from military service, get sentences of imprisonment quashed, or dispose of the granting of concessions; and the exact sum of money or the quality and price of the presents in return for which the help of the starets could be purchased was also known. If, after submitting their petition, well-to-do peasants, rich widows, financiers, or persons anxious for ministerial rank put money on the table, Rasputin stuffed it into the wide pockets of his velvet breeches; but he was just as ready to help a petitioner with empty hands. Every day [he received] petitioners who expected money from him. Grigori Efimovich gave generously. He had scarcely [stuffed] a bundle of banknotes in his pocket than he pulled them out again and gave them to a poor petitioner.

Besides [those] who came to Rasputin with gold and gifts, and [those] who came to receive them, there was still a third group of visitors. These were the women and girls who came to beg [favors] for someone closely connected with them. These women had heard that no gift could dispose the starets to help so readily as feminine charm. If he liked a suppliant who offered herself as a gift, he set in movement the highest authorities, and even the Tsar and Tsaritsa, although his protégée might be only a simple servant girl.

It seldom happened that such suppliants met Rasputin's advances with a refusal. Many boasted that the holy man had honoured them with his love. For at this time it was the supreme longing of many women and girls in St. Petersburg and the provinces to be admitted into the "holy of holies," as the starets' most intimate circle was called. On one occasion, when a novice refused to accede to Rasputin's desires, one of his disciples, a married woman, asked her in amazement: "How can one refuse anything to a saint? I have already belonged to him, and I am proud [of it]."

"But you are married! What does your husband say to it?"

"He considers it a very great honour. If Rasputin desires a woman we all think it a blessing and a distinction."

Rasputin and the Jews*

. . . Interceding for Jews soon became my principal . . . occupation. . . . I already began to fear that Rasputin was becoming an anti-Semite. . . .

At the time . . . the tsar was completely under his influence. Nicholas was fascinated by reactionary organizations and became a member of the Union of the Russian People which was organizing pogroms. Had Rasputin joined the reactionaries, that would have been fatal for the Jews. But after much wavering he came to our side. . . .

The most . . . energetic defender of Jews was Moses Ginsburg . . . who concerned himself with the Jewish question in St. Petersburg. . . . At one point in the course of the war Ginsburg . . . explained to me that . . . it was essential to put an end to the fearful persecutions of Jews in the regions of military operations.[1] Ginsburg had the impression that the Commander-in-Chief [the Grand Duke Nicholas] was trying to use the opportunity to wipe out the Jews once and for all. . . . "You have excellent connections," said Ginsburg. ". . .

* SOURCE: A. Simanovich, *Rasputin i Evrei, Vospominaniya lichnago sekretarya . . . Rasputina* (Rasputin and the Jews, Memoirs of Rasputin's Personal Secretary), Riga, n.d., pp. 52-57.
[1] The first year of the war was fought in Poland and Lithuania, where so many of the Jews lived.

Get Rasputin to help us. . . . Rasputin can do whatever he wishes. He can change the attitudes of all the ministers. We can not stand by while [the Grand Duke] and his helpers murder and plunder the . . . Jews in the regions of military operations, and while they are so persecuted throughout Russia. . . ." The talk with Ginsburg made a deep impression upon me. . . . I proposed that a conference be arranged between the Jewish representatives and Rasputin, so that they might personally become convinced about his views on the Jewish question. . . . The conference took place in Ginsburg's home. . . .

Upon his appearance in Ginsburg's salon, Rasputin was given a grand reception. Many wept. Rasputin was much moved. . . . He listened attentively to our complaints . . . and promised to do all he could [for the Jews]. To that he added: You all must help Simanovich [author of these lines and personal secretary to Rasputin] because he can bribe the right people. Act the way your fathers did when they concluded financial agreements even with tsars. What has become of you? You no longer act like your ancestors. The Jewish question must be solved by bribery or cunning. Be at ease where I am concerned. I shall do all I can." . . .

After the conference, dinner was served. Rasputin chose to sit by the side of the young and pretty wife of Ginsburg. The host, who knew Rasputin's reputation as a ladies' man, begged me to sit between his wife and Rasputin. . . . After the conference . . . Rasputin openly supported the Jews. . . . I tried in every way to exploit his sentiments. He often complained about the anti-Jewish activities of ministers and other leading figures. . . . He told me that the tsar was not as anti-Semitic as was generally believed. The word "Jew" had an unpleasant effect on the tsar. . . . This came from childhood experiences in the imperial family and what he had heard from governesses and servants. Rasputin told me that the Minister of the Interior once when playing with Nicholas, then crown prince, tried to frighten him with the words: "You just wait, the Jews will get you." . . . The crown prince screamed with fear. . . . Rasputin discussed the Jewish question ever more frequently with the tsar and the latter became ever more [tolerant].

I myself found a suitable occasion to plead the case of my co-religionists before the tsar. . . . Twenty Jewish dentists had been sentenced to jail on the grounds that they had acquired their diplomas only to evade the laws of Jewish settlement. . . . I asked representatives of the sentenced doctors to come to Rasputin. . . . They begged for his aid against Shcheglovitov, Minister of Justice. Rasputin said: "How can I help you? Shcheglovitov is so stubborn that he doesn't even carry out the tsar's orders when they are in behalf of the Jews. You must let Simanovich handle your case. He will outwit Shcheglovitov. . . ."

[Simanovich and Rasputin broached the subject to the tsar the following Sunday.] "Oh, those tooth yankers!" the tsar exclaimed. "But the Minister of Justice will not listen. . . ."

"Your Majesty," I interjected, "what does this mean, won't listen? The minister does not dare to contradict Your Majesty." Rasputin struck his fist upon the table and cried, "How does he dare not to carry out your orders?"

The tsar was visibly confused.

"Your Majesty," I said, "may I suggest that you sign the petition. After leaving Your Majesty, I shall take it to Tantsev [chief of the tsar's chancellery] and he will dispose of the matter." The tsar accepted my suggestion. The dentists were reprieved. They took up a collection . . . and bought Rasputin a sable coat.

The Collapse of Russian Morale*

[I recall the] first war months in Moscow. . . . I see again those moving scenes at the station: the troops . . . in cattle [cars]; the vast crowd on the platform . . . bringing . . . flowers and cigarettes; fat priests to bless the happy warriors. . . . . . . Here was a Russia . . . inspired by . . . patriotism. . . . It was, too, a sober Russia. The sale of vodka had been stopped, and an emotional . . . fervour took the place of the . . . intoxication which in previous wars had characterised the departure of Russian soldiers.

* SOURCE: R. H. Bruce Lockhart, *British Agent,* London, G. P. Putnam's Sons, 1933, pp. 95-159.

Among the bourgeoisie there was the same enthusiasm. The wives of the rich merchants vied . . . in [donating to] hospitals. There were gala performances . . . [for] the Red Cross. . . . Every night at the opera and the ballet, the . . . orchestra played the national hymns of Russia, England, France and Belgium, while the audience stood [patriotically] at attention. . . . Later, . . . the fervour evaporated, and the heavy-paunched Muscovites groaned audibly at an ordeal which lasted over half an hour. But in those early weeks of 1914 Russian patriotism had much . . . to feed [on]. The beginning of the war [bode well], and [at] the news of each Russian advance Moscow [rejoiced]. . . . Revolution was not even a distant probability, although . . . every liberal-minded Russian hoped that victory would [lead to] constitutional reforms. . . .

In St. Petersburg, it is true, these early Russian triumphs invoked . . . sneers at the failure of the Franco-British effort. . . . Pro-Germans spread . . . rumours about England's determination to fight until the last drop of Russian blood. In Moscow, however, . . . enthusiasm for the Russian victories was tempered by sympathy for the difficulties of France and England. . . .

On September 10 we attended . . . a gala performance . . . in honour of the capture of Lemberg. . . . The uniforms of the officers made a brilliant setting to the jewels and costly dresses of the women. . . . The curtain fell but the lights did not go up. . . . The atmosphere became electrical. "The Russians had won another victory. They had captured 100,000 prisoners. They had taken Przemysl." In the darkness rumour ran riot. Then the footlights went up . . . , a . . . girl of eighteen . . . came on to the stage. . . . She held a slip of paper.

The audience hushed itself. . . . Quivering with emotion . . . , the girl . . . read: "The following . . . telegram [is] from French headquarters." . . .

Then . . . she cried: "Je suis heureux de vous annoncer victoire sur tout le front.— Joffre."

The lights blazed up. . . . In a storm of cheering the orchestra struck up the Marseillaise. Bearded men kissed each other. Women . . . wept. . . . From the gallery above came the tramp of marching feet, and four hundred French reservists, singing in . . . unison, took up the refrain. They were leaving for France the next day. . . . It was epic. It was the last occasion on which Russia was to feel . . . confident about the outcome of the war.

The capture of Lemberg had softened the grim defeat of Tannenberg. But the Tannenbergs were to be repeated, and, although the Russians were to hold their own against the Austrians . . . , they were no match for the Germans. . . .

The decline in morale was . . . gradual, and, as it became clear that the war was to be a long one, life stabilised itself. In Moscow, . . . far . . . from the front, the spirit of the bourgeoisie was by no means discouraging. There was, it is true, little attempt to . . . make sacrifices. There was no [hostility toward] shirkers. . . . Places of amusement flourished . . . and, although the proletariat and the peasantry were deprived of their alcohol, no such restrictions were imposed on the well-to-do. . . . To [obtain] wine . . . required a permit, but, as the cost of living rose and since Russian officials were badly paid, permits were easily obtainable. In restaurants . . . one drank one's alcohol from a teapot instead of from a bottle. As control became more lax, even the pretence of the teapot disappeared.

On the other hand, . . . extremely valuable work was done by the so-called public organisations, represented by the Union of Cities and by the Union of Zemstvos, in providing the army with a whole network of hospitals and factories. Without this aid, the Russian military machine would have broken down far sooner. . . . Yet, instead of . . . encouraging the [patriotic] public organisations . . . , the . . . Government [hampered] their activities. It may be said that the public organisations were politically ambitious, that they were honeycombed with Liberalism and therefore a menace to the autocracy. Admittedly, both the Cities Union and the Zemstvos Unions were controlled by Liberals who had a deep suspicion of St. Petersburg. Admittedly, too, their headquarters were in Moscow, and Moscow was never popular with the Emperor. But, in the beginning . . . their enthusiasm for the war was single-minded, and the political aspirations, which came later, were the . . . result of a policy of perpetual pin-pricks. . . . The Tsar, dominated by a woman . . . obsessed with the one ambition to hand down the autocracy unimpaired to her son, never took the public organisations into his confidence. [That] Moscow became more absorbed in the internal political struggle than in the war itself was mainly the result of the Tsar's . . . obtuseness. . . . His failure to harness the loyalty of his . . . people

. . . eventually cost him his throne. . . .
Moscow, always much more anti-German
than St. Petersburg, was a . . . cesspool of
rumours of pro-German intrigues in high
places. . . . [Following is] the most popular
Moscow story of the war. The Tsarevich is
seen crying in the . . . Winter Palace. A
general . . . pats the boy's head.

"What is wrong, my little man?"

The Tsarevitch replies . . . :

"When the Russians are beaten, papa
cries. When the Germans are beaten, mama
cries. When am I to cry?"

Stories of this kind were repeated all over
. . . and did immense harm both among
the proletariat and the peasantry. . . .

. . . Although full of wounded, Kieff had
far more war-spirit than Moscow. . . .
Right up to the revolution, the nearer one
came to the front, the more optimistic was
the . . . sentiment. All the best of Russia
. . . was in the trenches. It was . . . not
the front which let the country down. . . .

I arrived at Kieff . . . on Good Friday.
. . . Every one seemed [happy]. The news
from the Austrian front, for which Kieff
was the base, was still good. Przemysl had
[just] fallen. . . .

. . . I . . . returned to a [depressed]
Moscow. . . . The [German] counter-
attacks had . . . begun, and refugees were
streaming into the city and taxing its housing resources to the utmost. . . . Socialist
acquaintances [reported] disorders among
the new conscripts in the villages. The
wounded did not like going back. The
peasants objected to . . . sons being taken
away from the fields. My English friends
in the provincial textile factories [were]
anxious about the Socialist agitation among
the workmen. It had become anti-war as
well as anti-Government. In Moscow . . .
there had been bread riots, and the Assist-
ant-Prefect had been stoned. Sandetsky, the
commander-in-chief of the Moscow district,
. . . who hated Germans had been [dis-
missed]. . . . The . . . reason . . . , it was
rumoured was [his] excess of patriotism.
The Empress, whose work for the wounded
was untiring, had given ikons to the Russian soldiers and money to the German and
Austrian prisoners. True or untrue as this

report may have been, Sandetsky had protested against the mollycoddling of prisoners
in high quarters. . . . The atmosphere was
unhealthy. Confidence in the Russian arms
had given way to a conviction of German
invincibility, and . . . the Moscow population [was] bitter [about] the alleged pro-
German policy of the . . . Government. . . .

On June 10 vast anti-German riots broke
out in Moscow, and for three days the city
was in the hands of the mob. Every shop,
. . . factory [and] house, owned by a German or bearing a German name, was
sacked. . . . The mob, mad with drink,
[looted] from the wreckage of some Ger-
man-named wine merchant, showed no
mercy. It cared nothing that its victims
were Russian subjects and in many cases
men who, in spite of their names, could
speak no German. At Zündel's, a factory
. . . , the German-speaking manager . . .
was killed on the spot. . . . For . . .
twenty-four hours the police could or would
do nothing. Fires broke out in many quarters. . . . Hooligans sacked the leading
piano store. . . . Bechsteins, Blüthners,
grand pianos, baby grands . . . , were
hurled from the various stories to the
ground.

On the third day, after some shooting,
the authorities were able to restore order.
But for the first time since 1905, the mob
had felt its power. . . .

The fall of Warsaw [climaxed] the disastrous summer campaign of 1915. . . .
There was a great increase of pessimism.
. . . [There were] rumours of Russians
[fighting] with nothing but sticks in their
hands. . . . At factory centres like Ivanovo-
Voznesensk there were anti-government
strikes [and] some . . . shooting.

. . . [On August 23] a Moscow newspaper came out with large headlines: "Official: Dardanelles Taken." Then followed
a graphic account [complete] with . . .
casualty lists. . . . [Vast crowds] knelt on
the Tverskaia Square to thank God for
this glorious victory. There was a manifesta-
tion before the [British] Consulate-General.
In vain I tried to tell the mob that the news
was false. . . . In the storm of cheering my
voice was lost. . . .

The next day there was general disappointment at the false report, and . . . with my French colleague, I called on the Prefect to demand summary action against the editor and the publishers. . . . He had . . . anticipated our just indignation. He had closed down the newspaper for the rest of the war. We expressed our gratitude. . . . [But] the paper [continued] to appear, having changed its name from *Evening News* to *Evening Gazette*. . . . The erring editor of the day before had signed the leading article of today. . . .

. . . The victory stunt had been operated in connection with the police in order to let the public work off steam. . . .

. . . The autumn advanced. . . . Blow succeeded blow . . . and if in St. Petersburg . . . few . . . believed in a Russian victory, Moscow [thought] the war could not be won unless the dark influences in the capital were eliminated. From this moment dates the first of the many resolutions demanding a ministry of national defence or of public confidence. At first these demands were modest enough. Moscow was prepared to accept legitimate . . . ministers who had no connection with the . . . parties in the Duma. It would at this stage have been simple enough for the Tsar to have formed a new Ministry which would have satisfied public opinion without going outside the usual circle from which he chose his advisers. . . . Those nearest him, however, saw the matter in another light. They told him that any concession now would be regarded as . . . weakness and that the appetite of the reformers would [increase]. This . . . argument . . . never failed to convince the Empress, and in consequence the Tsar's reply to those who were working hardest for . . . victory was to dissolve the Duma, to relieve the Grand Duke Nicholas of his command, and to dismiss Samarin, Sherbatoff and Djunkowski, the three Ministers [then] most popular in Moscow.

The dissolution of the Duma provoked the usual strikes and protests. But the assumption of the Supreme Command by the Tsar himself was the first milestone on the way to Golgotha. It was the most fatal of [his] many blunders, for as Commander-in-Chief he became personally responsible . . . for the long succession of defeats which, owing to Russia's technical deficiencies, were now inevitable.

The dismissal of Samarin and Djunkowski was the indirect sequel of an episode . . . which I . . . [witnessed]. One summer evening I was at Yar, the most luxurious nighthaunt of Moscow. . . . There was a violent fracas. . . . The cause . . . was Rasputin—drunk and lecherous—and neither police nor management dared evict him. [Phone calls were made and finally] Djunkowski, . . . Assistant Minister of the Interior and head of all the police [was reached]. Djunkowski [ordered] that Rasputin . . . be arrested. . . . He was led away, snarling and vowing vengeance. . . . Within twenty four hours Djunkowski was relieved of his post. Samarin's dismissal, which followed later, made a very painful impression. . . . He was then . . . Minister in Charge of Church matters. . . . [Only] a madman could accuse him of . . . lack of loyalty to the Emperor. Yet every Liberal and every Socialist respected him as an honest man, and the fact that the Emperor could . . . sacrifice [him] for a . . . Rasputin was accepted . . . as a complete proof of the Tsar's incompetence. "Down with the autocracy!" cried the Liberals. But even . . . reactionaries . . . said: "If the autocracy is to flourish, give us a good autocrat."

* * *

The story of the . . . months leading up to the first revolution is [one] of almost unrelieved pessimism: failures on the front . . . , boredom . . . in official circles in the rear, bewildering changes of ministers, impotent protestations by the Duma, increasing discontent . . . in the villages [and] in the trenches.

In St. Petersburg and even in Moscow the war had become . . . secondary. . . . The approaching cataclysm was . . . in every mind. . . . The ruling class, [fearing] disaster, sought to warn the Emperor. Political resolutions, passed now, not only by the Liberals, but by the nobility, were showered . . . upon the Emperor. There was no disloyalty in [them]. They merely begged the Tsar to [replace] his counsellors . . . with men enjoying the confidence of the country. . . .

. . . I was in almost daily contact with the men who, sorely against their wish, formed the first provisional government after the abdication of the Tsar. . . . They were appalled by the problem which confronted them as Russian patriots. The problem [as stated] by Maklakoff, . . . subsequent ambassador of the Provisional Government in Paris, [was]: A motor-car is going down a steep hill [toward] a . . . precipice. . . . You are in the back seat. Suddenly you realise that the driver has lost control. What are you to do?

. . . I found . . . St. Petersburg more depressing than ever. Champagne flowed like water. . . . The two best hotels . . . were thronged with officers who should have been at the front. There was no disgrace in . . . finding a sinecure in the rear. . . . And in the streets were the long queues . . . , waiting for the bread that never came. . . .

[In] December the . . . anti-government resolutions became bolder. In the factories the Social-Democrats and the Social-Revolutionaries were now conducting an active revolutionary propaganda. Goaded to fury by the [reactionary] inanities of Protopopoff . . . , Minister of the Interior, . . . the Zemstvo and Cities Unions defied his action in forbidding their Congress by passing a secret resolution which in the violence of its language exceeded all their previous political demands. There was, it is true, no word against the Emperor, but . . . the resolution declared that "the government, now . . . an instrument of the dark forces, is driving Russia to her ruin. . . . The country requires a government worthy of a great people. Let the Duma . . . justify the expectations of the people. There is not a day to lose!"

This document was only secret in so far as it was forbidden to be published. It was circulated in reneoscript in thousands of copies, both at the front and in the rear.

This resolution was passed just before Christmas. Two days before the end of the year Rasputin was assassinated. . . . [That] act was intended to save the old régime. Although for a moment it raised the hopes of the patriots, its only effect, viewed . . . in the light of history, was to assist the anti-war elements and to hasten the revolution.

Section 3

Rise of Bolshevik Power Amid Anarchy

THE MARCH DAYS

THE revolution started without an organization, without a plan. No political group in Russia at the time had anticipated either the scale of the March demonstrations or the early participation in them of the Petrograd army and naval forces. Equally astounding was the Tsar's abdictation on March 15 and the consequent collapse of the entire State and police apparatus in the capital and throughout the empire. The Duma remained as the last vestige of the old regime, but that body had never been permitted to consider itself authoritative; in addition, it did not represent the people. The Duma set up a Provisional Committee, later known as the Provisional Government, centered about liberals of the Milyukov stripe. But since it was associated with and initially accepted the idea of continuing monarchism, this government was at once suspect to the peasants, the workers, and the national minority peoples of the empire.

The spontaneously formed Soviet, made up of deputies from the factories and military units of Petrograd, and headed by an Executive Committee of Menshevik, Socialist Revolutionary, and Bolshevik leaders (the last being least influential), had had no previous governing experience. Because of the war the Soviet was far from certain what steps it might safely take without causing disorganization and total military catastrophe.

Thus, out of the chaotic March days there emerged the so-called "dual authority," which, in effect, was one authority neutralizing the other. The Provisional Government tried to carry on the war, keep the wheels of industry turning, and maintain the legal forms of the old regime until such a time as a Constituent Assembly could be elected. From the outset, however, it was confronted by the Soviet of Petrograd and its rapidly mushrooming replicas the country over which really represented the broad popular masses. But the Soviet was itself sharply divided into a leadership of intelligentsia and an inchoate mass membership. The former, though decidedly antimonarchist, still recognized the need for legal order and internal stability. The latter (soldiers, peasants, and workers), wanted early peace, land reform, and better conditions of labor. Therefore, even while it was agreeing that the war must go on in the name of national survival, the Soviet leadership yielded to the officer-hating mentality of the men in the armed services and issued Order No. 1 on March 14, which abolished the authority of officers.

THE DISSOLUTION OF THE ARMY

When the garrisons in Petrograd joined the rioters in March, the last props of the old regime collapsed. This swift decision of the soldiers may be ascribed partly to their general lack of confidence in the way the war was being conducted and partly to the intense class feelings of the men in the ranks, who readily identified the officers with the old order and themselves with the poor and hungry people of the capital. Then there was the factor of ennui from years of barracks' life, along with irritating drills, inspections, and the persecution by martinet officers. Order No. 1 and Kerensky's May 22 "Declaration of Soldiers' Rights" had led, respectively, to the establishment of soldiers' councils and to the appointment of political commissars[1] in the army. However, these measures did not immediately effect much change in military attitudes except among the Petrograd garrisons. These troops, unlike their front-line comrades, did not need to think of their actions in terms of national betrayal. At the front, discipline remained reasonably well intact for a few months, but the impact of events in the capital and throughout the country soon caused that to crumble.[2]

After Lenin's return to Russia in mid-April, Bolshevik agitation for ending the war became immensely effective and radiated swiftly through the entire army. In the words of General Loukomsky, Commander of the 1st Army Corps on the Northern Front:

If any rumors or reports reached the Provisional Government (usually coming from the regimental 'Committees') of a commanding officer having exceeded his rights and privileges, a searching inquiry was held at once, and the culprit, or any one simply suspected of being in fault, was punished and humiliated. All slander coming from these 'Committees' was . . . believed; even [highly-placed officers] were often dismissed without . . . serious grounds. . . . On the other hand, no measures whatever were taken against the excesses that were committed with regard to the officers. . . . The authorities pandered to the soldier masses. . . . When the new War Minister, Mr. Kerensky, visited [the Staff Headquarters] in Mohilev, a complete picture of the demoralization . . . of the Army was laid before him. He seemed to agree with the necessity of taking serious measures for restoring discipline, but categorically refused to re-establish capital punishment . . . , which had been abolished at the beginning of the revolution.[3]

---

[1] The latter were sent to regiments supposedly to cope with problems created by increasingly unruly soldiers' councils while insuring that the democratic spirit of the revolution be retained.

[2] Deputies elected to the Soviet from front-line units soon became infected with the virus of democracy rampant in the capital.

[3] See A. Loukomsky, *Memoirs of the Russian Revolution,* London, T. F. Unwin, Ltd., 1922, pp. 78-85.

Bolshevik propaganda was given inadvertent support by Milyukov's May 1 note to the governments of France and England, restating Russia's claim to Constantinople, and by the disastrous July offensive foisted upon an unwilling army by the government. These events, each being followed by demonstrations in Petrograd, seemed to bear out Lenin's charges that Russian blood was being cynically shed for the benefit of English, French, and Russian bankers and that the Mensheviks and Socialist Revolutionaries in the government were bourgeois politicians disguised as socialists.

To the peasants in uniform came news of the seizures of landed estates by fellow villagers. By the fall of 1917, many were deserting the front. "The soldiers," as Lenin said, "voted for peace with their feet—they ran away." When Trotsky traveled to Brest-Litovsk in January, 1918, to negotiate peace with the Germans, he found the Russian trenches to be "almost empty."

THE PEASANT—FUSE OF THE REVOLUTION

When news of the Tsar's fall reached the countryside, the peasants expected that they now would finally obtain their just shares of land. They seemed willing at first to wait for an orderly process of distribution. Traditional respect for the landowners died hard, especially since the vigorous peasant males, serving in the armed forces, were far from their native villages when the storm broke. The peasants, moreover, believed that the new government (how many understood the limitations of a provisional government?) would soon proceed to right the wrongs of centuries. While they were waiting for the government to act, the peasants organized communal and district land committees and elected deputies to peasant soviets.[4]

A congress of peasant soviets, organized by the Socialist Revolutionary Party, convened in Petrograd during May to ask that all the land then owned by landlords, the State, and the Church be divided among the peasants. The prominent Socialist Revolutionary, Victor Chernov, had initially sponsored such a program which he knew accorded with the sentiment of the peasants. By May, however, as Minister of Agriculture in a property-respecting government, Chernov preferred, or professed to prefer, waiting for the legal changes that only a constituent assembly would be empowered to introduce. At the same time, the peasant deputies in Petrograd, more educated on the whole than the villagers who had chosen them, were not properly reflective of steadily growing impatience of the masses. So the Executive Committee of the Peasant Congress acceded to Chernov's change of stand and agreed to postpone immediate action with regard to land reform. This hesitancy left the way to the peasants' hearts open for Bolshevik agitators who descended upon the villages to sow the seeds of class violence.

Lenin's slogans, linking the words "Land" and "Peace," had a major impact on the peasant revolution. The soldiers, as mentioned, were quick to respond. Soldier

[4] See V. Chernov, *The Great Russian Revolution*, New Haven, Yale University Press, 1936, pp. 142-153.

deputies to the peasant soviets called for prompt and violent measures against the landlords. Soldiers stationed in various parts of the country, coupled with ever-increasing numbers of deserters come home to claim their land, led the peasants in mass assaults on the manorial estates.

The government, failing to appreciate the current's swiftly growing power, tried to halt the spontaneous land seizures by organizing a Committee on Agrarian Reform and by setting up local committees of government officials and peasants. The futility of these measures may be inferred from an announcement of July 30 made by a high government official: "Everywhere fields are being seized . . . property is being stolen . . . forests are being chopped down. . . . Private owners are leaving their fields unsown. . . ."

LABOR AND MANAGEMENT

The industrial proletariat, by 1917, constituted less than 2 per cent of the total population, and most of these were concentrated in the few industrial centers of European Russia. However, they made up for shortage of numbers by their militancy, an attitude drummed into them by decades of Marxist and trade union agitation, in and around their places of work, and their experiences with strikes and mass demonstrations usually accompanied by bloodshed. If the peasant, at the outset of the revolution, was not certain who the enemy was and how to attack him, the workers had no trouble identifying their archfoes. Therefore, the thought that the factories belonged to the toilers was quickly voiced and soon acted upon.

POLITICAL DEVELOPMENTS

When the smoke had cleared, following the March days and the Tsar's abdication, the political configuration in Petrograd was about as follows: (1) All extreme conservative groups were entirely unrepresented in the two bodies—Provisional Government and Soviet—claiming authority. (2) There appeared to be a clear demarcation between the Kadet-dominated Provisional Government, remnant of the unrepresentative Duma, and the Socialists of the Soviet. The Soviet was unquestionably representative of the masses of the capital and, in terms of what it stood for, of most of the people of Russia. The Bolsheviks, with Lenin still abroad, were a minor faction in the Soviet and were not clearly opposed to the ideas set forth by the Socialist Revolutionaries and Mensheviks in the Soviet Executive Committee.

As the course of developments would soon reveal, the views of the Socialist Revolutionary and Menshevik leaders of the Soviet were much closer to those of the members of the Provisional Government than they were to the desires of those whom they supposedly represented. The radical tone of their speeches notwithstanding, they, like the Kadets, opposed making an end to the war and refused, short of sanction by an elected Constituent Assembly, to accede to demands for immediate land reform or to acknowledge the right to independence or autonomy for most of the national minority peoples.[5]

Lenin appeared upon the scene like a *deus ex machina* and quickly whipped the Bolshevik party into line behind a program calling for immediate peace, land reform, the right of Russia's subject nations to self-determination, and the institution of a government based on the soviets. His slogans stimulated mass pressure in Petrograd for replacing the Provisional Government with Soviet power and for bringing to an end the "imperialist war."

The May demonstrations, rising out of Milyukov's May 1 note to the Allied Governments, forced the Foreign Minister as well as Minister of War, Guchkov, out of the Provisional Government and moved the most prominent Socialist Revolutionary and Menshevik leaders to join with bourgeois elements in a coalition Provisional Government. The entry of these socialists into an unrepresentative government created the impression that they were willing to postpone the fulfillment of the popular desires for peace, for immediate agrarian reforms, and for greater freedom for the national minority peoples. The moderate socialists became increasingly insulated from the people at large, who now began to look ever more to the Bolsheviks for guidance. The July offensive, coupled with the resignation of the Kadets from the Provisional Government over the issue of Ukrainian autonomy, set in motion the vast demonstrations of July 16-18—the so-called July Days. The moderate socialist leaders, whether as members of the Provisional Government or of the Soviet, had clearly lost the confidence of the Petrograd masses.

The Provisional Government survived the July Days only because Lenin himself had underestimated the urgency of the popular movement and was not yet ready to risk taking power by means of the overwhelming forces placed so amply at his disposal.[6] For the moment, Bolshevik influence dwindled.

The Third Provisional Government was formed in August with Socialist Revolutionary Kerensky, now Prime Minister as well as Minister of War. However, the government continued to resist the popular demands. Bolshevik influence soon began to reassert itself in the capital and further permeate the rest of the country. Soldiers deserted in avalanches, and as conditions in industry and in the countryside became more and more chaotic, Kerensky and his cohorts began to move beyond mere coalition with liberal democrats and turned to conservative elements for help. At the same time, a left-wing faction broke away from the Socialist-Revolutionary Party.

General Kornilov, who hoped to re-establish discipline at the front and crush the "Soviet and Bolshevik traitors" in the rear, had been appointed Commander in Chief of the army by Kerensky at the end of July. In the ensuing weeks, that patriotic

---

[5] All parties agreed that Poland should become free, but Poland was then completely under domination of the Central Powers so that this was not too meaningful a concession.

[6] See S. W. Page, *Lenin and World Revolution,* New York, New York University Press, 1959, Chap. III.

general had become the dreamed-of "man on horseback" to landowners, capitalists, military men—all those who had been politically, if not materially, dispossessed by the revolution. Kornilov plotted to establish martial law in Petrograd by means of Cossack and Caucasian troops under his command, aided by a group of right-wing conspirators in Petrograd that was composed mainly of army officers.

A State Conference, convoked in Moscow late in August, was intended to display the unity of all factions, right and left, behind the government. At the conference, Kornilov was cheered to echo by the right, and denounced by the moderate left. Kerensky, though given an ovation by the left, vainly requested the soldiers' deputies present to show their respect for Russia's "first soldier." The Bolsheviks were conspicuous by their absence and by the one-day general strike they had called in Moscow to protest the meeting.

Kerensky was trying to maintain the forms of a government functioning under normal legal procedures in a State lacking both armed power and popular approval. Inevitably he took recourse to ill-considered measures of desperation. Fearing a *coup d'état* by the Bolsheviks, who in September attained majority representations in the Petrograd and Moscow soviets, Kerensky encouraged Kornilov to believe that he favored Kornilov's idea of setting up a military dictatorship. Then, apparently fearing that he himself might be deposed and all that the revolution stood for be wiped out, Kerensky abruptly dismissed Kornilov as Commander in Chief. In this act he had the approval of the majority of his cabinet, but the Kadet ministers resigned in protest. Despite his dismissal, Kornilov sent his troops against the capital. But his attempt at a *coup d'état* was thwarted largely by the railway workers who, upon instructions from the Soviet, blocked the passage of the troops some forty miles from Petrograd by sabotaging transport and communications. Kornilov's stymied forces were then met by propagandists who easily dissuaded them from marching against their class brethren. Petrograd itself had been fortified and barricaded and generally prepared for battle against the counterrevolution by the Soviet. Moderate socialists and Bolsheviks, including their leaders released from prison, had joined forces in organizing the defending military forces and a workers' Red Guard. Most of the officers involved in the Kornilov plot were quickly arrested.

Kerensky's government had survived once more but only at the cost of strengthening the Bolsheviks and hopelessly antagonizing the factions of the right. Still seeking some footing on the fast dwindling middle ground of moderation, Kerensky, in the last days of September, convoked a Democratic Conference of representatives of soviets, zemtvos, trade unions, and other groups but excluded the property-owning classes. The purpose was to consult with these delegates about the formation of a new government. Should the new coalition contain ministers from the Kadet party which had been in sympathy with Kornilov? The Conference was against it, but Kerensky thought otherwise and appointed Kadets to the cabinet. That action, along with the careless supervision that permitted Kornilov and his henchmen to escape from detention in the Ukraine and flee to the south of Russia, further exposed Kerensky as trying to play both sides of the fence.

Out of the Democratic Conference grew the so-called Council of the Republic, or pre-parliament, which sat from October 20 on. It was supposed to represent organized opinion and to guide the government for six weeks and then be replaced by the Constituent Assembly. But the Council was made impotent by class strife, and, in any case, it had little contact with the people or influence over the course of events either in Petrograd or anywhere else in the country. By October, Lenin was persistently demanding that his party use its preponderant strength in the capital to take power in the name of the Soviets before the Germans should capture the city and make an end to the revolution.

On the night of November 7, having won an almost bloodless victory, the Bolsheviks presented the Second All-Russian Congress of Soviets with governmental power. The Mensheviks and the right-wing Socialist Revolutionaries would have nothing to do with that illegal act and walked out of the session. The first Soviet Government was made up of a coalition of People's Commissars (Ministers) drawn principally from the Bolshevik party, but it also included some left-wing Socialist Revolutionaries.

CONSOLIDATION OF AUTHORITY

The easy November victory of the Bolsheviks in Petrograd by no means signified that they had the country behind them. Only one-fourth of the population voted for Bolsheviks in the November 25-27 elections of delegates to the Constituent Assembly. Most of those votes came from the urban proletariat, as well as from soldier-peasants just home from the front and their wives and neighbors whom they influenced. Still, if the majority did not support the party that controlled the Soviet power (more than half of the votes went to the right-wing Socialist Revolutionaries), it was not actively opposed to it either. The peasants on the whole were indifferent to what the politicians in Petrograd were doing as long as the latter did not prevent them from partitioning the land among themselves. Besides acknowledging the new order in the villages, Lenin's government was quick to enter upon peace negotiations with the Central Powers—a popular move—and to issue assurances regarding national self-determination which the national minority peoples mistakenly took to mean that they could look forward to political autonomy if not outright independence.

The discontented were for the moment relatively few in number and were made up of members of the dispossessed classes. Some army officers remained neutral while others, in the south of Russia, began by the end of 1917 to organize military forces for struggle against the illegal government. Against the threat of counterrevolution and to provide against the danger of further German penetration into Russia, the

Soviet regime proceeded to raise a new army. At first it was on a volunteer basis; later, as the counterrevolutionary movement grew in strength, it was by conscription. Mensheviks and Right Socialist Revolutionaries remained active in their opposition to the Bolshevik-Left Socialist Revolutionary coalition government.[7] Within the soviets and through their now illegal newspapers the moderate socialists directed a steady fire of criticism as they looked forward to the convention of the Constituent Assembly in January, 1918, in the hopes of establishing their legitimate claims to political power through that democratically elected body. They did not anticipate that Lenin would allow it but a token existence—one day of life. Until the spring of 1918, then, the Bolsheviks had a fairly free hand and, except for vigorous persecution of nobles and bourgeoisie (the clergy was not yet subjected to heavy attack), life for the vast majority of the people was generally free from governmental repression.

The "honeymoon" of Soviet power came to an end soon after the signing of the Peace of Brest-Litovsk in March, 1918. The treaty, which seemed to have exposed the entire former Russian Empire to German conquest, had numerous direct consequences that gravely endangered the survival of the Bolshevik regime. The Germans, already lords over Poland, Lithuania, Latvia, and Estonia, were now enabled to extend their military domain over the Ukraine and were obviously not content to stop there. In the Don-Kuban region a volunteer army, dedicated to the task of overthrowing the "traitorous" Bolsheviks, had come into being. In Siberia, the Czechoslovak Legion, fearful of the German advance and hastening to get out of Russia by means of the Trans-Siberian railway, turned on the Bolshevik contingents who tried to disarm them and seized control of the railway towns all the way to Central Siberia. That led to the establishment by Socialist Revolutionaries of a number of regional governments in Siberia which were later coordinated under a Directorate at Omsk. At the same time, intervention of the Allied Powers, partly as an extension of their war effort against eastward expanding Germany, was taking place in the coastal areas of Russia—in the North, the South, and the Far East—and began giving support to the anti-Bolshevik forces. On November 18, Admiral Kolchak, aided by the British, seized power in Omsk and was designated as the head of the White movement.

Within months the Bolshevik-held sector of the former empire had shrunk to an area roughly equivalent to the sixteenth-century domain of Ivan the Terrible and suffered, in addition, from critical shortages of food, chaotic conditions in the factories, and an almost total breakdown of transportation. "There were moments," as

[7] It was not until June, 1918, that the moderate socialist parties were excluded from participating in the All-Russian Central Executive Committee of the Soviet regime. In September, 1920, however, Mensheviks and S.R.'s were still permitted to sit in the Sixth Congress of Soviets. Soon thereafter most of the Menshevik and S.R. leaders were expelled from the country.

Trotsky later wrote, describing the situation in the spring of 1918, "when one had the feeling that everything was . . . crumbling, that there was nothing to hold on to." In the meantime, the Left Socialist Revolutionaries, infuriated by the Brest-Litovsk Treaty and above all by the sufferings of their peasant supporters, broke with their allies in the Soviet government and tried, in July, 1918, to oust the Bolsheviks by means of armed risings. When these failed, they resorted to assassinations. On August 31, Lenin himself was severely wounded by two shots fired at him point blank as he was leaving a factory meeting.

In view of such conditions, the Bolsheviks turned from the relatively permissive attitudes of their first eight months of power to the devices of unrestricted terror directed against all who would attempt to foment opposition. The principal instrument of the terror was the all-powerful Cheka[8]—the sword of the revolution. Felix Dzerzhinsky was the founder of this organization, which since that time, although under new titles (GPU, OGPU, NKVD, MVD-MGB), has served as the long arm of Soviet law and order. In June, 1918, Dzerzhinsky described the Cheka as "the defence of the revolution" on a par with the Red army. "And just as in the civil war the Red Army cannot stop to ask whether or not it may harm individuals, but is obliged to act only with the thought of securing the victory of the revolution over the bourgeoisie, so the Cheka too is obliged to . . . conquer the enemy even if its sword . . . sometimes falls upon the heads of the innocent." Given such a license to brutality, it is easy to imagine the types of men who became Chekists. Interrogation and wholesale murder of "bourgeoisie" went on night after night at Lubyanka, the notorious Cheka prison.[9]

In the spring and summer of 1918, Lenin, in whatever limited ways were open to him, had introduced elements of communism into Russian society. Given the then shattered condition of Russia's economy, such experiments evinced Lenin's desire to prove that his regime was actually a Communist one. He was presumably trying to impress the proletariat of Europe over which he soon hoped to acquire revolutionary leadership. So, Committees of Poor Peasants were established in the villages for the purposes of inciting the poor against the rich, or kulaks, and in order to requisition farm produce for the hungry cities. A few hundred agricultural communes and Soviet farms, or *Sovkhozi,* were set up, foreshadowing the later all-out collectivization. Factories were nationalized and placed under the direction of workers' councils. These provisions, adding up to what is known as War Communism, actually cut the total food and industrial production. However, since the war required the highest degree of centralization, the discipline imposed and the idealistic enthusiasm inspired by War Communism probably saved the Soviet regime. In fact, the socialistic meas-

[8] "Che" "Ka" are the Russian initials for the words Extraordinary Committee.
[9] See G. Solomon, *Sredi Krasnykh Vozhdei,* Paris, Michen, 1930, pp. 274-275, 282-284.

ures were soon moderated to conform with day-to-day expediency. Lenin was compelled to prompt the party fanatics to permit all but the richest propertied peasants to be left to farm their lands in peace, and the useless factory councils were replaced by former plant managers, or "specialists." These moves ran parallel to the recruitment of Tsarist officers to serve in the Red army, but under careful surveillance by political commissars.

Anything like real communism was much too drastic a change to be effected at a time when the very existence of Bolshevik power was so gravely threatened by the White armies pressing toward Moscow from the South and the East and on Petrograd from Estonia, while interventionist forces were aiding the Whites and landing troops on Russian soil. The social revolution had to be postponed. But by 1920 the Bolsheviks, having crushed their political and military opponents, were firmly in the saddle.

Chaos in the Capital—March, 1917 *

During the last days disorders have taken place in Petrograd, followed by . . . assaults on the lives of soldiers and . . . police.

I forbid every kind of assembly in the streets.

I warn the population of Petrograd that commands have been issued . . . to the troops to use their arms . . . to assure tranquillity in the capital.

HABALOV
Lieutenant-General
Commanding the Forces in
March 10, 1917   the Petrograd Military Area

The above proclamation was posted in the streets of Petrograd on the morning of March 11th. Its effects were quickly seen. Before evening there was some [four] hundred dead. . . . On the following morning a proclamation was posted from General Habalov that if all the workmen did not resume work by the morning of March 13th they would be arrested and sent into the

* SOURCE: J. Pollock, "The Russian Revolution, A Review by an Onlooker," The Nineteenth Century and After, New York, May, 1917, pp. 1068-1082. Used with the permission of The Twentieth Century, London.

ranks. . . . In less than twenty-four hours . . . Habalov was a prisoner and almost the whole of Petrograd in the hands of the populace and revolutionary soldiery.

In the midst of the most gigantic war one of the most momentous of known revolutions has been accomplished in . . . exactly seven days. . . . The first appeals made preserved the Emperor's authority, and the people showed no wish to change it; but events moved rapidly beyond this point. The immediate causes of the revolution are the reaction that has only gained in severity since the assassination of Rasputin, provocation by agents in the service of the Home Minister [Protopopov] . . . , and shortage of bread. It is the last that, acting on the exasperation produced by the two former, has brought about the explosion. . . .

The first bread riot in Petrograd took place on the 8th of March. . . . The rioting was so far confined to the Viborg side, the chief workmen's quarter of Petrograd. . . . On the 9th the rioters stopped the trams across the river. . . . Visits were paid to all the factories and the hands called out in a sympathetic strike against the sudden food shortage. . . . A prefect of police . . . who threatened the crowd was killed. Strong Cossack squadrons patrolled Petrograd. . . . [They] used their whips, but . . . told the crowd they would not shoot so long as they only asked for bread. Alarmed at the attitude of the Cossacks, the authorities on the 10th brought troops of the line into the streets to support the police. . . . [Protopopov] had the roofs at every important street corner garrisoned by police with machine-guns. . . . To Protopopov's disposition of the machine-guns the success of the revolution is due. . . . Placed in dormer windows and behind parapets, [they] were extremely difficult to train on their objective, and the police forces scattered throughout the city in innumerable small detachments were not in a position to support one another.

On the same day the first serious bloodshed took place, the police opening fire on a peaceful crowd opposite the Nicolas Station. . . . Sunday, March 11th, began nervously. There were soldiers everywhere in the streets. . . . By now the trams had all stopped. . . . No newspapers appeared. About 3.30 P.M. the troops began to clear the streets round the Nevsky at the bayonet point, and soon afterwards the police turned their machine-guns on to a crowd at the same place as the day before, but with more deadly effect. . . . The crowd . . . retaliated with pistol shots. . . . It was significant that soldiers were seen among the crowd firing on the police. . . . In the morning of Monday, March 12th, a detachment of gendarmes arrived to arrest the refractory soldiers. On this the battalion rose, overpowered the gendarmes, killed . . . some . . . officers, and at 8 A.M. left their barracks and rushed through the streets cheering. They were quickly joined by [other troop units]. First they marched to the artillery dépôt close by, then to the arsenal across the river, both of which they seized, burning the Courts of Justice on the way. The general in command of the . . . dépôt and several other persons were killed. . . .

When, soon after fighting began, it became apparent that no troops in Petrograd could be relied on by the Government, in the early afternoon the police began to fire on the soldiers, and among the troops adhesion to the revolutionary ranks became general. In order to avoid recognition many officers in the revolted regiments dressed like privates. There were by now no police on the streets, and crowds from across the river profited by the revolutionary troops' having overpowered the bridge guards to come into the centre and help to spread the spirit of revolution. Among their first objectives were the prisons where political prisoners were kept. These were released, but with them ordinary criminals also, . . . and some of the prisons were burnt. . . . Next . . . the police stations . . . were sacked [and set a-fire along with the main police archives]. . . . By night the revolutionaries were in possession of the whole city, except the Winter Palace, the Admiralty, and the telegraph and telephone stations. . . .

The guard regiments in Petrograd going over to the revolutionaries . . . now numbered between thirty- and forty-thousand. . . . Many [had] given their rifles away to the crowd. . . . When the immense excitement is considered, and the fact that, after years of reaction . . . all authority was suddenly removed from the troops and populace alike, it [was amazing how] little disorder occurred. There was no general looting, well-dressed ladies who ventured out or dodged the fighting to get to their homes were not molested, and though officers were stopped and [disarmed], they were not for the most part ill-used.

As early as Saturday, March 10th, Rodzianko, the President of the Duma, had sent a telegram to the Emperor begging him to take measures to avert disaster and to allay feeling. On the 11th he telegraphed again that the Government was paralysed, . . . that all public services were disorganised, and urged him to entrust the formation of a new government to someone enjoying the confidence of the country. On the morning of the 12th he telegraphed: "Position growing worse. Imperative take immediate measures. . . ." To these telegrams only one answer was received. On the morning of the 12th a decree was forwarded to Rodzianko from Prince Golitzin, the Premier, dated two days before from General Headquarters, and proroguing the Duma "to a date not later than April, 1917, dependent on extraordinary circumstances." It was clear that Nicolas . . . and his advisers were bent on crushing the popular will, and believed that this could be done. Faced by a desperate position, Rodzianko rose to the greatness of his task. . . . He assumed a responsibility which, had the revolution failed, would . . . have cost him his head, and disregarding the prorogation summoned a meeting of the Duma. The members of all parties but the Right met at half past two o'clock and and proceeded to elect a Temporary or Executive Committee for the establishment of order in Petrograd, which assumed and during the next three days kept control of the government. Rodzianko had already telegraphed to the generals commanding the various fronts, and had received answers from General Brusilov, on the south-western, and from General Russky, on the northern front, that were at least not hostile. . . . At one o'clock in the afternoon Prince Golitzin informed Rodzianko by telephone that he had resigned office, and was followed by almost all the other members of the Cabinet except Protopopov, who had vanished. The revolutionaries searched and pillaged the houses of ministers, the last-named only escaping a few minutes before their arrival. Before evening the president of the Council of the Empire, and former Minister of Justice, a man notorious for having debased justice . . . , was arrested, and the beginnings of a national government already existed in Russia.

Throughout . . . March 13th fighting in Petrograd was . . . heavy. The telephone was early captured and communication cut for the rest of the day. Every street corner became a [death] trap [of police-firing from] the upper part of the houses and [counter-firing by] soldiers and civilians [from] doorways below. Soldiers in motor-lorries or armoured cars dashed to points where the fighting was fiercest. . . . This gradually died out as the effect of an order from the Duma Committee that the owner and head-porter of any house from which firing took place would be held responsible.

These head-porters . . . were responsible to the police for the identity of every inmate in their houses, and one of their chief businesses was in fact spying for the police. . . . The latter could not now have mounted guns upon the roofs without their knowledge, and the prompt result of the proclamation proved its wisdom. . . . When in the course of the 13th and the morning of the 14th it became known that the troops at Tsarskoe Selo, Pavlovsk, Oranienbaum and Cronstadt had joined the people, and later that the garrison of Moscow too had thrown in its lot with the revolution, feeling had become quieter. The autocracy was left without serious defence, except in the unlikely event of the soldiers at the front declaring in its favour. Desultory but heavy outbursts of firing continued in Petrograd till Thursday night, March 15th, when a detachment of 500 provincial police suddenly arrived, overpowered the station guard, and marched through the city until dispersed by armoured motors. So recently as March 20th one or possibly more motor-cars ornamented with black flags have been dashing along the streets loosing off occasional belts of machine-gun cartridges at the passers. . . . But such piratical efforts are futile. Since March 14th the red flag flies everywhere in the capital.

[Estimates of the number of dead range from 2,000 to 10,000.] Many officers were murdered by their men in the Baltic fleet as well as in the army. Many policemen . . . were made prisoners and taken to the Duma; but very many more were shot on the spot and their bodies flung into the canals. In the provinces the revolution was of a paper character, being mostly executed in the telegraph offices. Normal life was scarcely interrupted for more than one day in Moscow, and even less in other cities. It is none the less believed that not a few policemen and officers were disposed of in various parts, victims it may be in many cases of private revenge.

Warned by the fate of others, ministers and lesser servants of the old regime hastened to give themselves up to the Duma or were hunted out of hiding. . . . The majority of the officers in Petrograd were quick to realise that the old order had passed away, and among the many processions of soldiers and employees who marched to the Duma to signify their adherence, none was more pleasing than that of a great number of officers, . . . generals among them, who on the 14th, after a meeting at the Army and Navy Club, went to the place themselves at the orders of the Duma Committee. . . . On the [same day] the Duma Committee appointed Commissioners to take charge of the various ministries and other public offices, and telegraphed the news to all the towns of Russia that it had temporarily undertaken the direction of affairs, and a municipal militia was established in the capital with its head office at the Town Hall.

Within a few hours of the appointment of the Executive Committee of the Duma, a Council [Soviet] of Workmen's Deputies was organised also at the Duma, composed of labour representatives, some soldiers, and a few stray sympathetic politicians. They divided the city into districts, to each of which a Commissioner was appointed, and representatives were invited to be sent from the factories and from every company. The object of the Commissioners was "the establishment of the popular power in the districts of Petrograd." "We call upon the population of the capital," their proclamation ran, "to gather round the [Soviet], to organise local district committees, and to take into their hands the direction of all local affairs." By the 14th of March the [Soviet] was consolidated and enlarged into the [Soviet] of Workmen's and Soldiers' Deputies, and was making a bold bid to get the power over the army into its hands. Order No. 1 posted throughout Petrograd on the 15th of March ordained that in all their political concerns the military were subject to the [Soviet], that committees were to be elected by every battalion or company to supervise the internal administration of the regiments, that all arms were to be under control of the committees and in no circumstances to be returned to officers as the Duma Committee had authorised, and that the orders of the Military Commission set up by the latter were only to be

obeyed when they did not contradict the orders and resolutions of the [Soviet]. On the 13th discipline was non-existent. Many of the soldiers had given up their arms to the crowd and were drifting listlessly about the streets watching the progress of the fight and in difficulties for food. On the 14th, though the food difficulty had increased, their behaviour was better; they paraded in companies, though still many without arms, and preserved some outward orderliness. The adherence too of the officers on this day had its effect, and soldiers even began to salute again. But with the publication of the [Soviet's] Order an immediate deterioration became noticeable. The semblance of order preserved the day before vanished and was replaced by a sullen and occasionally a threatening attitude. There were no longer signs of respect for the officers, and the men went about asking for food and collecting money to support soldiers' tea-houses that had taken the place of many cafes. Small squads went round searching private apartments for arms, without, or refusing to show, the authority they should have had from the Duma: a fact greatly to the advantage of criminals, who dressed themselves up as soldiers and carried off valuables from citizens who dared not resist. It was known that a strong party for the immediate conclusion of peace existed among the workmen, and the gloomiest anticipations, freely entertained, were intensified by reports of the enemy having broken the Russian lines near Dvinsk. . . .

From the very first day of the revolution, a news sheet was issued with the imprint of the "Committee of Petrograd Journalists" and distributed gratis in the streets. This had to compete with the fuller sheet of the [Soviet], which though sold at five kopeks enjoyed greater facilities for distribution, and it was not until Sunday the 18th that the publishers could arrange with the compositors to allow the regular papers to come out. The [Soviet] further forbade cabs . . . to ply for hire after 7 P.M.; but they have had difficulty in enforcing this rule. Over the tramways, however, the [Soviet] had complete control. . . . The theatres too are sought to be brought under the workmen's heel: the [Soviet] . . . refused leave to any to open until the burial of certain victims of the fight in the cause of freedom. . . .

By dint of much tact . . . on the part of the Duma Committee and of the new government announced by it on March 15 with Prince Lvov, the President of the Union of Zemstvos, as prime minister, an open breach with the [Soviet] has hitherto been avoided. Frequent reports indeed are spread of the harmony reigning between the two bodies. But the mischief done in the first two days by the [Soviet] has spread very wide, and may prove irreparable. While many of the troops have returned to their duty, and fair discipline is kept, . . . the peace party among the Socialists have not relaxed their efforts, and have succeeded in affecting some at least of the soldiers at the front. . . . On March 23 the papers contained . . . appeals to the army and the nation from A. I. Guchkov, the new Minister of War, and from the whole cabinet. . . . [They call] upon citizens to do their duty at the front and at the rear. . . . They inform the nation that . . . should the Germans be victorious their victory will be gained not only over the Russian State but over the newly won freedom of the Russian nation. They . . . beg the soldiers to trust and follow

their officers, who shared danger and hunger, and freely laid down their lives with their brothers. . . . Nevertheless . . . rumours circulate that soldiers are leaving the Front and that the officers are helpless to control them. The extreme Socialists [Bolsheviks] make no secret of their desire. Their programme is "Down with the war at any cost . . .". In the third number of *Truth* (*Pravda*), the Moscow organ of this party, it is declared: "We hate every kind of despotism. We hate the despotism of William and . . . of Lloyd George . . . just as we hate the despotism of the Romanovs." . . . The fifth number (March 22) . . . calls upon the soldiers in the trenches to raise the red flag, sing the International, . . . and fraternise . . . with the [enemy]. . . .

Meanwhile, [Nicholas II having abdicated], the government, appointed by the Executive Committee of the Duma, remains both in fact and in name temporary. On March 19 it announced that in due time a Convention would be summoned to decide the future constitution of the Russian State. In view of the large number of men at the Front, it is hard to see, even in the best case, how this can be before the end of the war.

The Soviet of Soldiers' and Workers' Deputies*

Neither the Bolsheviks, nor the Mensheviks, nor the Workers' Group, nor the Social Revolutionaries . . . led the workers of Petrograd on to the street. It was someone mightier than they: Tsar Hunger.

It began with ordinary food riots. The bakeshops lacked sufficient bread. Long queues, at first chiefly of women and boys, took out their resentment on the bakers, suspecting them of hoarding flour for purposes of speculation. . . . There were disorders, there was still no revolution. There

*SOURCE: V. Chernov, *The Great Russian Revolution*, New Haven, Yale University Press, 1936, pp. 101-109.

was no leader, but every revolutionary and democratic group, organized or unorganized, rushed headlong into the movement, trying to attract as many people as possible and to inspire it with definite and militant political slogans. . . . During these days, several attempts were made to create interparty centers to make up for the weakness of the several illegal party organizations. Personal conferences were held by leaders of the trade-union movement, of the cooperative, cultural, and educational organizations with deputies of the extreme Left of the Duma and prominent representatives of the revolutionary parties.

At these conferences an old Social Democrat, Cherevanin, first suggested that the Soviet of Workers' Deputies must be organized at once. The idea was already in the air. . . . There had been reports of elections to the Soviet in some factories. As soon as the idea of reestablishing the Soviet was presented and welcomed by the leading groups of the intelligentsia, regardless of party, the movement at once became universal. However, deputies chosen at individual factories still had no common rallying point and did not even know where to assemble. Indeed, there had been no time to deal with that question. Street agitation, meetings, attempts to arrange fraternizing with the troops drew people into a whirlpool of activity and left no time for anything else. It was only [on March 12], when certain military units began to pass to the side of the people, . . . that a crucial event occurred. The recently arrested members of the Workers' Group and many other political prisoners had been freed from prison by the people. Headed by a worker, Kuzma Gvozdev, they appeared at the Tauride Palace. With the socialist deputies in the Duma and other influential members of the labor movement, they formed a provisional Executive Committee of the Soviet of Workers' Deputies, a kind of organizing bureau, which at once informed the wards that on that same evening all the deputies were to assemble for the first meeting of the Petrograd Soviet.

Soviet democracy had set up its organization. . . .

. . . The duties of the Soviets were not clearly defined. They were simply rallying points of revolutionary energy. . . . The Soviets were improvised organizations due to the absence of stable, well-established, and distinct *parties*. In Russia, true enough, there was no lack of parties. Rather, they were overabundant. But they included only the small world of professional revolutionaries and the "cream" of the working class. For the toilers as a whole they scarcely seemed to exist, or belonged to the sphere of legend. Nor did Russia possess those broad trade-union organizations without which the working class is only "human dust." Hence the Soviets arose as a temporary substitute for the trade-union and political organizations of the working class.

. . . Their only task was to spread the "sacred spirit of revolution" throughout Russia, . . . to . . . destroy in embryo all [Rightist] attempts to rebel against the revolution, and finally to see to it that the Provisional Government which had issued from the revolution served the revolution in program and personnel. That was all. The Soviets never had a very definite constitution; elections to them were always rather chaotic and unorganized. . . . The Soviet least resembled . . . a regular government institution.

All this, in a transitional period, by no means prevented the Soviet from being the only active law-creating force. Let us not forget that the Provisional Committee of a private conference of members of the Imperial Duma in these very days defined its mission as that of *negotiator* between the people and the old government, and was trying, through agreement with the latter and by broad concessions exacted from it, to save what it could of the old order. . . . Soviet democracy was poorly informed of these backstage agreements. . . .

What *was* Soviet democracy doing? It was not seizing power, nor declaring itself the government. It was acting as an immediate, revolutionary, law-creating force. . . . The Provisional Executive Committee of the Soviet of Workers' Deputies, . . . a self-created organizing bureau, was already functioning as a government in . . . many matters, simply because there was no one else to decide them. First, it organized a provisional military staff from a large number of Leftist officers. . . . It organized a provisional food commission. . . . The military staff attempted to introduce some order and leadership into the torrential movement of the soldiers, sailors, and armed workers. . . . It [sent flying squads of armed men] . . . throughout the city, to seize . . . strategic points, railway stations, police stations, secret police headquarters, telegraph, telephone, various barracks, to arrest [officials] of the old government, and clear garrets of police [and] machine guns, disarm patrolmen, etc. The food commission undertook [to fix] prices for . . . over-dear articles like butter. . . . It . . . took [immediate] measures to secure . . . provisions for the military forces which had joined the revolution. . . . A hungry sea of soldiers without officers and provisions meant danger of looting and anarchy. At the first session of the Soviet one other measure was taken: Petrograd was divided into wards and . . . Soviet commissars were dispatched to them to supervise the election of "ward committees" as the local organs of popular government, and to form an armed working-class militia, made up of one hundred men per thousand of factory personnel. Finally, the Soviet reorganized radically. Having begun as the Soviet of Workers' Deputies, it immediately become such a powerful center of attraction for the military units that it could not hold to its previous form. At the first session the Soviet welcomed [many] delegations from all sorts of military units. They proclaimed their complete solidarity with the working class. . . . The Soviet [was] joined by the entire Semenov Regiment, [famous for crushing] the Moscow insurrection of 1905. . . . It was now determined to transform the Soviet of Workers' Deputies into the Soviet of Workers' and Soldiers' Deputies . . . , each battalion to send one delegate.

Within a few days the Soviet was turned into a gigantic workers' and soldiers' preliminary parliament. [It soon had 3,000 members.] Each decision was instantaneously reported to barracks and working class quarters by a thousand channels. This was an [irresistible] force. . . .

Small wonder if Rodzianko could not secure a train to go to the Tsar without the Soviet's permission. . . .

. . . Only the Soviet could stop the general strike, and reopen the factories. It alone could restore street-car traffic. Controlling the entire printers' union, it alone could permit the appearance of newspapers, of all or some. The Provisional Government had to appeal to the leaders of the Soviet as soon as it was organized and wished to publish its first declaration. When the military units of Petrograd became a component part of organized Soviet democracy, the Soviet was transformed into the only real source of power. At its first session the Soviet resolved that measures be taken immediately to remove all public financial resources from the control of the old government. By virtue of this *Soviet* decision revolutionary sentries occupied and guarded the State Bank, Central and Provincial Treasuries, Mint, Engraving Office, etc.

. . . On March [16], a conference of representatives of the Petrograd banks requested the Soviet "to permit the banks to be opened immediately." . . . Grand Duke Michael requested the Soviet to grant him a special train from Gatchina to Petrograd. He was told that "because of the high cost of coal, citizen Romanov may buy a ticket and travel in an ordinary train [like] other citizens." From morning to night the Soviet was besieged by "a mob of outsiders, of people with [problems], . . . all kinds of businessmen, . . . weeping women." The Executive Committee . . . was appealed to in all kinds of matters, including divorces and legal disputes. . . .

. . . Sukhanov[1] says that "the Soviet apparatus of administration began involuntarily, automatically, against the Soviet's own will, to displace the official governmental machine, which had less and less to do. . . . We had to . . . take over various functions of administration, while . . . maintaining the fiction that the government was being run from the Marinsky Palace."

---

[1] A socialist participant in the events, later famous for his seven-volumed *Notes on the Revolution*.

Breakdown of Military Discipline*

. . . By evening [there were many] rumours [about] our . . . battalion: it had refused to join the revolution . . . ; it had been among the first units to join . . . ; the soldiers had killed . . . the officers; all the officers were safe, and so on.

I decided that . . . my duty was to present myself to the [battalion] commander . . . and [discover the truth]. . . . [Next morning] I took a taxi to the barracks. . . . At the gates [sat] a soldier . . . , rifle across his knees, [smoking] a cigarette. He wore no belt. For over a century there had not been an instant, day or night, that [the] sentry had not stood . . . trim, [and] erect. . . . As you passed he would salute with mechanical precision. [This] slovenly [seated] fellow . . . [symbolized] the disappearance of an . . . era. He paid not the slightest attention to me. . . .

Bronevsky . . . [was] surprised [to see] me. He was pale. . . . "Come to my room and let's talk. Only, be careful," he whispered. "We are prisoners here and watched continually." He let me in, looking cautiously . . . out of the window. A soldier was standing not far away. "See that fellow there? He's . . . watching me through the window. It's better than the first days, though. . . . A man [stayed] in our room the whole time to hear what we were saying. . . ."

[Briefly he told me the story.] The battalion had joined the revolution. . . . The Commander . . . was wounded . . . by a shot. . . . Another officer, Captain Romanov, was arrested by the men . . . because his name was [accidentally] that of the reigning dynasty. . . . A few officers [went] into hiding . . . and some left immediately for the front to rejoin the regiment there. He himself happened to be on leave from the front and had arrived the

night before. . . . He found one young officer alone, Lieutenant Miassoiedov, in charge of the battalion. The men had immediately elected Bronevsky as their new commander; his appointment was endorsed by telegram from the front, and thus he stayed. His election did not surprise me, as he was a great favourite with the soldiers because of his kindness. . . .

"And now you have come," he concluded, "the question is what they are going to do with you. There is a committee of soldiers which controls everything here, and we are only constitutional sovereigns who reign but do not rule."

"What can they do to me?" I asked. "And besides, I don't think they know I'm here. The sentry did not see me."

"Don't you worry. He has . . . already reported you to the committee. He may have let you in, but he will not let you out. You are a prisoner here until your fate is decided, and that will depend upon your popularity. They will do one of three things: . . . murder you, arrest you . . . , or elect you one of their officers."

. . . Lieutenant Miassoiedov came in and [told me] that the committee was already debating my fate. The suspense lasted three days and at last, on March [24], Bronevsky announced that I had been elected. . . . A sergeant who had served under [me had] told the committee about the time . . . in 1916 when, . . . against the orders of the commander of the regiment, I had given my men permission to go on leave. Presently two members of the committee came to see me . . . and asked me . . . if I would do them the honour of remaining with the battalion. That . . . evening we learned that five officers of the Moscow Regiment who had been elected by their soldiers the day before had been murdered by them during the night.

Our functions were now divided: Bronevsky, as commander, had the general super-

* SOURCE: A. Lobanov-Rostovsky, *The Grinding Mill,* New York, Macmillan, 1935, pp. 205-210.

vision of affairs and the task of keeping in touch with and receiving instructions from the superior officers of the Petrograd garrison. Miassoiedov, who showed a talent for debating and politics, was the liaison officer with the committee, and I was . . . placed in charge of the routine administration and office work.

Thus we started our "constitutional rule" over a thousand increasingly unruly soldiers. . . . At first we had no reason to complain of our men; they were disciplined and polite and for a while . . . cooperation seemed possible. But soon disorganizing tendencies developed. . . . The trouble was that there were two . . . competing sources of authority above us. . . . The Provisional Government . . . gave us instructions through the Ministry of War or through the headquarters of the Petrograd Military District. We officers were bound to follow these instructions. On the other hand there was the self-appointed Petrograd Soviet of Workers' and Soldiers' Delegates which controlled the equally self-appointed regimental committees such as our own committee. The soldiers on their side gave their entire allegiance to the committees. The Soviet and the committees were aiming at the overthrow of the Provisional Government and therefore pursued a policy of hindering its work. . . . Let an order come from the superior military authorities, and the committees would vote against it regardless of whether it was good or bad. Thus we found ourselves between two fires.

Furthermore, we were completely paralyzed by the famous Order Number 1, which had been endorsed by the Minister of War and hence had become law for us. This document, issued by the Soviet on March [14], for the very purpose of breaking up the existing army, said in substance that a committee was to be created immediately in every existing military unit. These committees were to be responsible to the Soviet, and orders from the superior military authorities or the officers were to be obeyed by the soldiers only if they were not contradictory to the orders of the Soviet. All arms . . . were to be at disposal of the committees alone and under no circumstances delivered to the officers. . . . All conflicts between officers and soldiers were to be judged by special courts set up by these committees.

. . . With two sets of conflicting authority there was . . . complete disorganization and paralysis. How the system worked may be seen from entries in my diary:

On March [28] I note that some drunken members of the committee entered the officers' mess and smashed the billiard tables. While passing through the main entrance to the barracks I saw that the sentry had quietly put down his rifle and gone away. . . . Walking down the street I saw the Kexholm Guards Regiment passing. I stopped to salute the colours and was immediately surrounded by a crowd of soldiers who began booing . . . and calling me a counter-revolutionary. . . . The attitude of the soldiers is on the whole correct and about 50 per cent still salute the officers. . . .

On March [30] it is our turn to express support of the revolution. The battalion, always well drilled, presented a martial appearance, but the large red banners carried by the men were in curious contrast. . . . With a great blare of brass we entered the enormous hall of the Tauride Palace.[1] . . . A poorly dressed man . . . climbed up on a table and began to speak. It was Tcheidze, the Georgian Socialist leader, now President of the Soviet. . . . After extolling . . . the democratic republic, . . . he shouted . . . : "Soldiers, beware of your officers. Watch them that they should not betray your interests. Remember, you have made the revolution. You are now all-powerful. . . . Impose your will on your superiors. Beware of the bourgeois. Beware of all the middle-class leaders of the revolution—of Miliukov, of Rodzianko, of all orators who will speak after me. Don't listen to them. . . . You have obeyed your generals long enough. Now I am general of the revolution, so obey me." . . .

The immediate result of Tcheidze's speech was a noticeable let-down in discipline and an increase in hostility of our

[1] Meeting-place of the Soviet.

men towards us. The very next day the committee voted that all pictures in the mess, portraits of sovereigns and battle scenes, should be taken down and burned . . . in the courtyard. Some of these pictures had real artistic value. With great difficulty Bronevsky dissuaded the committee from this act of vandalism, and it was finally agreed that the paintings should be covered up.

Rural Storm Warnings*

. . . Victor [Chernov] had to interview numerous [discontented] peasant delegations from the provinces. . . . The Peasants' Congress had been set up to divide the land equally among the people so that in principle private estates were already abolished. In actual fact the peasants couldn't acquire the land until the Constitutional Assembly had passed a resolution.

But now the peasants were getting impatient . . . , and in some districts they had seized the land by force. Something . . . had to be done . . . quickly. With the harvest season approaching there was bound to be trouble between themselves and the big landowners.

"We can't wait any longer. If they don't give us legal rights we'll take our land by force."

One old peasant with . . . mistrustful eyes [struggled] towards us. He [bowed to] Victor. . . . [Then he] began to speak:

"We know this Provisional Government intends to help the peasants, and we're relying on you as our Minister of Agriculture. We've all read your circular about refusing further [unauthorized land] transactions and we've done as requested. But now our landlords have shown us an order from the Minister of Justice which cancels your decree. And as you both belong to the same government we don't know whose word counts most! Naturally, we're anxious to take your instructions, but our landlords will only recognise that order from the Minister of Justice. Well, what's to be done about it?" he demanded with a malicious half-triumphant look in his eyes.

"I'm afraid the final solution rests with the Council.[1] . . . They're the only people who can make this decree law," replied Victor, becoming very red and embarrassed.

It was such an awkward situation and these people were obviously right up to a point. What they didn't understand were the intricacies of Party Politics (even in a Revolution!) and the necessity of coalescing wherever possible, with the *bourgeois* and upper classes. So we tried now to persuade them to await the Council's decision.

"You needn't be afraid of their decision, because the majority[2] are your own representatives, so that it'll really be you peasants who are deciding this for yourselves. Meanwhile, local committees in each village must decide on farming prices and land dues, etc."

Victor knew how to talk to peasants. He used . . . simple phrases. . . . The delegates [listened] attentively and I think in the end he managed to convince them.

"Oh, yes, I get your meaning," said one man truculently. "You fellows defending *our* interests are in a darned tight squeeze at the moment—you're powerless. Well, you can tell the other lot that we've already claimed the land. The land's ours now, d'you hear that? If any . . . landlord tries to stop us we'll set fire to the fields!"

---

* SOURCE: Olga Tchernoff, *New Horizons,* London, Hutchinson & Co., Ltd., 1936, pp. 41-43, 67-69. Olga Tchernoff, or Chernov, was the wife of Victor Chernov.

[1] Referring to the Council of Ministers of the Provisional Government.

[2] The majority in the Provisional Government were Socialist Revolutionaries.

So they returned . . . to their villages, more or less satisfied for the time being. Although who knew for how long? And even if these delegates felt satisfied, would they be able to reassure the great mass of peasants, already exasperated by this long period of waiting? . . .

Victor mopped his forehead, he was sweating all over.

"Did you hear that . . . fellow? . . . Our Party[3] really seems to be doing everything to turn the peasants against [it]."

[3] The Socialist Revolutionary Party.

The Peasant's Wrath Unleashed*

The mighty wave of the . . . Revolution did not, at the outset, break on the shores of our life in the Borderlands. For long only . . . insignificant backwashes betrayed its vicinity and magnitude. . . .

I remember those first days of March 1917. The first "procession of freedom" marched through [our village] and was composed of some fifteen students and few scores of Jews and Jewesses. At the head, under a red flag . . . , ran the local judge, . . . a little dry old man, an eternal dreamer . . . of the Left, for years persecuted by the . . . Government. . . . The procession waded . . . through [the] mud, singing out of tune "Rise, working men!" . . . The peasants stood on the sidewalks, gazing [contemptuously] at the red symbol . . . and at the shrieking Jews. . . . As we passed them we exchanged greetings and observations. . . .

"Good won't come of it, sir! Without a Tsar, there won't be any order or sense. Who'll be head of the State?" they said, gloomily. . . .

The removal of the Tsar's portraits from the village went off peacefully. . . . For the most part the portraits were not destroyed, but carefully packed . . . away to await a new turn of events and the return of the old authorities. The names of the village and district officials were changed, the police were replaced by militia. That was all.

But Spring . . . was drawing nearer . . . , and . . . the ferment was spreading. Insidious agitators appeared. They crawled into cottages, they burrowed into the country. Each carried the . . . terrible watchword, . . . "Land!" This swarm of political offenders, ex-convicts, . . . village schoolmasters and . . . visionaries . . . mingled with the vilest types of the towns, promised, as they fluttered their red papers, an equal division of land, without purchase, within four months.

"Why four months?" asked the peasant suspiciously.

"Because the masters don't agree: they have to be convinced first."

The peasant [scratched] his head. . . . . . . He went out to the fields to look at the great and fertile manor corn-lands, . . . stretching further than his eye could reach; then at his own narrow, badly cultivated, tiny ribbon of field. . . . Finally, tired of thinking [about it], he would go home; and there the case was taken up by his wife.

The village women played a large part in awakening peasants to a consciousness of their power. For the moment, frankly attracted by the unexpected equality of rights which fell to their lot, . . . they . . . became finished agitators. No one coveted as greedily what belonged to the manors. . . . At the village meetings no one could out-talk the women, and no one restrain them. . . . Stretching out their hands towards the manor, white on the hill, [they] shrieked: "We must have land! We won't have the squires!" They were . . . assisted

* SOURCE: Sophia Kossak-Szucka, *The Blaze, Reminiscences of Volhynia, 1917-1919*, London, G. Allen and Unwin, Ltd., 1927, pp. 22-51.

by soldiers on furlough, by deserters—daily more numerous—and by callow youths. Every cottage [was] divided into two [warring] camps. . . . The . . . older heads . . . passively resisted, and checked the movement, but gradually yielded . . . carried away by the young. . . . A conflagration [began] to . . . [envelop] all Volhynia, all Podolia, all the Ukraine . . . and stood like a wall between manor and village. Then in those fields, outwardly calm, you could hear . . . a harsh voice from underground, crying of . . . a hunger mightier than any other. . . . "Land! Land!"

That cry went everywhere. . . . "Give us . . . our land!" was to be read in every face. . . . It was a primal element . . . rising [like] a . . . wave . . . to sweep all before it. Questions, as burning as the fundamental one, came to the fore. It was not enough to distribute the land: how and to whom was it to be distributed?

Firstly, the *intelligentsia* and the present landowners must be struck out; next, domestic servants and the landless class, because the landless class is purposely created not to possess land, as its name shows. If more still must be struck out, then everybody who has several sons, because such would get too much through the division per head. (This was within a resolution of a village meeting.)

But how were all these obstacles to be got rid of? What was to be done in the event of resistance? An abyss [yawned], dark, throbbing with thoughts that dared not be named. . . . Nothing as yet was essentially changed; everything, apparently, was going on as it had . . . for years. But men were already living together like wolves, . . . their eyes greedily seeking to discover the hidden thought in their neighbour's face. No day passed without a fight, no hamlet was without a murder. . . .

It was thus that sacred and long-dreamed freedom descended upon the Ruthenian nation.[1]

In the beginning of May 1917 the newly nominated commander of the militia,

[1] The inhabitants of Belo-Russia and the Western Ukraine are often referred to as Ruthenians.

Vlasov, came to Skovroodki. He was the first Bolshevik with whom we came into contact. He was a clever . . . agitator, unscrupulous and well aware of the end at which he was aiming. He soon showed his hand. At the first village meeting, when to his seemingly innocent inquiry as to why the village cattle were in the fallow field and not in the meadow, the peasants answered, "Because the squire won't allow it," he expressed astonishment. "But how can the squire not allow it? The squire is one, and you are many."

It was the first occasion that such sentiments had fallen from the lips of a Government official. From that moment two worlds were openly at war. The one side was represented by a vagrant from the outer world, a doctrinaire, deluding the mob and himself; the second by the intellectual Polish squirearchy, men who for centuries had been rooted in the country. . . . I still cherished [childish] delusions. In spite of all that was trembling, . . . I felt safe and strong in Novosyelitsa! The proprietor enjoyed an almost royal prestige, confirmed by centuries, and my husband, Stefan, his representative, respect and confidence. We had never harmed anyone. Who could threaten us?

We calmly planned a plausible parcelling out of a part of the fields, a peaceful life in common with our neighbours, one that should be ever better and more intimate. We did not sufficiently appreciate Vlasov's importance. We laughed at his outbursts of zeal in the direction of socializing women and destroying the Orthodox churches, of which the older peasants told us in great excitement. Our attitude to this foreign vagrant was like that [of] an immemorial forest [toward] a wretched . . . shopboy flicking at . . . mighty trunks.

Every district simultaneously received [many] Vlasovs. The temporary Kadet Government, wavering and weak, was still nominally at the helm; but the extreme Left, whose rule was now approaching, was already openly bringing forward its plan for a radically reorganized mode of action. Two Governments existed—a real and an official one. Every functionary received double instructions: one, officially proclaimed in print, was sensible, sober, and almost impartial; the other, the secret one, . . . was [quite] different. . . . Every order had a double meaning. The *intelligentsia,* naively blind at this juncture, was for long unable to find its bearings. . . . With a touching readiness to adapt itself to the new order, loyally supporting the printed commands, it kept turning to the authorities with the request for their decision in the frequent disputes which occurred. The authorities speedily decided questions, but in a manner wholly unexpected by the injured parties. When, for example, our neighbour, . . . Kopec, complained to the Commissar that the peasants' cattle had grazed to the ground two fields of white clover, the Commissar drove to the spot, investigated the damage . . . and ordered Kopec to give the peasants one more field, this time of red clover, as no white clover was left, "and the villagers' cows must have good pasture."

At this time our antagonist, Vlasov, was energetically organizing, . . . "judicial trials of the squires." . . . Having invited the proprietor, or the manager representing the proprietor, to the village meeting, Vlasov then summoned the villagers to a public declaration of all their complaints . . . against the "squire," [so] that the meeting should pass judgment. It so happened that in Novosyelitsa and Skovroodki, as well as in Pohoryla, the peasants could . . . adduce nothing against the squire. In vain Vlasov . . . reminded them of this or that. "Think hard, comrades," he said: "perhaps a year ago, or perhaps two years ago, your squire did you some wrong? . . . Don't you recall anything? How odd!"

The squire, meanwhile, sat at the extreme edge of the circle, as if he was the player "out" at a game, and waited while the mob . . . deliberated. The women . . . trembled with eagerness to lay hold of some great "wrong." It was in vain. . . . The Ruthenians had a deeply rooted feeling of justice, and several months more of skilful propaganda were needed to eradicate or warp it.

The Petrograd vagabond had a harder fight than he had expected. Confident of the final result, he slightly shifted his position. He attacked the lower agricultural officials, who were nearly always unpopular among the people. Therefore, on July 1st, at a village meeting in Pohoryla, a resolution was passed by which the manorial overseer of the fields was deprived of the right to go out into the fields after eight in the evening and earlier than six in the morning. Any peasant who met him during the forbidden hours had the right to set upon him and drive him off. Likewise, the night watchman was suppressed as unnecessary. Were we living among thieves?

The village committees expelled farm servants, even domestic servants; they suspended the activities of the bailiffs, treasurers and foresters. Vlasov's friend and adjutant, a sailor from Kronstadt named Hrynyuk, a native of the Village of Kruhliki, belonging to Novosyelitsa, proclaimed the "Independent People's Republic of Kruhliki," of which apparently he was the head.

*   *   *

. . . The horizon darkened every day. . . . Each day the *Kiev Daily News* brought us a fresh list of destroyed manor-houses and [horribly mutilated] victims in the province of Kiev and Trans-Dnieper Ukraine. . . .

Every day we looked fearfully for names . . . of our friends and kindred. . . . Old and beautiful Lashki fell the first victim to outrage in our district. It was begun by the soldiers of the Chuguyew regiment . . . stationed [nearby]. That regiment, formerly [of] good reputation, was by now a . . . Bolshevized rabble. . . . The doors were smashed open and the cellar [was] found. . . . Here was real treasure, . . . an enormous quantity of old wines, vodka and mead. On the news that soldiers were in the manor-house the villagers rushed to the spot and assisted at the removal of . . . barrels and . . . bottles. The soldiers heaped up the wagons as high as they could and, as they drove off, said to the peasants: "It's your turn now." [Soon] the village was lying dead-drunk. In the morning the mob went back to the house. . . .

The sack of the manor began. Beautiful articles of furniture and crystal candelabra were flung through the windows, part of the roof was pulled off, doors were torn off their hinges, . . . the turquoise and gold Empire ceilings pulverized. . . . The shouts of mirth and triumph could be heard even in our own park. They were not to be without an echo. It was not for nothing that the Novosyelitsa peasants stood out in the road and, catching pleasant distant sounds, greedily sniffed the odour of old brandy and cognac. . . .

[But] the Chuguyew soldiers were recalled from the district. The peasants were not [yet] bold enough to begin the attack alone.

The peasants' courage, indeed, was for the moment only equal to breaking boughs and cutting down the smallest trees in the park. Each day long strings of women in shawls marched up from the . . . village, and returned laden with armfuls of wood. In the beginning they restricted themselves to the outskirts of the park and fled when they saw an official or servant. But as the wave of mob violence approached us, the women came closer and became . . . increasingly insolent. When . . . walking in the garden [I would see] the well-known Varka or Paraska [and] wish her [an] affectionate . . . "Good Morning," entirely forgetting the actual state of affairs. Sometimes the woman who was thus unexpectedly addressed would answer automatically, although unwillingly: "Good Morning, madam." More often she would turn her back on me and silently go away.

The silence of these women was of a restrained hatred. We were their accursed enemies. We realized that now there was hardly a man in the village who did not wish our death. Such a simple thing to give a cordial greeting to a neighbour. . . . But that now belonged to a dead past. Why had this come to pass . . . ? Our souls also became filled with hatred . . . for those who had come into our tranquil little nook and changed our peace to war. . . . Not one shadow now remained of the old relationship. And yet so short a time ago we were dearly loved. . . . I knew then, as I know today, that the process by which the change had come about was a natural one, independent of the will of the unenlightened and passive mob. It is better to have a good squire than a bad one; but nobody can deny that it is better not to have a squire at all than to have even the best of squires. The moment that the agitators persuaded the peasants that it was possible not to have squires at all, that in driving them out they were securing their sacred rights, at that moment the sentence was passed from which there was no appeal.

Whose words could compare with those of the agitator? Not even God's, for He had said: "Thou shalt not steal," while the stranger . . . with the Red newspaper in his hand, said: "What belongs to others belongs to you." Who could be more liberal than he?

The good squire was got rid of in a more brutal fashion than the bad or indifferent one. He, strong in his conviction of a clear conscience, indignant at what he looked upon as ingratitude, resisted the inundation longer, defended himself more determinedly. To the end, in spite of all, he would not believe that the peasants would touch him. The peasants, albeit ignorant and narrowminded, knew by instinct that a good man will not take revenge, and therefore they were less afraid of him in the event of a future reversion to the old order than they were of an indifferent or a hard squire. . . . Acting against their consciences, they let loose all the brutality . . . of which they were capable in order to stifle conscience.

Simultaneously with the tree-breaking in the park began the pasturage of horses on the lawns. At first this was carried on cautiously at dead of night, in the most distant sweeps of the park, but as events marched on, so it came nearer and grew bolder. By October the whole village was taking wood out of the park and pasturing livestock there, as though it had been [an ancient] privilege. We stopped sitting on the terrace in the evening to avoid hearing the singing and laughing of the peasants driving their horses to night quarters through the main alley. The exaggeratedly loud laughter and songs were intended as a provocation and a hymn of triumph. A little later they began to pasture animals on the great lawn in front of the palace, close to our windows. Horses and cows gazed through the panes of the great parapeted windows. Choking down for the hundredth time our anger . . . , we dressed in semi-darkness, and purposely waited to draw up our blinds until the moment when we expected the peasants would have driven the horses from their pasture. But the peasants soon saw through this artifice, and ostentatiously sat themselves down before the house till we drew up the blinds. Then, yawning and stretching themselves with the utmost deliberation, they fastened their sheepskin coats and belts, . . . mounted and rode slowly away.

This state of things was torture. The sense of our humiliating powerlessness played havoc with our nerves.

*   *   *

. . . Neighboring Podolia [was] now only smoking ruins. Through an immense expanse of country, hitherto thickly dotted with manor-houses, where farming had been carried out in a highly scientific manner, not one farm remained, not one large dwelling-house.

. . . Manors . . . were pulled down to the last brick, gardens despoiled to the last tree, places made ploughed fields so that the owners might have nothing to which to return and be unable to recognize the spots where they were born. Here and there a tall chimney would be left as the only trace of the late property. . . .

. . . I remember the . . . destruction of a well-known manor-house in the district of Ploskirov. The rioting villagers were drinking from early morning, [preparing] to start for the manor. In the old white house all the family were gathered round the death-bed of the proprietor's mother. . . . They [were] praying God to let her die before she found out what was threatening her children. . . . They knew from the savage shouts . . . drawing near that disaster would soon be upon them. A howling mob surrounded the house and demanded that the master should surrender. Alarmed by the uproar, the old lady found out from the servants the cause of it. She started from her bed, grasped the crucifix which . . . had [been] placed in her hands and went out . . . to the [frosty] veranda. . . . Between the rabble and the terrified inhabitants of the manor stood that tall apparition clad in a long nightdress, a cross in her emaciated hands. "Men and women!" she cried out, "I am about to face God's judgment-seat. In an hour's time . . . I shall bring my charge against you to God Himself. When I am dead I shall haunt you. . . . Be off with you! Be off! . . ."

The mob retreated, panic-stricken.

A Mill Manager's Dilemma *

. . . The English mill owners and mill managers . . . were trying to keep their plants going. . . . The workers . . . had no idea what freedom meant, but most of them took it as an invitation not to work. There was a daily drama in every mill yard. . . . One . . . with . . . 3,000 workers had immediately elected its own Soviet, which was insisting that it should now have a say as

to how the mill should be run. It . . . drew up a list of demands which, aside from the orthodox stipulation of an eight-hour day, demanded an impossible increase in wages forthwith. . . . [Under the Tsar] entire families of workers [had] one badly ventilated room, and the dark, dirt and wet inside the mill . . . were no better. But this was the opposite swing of the pendulum; and they were demanding things which the mill managers . . . could not give. The

* Source: N. Farson, *The Way of a Transgressor,* New York, Harcourt, Brace, 1936, pp. 255-256.

English mill managers had no force to use against these demands of the Workers' Soviets except ridicule and tact—and their policy soon turned from flat opposition or attempt at compromise to one of yielding as slowly and as gracefully as possible to each new demand.

The reason . . . was that no one knew where this Revolution was going to lead the working class. The workers themselves had no knowledge of outside conditions and working hours; and the more cynical among their leaders thought that the only way to see how far they could get was by trying it on. As soon as the Englishmen thought they had come to some decent arrangement with a Workers' Soviet . . . , the extremists . . . were immediately demanding further concessions.

It was enough to drive a man mad.

I watched an Englishman go through this ordeal day after day, trying to reason with his workers in the mill yard. . . . He stood on a table and harangued the crowd. Using simple comparisons he tried to explain to them why they would have to be content with certain concessions. . . . The price of labour, for instance, was just like the price of wool. . . . Now, they would not pay several thousand roubles a *pood* for their wool, would they? No, growled the workers, they certainly would not! Then, he demanded, why ask the mill to pay them such ridiculous prices for labour?

For a moment the mill crowd would look thoughtful, and some of the steadier hands . . . would begin nodding their heads. Perhaps, for a moment, the Englishman would carry his point, and the Workers' Soviet would be satisfied because it had just managed to get some concessions which increased its prestige in the workers' eyes. But always, often before the Englishman had got down from the table, a wilder spirit would jump up.

"Fools!" he would yell at the crowd. "Why stand here and talk about it? The mill is ours. We will . . . throw out these foreigners and run the mill ourselves. "[Down with the bourgeoisie]!"

The Factory Workers and the Bosses*

Pravda
June 8/June 21, 1917

*The Revolution and the Strike
of the Laundresses*

In the May 24/June 6 session of the Workers' Section of the Soviet of Workers' and Soldiers' Deputies the following was resolved: (1) To give organized protection to the striking laundresses while they picket the laundry plants to prevent strike breakers from being hired. (2) In the event of a lockout, to requisition these plants by means of the Soviet and the trade unions and turn them over to the regular workers so that these laundries may be municipalized at the earliest possible moment.

The strike has been going on for twenty-six days. The bosses have agreed to all demands, but refuse to pay wages for the time the workers have been on strike. They want to throw the blame on the workers, claiming that the workers did not want to take the peaceful road to settlement. But the bosses forget that it was they who wanted no peaceful settlement. That left the workers but one means; to strike, and only that way were we able to extract from the bosses these pitiable concessions. When the strike began they dawdled for two weeks and proposed no negotiations with us. They said that they were closing their laundries for three months, in order to sell their equipment, and thus wanted to frighten the workers. But they forgot that the days of monarchy have passed and with it their unlimited power and that the workers are now strong. The bosses even now threaten

* SOURCE: Items from the Bolshevik Press, June to November, 1917.

the workers with closing and are already closing their plants. The workers cannot requisition the plants with their own strength. They request that comrades more experienced in such matters help them to take the practical steps to requisition; help them actively because the bosses sit in ambush;—protected. Armed troops have been sent and don't allow us to go in.

Many factories have contributed funds for the striking laundresses.

Pravda
June 28/July 11, 1917

The Congress of Factory Inspectors

On June 10/23 the congress of factory inspectors began in Moscow. It was convened to take up questions of legislation with regard to protecting labor, the execution of inspection, etc. . . . All workers know what the factory inspection was and what it still is. . . . It was established by the tsarist government [to pacify the workers] after consultation with the industrialists only and was meant to serve their interests. In conflicts between labor and capital the government inspectors went against the workers, took part in persecution of workers' organizations and even had contacts with the secret police. The inspector who was too obviously partial to the interests of the workers soon lost his job. . . .

Not improvement and reform of the State inspectorate, but a basic transformation of it is the workers' slogan. The factory inspectors must depend not on the government and the business men but on the workers. . . . Down with bureaucratic inspection! . . . It must be the task of all workers' organizations to struggle for elected factory inspectors.

Rabochi Put'
September 7/20, 1917

The Soykin Printing Shop

For a long time something rotten in the printing shop had been observed by the factory committee. Nothing was done to repair or replace machines or to replace worn out parts. The factory committee gave the factory administration an estimate [of the cost in rubles] of the essential improvements needed, but this estimate was pigeonholed. Attempts to bring a state of order to the enterprise was met with the fiercest opposition by the factory administration. A picture of sabotage on the part of the owners was becoming clear. But only now and quite by accident has the desire of the administration become evident to the workers. They mean to sell all the machines to speculators who in their turn expect to sell the machine parts to various factories. A major printing house destroys itself. Hundreds of workers will be thrown on the street, and this just at the time when the elections to the Constituent Assembly is nearing and the services of the printing houses will be especially needed.

The bourgeoisie are preparing for the elections. The working class must also prepare. It is necessary at once to proceed to the requisitioning of the printing house and to the confiscation of all printing houses which are closed and sabotaged like that of Soykin.

The Aivaz Factory

During the Kornilov days the workers organized to protect the factory from counter-revolutionary arsonists. They set up a guard of . . . persons working secretly and a guard of . . . persons operating openly, working in three shifts. Now the factory management has declared that it will not recognize the status of the factory security personnel. From the outset the technical director of the factory, Kurpevich, even maintained that the workers had no right to set up a workers' guard; to take such authority upon themselves. But the factory committee refused to ignore either the combustible condition of the plant or the order of the committee on counter-revolution. Then the director declared that he would recognize the guard but would refuse to pay the workers for time spent in watching for fires. That is, they could guard our factory —but at the workers' expense.

The factory committee decided to stand its ground and to present its case to the committee for struggle against counter-revolution.

Rabochi Put'
October 20/November 2, 1917

Conflict in the Petrov Factory

In the factory a conflict has risen over the non-payment of wages to the members of the factory-shop committees and of the Soviet of Workers' and Soldiers' Deputies.

The behavior of the management [offended] the workers with the result that several members of the administration were carried out on stretchers. The management replied by closing the factory. . . . If the management refuses to open the factory, the factory committee will take the decision to sequester it.

Marx's Missionary*

. . . I came upon a large square. A large crowd were gathered . . . , their faces raised towards a first floor balcony, where I could perceive the figure of a man gesticulating. He was a solidly built man and had a clear compelling voice, his sentences were . . . punctuated by dramatic gestures with his right hand.

"These traitors are lying . . . ! You'll never get peace or land while your class enemies are in power. *Your* worst enemy at the moment is the Provisional Government, . . . a rotten lot of *bourgeois* socialists. Turn them out comrades! Fight for the great Russian proletariat! Fight for a free, classless State!" The speaker ended with an imperative gesture of his right hand, as though he meant to sweep the *bourgeoisie* out of existence. He turned round . . . it was Lenin!

His speech did not merely fire the crowd with a momentary enthusiasm. Its effect was more lasting and profound—altogether different from that of other speakers.

He spoke entirely as an intellectual, never deigning to lower his speech to the crowd's level. He used complicated Marxist terms which were obviously unknown to this working class gathering. But, strangely enough, these words produced a magical effect. . . .

* SOURCE: Olga Tchernoff, *New Horizons*, London, Hutchinson & Co., Ltd., 1936, pp. 60-61.

His philosophy seemed so logical in its formidable simplicity. He had rooted his beliefs deep down in the people . . . *class hatred*. Oh, yes, it was only too obvious!

"Wipe out the past, comrades. You are the Russian proletariat, it's you who must help build the new world—it's you who must institute freedom and peace!"

Proletarian justice. This was their new religion, something tangible, something eternal!

Lenin suddenly disappeared before the crowd had time to applaud him. . . . Some of his followers had already hustled him into a waiting car. . . .

Then a woman . . . in black got up on the stands and began shouting [hysterically].

"They mean to go on with this war. They want to sacrifice *your* blood and end the revolution!"

The crowd, who had remained silent during Lenin's speech, now gave vent to their rage.

"There's been too much bloodshed. What we want is peace!"

"Yes, peace, food and land enough to live on. . . ."

"Peace. We want peace at once . . . ," yelled the mob.

"Down with the bourgeois traitors!" screamed the woman in black.

Democracy's Last Gasps*

The Democratic Congress

When the counter-revolution, headed by
. . . Korniloff, was at its height . . . the
Executive Committee of the All-Russian Soviets demanded the holding of a Democratic Congress, which was to be a fore-
runner of the Constituent Assembly and
was to make further counter-revolution impossible. . . .

. . . About a month later 1,600 delegates
from all parts of Russia answered the sum-
mons. . . .

On the stage [of the Alexandrinsky The-
atre] sat the presidium . . . , behind them
the entire Petrograd Soviet and in the main
theatre and galleries sat the delegates. Almost every revolutionary leader was present, and there were representatives from the
All-Russian Soviets of Soldiers and Workmen, the All-Russian Soviets of Peasants,
. . . Labor Unions, . . . Railroad Employees, . . . Commercial Employees, Liberal
Professions (doctors, lawyers, etc.), Zemstvos, Cossacks, Press, and Nationalist Organisations, including Ukrainians, Poles,
Jews, Letts, [etc.]. No body just like it had
ever met in Russia before. . . .

. . . The Congress was formally opened
by President Tcheidze, and Kerensky came
forward to make his address. . . .

Only persons of great intensity can make
an audience hold its breath . . . the way
Kerensky did. . . . He was clad in a plain
brown soldier's suit without so much as a
brass button . . . to mark him Commander-in-Chief of the . . . Army and
Navy and Minister-President of the Russian
Republic. Somehow all this unpretentious-
ness accentuated the dignity of his position.
It was characteristic that he should ignore
the speakers' rostrum and proceed to the
runway leading from the main floor to the

stage. It produced an effect of unusual inti-
macy between the speaker and his audience.

"At the Moscow Conference," he began,
"I was in an official capacity and my scope
was limited, but here I am Tovarishch
[comrade]. There are people here who con-
nect me with that terrible affair. . . ." (He
was referring to the Korniloff counter-revolution.)

He was interrupted by shouts of "Yes,
there are people here who do!"

Kerensky stepped back as if struck, and
all the enthusiasm went out of his face.
. . . Deeply conscious of the coldness, the
hostility even of his audience, he played on
it skillfully. . . .

"After all, it doesn't matter what you
think about *me*—all that matters is the revolution. . . ."

Yes, that was true and everybody in the
audience felt it for the time he was speaking. When he finished they rose in a tremendous ovation.

Dramatically he stepped from the stage,
traversed the long aisle in the centre of the
theatre, mounted the Tsar's own box and
raising his right hand as if to drink a toast,
spoke again: "Long live the Democratic Republic and the Revolutionary Army!" And
the crowd shouted back: "Long live Kerensky!"

This was the last ovation Kerensky ever
got. . . . Russians are never convinced by
phrases. . . . They were disappointed in
Kerensky's speech. He was charming, but
he had not told them anything. There were
many details about the Korniloff affair
which they wished [clarified]; they also
wanted desperately to know what had been
done about a conference of the Allies to
discuss war aims, and he had not mentioned
it. . . . His influence was [soon] gone, and
they threw themselves into the struggle of
deciding the issues for which they had
come.

For nine days the Democratic Congress

---

* SOURCE: Louise Bryant, *Six Months in Red
Russia*, New York, George H. Doran, 1918, pp.
59-78.

continued. Hundreds of delegates spoke. . . . At first, the Chairman tried to limit their speeches, but the audience [protested]. "Let them say everything they have come here to say!"

It was amazing. . . . Often a peasant . . . would give [an hour's] talk and keep the close attention of his audience. Not one speaker had stage fright. Few used notes. . . . The gigantic problem was to weave a general satisfactory programme from their widely divergent desires. . . . The sessions often lasted until 4 in the morning, but the hunger for truth . . . never lessened. There was the same earnest groping for solution in the grey dawn as in the flaring sunset. . . .

Flashing out of that remarkable gathering was the striking personality of Leon Trotsky, . . . vehement, serpent-like, he swayed the assembly as a strong wind stirs the long grass. No other man creates such an uproar, such hatred at the slightest utterance, uses such stinging words and yet underneath it all carries such a cool head. In striking contrast was another Bolshevik leader, Kameneff. . . . His way of expressing his opinions was as mild as Trotsky's was . . . inflammatory. . . .

Not . . . to be overlooked were the twenty-three . . . women-delegates, notable among them Marie Spiridonova, the most politically powerful woman in Russia or in the world, and the only woman the soldiers and peasants are sentimental about.

The one thing that the Congress completely agreed upon and instructed the Preparliament which was to follow it to do, was to issue an appeal to the peoples of the world reaffirming the Soviets' formula of last spring for peace "without annexations and indemnities" on the basis of self determination of peoples.

A . . . sore point in all the speeches was the subject of capital punishment in the army; it was always causing an unpleasant stir. . . . The gathering was firmly against the re-establishment, but it was never actually put to a vote.

The quarrel over coalition wrecked the assembly and almost broke Russia.

A resolution put up by Trotsky and read-ing: *We are in favour of coalition of all democratic elements—except the Kadets* carried overwhelmingly and showed the real feeling of the country.

Every one knows now that it was the most tragic thing in the world that that decision was not left.

Unfortunately just after the resolution was passed, word was brought that Kerensky was about to announce his new cabinet containing representatives of the Kadet party and several Moscow business men known to be particularly out of harmony with socialistic aims. Tseretelli hurried to the Winter Palace and told Kerensky . . . that without the sanction of the Democratic Congress, the formation of such a cabinet would lead directly to civil war.

The next morning Kerensky appeared before the Presidium, and threatening to resign, painted such a tragic picture of the condition of the country, that the Presidium returned to the Congress with a resolution to immediately constitute the Preparliament with full power to authorise the constitution of a coalition government, if it thought absolutely necessary, and to admit into its own ranks representatives of the bourgeoisie proportional to their representatives in the cabinet.

Tseretelli, Dan, Lieber, Gotz and other politicians upholding the Provisional Government, spoke again and again for the measure. Lunacharsky and Kameneff spoke against the wording, claiming that Tseretelli had not read the same motion which had been agreed upon at the meeting of the Presidium. Whereupon Tseretelli's usual self-control deserted him and he cried: "The next time I deal with Bolsheviki I will insist on having a notary and two secretaries!"

The Bolshevik Nagine shouted back that he would give Tseretelli five minutes to retract his words, and Tseretelli remaining stubbornly silent, the Bolsheviki used this as an excuse for bolting the assembly. They left the hall amid [a] tremendous uproar. Men ran into the hallways, screaming, pleading, weeping. . . .

This split over coalition marked the beginning and the end of many things, and was a real blow to the democratic forces brought together for self-protection during the Korniloff attempt. When the measure was finally voted on, the delegates were not allowed a secret ballot. . . . Over night a terrific change came over that once peaceful gathering. When Spiridonova got up and told her peasants that this measure cheated them out of their land, [an] ominous roar followed. . . . As I watched that change it came to me what the passage of the measure really meant. It meant civil war, it meant a great swinging of the masses to the banners of the Bolsheviki, it meant new leaders pushed to the surface who would do the bidding of the people, and old leaders hurled into oblivion, it meant the beginning of class struggle and the end of political revolution. . . .

The next evening coalition passed by a small majority and the delegates filed out into the rain . . . after having arranged the election of the Preparliament.

The Preparliament and the Council of the Russian Republic

The first meeting of the Preparliament took place in the shabby old hall of the Petrograd City Duma on [October 20], and showed that the moderate socialist machine was still in control by the election of Tcheidze as President. Another indication of the drift toward the right wing was the decision to discuss the question of the constitution of the government in *secret session,* in face of the combined protest of the Bolsheviki, Menshevik Internationalists[1] and the left wing of the Socialist [Revolutionaries].

During the secret session Tseretelli arrived from the Winter Palace with a report of the alliance, hastily concluded, between the moderate socialists and the bourgeoisie, announcing the bourgeoisie would enter the Preparliament in the proportion of 100 members to each 120 democratic members; that a coalition government would be formed; and that the government would not be responsible to the Preparliament. Then, coalition being a fact, everybody entered into violent debates upon the subject,

[1] A left-wing faction of the Menshevik party

which were terminated by [Katherine Breshkovskaya] announcing in a trembling voice at 2 o'clock in the morning that coalition was right because human life itself is based on the principle of coalition. . . .

The next day a heated debate took place upon the question of the death penalty in the army, followed by passionate addresses by every one altogether upon coalition, the dissolution of the Duma, peace, the threatening railroad strike and the land question which ended in the resolution of the Socialist Revolutionists insisting that the first task of the new government should be the immediate placing of the land under the authority of the General Peasant Land Committees.

At one time such pandemonium reigned that a violent discussion between Trotsky and Tcheidze ended because neither one could hear what the other was saying. In the lull that followed [Breshkovskaya] rebuked the delegates, saying that they had come together to save Russia and that not a single step had been taken.

Avksentieff, at that time president of the Peasants' Soviets, but now completely out of power, declared that if the land amendment had anything to do with endangering coalition the Socialist [Revolutionaries] would retire it. The whole matter was finally disposed of by the representative of the Land Committee himself who got up and remarked bitterly that the whole business was utter absurdity and that the Peasants' Land Committee would have nothing to do with it, whereupon the resolution was rejected. At six o'clock in the morning the delegates went wearily home. . . .

The next morning Tseretelli announced that the official name of the *Preparliament* would be the *"Council of the Russian Republic,"* and that it would meet in the Marinsky Palace after a few days. . . .

For weeks the Council of the Russian Republic held futile sessions. On the very first evening the Bolsheviki, through their spokesman, Trotsky, hurled a bomb into the gathering from which it never recovered. They accused the . . . propertied classes . . . of being represented out of proportion to their numbers as shown from the elections held all over the country, and charged them with the deliberate intention of ruining the Revolution; appealing to the soldiers, workers, peasants of all Russia to be on their guard, the Bolsheviki left the Council never to return.

After that the Council sat day after day, a hostile, divided house, unable to carry out a single measure. The Mensheviki, Menshevik Internationalists, Right and Left Socialist [Revolutionaries], sat on one side, the Kadets on the other, and the vote on every important measure was a tie. Orators from the right got up and heaped recriminations on the left, orators from the left screamed curses on the right. And all this time the mass of the people left their old parties and joined the ranks of the Bolsheviki. Louder grew the cry: *All power to the Soviets!*

Every few days Kerensky would appear and make impassioned addresses without any effect whatever. He [was] listened to with indifference: the Kadets often choosing this particular time to read their papers. During one of the last speeches he made in the Marinsky Palace, begging them to forget their differences and somehow pull together until the Constituent Assembly, he was so overcome with the hopelessness of the situation that he rushed from the platform, and having gained his seat, wept openly before the whole assembly.

All those who understood the condition of Russia at that time knew that Kerensky was the symbol of a fictitious union of parties, but how long he could remain so no one could foretell. He was ill and carrying the weight of all Russia on his frail shoulders. Moreover, he had been betrayed by the very Kadets he had worked so hard to keep in the government. The Bolsheviki were offering a definite programme containing the wishes nearest to the hearts of the people, and the people were going over to the Bolsheviki.

One thing might have saved that pitiful Preparliament even in the last days, and that was the *Allied Conference to Discuss War Aims* which new Russia had demanded at the beginning of the revolution and which was to be held in June, was postponed to September, then to November, and finally, apparently, given up altogether. With the final decision of the Allies . . . , the last shred of influence of the Council of the Russian Republic disappeared. All Russia was slowly starving, another terrible winter was coming on, and there was nothing definite to hang their hopes on. [Kerensky himself] told me, a few days before the Provisional Government fell, that the people had lost confidence and were too economically tired to put up further effective resistance against the Germans.

"The Constituent Assembly must be the deciding factor, one way or the other," he said. He hoped that he could hold the country together until then, but I do not think for a moment that he thought he could hold it any longer. I do not think he dared prophesy what would come out of the Constituent Assembly when it did meet.

On [November 7] the meeting of the All-Russian Soviets was due to be held in Petrograd. That that tremendously powerful body would demand immediate action on all the burning issues there was no doubt and that if the Provisional Government refused those demands they would take over the power there was also no doubt. Kerensky believed that he ought to prevent this meeting by any means possible, even by force of arms. He did not realise how far the Bolshevik influence had spread. The masses moved fast in those days and the army had gone solidly Bolshevik.

Kerensky took into account, however, that the Petrograd garrison was composed largely of Bolsheviki and so . . . he ordered this garrison to the front to be replaced by troops less Bolshevik. Naturally, the Petrograd garrison protested and appealed to the Petrograd Soviet. The Petrograd Soviet appointed a commission to go to the front and confer with General Tcherimissov, and demand of him that if he did send regiments to replace the Petrograd garrison the Petrograd Soviet should be allowed to choose them. This General Tcherimissov flatly refused, saying that he was the Commander-in-Chief of the army and that his orders should be obeyed.

In the meantime members of the Petrograd garrison held a meeting and elected the now famous Military Revolutionary Committee, and demanded that a representative of the committee be allowed in the General Staff of the Petrograd District. This proposition the Petrograd Staff refused to consider. In reply the Petrograd garrison declared that it would take no orders from anybody unless countersigned by the Military Revolutionary Committee, as they maintained that the General Staff was secretly taking measures to disperse the meeting of the All-Russian Soviets [by violence].

On [November 5] Kerensky announced before the Council of the Republic that an order had been issued for the arrest of the Military Revolutionary Committee. The next night several of the members of the Pavlovsk regiment secreted themselves in the office of the General Staff and discovered that plans were being made to seize the city with the aid of the Junker regiments, and forcibly prevent the meeting of the All-Russian Soviets scheduled for the following day. That night Kerensky ordered all the extreme radical papers and the extreme conservative papers suppressed. But it was too late; it was like sweeping back the sea with a broom. The Soviets had become the ultimate political expression of the popular will, and the Bolsheviki were the champions of the Soviets.

After the Pavlovsk regiment discovered the plans of the Provisional Government, they set sentries and began to arrest all persons entering or leaving the General Staff. Before this time the Junkers had begun to seize automobiles and take them to the Winter Palace. They also seized the editorial offices and the printing shops of the Bolshevik papers. During all this confusion a meeting of the old Executive Committee of the Soviets was taking place at Smolny. The old Central Executive Committee was composed largely of Mensheviki and Left Socialist [Revolutionaries], and the new delegates were almost solidly Bolshevik. There was nothing to do but speedily elect a new Central Executive Committee.

The next afternoon I started out as usual to attend the regular session of the Council of the Russian Republic. One glance around the square before the Marinsky Palace assured me that the long looked for storm of civil war had come. Soldiers and sailors were guarding the little bridges over the Moika, a great crowd of sailors were at the door of the palace and barricades were being hastily constructed. Word flew round that they were arresting the Council of the Republic. As a matter of fact no one thought the Council of the Republic was important enough to arrest. What really happened was tragically funny. A big Cronstadt sailor marched into the great elaborate red and gold assembly chamber and announced in a loud voice: "No more Council! Go along home." And the Council went—disappearing forever as an influence in the political life of Russia.

The One-Day Assembly*

. . . January 18, 1918: It was the opening of the Constituent Assembly at the Tauride Palace. . . .

The grand amphitheatre was crowded. As usual, soldiers and sailors, workers and peasants invaded the public galleries. People were shouting [their views] at the top

* SOURCE: Olga Tchernoff, *New Horizons*, London, Hutchinson & Co., Ltd., 1936, pp. 100-105.

of their voices, . . . trying to argue above the din. . . .

. . . Least perturbed was the speaker. . . . This man was Chvetzov, a Socialist [Revolutionary] and President of the Old Provisional Government. It was his duty to open the session of the Assembly. He rang for order several times. . . .

Then a young Bolshevik strode on to the platform, tore the bell from his hands and gave it to Sverdloff, a member of the Government, who forthwith rang and declared the Assembly open.

The tumult gradually abated. Some began singing the *Internationale*. The most important matter for today was the . . . election [of the] President of the Constituent Assembly.

Two candidates came forward. Marie Spiridonova, put up by the Bolsheviks, was the leader of our old Left-Wing [Socialist Revolutionary] comrades who had rallied to the Bolsheviks. . . . Her grave features and far-off expression made her seem like some Byzantine ikon. The other candidate was Victor Tchernoff, the leader of the Socialist [Revolutionaries].

He was elected president with 244 votes. . . .

When the results were known a fresh uproar started. An angry murmur came from the Left-Wing Socialist [Revolutionaries]. Boris Kamkoff [1] slammed his desk, producing a deafening noise. . . .

Victor was then installed in the . . . presidential chair. . . . He picked up the bell, it was his only weapon against a riotous hall!

Then he began his opening speech. It was a declaration of Party policy, modified by his own views as much as possible. He had never been in complete agreement with the Socialist [Revolutionaries], but had felt obliged to follow their official policy. Now, for the first time, he began enlarging on his individual ideas, and this gave his speech a certain duplicity of meaning. It was an amazingly calm, academic . . . speech in the midst of such an audience; but I'm afraid it had a mixed reception.

"The Constituent Assembly must mould itself to the people's will!" decreed Victor.

"A bullet through his head, that's what they want!" yelled a soldier, raising his rifle and pointing at Victor.

"The People" was like a red-hot iron to the Bolsheviks! The people, just a *bourgeois* invention! All that counts is the will of the proletariat. . . .

Under the menace of raised rifles Victor

continued his speech resolute and calm, in appearance at any rate.

He had irritated the Right-Wing [Socialist Revolutionaries] by his internationalist theme, incensed the Bolsheviks by proclaiming that the people were against a proletarian dictatorship.

Nevertheless, he succeeded in finishing his speech and in quelling the tumult to some extent. This . . . despite the . . . jeering soldiers who surrounded the platform trying to drown his speech with coarse . . . remarks.

Lenin sat in the midst of the people's commissars. He was very pale and tried to hide his emotion by a sardonic smile. He laughed from time to time, then he shut his eyes and pretended to be dozing. His nonchalant attitude expressed utter boredom. . . .

Different speeches followed. [To] a Bolshevik speaker . . . the people listened more attentively [but] when their opponents tried to speak the uproar was renewed. Boukharine, a young Bolshevik, railed against the democratic principles in a sarcastic . . . speech.

"From this platform we'll proclaim war on the whole *bourgeois* republic. In the future there's only one dictatorship, that of the proletariat!"

"The people don't exist!" cried another Bolshie. "It's a fiction invented by the ruling classes."

Tzeretelli, an ex-Minister of the Provisional Government, was received with threats and menacing gestures when he got up on the platform.

"Traitor! Capitalist! . . . look at him, comrades! He's the man who restored the death penalty!"

Victor rang the presidential bell, and called for order. But his voice was quite lost in the *fracas*.

Tzeretelli remained calm. . . . He waited until the first access of rage had passed and then began speaking again. His stern, impressive manner even managed to impose silence.

He accused the Bolsheviks of having ruined the Revolution, of having destroyed public liberty and of violating the people's

[1] One of the Left S. R. chieftains.

will. Even his enemies were impressed by this passionate speech. But in the end, just as before, their anger burst into a wild chaos of derision and dissension.

Roudneff, the ex-Mayor of Moscow who had directed the October attack during the Bolshevik *coup d'état,* got up on the platform, but he had to be persuaded to leave, as the mere sight of him infuriated the Red soldiers and started a fresh onslaught from the Bolshevik quarters. Indeed, the soldiers had now become a quite uncontrollable menace in the Assembly. No one, save their own favourite speakers, were allowed a hearing.

"Stop the session. We've had enough of your *bourgeois* speakers! We want to get down to action. Where are our own members? Let's hear what they've got to say!"

Indeed, the hall began to resemble a battlefield. Chairs and tables were overturned, pictures torn from the walls, in every row there were groups of soldiers trying to heckle the speakers, their rifles cocked threateningly towards the platform. The sailors' faces were distorted with rage. . . . Their impatient . . . hands never left the trigger. . . . I grew more and more alarmed. Surely disaster was inevitable if the session was continued, but no one else seemed to take much notice.

The members remained motionless. The President rang his bell, and the speaker went on. . . .

A sailor . . . clambered up on the platform and touched the President's arm. He said he's been ordered to clear the room.

"By whose orders?" asked the President in surprise.

[The sailor] cried that that was of no importance, but that in any case the Guard was tired and that they were going to cut off the electricity.

"Comrade, the members are just as tired, only it's their duty to settle the agrarian problem as the people wish. We must come to some definite decision," said Victor quietly.

At this [the sailor's] companions began shouting loudly: "That's enough! We're all tired, we don't want to listen to your people. . . . Come on, boys, we'll cut off the light, . . ."

More cries of derision followed, coming mostly from the armed troops scattered about the hall.

Then in a firm . . . voice, Victor summarised the agricultural reforms which were to be included in the Constitution. It would become a fundamental law, unable to be modified or adapted by local interested parties. This bill was the proud work of the Socialist [Revolutionary] Party. The Assembly now had to vote on its adoption.

So he went on reading it out, article by article, interrupted from time to time by cries of: "That's enough!" "Chuck him out, comrades!" and always menaced by the soldiers' rifles.

But luckily the peasant delegates' attitude imposed comparative silence. Although bored and weary after the other speeches, their faces lit up and they seemed enthusiastic directly Victor began to speak. At last the Russian peasants' . . . happy dream was about to become law. . . .

"Private property is abolished! The land would be distributed among the peasants!"

This announcement even silenced the Guards' anger for the moment.

Four o'clock in the morning: the President and delegates had no resistance left. They knew they were losing ground at every step. But . . . the treasure had been saved, for there was a unanimous vote in favour of the agricultural bill.

There followed another debate on free speech and the censorship of the Press. Then the question of separate treaties with the Allies was brought up. But this was their last effort; at the moment nothing could save the Assembly.

Chaos had broken loose. It was redoubled since the agricultural vote. Again the President rang for order and again he was shouted down by the howling mob. He was like a captain on the bridge just before his boat went down.

He announced that the session was over and they would continue on the morrow.

A well-known Bolshevik came up to Victor and said in a low voice: "You'd better go out by a secret door, there's a crowd round your car waiting to assassinate you!"

So the Tauride Palace emptied itself slowly. I saw delegates scurrying across the courtyard, glad to have got out unharmed.

Defeat of the Left Socialist Revolutionaries*

Life in St. Petersburg [in late February, 1918] was a curious affair. The Bolsheviks had not yet [established] iron discipline. . . . They had, in fact, made little attempt to do so. There was no terror, nor was the population . . . afraid of its new masters. The anti-Bolshevik newspapers continued to appear and to attack the Bolshevik policy with violent abuse. . . . The bourgeoisie, still confident that the Germans would soon send the Bolshevik rabble about its business, was more cheerful than one might have expected. . . . The population was starving, but the rich still had money. . . . Cabarets were crowded. On Sundays . . . there were trotting races. . . . The only real danger to human life during these early days of the Bolshevik revolution [were] the Anarchists—bands of robbers, ex-army officers, and adventurers, who had seized some of the finest houses in the city and who, armed with rifles, . . . and machine-guns, exercised a gangsters' rule over the capital. . . . The Bolsheviks seemed quite incapable of dealing with this pest. For years they had been crying against the Tsarist suppression of free speech. They had not yet embarked on their own campaign of suppression.

I mention this comparative tolerance of the Bolsheviks, because the cruelties which followed later were the result of the intensification of the civil war. For the intensification of that bloody struggle Allied intervention, with the false hopes it raised, was largely responsible. . . . Our interven-

* SOURCE: R. H. Bruce Lockhart, *British Agent*, London, G. P. Putnam's Sons, 1933, pp. 238-317.

tion intensified the terror and increased the bloodshed.

On Saturday, March 3rd, the . . . peace was signed . . . at Brest. . . . At the same time the Bolsheviks announced the formation of a new Supreme War Council and issued an order for the arming of the whole people. Trotsky was appointed President of the new Council. . . .

. . . One of Trotsky's first tasks as Commissar for War [was] to rid Moscow of the Anarchist bands. . . . [On] . . . April 12 he [raided] twenty-six Anarchist nests. . . . Over a hundred were killed. . . . Five hundred were arrested. . . . The Bolsheviks had taken their first step to enforce discipline.

*   *   *

. . . [The assassination of Count Mirbach, the German Ambassador was] accompanied . . . by [a] revolt against the government. . . .

. . . After the [November] revolution, the extreme wing of the Russian Social-Revolutionary Party joined . . . with the Bolsheviks [in forming] the new Government. They received a few . . . Commissariats, retained their places in the Soviets, and were strongly represented in the All-Russian Central Executive Committee, which, when the Congress of Soviets is not sitting, is the supreme . . . power of the Russian Socialist Federative Soviet Republic. For the first eight months . . . the Soviet Government was . . . a coalition.

. . . The Left Social-Revolutionaries were quite as extreme as the Bolsheviks in their hatred of capitalism and Imperialism. They were . . . as violent . . . in [denouncing] the Allies. In internal politics, while they differed from the Bolsheviks on agrarian questions, they upheld the Soviet system and supported the Bolsheviks in the prosecution of the civil war. Two members of the party . . . [early in] the Bolshevik regime [were] the most successful military commanders of the new Government.

Unlike the Bolsheviks, however, the Left Social-Revolutionaries were not prepared to go to any lengths in their desire for peace. They had been opposed to the Brest-Litovsk Peace and, although they retained their representatives in the government, had never accepted it. They drew most of their support from the Ukraine, which had been occupied by the Germans, and the Germans were hard task-masters who had installed a dummy . . . Government and restored the land to the . . . landowners.

The Left Social-Revolutionaries had not accepted this situation and ever since the peace they had [waged] partisan war in the Ukraine against both the . . . landlords and the German troops of occupation. By both sides this miniature warfare was conducted with appalling cruelty. Goaded . . . to despair by the sufferings of their compatriots in the Ukraine, the Left Social-Revolutionaries protested . . . against the servile attitude of the Bolsheviks before the Germans. . . . As even the official Press had to admit, almost daily, some fresh German breach of the Brest Treaty, considerable point was given to the caustic comments on the cringing tone of Chicherin's[1] mild protests and the barely civil replies of the German Ambassador.

The real difference between the two Russian Government Parties was that the Left Social-Revolutionaries regarded Germany as the chief menace to the revolution. The Bolsheviks, or rather Lenin, for he alone saw clearly in this confused atmosphere, were determined to do nothing which might endanger the fragile fabric of their peace. They were now more afraid of Allied intervention than of further aggression by the Germans. The two parties were of course

[1] Chicherin was Commissar of Foreign Affairs.

at heart both anti-German and anti-Entente. The situation, however, was not without its comic side. While the Bolsheviks were publicly denouncing the activities of the Left-Social-Revolutionaries in the Ukraine, they were supplying them secretly with the funds for their partisan warfare against the Germans.

[Another] grievance . . . divided the two Parties. Among the peasants the chief supporters of the Left Social-Revolutionaries were the Kulaks. Partly . . . to strengthen their own position in the country, and partly to obtain more grain, the Bolsheviks had organised so-called Poverty Committees, . . . of poorer peasants, who were encouraged to attack the richer Kulaks and to seize their grain.

[Such] dissensions were bound to come to a head. Secretly, the Left Social-Revolutionaries began to . . . [plan] for the overthrow of the Bolshevik Government and for a renewal of the war with Germany. By July 4th, the opening day of the Fifth All-Russian Congress, the . . . situation was ripe for . . . explosion.

For this Congress the Left Social-Revolutionaries had made special preparations. In spite of Bolshevik manipulation at the elections, they [returned] about one-third of the 800 delegates present, and for the first time since November, 1917, the Bolsheviks were confronted, in their own carefully hedged-in Parliament, with a real official opposition.

The Congress took place in the Moscow Opera House. . . . On the right [sat] the Bolshevik majority, . . . mainly . . . soldiers . . . ; on the left the . . . opposition, whose brawny arms and loose shirts proclaim their village origin.

On the . . . stage, . . . sit the members of the Central Executive Committee— . . . about one hundred and fifty intellectuals, [mainly] Jews.

At a long table across the front of the stage is the Presidium, with Sverdloff, the President, in the centre. . . . At this table, too, sits Zinovieff, the President of the St. Petersburg Commune. . . . On the right of Sverdloff sit the Left Social-Revolutionary leaders; Kamkoff, . . . and . . . Maria

Spiridonova. . . . In 1906, while still a girl, she had [assassinated the] Councillor of the Government Administration of Tamboff. . . . [Her suicide] attempt . . . failed, and she was . . . raped by the Cossack soldiery. She had been condemned to death, but . . . on account of her age, the Tsar had changed her sentence to . . . penal servitude for life. [Her] almost fanatical expression . . . shows that her sufferings have affected her mind. . . .

Behind the Presidium table . . . are . . . the other members of the Central Executive Committee. . . . Here are to be found the real Bolshevik leaders. . . . They are present in full force. . . .

In the boxes and galleries . . . are the . . . supporters of the various delegates. Admission is by ticket only, and every entrance . . . is guarded by Lettish soldiers. . . . I [am] in the . . . box . . . with . . . members of the Allied Missions. Just above us are the representatives of the German, Turkish and Bulgarian Embassies. . . .

From the first the atmosphere is charged with electricity. . . .

The real battle comes on the second day. . . .

Spiridonova . . . rises, and . . . her first words [reveal] that this is no ordinary Congress, that today the Bolsheviks and the Left Social-Revolutionaries have come to the parting of the ways. . . . She bitterly attacks Lenin. "I accuse you," she says, addressing Lenin, "of betraying the peasants, of [using] them for your own ends. . . ." She appeals to her followers: "In Lenin's philosophy," she shrieks, "you are only . . . manure." Then [hysterically] she turns on the Bolsheviks: "Our other differences are only temporary, but on the peasant question we are prepared to give battle. When the peasants . . . are . . . oppressed . . . , in my hand you will still find the same . . . bomb. . . ." The end of the sentence is drowned in . . . applause. . . . Peasants stand up . . . and shake their fists at the Bolsheviks. Trotsky . . . tries to speak. He is howled down. . . . Sverdloff rings his bell and threatens to clear the theatre. . . . Then Lenin walks slowly to the front of the stage. On the way he pats Sverdloff on

the shoulder and tells him to put his bell away. Holding the lapels of his coat, he faces the audience—smiling, supremely self-confident. He is met with jeers. . . . He laughs good-humouredly. Then he holds up his hand, and . . . the tumult dies. With cold logic he replies . . . to the criticisms of the Left Social-Revolutionaries. . . . His remarks produce another storm. . . . Again Sverdloff . . . grasps his bell. Again Lenin raises his hand. His self-confidence is almost irritating. Then . . . he proceeds as . . . though he were addressing a Sunday-School meeting. To the taunts of servility towards the Germans he replies that the Left Social-Revolutionaries, in wishing to renew the war, are carrying out the policy of the Allied Imperialists. . . . He defends the Brest Treaty, points out how bitter a humiliation it has been, but underlines the grim doctrine of necessity. . . . Gradually the sheer personality of the man and the overwhelming superiority of his dialectics conquer his audience. . . . The speech ends in a wild outburst of cheering, which, although many of the Left Social-Revolutionaries must know of the preparations for the morrow, is not confined to the Bolsheviks.

The effect on the Left Social-Revolutionaries, however, is only temporary. Lenin is followed by Kamkoff, a brilliant orator. . . . He spares no one. . . . He turns towards . . . the Germans. . . . "The dictatorship of the proletariat," he thunders, "has [become] a dictatorship of Mirbach. In spite of all our warnings the policy of Lenin remains the same, and we are . . . not . . . independent . . . , but the lackeys of the German Imperialists, who have the audacity to show their faces even in this theatre."

. . . The Left Social-Revolutionaries are on their feet shouting . . . "Down with . . . the German butchers! . . ." Hurriedly Sverdloff rings his bell and declares the session closed. . . .

The debate . . . of the fifth of July was not . . . resumed on the . . . sixth. . . . The stage revolution of yesterday had transferred to the barricades. . . .

. . . The Left Social-Revolutionaries had assassinated Mirbach, hoping . . . to provoke Germany into restarting the war. . . .

In the meantime [they] had assembled such troops as they could persuade to support them. . . . For an hour they enjoyed a slight success. They arrested Derjinsky.[2] They captured the telegraph office. Then [they sent] telegrams all over the country to announce the success of their *coup d'état*. . . . So feeble was their military effort that the vast majority of the Moscow population never realised until the next day that an attempted revolution was in progress.

[In the meantime Trotsky] had called in two Lettish regiments from the suburbs.

[2] Chief of the Cheka.

. . . Within a few hours the Left Social-Revolutionary troops . . . laid down their arms. . . .

The only effect of this *opéra bouffe* . . . was to strengthen the . . . Bolsheviks and the peace party. The repercussion in the country was insignificant. A few days later Muravieff, the commander-in-chief of the Bolshevik forces on the Volga, attempted to move his troops against Moscow. By this time . . . the failure of the *coup d'état* in Moscow was known, and he was arrested by his own men. He ended his life . . . by shooting himself in the presence of the Simbirsk Soviet. Spiridonova and Cherepanoff were imprisoned in the Kremlin.

The Building of the Red Army*

Before the revolution our party had a military organization and it had a twofold aim: (1) to carry on revolutionary propaganda in the army and (2) to create within the army itself bases of operation for the overthrow of the State power. Since the revolutionary excitement seized the entire army, the organizational role of the Bolshevik cells in the regiments was not especially noticeable. But it was an important role because it enabled us to pick out small but determined elements, whose significance is so great at the critical moments of the revolution.

The revolution grew directly out of the war; one of its most important slogans was the end to war and this was accompanied by feelings of war-weariness and revulsion toward war. At the same time the revolution itself produced new military dangers which became even more menacing. Out of this grew the extraordinary external weakness of the revolution in its initial phase. The almost *absolute defencelessness of the revolution revealed itself* particularly

* SOURCE: L. Trotski, *Die Geburt der Roten Armee* (The Birth of the Red Army), Vienna, 1924, pp. 7-16.

during the Brest-Litovsk negotiations. Russians did not want to go to war, believing war had been ended for all time; the peasants took possession of the land; the workers expanded their organizations and seized the factories.

So there came about the gigantic experiment in pacifism in the Brest-Litovsk period. The Soviet Republic declared that she would not sign a peace of violence but would also not wage war and ordered demobilization. . . . The Germans resumed their offensive . . . and the masses began to understand that we had to defend ourselves with armed might. . . . General Hoffmann's offensive helped us to undertake the serious creation of the Red Army.

At first, however, we did not yet dare to introduce a forced draft. We did not have the political and organizational possibilities for mobilizing the soldiers just discharged. The army was built up on the voluntary principle. Naturally, along with the sacrifice-minded working class youth, the army also became full of numerous vagabond types. . . . Our best regiments . . . were unstable and unreliable. . . . The resistance strength of our regiments was minimal; one city after another, in the summer of 1918, was falling into the hands of the Czechoslovaks and the Russian counter-revolutionists who joined forces with them. Their center point was Samara. They conquered Simbirsk and Kazan. Nizhni-Novgorod was menaced. After crossing the Volga they were preparing their advance upon Moscow. At that moment (August, 1918) the Soviet Republic made extraordinary efforts toward the building and reinforcing of an army. The method of mass mobilization was employed by the Communists for the first time and a centralized apparatus of political direction and education was set up among the troops of the Volga front. Along with that, in the Moscow and in the Volga regions, attempts were made to mobilize several age classes of workers and peasants. Small companies of communist troops assured the execution of the mobilization. In the Volga guberniyas a strong regime was introduced which corresponded to the dimensions and the immediacy of the enemy threat. At the same time intensive agitation was carried on in speech and in print. The Communist troops moved from village to village. After the first waverings the mobilizations expanded greatly. These were accompanied by a hard struggle against the deserters and those social groups who inspired them— the rich peasants, . . . the clergy and the remnants of the old bureaucracy.

Communist workers of Petrograd, Moscow, Ivanovo-Vosnessensk, and so on were brought into the newly created troop units, and attained the status of commissars—i.e., unit revolutionary leaders and direct representatives of the Soviet power. The revolutionary tribunals, by way of a few judgments that set examples, showed . . . that the socialist fatherland, when in mortal danger, demanded absolute obedience. . . . Within a few weeks, a combination of agitation, organization and repression had . . . made a real army out of the wavering masses. [Kazan and Simbirsk were retaken by us in September.] . . .

In the meantime the military-administrative apparatus was being developed throughout the entire country in close connection with *guberniya*, district and local soviets. The territory of the Republic, carved out by the enemy, but still vast, was divided into sections, each of which was composed of several guberniyas. Thereby the needed centralization of administration was achieved.

The political and organizational difficulties were still immense. The psychological about-face from the destruction of the old army to the construction of the new was obtained at the cost of constant internal irritations and conflicts. The old army had adopted a system of elected soldier committees and elected officers who were actually subordinated to the committees. That system naturally had a revolutionary-political but not a military purpose. From the point of view of combat . . . it was a monstrous . . . system, though useful in its time to . . . rid the army of its upper class command personnel [and] dissolve the army. . . . The system of elections could in no way provide the revolutionary army with an effective and authoritative officer group. The Red Army was built from the top down, upon the principle of the dictatorship of the working class. The commanding personnel was chosen and controlled by the organs of the Soviet regime and the Communist Party. . . .

At the beginning the volunteer units served as a necessary and adequate weapon. The struggle against the counter-revolution which had not yet had time to coordinate its efforts and arm itself, was carried on by independent small units. Such a struggle required self sacrifice, initiative and independence. The more the war's arena broadened . . . the more the war demanded proper organization and discipline.

The indignation against the bureaucratic centralism of Tsarist Russia was a powerful force in the revolution. Districts, guberniyas . . . cities, tried as much as they could to assert their independence. The idea of "local power" took on a chaotic quality. . . . Among the masses this represented a healthy reaction to the old regime's stifling of all initiative. However, as the counter-revolution gathered its forces and as other dangers grew, these primitive autonomous tendencies became ever more dangerous, in political as well as in military matters. . . .

The year 1918 and a large part of 1919 passed in a . . . persistent struggle to create a *centralized disciplined army.* . . .

The selection and training of the *command* personnel offered the greatest difficulties. We had at our disposal . . . old traditional officers—leftovers from the war —in addition to the commanders whom the revolution had selected during the initial period of volunteer recruitment.

Of the old officers there remained with us the few persons who grasped or sensed the meaning of the new epoch, or the professional militarists, rigid, unprincipled fellows, who lacked the courage to join the Whites. Lastly there were some active counter-revolutionaries who had become turncoats.

With the first steps of the army's construction the question of what to do with the former officers of the tsar's army became acute. We needed them as . . . connoisseurs of the military art without whom we would have had to start *from scratch.* In that event our enemies would scarcely have given us the opportunity to bring our self-education to the required level. We would have been unable to construct a centralized military apparatus without calling upon the numerous representatives of the old officer class. Now they belonged to the army not as representatives of the old ruling class but as office holders of the new revolutionary class. Naturally, many deceived us and went over to the foe and took part in mutinies, but by and large the spirit of their class opposition was broken. Nevertheless they were still bitterly hated by the simple masses and this issue became a source of outraged opinions. However, we did not need such officer personnel among small local troop units [where they might have been lynched]. In the final analysis we wanted to break the resistance of the counter-revolutionary elements of the old officer class in gradually assuring its loyal elements the opportunities for work in the Red Army. . . .

The most important role in the creation of the command apparatus was that played by the institution of the *commissars.* These were supplied by the revolutionary workers, the communists, and partly—in the initial period—by the left S.R.'s (until July, 1918). The role of commander was thus in a certain sense divided. The commander retained the purely military leadership. The political-educational work was concentrated in the commissars. Above all, the commissar was the direct representative of the Soviet regime in the army. The task of the commissars was that of creating conditions whereby—without hindering the purely military function of the chief or lessening his command authority—he could assure that such authority could not be used against the interests of the revolution. . . . From the ranks of the commissars came many revolutionary commanders.

At the very outset we undertook the task of creating a network of *military school institutes.* At the beginning they revealed the general weakness of the military organization. The brief course of a few months did not turn out real commanders but only average Red Army men. Since at that time masses of completely untrained men were sent into battle, these briefly trained Red Army men were given command posts and even became company leaders. We eagerly sought out the former noncommissioned officers of the tsar's army. They for the most part came from the propertied elements of city and country and were largely the literate sons of the richer peasant families. They bore an innate hostility toward the golden epaulettes of the noble and intellectual officers and stood apart from that group. They gave us many outstanding commanders and army chiefs. . . . But this group also provided the counter-revolutionary mutineers and the White Army with many commanders. . . .

The role of *propaganda* in the Red Army is known to all. The political work that preceded every stage of the political and military development required a much ramified army apparatus. Of that the most important organs were the above-mentioned commissars. The bourgeois press of Western Europe distorts the matter by describing propaganda as a kind of diabolical invention of the Bolsheviks. Propaganda plays an enormous part in all armies of the world. The political apparatus of the bourgeois army is much more powerful and much richer than ours. The advantage of our propaganda lies in its content. Our propaganda closes the ranks of the Red Army but splits those of the opposition, not because of any special techniques . . . but because of the communistic idea which is its essence. We advertise this military secret openly and everywhere without fear that our opponents will plagiarize it.

The technical equipment of the Red Army mirrored . . . the general economic situation of the country. In the first period of the revolution it had at its disposal the material heritage of the imperialist war. That was . . . colossal but also very chaotic. There was too much of certain items, too little of others. Besides, we didn't really know what we had. The top administrative officials [of the former government] concealed the little about which they knew. The "local authority" [when the dissolution of central power began] seized whatever was in its territory. The leaders of the revolutionary volunteer forces supplied themselves with whatever came to hand. Station masters missent whole carloads of ammunition and entire trains failed to arrive at their destinations. The initial period also saw a dreadful wasting of the supplies of the imperialist war. Individual battalions or regiments dragged parts of armored equipment and airplanes with them while lacking bayonets and even cartridges for their guns. War industry was at a standstill as early as the end of 1917. Only in 1919, as the old supplies began to run out, was work begun to restore war industry. In 1920 practically all of industry worked for the war. We had no supplies. Every gun, every bullet, every pair of boots went directly from the machine . . . to the front. There were situations—and they lasted for weeks—when we had to count every bullet, and the late arrival of an extra munitions train meant the retreat of whole divisions. . . .

Although the prolongation of the civil war led to the collapse of the economy, the supplying of the army improved steadily; partly because of the intense industrial effort, partly because of the better organization of the military economy itself. . . .

The unity of the army and its power grew steadily. At the beginning not only peasants, but workers, too, did not want to join the army. Only a very thin layer of selfless proletarians consciously accepted the task of creating the armed might of the Soviet Republic. . . . The mood of the peasants was always wavering. Whole regiments of peasants—true, they were usually quite unready politically and technically—surrendered without a struggle in the early phases [of the civil war]. Then, when the Whites enlisted them under their banner, they came back to our side. Sometimes the peasant masses sought to express a certain independence and hid out from Reds and Whites in the forests and created their "green" troops. But their disunity and political helplessness doomed them to defeat in advance. . . . The peasant mass swayed first to this then to that side. In the end the peasants supported the working class. In the backward guberniyas, as in Kursk and Voronezh, where there were thousands and thousands of deserters, the mere appearance of troops on the guberniyas' borders . . . swept the deserting swarms of yesterday into the Red Army. The peasant supported the worker against the landlord and the capitalist. In this sociological fact lay the final reason for our victories.

The White Catastrophes*

Admiral Koltchak and His Army

We have seen how in May and June, 1918, the Czechs, passing eastward through Siberia, turned back and, seizing the trans-Siberian, captured the Volga towns, whence they were with difficulty driven by the Soviet in the early autumn of 1918. We have glanced at the welter of Siberian White "Governments" which finally, in November, 1918, were overthrown by Koltchak's *coup d'état,* the Admiral thereby making himself "Supreme Ruler" of Russia, in which capacity he was acknowledged by Denikin and all the other White generals. . . .

. . . Had there been any real popular feeling in favour of an anti-Bolshevik government, Koltchak must have succeeded. He held the . . . only main artery across Siberia—the trans-Siberian; he was based upon the open sea at Vladivostok, and through that port eight nations poured men, money and munitions to his aid. . . .

. . . With all this . . . Koltchak was unable to maintain himself, and the reason is not far to seek. The civil war in Siberia was no civil war at all in the proper sense of the word. It was a war fomented and maintained by Britain, France, America and Japan for their own purposes under the pretext of aiding the Russians to set their house in order. . . . U.S.A. Commander-in-Chief in Siberia, General W. S. Graves, writes:

"At no time while I was in Siberia was there enough popular support behind Koltchak in Eastern Siberia for him or the people supporting him to have lasted one month if all Allied supports had been removed." . . .

Koltchak was suspected, not without reason, of Tsarist leanings. Certainly he was entirely devoid of any bias in favour of

* Source: A. Gordon, *Russian Civil War,* London, Cassell & Co., 1937, pp. 241-267.

democracy. He hated and in return was hated by the Social Revolutionaries, who at that time were far and away the largest political body in Siberia. From the first his regime was distrusted and detested by all but the military clique who created it.

The French looked upon it with deep suspicion, scenting British intrigue. . . .

The Czechs—the backbone of the armed forces in Siberia—were profoundly hostile, and on November 20 the Czech National Council published a manifesto expressing their hostility. "The *coup d'état*"—so ran the document—"goes against those elementary laws which should be the foundation of all governments. We who are fighting for the ideal of liberty . . . , will not give our help or sympathy to *coups d'état* which are in opposition to those principles."

But deepest and most ominous of all was the hostility of the common people, who received this new dictatorship with a mistrust and alarm that grew in intensity. . . . All the old vices of the Tsarist regime came back. . . . Floggings and shootings once more became the basis of army organization. The officers gambled, drank, and stole military supplies, whilst the men starved.

The anti-democratic colour of the new government became clearer every day. Representatives of workmen were no longer admitted to official receptions, and the agrarian policy of the government plainly showed that the clock had been set back to pre-revolutionary times.

Meanwhile a White Terror was inaugurated, far worse than anything perpetrated by the Reds. . . . Not merely suspected Bolsheviks, but Socialists of any kind, even Liberals and Democrats, were slaughtered in thousands. . . . In one village on the Amur a number of intelligentsia—Democrats—had taken refuge. . . . Koltchak's governor . . . encircled the place with White troops; a hole was made in the ice on the river and the entire population driven under the ice.

Everywhere the peasants were plundered, shot, hanged, thrashed and deprived of their land. Whole villages were exterminated. . . . In four days (January 17-21, 1920) 800 political prisoners were murdered . . . at one place, . . . some by rifle fire, some by the sword, some by poison. Some were even burnt alive at the stake by way of variety, "to prevent the executioners from being bored."

Koltchak himself was not the instigator of the worst of these excesses but rather their victim. Surrounded . . . by a gang of the worst types . . . he . . . was tortured by ill health. . . . Racked with pain, he was heavily drugged with morphia. His mental faculties failed. . . .

. . . Soon the bitterness of the Czechoslovaks . . . became so acute that . . . their civilian chief at Vladivostok, publicly pronounced the new regime to be . . . a government of assassins. The Supreme Ruler was informed that the Czechs would no longer support him and that it was their intention to quit Siberia forever. It was only with the greatest difficulty that they were induced to take over the task of policing the railway pending the arrival of transports at Vladivostok. . . .

This sick misguided man, who would sit for hours on end under the influence of morphia, muttering wildly to himself, was for a time held out by the British as the one strong man who was going to save Russia. . . .

During the winter of 1918-1919 forced mobilization took place throughout Siberia. "The methods adopted were of so harsh a character that recruiting expeditions resembled punitive expeditions rather than the effort of a friendly government to win the support of its subjects." The process placed at Koltchak's disposal a force some 200,000 strong. Arms and munitions were plentiful: 100,000 rifles and 200 guns were received from Britain alone. Thus backed, the Supreme Ruler saw himself, as Denikin in like case a few months later was to do, marching irresistibly into the Kremlin. The parallel was even closer. Koltchak, like Denikin, spurned the wiser counsel of his one brilliant field commander. Gaida, the meteoric young Czech who at the time commanded the Siberian armies, begged the Admiral to dig himself in and to consolidate and organize the vast and chaotic territory over which he ruled. Koltchak would have none of it. His one cry was: "To the Volga!"

On March 1, 1919, Gaida perforce gave the order for the 800-mile front to advance. Although for a while the offensive was brilliantly successful, it was doomed before it began, notwithstanding that in numbers and in equipment alike the Whites held an overwhelming advantage. But whilst the Reds were a . . . fanatical and homogeneous fighting force, the Whites were apathetic . . . and disgracefully served by their officers. . . .

A . . . correspondent of the *Manchester Guardian* . . . wrote: "The majority of the officers had a rooted objection both to fighting and working . . . the only martial ardour which they showed was exhibited in the restaurants of Vladivostok and Omsk when, late in the evening, they sometimes covered the members of the orchestra with their revolvers and made them play *'God Save the Tsar.'* . . . Many officers swindled the men of their food and clothes in the good old way."

At the time of the offensive Omsk was crowded with officers. The staff alone numbered 2,000. Officers openly evaded being sent to the front, even . . . jumping off the train after it had set out. British officers on the spot were utterly disgusted. . . . Major Hodges writes . . . : "I think most of us were secretly in sympathy with the Bolsheviks after our experiences with the corruption and cowardice of the other side. It was revolting to see wounded men dragging their way from station to hospital over dirty streets for perhaps a mile or two while officers rode scornfully by in droshkies or motor cars."

Corruption and peculation were on an enormous scale. Of the vast quantities of clothing and equipment that came up from Vladivostok very little ever reached the front. In the summer of 1919 half a million caps were indented for—and duly charged to the Treasury. When Koltchak inspected the front in July he found the men still wearing . . . winter caps of fur. Not a single one of the others had reached the line. Gaida's army was drawing rations from Omsk for 275,000 men. The actual strength was 100,000. . . .

Gaida commanded the northern sector in person, and here the peasants over whose fields the advance proceeded received decent treatment, thanks to the Czech general's democratic instincts. Elsewhere along the front looting, flogging, hanging, and terror marked the advance of the White armies.

The line rolled forward an average depth of 200 miles. By mid-April Gaida was nearly at Kazan, the centre nearly at Samara. . . . Presently the Siberian armies, backed as they were by so rotten and chaotic a base, and with the infuriated peasantry in rebellion behind them, gave way. Disgusted by their leaders and sick with the hopelessness of their cause, an entire division of the White Army went over to the Bolsheviks early in May. . . .

Perm fell, then Ekaterinburg. By August the Whites were back across the Tobol river and the Soviet armies—massed now against Koltchak—were advancing 16 miles a day. The Siberian Army was . . . disintegrating. Only by sheer military genius could Gaida prevent his entire northern army from being encircled. . . .

Koltchak chose this moment to break with his brilliant subordinate. Instead of proper supplies—most of which never got further than Omsk—the Supreme Ruler had been sending, to Gaida's disgust, cases of Anti-Semitic leaflets to be scattered from aeroplanes. He also objected strongly to the way in which Gaida was allowing the peasants to retain possession of their land.

A furious quarrel took place between the two men on July 12, 1919, on which the Admiral . . . lost control and screamed insults at the young Czech leader.

"What else could one expect of a so-called officer who has never even been to a military academy?"

"And what about you?" Gaida shouted

back. "Because you once commanded a few ships do you think you can govern an empire?" . . .

[On November 15, 1919] the Red Army marched into Omsk, [capturing] enormous stores of material and munitions, as well as 40,000 troops. . . .

. . . The Bolsheviks sent a sarcastic message to General Knox thanking him for the generosity of the British in equipping the Soviet troops so handsomely!

The Defeats of Yudenich and Denikin

In the high summer of 1919, yet another White Government—the "North-Western Provisional Government of Russia"—was set up . . . on the eastern fringe of Esthonia, by another of the ex-Tsarist generals, Yudenich, acting in cooperation with Koltchak and in concert with the Allies. . . . It would be truer to say that the new government was the direct creation of the British. . . .

The moment for this further attack on the Soviet was as well chosen as the place. Denikin was advancing upon Moscow with terrifying rapidity, whilst almost the entire mass of the Red armies had been poured across the Volga to crush Koltchak. The Soviet western front was but lightly held. . . .

. . . Yudenich launched his attack on Petrograd on October 11, 1919. . . .

Within five days Yudenich had swept forward so swiftly as to have reached Gatchina, less than 30 miles from Petrograd. A desperate situation now confronted the Soviet. . . .

The city itself was in dire confusion. Zinoviev, the President of the Petrograd Soviet, . . . was in a state of panic. . . . Everyone in authority was running round in little circles. . . .

But the common people were . . . ready to save their city. . . . They only needed a lead. Trotsky flung himself into the task like a demon. In a fiery broadcast to the world the War Commissar trumpeted defiance to the "pack of bourgeois curs who are worrying the body of Soviet Russia from all sides."

[Soon a] change came over the scene. . . . Working men and women in thousands flocked out of the city to dig trenches, erect barricades, fix wire. Every man who could carry arms and had arms to carry was mobilized and flung against Yudenich's lines at Tsarskoe Selo. . . . There was no quarter . . . no prisoners. . . . Yudenich . . . counter-attacked . . . with all the strength of his British tanks and guns. But against him were . . . workmen and students and peasants, dying for an ideal. With bare hands they stormed the tanks. . . .

Meanwhile, the British naval flotilla in the Baltic was rendering yeoman service to the Whites [by bombarding Red positions]. . . .

In [an] Order of the Day, Trotsky thus commented on this achievement to his troops:

On all the fronts you meet the hostile plots of the English. The counter-revolutionary troops shoot you with English guns. In (White) depots you find supplies of English manufacture. The prisoners you have captured are dressed in uniforms made in England. The women and children of Archangel and Astrakhan are maimed and killed by English airmen. . . . But even to-day, when we are engaged in a bitter fight with Yudenich, the hireling of England, I demand that you never forget that there are two Englands. Besides the England of profits, of violence . . . , there is the England of labour, . . . of high ideals. . . . It is the . . . England of the Stock Exchange . . . that is fighting us. The England of labour and the people is with us.

Three weeks later . . . Trotsky was decorated with the "Order of the Red Banner" . . . for saving Petrograd. . . .

All this time . . . the advance of the Volunteer Army upon [Moscow] was acquiring . . . spectacular momentum. . . .

Denikin, . . . was at the zenith of his power. . . . British supplies . . . poured into the Black Sea bases. . . . Vast quantities of it were quietly looted by the White generals and turned into cash.

So through the late summer and early autumn of 1919 the iron flood rolled nearer

and nearer to Moscow. On the very day (October 16, 1919) that Yudenich reached the furthest point of his advance on Petrograd, Denikin's centre reached the high-water mark of its advance on Moscow . . . just past Orel. The Whites were now less than 200 miles from their goal, and the press of the whole world daily predicted the inevitable end. . . . In Moscow all was gloom. . . .

* * *

Whatever [strategic] mistakes the Reds . . . made, those of Denikin and his White colleagues were still more catastrophic. Wrangel, the one brilliant commander among the White generals, was hobbled by the jealousy of Denikin, and left behind to eat his heart out at Tsaritsyn on the extreme right of the 1,200-mile White front. . . . Wrangel comments bitterly in his *Memoirs*: "[Denikin's Army] took Kiev, Kursk, and Orel. . . . All Southern Russia, with its wealth . . . was in . . . Denikin's power, and we heard of new successes daily. But . . . we . . . had bitten off far more than we could chew. Our front was too long in comparison with the number of our forces, we had no organized bases, and no strongholds in our rear."

. . . More ominous . . . was the presence of a hostile countryside behind the lines of the White armies. . . . The population of 30,000,000 was seething with unrest. Even those who distrusted Bolshevism grew to distrust the White regime still more, whilst the peasants, fed on a diet of looting, flogging and hanging by the White generals, sickened to a mad hatred that flared into open revolt at every opportunity. Roving bands of brigands, under wild leaders like Makhno and Gregoriev, carried a predatory warfare across the thrice-ravaged lands of the south, burnt stores, sacked towns and cut the railways. Red partisans harried the lines of communication.

As the advance continued, the muddle into which Denikin's organization had drifted grew indescribable. The further the centre drew ahead from its base the worse became the chaos. A lurid light is thrown on the picture by one of Wrangel's dispatches to the White Commander-in-Chief:

The continual advance has reduced the Army's effective force. The rear has become too vast. . . . The war is becoming to some a means of growing rich; re-equipment has degenerated into pillage and peculation. Each unit strives to secure as much as possible for itself and seizes everything that comes to hand. What cannot be used on the spot is sent back to the interior and sold at a profit; . . . many officers are away on prolonged missions, busy selling and exchanging loot. The Army is . . . fast becoming a collection of tradesmen and profiteers. Nearly all the officers have enormous sums of money; . . . there has been an outbreak of debauchery, gambling and wild orgies.

Denikin himself describes how, after a smashing defeat of the 8th and 9th Soviet armies, the Cossack cavalry, instead of exploiting their success, turned back: "Long files of wagons laden with booty trekked to the Don villages, thousands of fighting men trailing behind. Soon only about 2,000 men remained in the ranks."

Yet at the very times these orgies of lust and robbery were going on, with White generals voyaging about in their luxury trains [entertained by] orchestras and vaudeville performers, . . . the most ghastly scenes of suffering were being enacted behind the White lines. . . . Wrangel . . . reports: . . . "I found the railroads blocked by trains and abandoned ambulances without any staff, but full of sick and wounded who had eaten nothing for . . . days. . . . Crowds of refugees . . . are . . . dying of cold and hunger."

It was upon this welter of muddle and misery that the final herculean effort of the Soviet forces suddenly descended in a series of attacks. . . . The retreat became a rout. . . . By December 9 Wrangel—to whom Denikin had at last been reluctantly compelled to give the command in the centre in place of the drunken Mai-Maevsky—was forced to report: "The bitter truth is that there is no longer an Army." . . .

It was neither superior generalship nor preponderance in men or munitions that defeated Denikin. . . . The two armies were roughly similar in number, whilst in munitions and equipment the Whites had the overwhelming advantage, backed as they were [by the British]. In leadership Denikin's armies should have had the advantage, commanded as they were by the cream of the Tsarist generals and . . . officers, whilst the leaders opposed to them were mostly mere amateurs like Voroshilov. . . .

The crushing defeat of the Whites was not even wholly due—though this was a [vital] factor—to the qualities of the . . . heads of the Soviet State—the stubborn cunning of Stalin, the brilliance and audacity of Trotsky, and, above all, the master brain . . . of Lenin.

The victory was mainly won by the common people.

Whether behind the White lines or within the girdle of steel where the Reds still held sway, the masses were the great obstacle to Denikin's progress. For this the White commander was himself largely to blame. It was so obvious that he was a mere instrument of the old regime, and that his victory would be the signal for the immediate return of the landlords and the industrialists. During the years since the overthrow of Tsarism the peasants had in effect become the owners of the soil they tilled. Denikin's victory meant its return to the former owners. This in itself was sufficient to make deadly enemies of the millions of peasants of the South, nor could all the arguments of the White generals with whip . . . or rifle-butt gainsay it. Indeed, the crueller the oppression of the Whites the more stubborn the resistance of the peasants and the more embarrassing their guerrilla attacks on the long lines of communication.

Working with and through the peasants within the occupied territories was the powerful leaven of the proletariat especially those who—small in number but potent in influence—were consciously Communists. In spite of every sort of oppression, the industrial quarters of all the cities in Denikin's power were seething centres of hostility, forever bursting into paralysing strikes or open revolt that crippled the nerve-centre of the White organization.

On the other hand, the workers and peasants in the Soviet territories fused into a . . . unity. . . . Politics entered into it relatively little. It was a question of survival. Blockaded by land and sea, shut off from every source of supply save those within their shrinking confines, the Russian people saw the fight with Denikin as a . . . choice between life and death, and acted accordingly.

This feeling was [skillfully] played upon by the Soviet chiefs. Propaganda was developed into a fine art. Instead of concealing defeats, the Council of People's Commissars blazoned them abroad. Pictorial diagrams showed an illiterate population the daily constriction of the steel girdle that was crushing the very life out of Russia. Day by day the people saw the advance of the machine guns . . . that were to purge them of their treason to the comity of capitalism. Every art of the agitator and the propagandist was devoted to exploiting the will to live of a people to whom a White victory meant death by violence and a long continuation of the blockade, death by starvation or pestilence.

With their backs to the wall the entire mass of workers gave their lives into the keeping of Lenin and his lieutenants. Never in modern history has a nation been so mobilized for resistance, so welded into a vast military machine. There existed the most complete . . . centralization. Under War Communism every man, every kopek, every ounce of material came under the absolute dominion of the Council of People's Commissars—which meant Lenin.

With many blunders, with heartbreaking sacrifices, with nerve-racking disasters the Soviet machine organized itself for victory. . . . The machine moved swifter and swifter. . . . As the year 1919 died, its momentum grew irresistibly. The New Year saw it sweep the last of the White forces from Russian soil, save for the distant peninsula of the Crimea, where the shattered remnants of Denikin's armies, deserted by their leader, made a last attempt [under Wrangel] to regain Russia.

Communist Saturdays*

The *Pravda* . . . of May 17 [1919] published an article by Comrade A. J. . . . This article is so important that we reproduce it here in full. . . .

The letter of the Central Committee of the . . . Party on working in a *revolutionary way* gave a powerful impetus . . . to the Communists. The . . . enthusiasm carried many Communist railway workers to the front, but the majority of them could not leave their . . . posts or find new forms of working in a revolutionary way. Reports from the localities about the tardiness with which the work of mobilization was proceeding and the prevalence of red tape compelled the Moscow-Kazan Railway subdistrict to turn its attention to the performance of railway services. . . . Owing to the shortage of labour and the inadequate intensity of work urgent orders and repairs to locomotives were being held up. At a meeting of Communists and sympathizers of the Moscow-Kazan Railway subdistrict held on May 7, the question was raised of passing from words to deeds in helping to achieve victory over Kolchak. The following resolution was moved:

"In view of the grave . . . situation, the Communists and sympathizers . . . must spur themselves on again . . . and put in six extra hours of manual labour on Saturday. . . . [Since] Communists should not spare their health and life for the gains of the revolution, this work should be performed without pay. *Communist Saturdays* to be introduced throughout the subdistrict and to continue until complete victory. . . ."

* SOURCE: V. I. Lenin, *Selected Works* (2 vols.), Moscow, 1951, II, Part 2, pp. 214-220.

After some hesitation, the resolution was adopted unanimously.

On Saturday, May 10, at 6 P.M., the Communists and sympathizers turned up to work like soldiers. . . .

The . . . team spirit . . . during work [was] extraordinary. When the workers, clerks and head office employees . . . caught hold of a forty-pood wheel tire of a passenger locomotive and, like industrious ants, rolled it into place, one's heart was filled with . . . joy at the sight of this collective effort, one's conviction that the victory of the working class was unshakable was strengthened. . . .

When the work was finished . . . a hundred Communists, weary, but with . . . joy in their eyes, greeted their success with the solemn strains of the "Internationale." . . .

How the work is done by these communist subbotniks[1] is described by Comrade A. Dyachenko in an article in *Pravda* of June 7, entitled "Notes of a Subbotnik Worker." . . .

It was with great joy that I got ready with my comrade to do our subbotnik "bit" on the decision of the railway subdistrict committee . . . and . . . give my head a rest and my muscles a bit of exercise. . . . We were told off to the railway carpenter shop. We got there . . . and found that there were thirty of us.

[1] Saturday workers.

. . . And in front of us lay a "monster," a steam boiler weighing no less than six or seven hundred poods; our job was to . . . move it . . . a quarter or a third of a verst, to its base. We began to have our doubts. . . . However, we started on the job. Some comrades placed wooden rollers under the boiler, attached two ropes to it, and we began to tug away. . . . The boiler gave way reluctantly, but at length it budged. We were delighted. After all, there were so few of us. . . . For nearly two weeks this boiler had resisted the efforts of thrice our number of non-Communist workers. . . . We worked . . . strenuously, rhythmically, to the command of our "gangboss,"—"one, two, three," and the boiler kept on rolling. . . . It was getting dark, but we had yet to overcome a small hillock. . . . Our arms ached, our palms burned, we were hot and pulled for all we were worth—and making headway. The "manager" stood round and somewhat shamed by our success, clutched at a rope. "Lend a hand, it's time you did!" A Red Army man was watching our labours; in his hands he held a concertina. What was he thinking? Who were these people? Why should they work on Saturday when everybody was at home? I . . . said to him: "Comrade, play us a jolly tune. We are not bum workers, we are real Communists. Don't you see how fast the work is going under our hands? We are not lazy, we are pulling for all we are worth!" In response, the Red Army man carefully put his concertina on the ground and hastened to grab at a rope end. . . .

A Journalist in a Soviet Prison*

In this old Czarist prison [thousands] of politicals and criminals are herded together. One meets former dignitaries of Church and State, senior Czarist Officers, revolutionaries of all sorts, savants, artists, factory

* SOURCE: "The Case of Mrs. Stan Harding," *The Nineteenth Century and After*, Vol. 92, July-September, 1922, pp. 1-15. Mrs. Harding, a British subject, was arrested on a false charge by the Soviet Government in June, 1920, was refused a trial, and was thrown into prison.

workers, prostitutes and prison spies. The Buturky is like a great hotel where people from all parts of the country are constantly coming and going—though not at their own discretion.

Many Buturky inmates had not the least idea what their offence was, or even if they were supposed to be "criminals" or "politicals." [One woman, ignorant for months of the charges against her, tried to hang herself. Worried about the fate of her four little children, she] refused to be comforted by the assurance that they had *perhaps* been taken to some home for "counter-revolutionary" babies. [An] old peasant woman had been arrested on the mere allegation that she was the wife of a man she had never seen. This poor old peasant shrilled her wrongs till we wearied of her. Was it our fault that it was a crime to be or not to be the wife of Pavlo Sergevitch?

Among my fellow prisoners were many men and women devoted to the cause of freedom who had suffered long imprisonment in Czarist days; some still bore the marks of [their former] fetters. Few of us in England realise the incomparable tragedy of these people. They breathed for a moment the fresh air of freedom after the downfall of Czardom; then [came] the Bolsheviks [and] they were flung back into their [dungeons], or, if they managed to elude arrest, returned to the old life of dodging the sleuth and the *agent provocateur*. They often compared Czardom with what they called "this Pharaonian Communism." "The Che Ka," they said, "maintains an army of agents which compares with the political police [of] Czarist times. [But it] shoots and arrests people with a recklessness never known in the old days. No proof is needed; suspicion is enough. The Terror is far, far greater, so that people who would have scorned to save themselves by betraying others do so now. One must fear treachery far more; under Bolshevism it has been exalted into a civic virtue." And this is the real atrocity of Bolshevism—this miasma of lying and cowardice which emanates from the Che Ka is the ruin of Russian character by the Terror.

I know of women [jailed for long periods] in the hope [that they'd] betray the whereabouts of some relative. One prisoner, an old Czarist officer, who often put in a good word for the Bolsheviks, said to me: "What will you? Every absolutist State has its own methods." He said the Soviet has the strongest government since the Roman Empire, and would, he hoped, cure Russian intellectuals of the West European notions on the freedom of the Press.

Trade Union officials were in great num-

bers at Buturky. [Also numerous were] factory workers arrested in connection with the Soviet elections. Many had received a police warning on the eve of some election that if anything went *wrong*—in short, if there was any opposition to the Communist candidate—they would be *held responsible*. And they found themselves in prison as the result of some such electoral "hitch."

The Bolsheviks [claim to] represent the enlightened proletariat of the town, as opposed to the backward peasant masses. [In] fact the town proletariat has dwindled [rapidly] under Bolshevism; the workmen have fled to the country, where the tyranny of the Che Ka is less formidable. Let the Bolsheviks support their claim to represent the city workers by permitting elections with secret balloting. The Communists [discount] the validity of representative institutions in other countries [by pointing to] the influence of a money-controlled Press on electoral results. In Russia no Press except the Bolshevik Press has printed a word for years, so that if their theory is correct they should sweep the country. They know that their rule could face no such test.

At this prison I gained some understanding of the causes which have enabled Lenin to rule Russia so long.

In 1917 the army sold its tired soul for the promise of peace—oh, the fallacy!—to Lenin, who was thus able to possess himself of the machinery of State, which he used relentlessly to crush his opponents. The Che Ka absorbed the Okhrana (the Czarist political police), and *this amalgamated Czarist and Bolshevik police possessed between them the dossiers of every one in Russia who concerned himself . . . with politics.* [Thus] the Bolsheviks were able to [seize] all [their] political opponents, who, they tell us, are such "poor stuff." I believe that the race which dies for ideas is more numerous in Russia than anywhere else. [There are] many men and women willing to undergo martyrdom [and], if necessary, to expose their families to [police] persecution; but they have been disorganised, and exterminated by the ferocious persecution which the Soviet Government has undertaken in the interest of unity of political dogma. Now, the main asset of Bolshevik power is the fact that some millions of people may be expected to die of hunger in Russia, and that the Red Army and the special regiments of the Che Ka do not mean to be among those millions; they know that as long as the Bolshevik dictatorship is prolonged they will occupy a favoured position as the instrument of that dictatorship, and that their food situation will be the best in Russia.

Here in England people sometimes suggest that, if only we recognised the Bolsheviks, their policy would [become] more liberal; that some sort of constitutional government might be evolved, and then perhaps one day Lenin and Trotsky would resign in deference to the vote of [a] representative assembly. The Russian rulers might amnesty the Russian nation—and the Russian nation might amnesty its present rulers.

The Bolsheviks themselves have no such illusions. I often think of a remark made by my incognito [Che Ka agent], in a conversation on the train during my journey into Russia. Speaking of the Paris Commune he said: "And if *we* fall the people will stick pins in our eyes." Listen to Trotsky on his resignation: "If we go, we will slam the door for the world to hear!" That at least rings true.

They do not mean to go.

The existence of any sort of representative institutions such as might even be created by genuine Soviet elections would bring about the downfall of the present rulers. The abolition of the Che Ka would have the same effect. Therefore the Soviet will never allow genuine elections, and the Che Ka, though it may take fresh *aliases,* will remain, and will continue [to crush] all who oppose the Bolshevik dictatorship; it will concentrate its terror in turn on the professional classes, the trade unions of the town, the peasants and the priests.

Nor do I believe that the Bolsheviks would long tolerate the situation that would be brought about by granting to foreigners important concessions affecting basic industries and services, such as mining, forestry, and transport. Such concessions would create large classes of skilled workmen, who would owe to the foreign concessionaire their salvation from the surrounding misery, and who would be less amenable to the dictates of the central Government. My experience of Soviet faith convinces me that, rather than allow a situation to develop which would jeopardise their power, they would break any pledge and cancel any concessions.

They rule by terror—no Russian Communist disputes the fact—and the end of the Terror would be the end of their rule.

A Letter from Moscow*

Moscow, mid-June, 1920

. . . The Russian worker, whether day laborer or intellectual, receives a monthly wage of 2400 to 4200 rubles and, in most factories, workshops and government offices, also gets some soup and grits or vegetables daily. Naturally, he can't exist on

* SOURCE: "Briefe aus Sowjetrussland, Juni, 1920." (Letters from Soviet Russia, June, 1920), *Die Grenzboten,* 79 Jahrgang, Drittes Vierteljahr, Berlin, 1920, pp. 15-19.

such a ration and is forced to buy victuals from black market dealers at the so-called *Sukharevka* [second-hand market]. How much his wages are worth is shown by the following black market prices: one pound of black bread; 400 rubles, . . . one pound of butter; 3,000 rubles. . . . A pair of boots cost 15 to 20,000 rubles, a suit almost 100,-000 rubles. . . .

A year ago the prices in Moscow averaged a fraction of what they are today. The former bourgeoisie have, in the meantime, been completely wiped out, but the Bolsheviks have realized that they can achieve nothing without specialists. On the other hand, hunger has forced the bourgeoisie to work for the Bolsheviks. Perhaps it is the influence of former bourgeoisie employed in Soviet bureaus that pushes the Bolsheviks more rightward with every passing day. So, recently, free-trading has been permitted in the so-called home-work shops. In such shops, in which only home work may be sold, one can of course buy anything, . . . French perfumes, latest model dresses, liquor, food, and the like. At the last congress [of Soviets] in Moscow the resolution was adopted that the once so-favored revolutionary committees and communist controls in the factories be abolished and the personal director system be re-introduced. Naturally the old specialists are the new directors. The latest decree of the Bolsheviks was the declaration of furniture as private property. . . . Less than a year ago they were still asserting . . . that furniture was common property.

The *Sukharevka* sells everything. . . . [There the former rich] are selling their last items. . . . It is typical of the proletariat that the most beautiful grand piano sells for half the price of an ordinary phonograph and that both can be had for a trifle compared with the astronomical prices of food. The formerly richest and most spoiled are now satisfied if they get some black bread and potatoes each day. . . . An acquaintance of mine, formerly . . . owner of a palace in Moscow, . . . was given, as his place of residence, the bathroom of his former home. . . .

The Bolsheviks are making great efforts for the schools. They try above all to offer something to the proletariat and the utmost is done for children from four to eight. These are taken care of in kindergartens where the teachers have them making figures in clay, and the like. These children get the best of foods—caviar, sausage, . . . butter . . . in sufficient quantities. They get good clothing and free shoes and laundry. They even provided the kindergartens with fine porcelain and . . . beautiful linens and carpets from the mansions of the rich. . . . Tons of the porcelain are smashed by the children. The linens, napkins and the like are replaced by the teachers with ordinary rags and sold on the second-hand market. . . . The schools are not really educational institutions because nobody thinks about learning, but only about feeding. Hygienic conditions are . . . disregarded, for the children come to school . . . with collars of lice around their necks. . . . The scarcity of soap makes it impossible for the parents to wash the children or the children's clothes. In addition, the parents work so hard and come home at night so tired that they are not capable, as before, of caring for their children.

Some of the peasants say they are very satisfied with the Soviet regime. But the peasant is not better off than the city folk. He has enough to eat. . . . He has trunks full of money (old tsarist money; he wants no part of Soviet money) because he can't for any price buy the things he needs for his daily work,—sickles, plows, . . . horseshoes, farm machinery, etc. He has no petroleum, no matches (a box of matches cost 100 rubles for which one can buy a piano). He is harassed by the Committees of the Poor which the Bolsheviks initially installed in each village. He has seen how the commissars of the Committees, almost all of whom were selected from among the former drunkards and idlers, have gradually enriched themselves at the cost of surrounding landowners. So each of these commissars . . . has a piano in his shack and satin and plush furniture in his . . . stables or pig pen, whereas the hard-working peasant, rich on paper, has in truth become very poor. Anything he grows more than he personally needs (that doesn't happen any more) is taken from him at fixed prices; i.e., he gets nothing for his surplus. Also, through various decrees, he is hindered from increasing his livestock. Since he is required . . . to hand over every excess head of cattle, he slaughters such cattle at night, often risking his life to do so, and sells the meat to the city people. His greatest scarcity is salt (a pound costs 1,000 rubles). The peasant can't salt his winter provisions. He eats all meals without salt and would gladly trade his whole produce for salt.

The marriages in present-day Russia are interesting. Either party may assume the name of the other. The ceremonies are simple and very fast. . . . As a present the Soviet regime adds [a measure] of thin cloth, a samovar and other paraphernalia. Many marry just to receive these items and later sell them for high prices on the black market. Divorce is as easy as marriage. [It takes five minutes.] . . . A general phenomenon, probably due to years of unbalanced diets . . . is the female's lack of fertility. . . .

An overthrow in Russia is . . . only a matter of time. However, the people . . . are extremely apathetic and worn down and the government is by that token much stronger and more watchful. In order to guard against the unexpected, the best workers of the Moscow telephone office were shot long ago. But the present employees are still not trusted, and all of Moscow has been wired with an extra network of telephone lines that operates independently of the regular office and serves only communist officials. Still not satisfied, small radio stations have been set up on all corners of Moscow and in the Kremlin.

John Reed in 1919*

It is still fashionable, after a whole year of the Soviet Government, to speak of the Bolshevik insurrection as an "adventure." Adventure it was, and one of the most marvelous mankind ever embarked upon, sweeping into history at the head of the toiling masses, and staking everything on their vast and simple desires. Already the machinery had been set up by which the land of the great estates could be distributed among the peasants. The Factory-Shop

* SOURCE: John Reed, *Ten Days That Shook the World*, New York, Modern Library, 1935, p. xii. This book is a classic account of the Bolshevik seizure of power. Reed, an American correspondent, lies buried in the Kremlin.

Committees and the Trade Unions were there to put into operation workers' control of industry. In every village, town, city, district and province there were Soviets of Workers', Soldiers' and Peasants' Deputies, prepared to assume the task of local administration.

No matter what one thinks of Bolshevism . . . the Russian Revolution is one of the great events of . . . history. . . .

In the struggle my sympathies were not neutral. But in telling the story of those great days I have tried to see events with the eye of a conscientious reporter, interested in setting down the truth.

J. R.

New York, January 1st, 1919

John Reed in 1920*

One day in Red Square, Jacob Rubin, an American Socialist accidentally encountered John Reed. Reed exclaimed:

* SOURCE: J. H. Rubin, *I Live to Tell*, Indianapolis, Bobbs-Merrill, 1934, pp. 217-219.

"This is the first time I have had a chance to speak out. My God, you don't know what that means. . . . There is no freedom here, no justice, no opportunity, not even enough bread for the masses, and no hope. I am horribly . . . disillusioned."

With tears streaming down his face, he began telling me the story of his life. . . .

"What have I gained, Rubin? I sacrificed my friends, my family, myself. And for what? Are the people here any better off than in the United States? No! Has Communism accomplished anything? No! I have been a Socialist all my life. . . . But I can see now that . . . human beings will not be ready for Socialism for thousands of years. Look at your Communist leaders . . . when they are in power! Except for Lenin and Trotsky and a few others, they are grafters, politicians, theorists or . . . fools. Everybody knows that the heads of the *Cheka* are accepting bribes, stealing, even killing people to get their wealth.

"Who holds the important positions in the government and in the factories?— Members of the Communist Party, political job-holders . . . dreamers who spend their time drinking tea and making speeches or working for the party. . . .

"In the United States I hated the Capitalistic system, but I was at liberty to get up on a street corner and express myself. Here, where they are trying to free the whole world, I can't even criticize the government or say a word of sympathy—not for the Capitalists, not even for the Menshevik Party. . . .

"When I have guests in my own apartment, I am afraid to say anything about the government or the officials for fear that one of them may be a spy. . . .

"To-morrow night I want you to come to my apartment. . . . You will meet all the intelligentsia of Moscow. . . . They all think I'm still a Communist—and I'm afraid to tell them otherwise."

Section 4

NEP and Planned Economy

FROM LENIN TO STALIN

At the beginning of 1920, Lenin insisted that the extreme measures of regimentation, requisitioning, and rationing that had prevailed during the course of the civil war be continued so that Russia's economy might be restored to normalcy as soon as possible. Lenin failed to realize that it was mainly the idea of saving Russia that had enabled the people to sacrifice so much for so prolonged a period. The peasants had grudgingly given up their surplus grain to forced requisitions by the government. The industrial workers had done without necessities and had labored at whatever jobs the government had found it expedient to assign them. Peasants and workers had believed that once the war was won they would finally have become the masters of Russia.

Whatever Lenin's purposes, the masses, once the armies of Kolchak and Denikin had been destroyed, no longer had the strength of will to accept the strains of War Communism. In the meantime, the Bolshevik party had established a bureaucratic grip extending to all phases of Soviet life. In the soviets, power had shifted to the executive committees. Within the party, authority had moved from the members to the cadres. In the factories, it was no longer the workers but the party bureaucrats who were in charge. The Central Committee itself was fast becoming a rubber stamp of the Politburo. During the war the urban workers and the party rank and filers had sacrificed their democratic right to complain, recognizing the need for absolute unity in fighting off the enemies of the Soviet Republic. But by late 1920, especially after the latest invaders, the Poles, had been driven out of Russia, they began to long for the freedom to speak their repressed thoughts regarding the affairs of their—the people's—State.

In February, 1921, the food rations of the Petrograd workers were reduced. That incident served to spark large-scale strike action against an arbitrary government. A large number of workers were shot down by government troops. The ferment in Petrograd spread to Kronstadt and thus the growing disenchantment with the Bolshevik party was reflected by the sailors in addition to workers and peasants.

The island of Kronstadt was the naval base that protected Petrograd. The Kronstadt sailors enjoyed a long tradition of revolutionary heroism and decided to become the clarion of protest against the party's gag upon all dissenting voices. Relatively insulated from the mainland on their island and in their battleships, the men of Kronstadt, though not the same as those of 1917, still were motivated by the revolutionary-democratic *esprit de corps* of that climactic year. At the same time, they did not realize how totally bureaucratic the regime had become and how little tolerance there would be to demands from below. So, foolishly or courageously, they challenged the overwhelming power of Lenin's regime and were crushed without mercy. But Lenin realized that limitless popular sacrifices could no longer be expected. At the Tenth Party Congress, in March, 1921, he introduced his New Economic Policy that gave the peasants the right to sell their surplus grain on the open market, and permitted small business to resume activity. Also foreign capitalists were given permission to exploit Russian natural resources in return for fees paid to the Soviet government. However, the state retained "the commanding heights" of production, holding onto all large enterprises. By paying the workers of mines, railroads, and so on in depreciating money, and selling abroad the goods produced, the government was able to raise the national economy to a viable level.

Lenin's retreat came not a moment too soon. To the drain of six years of war and the undermining of the productive capacities of farms and factories, caused by the dislocating demands of War Communism, the year 1921 added a disastrous crop failure. Millions died in Russia's most horrible famine. But for generous aid, provided largely by the American Relief Administration, the number that died might well have been doubled or trebled.

By 1923 Russian economy was in the process of rapid recovery, thanks in large part to the devotion and sacrifice of party members and industrial personnel. Underfed, underpaid, if paid at all, they labored under execrable conditions of life, whilst all about them they saw the prospering NEPmen, the peasants, and even foreign concessionaires. But the revolution had been fought for and won by the proletariat. So thought many Communists who saw all but the proletariat getting richer day by day. The very bourgeoisie, whom the revolution had supposedly dispossessed, were brazenly flaunting their newly gained wealth. Bitter arguments about this raged within the party councils, but until Lenin died they remained, so to speak, under the lid. When the great leader died in 1924, the question of what should be done rose to the surface and soon merged with that of who should do it. Policy lines with regard to the course to be pursued became identified with various factions in the period from 1924 to 1927.

The left wing of the party, headed by Trotsky, proposed the immediate introduction of socialism along with a resumption of active efforts in behalf of the world revolution via the Communist International. The right wing, led by Bukharin, Rykov (nominal head of the government), Tomsky, and Yenukidze, considered it necessary to permit Russia, and the peasants in particular, to make further progress by means of the profit incentives provided by the NEP. Stalin favored an intermediate position that came to be known under the title of Socialism in One Country. That policy, already initiated by Stalin's apparatus, aimed at an early but not immediate scrapping of the NEP and an offensive against the wealth-accumulating kulaks. It rejected the idea of throwing Russia's weight into the struggle for world revolution. By 1927, Stalin and his program had triumphed. The militantly fanatical Trotskyites had been expelled from the party and the Rights were soon thereafter isolated and forced to submit.

Stalin's victory may be ascribed to a number of factors. The party was a bureaucratized apparatus as early as 1921. In 1922 Stalin was appointed General Secretary of the party and proceeded to convert it into his own political machine. Control over the country's soviets gave him the majority of the votes in the Central Committee and the power to determine party and State policy. His opponents, cut off from the "grass roots" of the party and handicapped further by ideological disunity, could never muster sufficient support against him. Stalin also controlled all of the media of mass communication. Thus, while his views were widely propagated, those of his opponents were left practically no channels through which to reach the public. Above all, as party boss, Stalin commanded the vast army of police that could be used to terrorize the populace into conformity.

The power of the purge, initially sponsored by Lenin to keep the party free from fractionalism, Secretary Stalin employed to weed out opposition-minded members, at first mainly small fry. At the same time he was able to draw into the party new youthful members from factories, mines, and farms, among them being Nikita Khrushchev. These, after brief courses in Marxist-Leninist theory (Stalin's version), were trained for the task of leading the conversion of their agrarian country into an industrial power. Such doctrinaire activists had no roots in the internationalistic-minded theorizing party of the pre-revolutionary decades and felt no ties to its veterans of exile and underground struggle. Whether they sincerely believed in the virtues of the projected Socialism in One Country or because they looked to exalted careers in the Soviet hierarchy of bureaucrats, they preferred the plan of Stalin to that of Trotsky. Trotskyism, spelled out, meant that Russian (that is, their) lives and Russian (that is, their) effort would have to be expended to save the rest of the world from capitalism. Nevertheless, considering themselves to be proletarian Marxists, they hated all who stood for private gain and were, on the whole, willing to turn against the Bukharin school of thought once Stalin gave the signal that the Right was wrong. Thus they became ready tools for Stalinism, which, in the final analysis, could only be achieved through the use of violence, particularly against the peasants.

Last but not least, Stalin was a master of intrigue and propaganda. Having little or no personal attachment to his comrades and being more concerned than they with personal victory against that of some doctrine, he was able, as none other, to play the ideologists against one another. "He is an unprincipled intriguer," was Bukharin's comment to Kamenev in 1928. "At any moment he will change his theories in order to get rid of someone." In his crafty game of intraparty politics, Stalin skillfully employed the Lenin-wrought tradition that loyalty to the party preceded all other considerations. Thus disarmed, the oppositionists in the party hesitated too long before attempting to come out firmly against the emerging dictator. Stalin also violated a basic conception of intraparty relationships established by Lenin: no Bolshevik, prior to Stalin's captaincy, would have employed smear tactics against his comrades, not to mention anti-Semitism, in order to undermine such stalwarts as Zinoviev, Kamenev, and Trotsky within the party and defame them before the general public. In the final stages of his struggle against Trotsky, his most articulate and most illustrious opponent, Stalin went so far as to turn anti-Soviet actions by the British, Polish, and Chinese governments—Trotsky having blamed Stalin's policies for those defeats—into a war scare, thus playing upon the deeply rooted Russian fear of invasion. Using the press, the radio, and the terror technique of having harmless suspects arrested en masse, he produced an image of himself as the true defender of the republic and of socialism, while maligning Trotsky and his cohorts as traitors to the party and the fatherland.

BRAVE NEW WORLD

In retreating from War Communism to the partial capitalism of the NEP, the Communist party retained the "commanding heights" not only over industry, but also over the minds of the generation which had come of age in the course of the revolution. The party and of course the schools, now geared to its doctrine, gave ideological guidance to its missionaries of collectivism, and this teaching was rewarded by the single-minded support of many thousands of young people who were determined to make the thing work and let nothing of the past stand in their way. If, for the moment, the economic patterns still reflected that which had been, a new code of morals and a new outlook on life, based on Marxist-Leninist thought, soon came to prevail. Traditional precepts, and the largely older people who tried to maintain them, were ruthlessly swept away.

The new yardstick of privilege was "class." Those of the wrong classes, of the "former people"—and even their children, who could not have been guilty of the pre-revolutionary injustices—were made social outcasts and forced to subsist, if they could, in the rapidly shrinking fringe areas of a society becoming increasingly totalitarian and geared not to the needs of the present, but to the goals of the future. Wages were poor, housing was in pitifully short supply as millions of people from the rural areas and many Jews, previously restricted to the fringe areas of the empire, came to live in the urban centers. There were long waits on lines, whether for food or for free abortions. In addition to their regular work, citizens were called upon to perform unwonted civic duties. The less dedicated were quick to complain about such annoyances. But the young Puritans took them in stride as part of the price to be paid for the joy of participating in shaping the world to come.

SOCIALISM IN ONE COUNTRY

The decade of the first two Five-Year Plans (1928-1932, 1933-1937), brought with it awesome industrial accomplishments, immense popular suffering, and a distortion of human values comparable only to that taking place in Germany at the same time under Hitler. Whatever the madness of Stalin's method, his manner of modernizing the Soviet Union economically and militarily has notable precedents in Russian history. Ivan the Terrible (1547-1584) and Peter the Great (1689-1725) likewise permitted no merciful impulses to deter them from strengthening the power of the Tsar and of the State. If Stalin appears to have acted more monstrously than they, that may be due to the greater scope of his task in a far more populous nation than his predecessors ruled over. Also, he exploited, besides the historically enshrined absolute power and the age-old Russian fear of invasion that sanctioned it, the technical means of a modern State. Through his devices of terror and propaganda, Stalin was able to reach almost every one of his 200 million subjects.

Stalin operated through the powerful dynamism of the Communist party—"the party of the proletariat, of the Soviet people, of the entire world, the party of the future," as its adherents saw it. That party had risen from nothing to seize power over a vast empire and to strike fear into the hearts of the ruling groups throughout the world. It had stood fast against counterrevolution, foreign intervention, total national exhaustion, and famine mainly because it had been bound together by iron discipline under Lenin. After Lenin, Stalin had preserved its vital unity at the expense of factional elements which had threatened to disrupt it. The party seemed invincible and almighty as long as it was monolithic, and Stalin alone seemed able to guarantee that it would so remain.

The Bolsheviks, whether 1905ers or graduates of War Communism or members of the Young Communist League, whether idealists for the cause or career-minded opportunists, were loyal. Since Stalin's will had become that of the party—itself the disembodied and seemingly successful instrument of historical progress—the average Bolshevik, the younger ones, who knew only of victories, especially, had no need to ask themselves whether or not the ends justified the means. If millions perished in their execution of Stalin's orders, theirs was not to reason why. If one of them faltered in carrying out the orders, however absurd or brutal in substance, then it was he, not Stalin, (that is, the party) that had erred. If in failing to maintain discipline one or another party member paid with self-abasement, imprisonment, or death, then that too was somehow and inevitably just.

Stalin did not introduce the planned economy with the anticipation that it would lead to millions of deaths and deportations. The First Five-Year Plan was initiated in 1928 and called for a dizzying pace of construction and production in basic industries. That, accompanied by a government offensive against the last remnants of private trade, meant a drastic reduction in the amounts of consumers' goods available. Workers lived in verminous barracks hastily thrown up around newly constructed factories. Never having owned property, the workers did not consider themselves deprived of anything specific and had at least the solace of believing that out of their curses and sacrifices would rise a society built to the needs of the little people of the U.S.S.R., if not of the entire world. But to most of the peasants, Socialism in One Country brought a bitter harvest. In the summer of 1929, in order to hasten the process of collectivization—designed, in part, as a kind of supertax to pay for the industrialization—Stalin ordered that the kulaks, already under severe attack, be "liquidated as a class." That order was soon enough executed by the combined forces of Communists sent from the cities and the village poor. The kulaks and their families were transported to remote prison camps and their land absorbed into the rapidly formed collective farms. That, however, left numerous lesser-propertied peasants who were also expected to join the *kolkhoz* but refused to give up their land and animals. The term "kulak" then became elastic, and all who resisted collectivization became enemies of the State. What ensued was an unequal war as the organized and well-armed forces of the State and the party attacked the helpless peasants, with the rich farm regions of the Ukraine as the major battle area. Stubbornly, the peasants hid their grain or let their crops rot in the fields. They neglected their animals or slaughtered and sold them. Thus to the ever-mounting terror in the villages, as peasants were tortured, shot, and transported, was added the tragedy of a man-made famine which claimed perhaps ten million lives. All through the nightmarish events of 1931-1933, food, some of it taken right out of the famine areas, was exported from the U.S.S.R. so that the importation of needed machinery would go on unimpeded.

The village horrors, ironically enough, had descended to their most barbaric levels at just about the time when the First Five-Year Plan, stumbling along on a costly trial-and-error course, had managed to establish the industrial basis for a richer Soviet economy. "Life is getting better and more joyful," was a prominent propaganda phrase of that period, and, indeed, throughout most of the Second Five-Year Plan (1933-1937), all manner of new goods and services began appearing in the cities and particularly in Moscow.

Despite the phenomenal progress in industry and the successful institutionalizing of the *kolkhoz* by 1934, the high cost of the accomplishments, in terms of lives lost in the food-producing regions as well as in mine and factory accidents, had led to open criticism of Stalin among the party leaders. Proposals were made that Stalin be deposed as General Secretary. In a moment of despondency, he himself offered to resign from his post, declaring before the Politburo that he might have become an obstacle to the party's unity. His offer, however, was not accepted, and before his opponents could organize their forces—hesitant as ever to act decisively in view of the specter of party disunity—Stalin had recovered his composure and was on the offensive against his critics.

Nazi Germany and Japanese aggressiveness along the Soviet-Manchurian border posed an obvious threat to the security of the Soviet State. In January, 1934, Stalin justified the costly tempo of his program to the Central Committee by stressing Russia's need for obtaining the military means of survival without delay. The purge, hitherto used by Stalin as a means for expelling doubters and "troublemakers" from the ranks of the party, if not from the U.S.S.R., was now turned into a device for their extermination by the G.P.U. or for their isolation from society by dispatch to the rapidly mushrooming forced-labor camps.

In December, 1934, Sergei Kirov, the popular head of the Leningrad section of the party, and generally regarded as Stalin's successor, was assassinated. Whether or not Stalin himself had arranged the murder, it became a pretext for "uncovering" a network of plotters against the life of Stalin and therefore against the security of the State.

Behind a façade of well-publicized trials of outstanding Communists and other Soviet leaders, held in Moscow from 1936 to 1938, the grim process of liquidation eliminated virtually all persons of some importance in whom any spark of conscience, any suspicion of less than unquestioning loyalty to the leader, could be surmised. The average citizen, cowed by the rampant police terror and having only such information as the centrally controlled press, radio, schools, and literary propaganda provided, either accepted the situation apathetically or really believed that Stalin was taking the tragically necessary steps to defeat the traitors to the country and the revolution. If even the old Bolsheviks, the generals of the Red army, and the chiefs of the G.P.U. freely confessed their involvement in the intrigues of the exiled Trotsky and were ready to restore capitalism in league with the German and Japanese militarists, then whom besides Stalin could one trust? It should be added that tens of millions had better lives and richer hopes for the future as a direct consequence of the existing order. Such persons applauded whatever drama the regime found it expedient to stage without concerning themselves about what went on behind the scenes.

After the purges, opposition to the regime was no longer voiced in the U.S.S.R. The word of Stalin had become the law—the writ—and comrade Stalin had risen to the status of an all-knowing father and leader, a man without flaws or faults. This truth, larger than all others, was many times daily impressed upon the minds of the people.

In attaining supreme power, Stalin had used the method of divide and rule. City had been pitted against country, poor peasants against the rich. More efficient workers, or Stakhanovites, had been favored against the ordinary and less efficient. Within the party itself, the largely youthful zealots and cynics were turned against those whose hearts bled for the suffering masses or against those who had known Stalin before his apotheosis and therefore were still able to cast a critical eye upon the way things were going.

The frantically paced economic program coupled with property deprivation and ubiquitous police surveillance made the nerves of the people taut. Stalin, by the time of the Second Five-Year Plan, was able to gain their gratitude simply by granting some relief from the pressure or even for holding out hope that relief might one day come. So, for instance, he was praised in 1933 for permitting the recently collectivized *kolkhoz* members to farm small plots of land as individuals, and, in 1936, just as the last traces of individual freedom were about to disappear, his promulgation of history's most democratically worded constitution gave hope that he sincerely meant to restore it when the time was ripe. A master of mass-conditioning, Stalin turned the Soviet people into fear and guilt-ridden idolaters who found a large measure of emotional security in equating Stalin to some superhuman force.

To introduce the planned economic system, it had been necessary to kill off and incarcerate millions and to alter the moral and emotional responses of centuries. But, by 1939, the U.S.S.R., rich in natural resources, had been converted into a mighty mechanism of ideologically guided technology so efficient that it was able to withstand the Nazi invasion and, out of the disasters wrought by World War II, rise swiftly to productive heights that would astound the world.

Protest Against the Bureaucratic Party*

By 1921 the . . . workers and peasants were expecting to be released from the rigours to which they had submitted for the sake of internal unity. . . . When therefore Lenin showed no inclination at all towards restoring workers' liberties and control over industry unrest became very widespread.

On the political field, this . . . dissatisfaction showed itself in the programme of the Workers' Opposition.[1] In Petrograd, the workers' protest meetings were dispersed by the Government so that they were forced to resort to strike action. . . .

. . . The strikers' demands appeared [in

* SOURCE: A. Ciliga, *The Kronstadt Revolt*, London, Freedom Press, 1942, pp. 3-15.

[1] The Workers' Opposition consisted of Communists in the trade unions who believed that the unions, not the party bureaucrats, should conduct the administration of industry.

proclamations posted] in Petrograd on February 27th:

"A complete change is necessary. . . . The workers and peasants need freedom. They don't want to live by the decrees of the Bolsheviki: they want to control their own decision.

Comrades, . . . demand [the following]:

Liberation of all arrested socialists and non-partisan working-men;

Abolition of martial law; freedom of speech, press and assembly for all . . . who labour;

Free election of shop and factory committees, . . . of labour unions and soviet representatives. . . ."

Arrests and suppression [were] Lenin's [answer]. The Government Committee of Defence of Petrograd issued an order: "In case crowds congregate in the streets, the troops are ordered to fire. . . ."

The Kronstadt sailors were disturbed by the events in Petrograd. Sympathy with the strikers was first expressed by the crews of the warships *Petropavlovsk* and *Sevastopol,* which in 1917 had been in the forefront of the revolutionary struggle. The movement spread throughout the fleet and then to the Red Army in Kronstadt. The Kronstadt sailors and workers had sent delegates to Petrograd to report on the events there, and it was on hearing the very unfavourable report of this delegation that they presented the Petropavlovsk resolution to a mass meeting of 16,000 sailors, Red Army men and workers. The resolution was accepted unanimously except for [the] votes . . . of Kuzmin, the Commissioner of the Baltic Fleet; Vassiliev, the chairman of the Kronstadt Soviet, and Kalinin, [later] President of the USSR. . . .

[Following is] the resolution which served as a programme for the Kronstadt movement. . . .

1. . . . The present soviets do not express the wishes of the workers and peasants to organise immediately re-elections to the soviets with secret vote, and with care to organize free electoral propaganda for all workers and peasants.

2. To grant liberty of speech and of press to the workers and peasants, to the anarchists and the left socialist parties.

3. To secure freedom of assembly for labour unions and peasant organizations.

. . .

5. To liberate all political prisoners of Socialist parties as well as all workers, peasants, soldiers and sailors imprisoned in connection with the labour and peasant movements.

6. To elect a Commission to review the cases of those held in prisons and concentration camps.

7. To abolish all "politodeli" [political departments] because no party should be given special privileges in the propagation of its ideas or receive financial support from the government for such purposes. Instead there should be established educational and cultural commissions, locally elected and financed by the government.

. . .

9. To equalize the rations of all who work with the exception of those employed in trades detrimental to health.

10. To abolish the communist fighting detachments in all branches of the army, as well as the communist guards kept on duty in mills and factories. Should such guards or military detachments be found necessary they are to be appointed in the army from the ranks, and in the factories according to the judgment of the workers.

11. To give the peasants full freedom of action in regard to their land and also the right to keep cattle on condition that the peasants manage . . . without employing hired labour.

. . .

13. To demand that the press give the fullest publicity to our resolutions.

14. To appoint a travelling commission of control.

15. To permit free artisan production which does not employ hired labour.

The Innocents of Kronstadt*

The Committee of Defense took up the systematic cleaning of [Petrograd]. Numerous workers, soldiers and sailors, suspected of sympathising with Kronstadt, were [arrested]. All Petrograd sailors and several Army regiments thought to be "politically untrustworthy" were ordered to distant points, while the families of Kronstadt sailors living in Petrograd were [held] *as hostages*. The Committee of Defense notified Kronstadt [of the following]: ". . . the arrested are held as hostages for the Commissar of the Baltic Fleet, N. N. Kuzmin, . . . and other Communists. If the least harm be suffered by our detained comrades, the hostages will pay with their lives."

"We do not want bloodshed. Not a single Communist has been shot by us," was Kronstadt's reply.

Kronstadt revived with new life. Revolutionary enthusiasm rose to the level of the October days. . . . Now for the first time since the Communist Party assumed exclusive control of the Revolution . . . Kronstadt felt itself free. A new spirit of . . . brotherhood brought the sailors, the soldiers, . . . [and] the factory workers . . . together. . . . Even Communists were infected by the fraternisation . . . and joined in the work preparatory to the . . . elections to the Kronstadt Soviet.

. . . The radio of March 6 sounds the keynote of Kronstadt's call [to Petrograd]:

"Our cause is just: we stand for the power of Soviets, not parties. We stand for freely elected representatives of the laboring masses. The substitute Soviets manipulated by the Communist Party have always been deaf to our . . . demands; the only reply we have ever received was shooting. Comrades! They . . . pervert the truth. . . . In Kronstadt . . . power is exclusively in the hands of the revolutionary sailors, soldiers and workers—not with counter-revolutionists led by some Kozlovsky, as the lying Moscow radio [tells you]. Do not delay, comrades! Join us . . . ; demand admission to Kronstadt for your delegates. Only they will tell you the whole truth and will expose the [lies] about Finnish bread and Entente offers. . . ."

The Provisional Revolutionary Committee . . . of Kronstadt . . . was exclusively proletarian, consisting . . . of the following 15 members [only a sample given here]:

1. PETRICHENKO, senior clerk, flagship *Petropavlovsk*
2. YAKOVENKO, telephone operator, Kronstadt District

. . .

13. PAVLOV, naval mining worker

. . .

15. KILGAST, deep sea sailor

Not without a sense of humor did the Kronstadt *Izvestia* remark . . . : "These are *our* generals, Messrs. Trotsky and Zinoviev, while the Brussilovs, . . . the Tukhachevskis, and the other celebrities of the Tsarist regime are on *your* side."

The Provisional Revolutionary Committee enjoyed the confidence of the whole population of Kronstadt. It won general respect by establishing . . . the principle of "equal rights for all, privileges to none." The . . . [food ration] was equalised. The sailors, who under Bolshevik rule always received rations far in excess of those allotted to the workers, themselves voted to accept no more than the average citizen and toiler. . . .

The . . . generous attitude of the Revolutionary Committee toward the Kronstadt

* SOURCE: A. Berkman, *The Kronstadt Rebellion* Berlin, Der Syndikalist, 1922, pp. 18-38. Russian-born Alexander Berkman was deported from the United States to Soviet Russia for being an anarchist. Aboard the deportation vessel on December 24, 1919, he resolved to consecrate the remaining years of his life "to the service of the wonderful Russian people." Less than two years later he left Russia disillusioned and determined to destroy the "Bolshevik myth."

members of the Communist Party—few of whom had been arrested in spite of Bolshevik repressions and the holding of the sailors' families as hostages—won the respect even of the Communists. . . . Many Kronstadt Communists publicly announced their withdrawal from the Party as a protest against its despotism and bureaucratic corruption. . . . The Executive Committee of the Communist Party of Russia considered its Kronstadt Section so "demoralised" that after the defeat of Kronstadt it ordered a complete re-registration of all Kronstadt Communists.

* * *

. . . [Kronstadt] felt itself the true defender of the Revolution. . . . The sailors did not believe that the Government would attack them by force of arms. . . .

In Petrograd there were persistent rumors that the Government was preparing military operations against Kronstadt, but the people did not credit such stories: the thing seemed [too] outrageous. . . . The Petrograd workers knew little of what was transpiring in Kronstadt, the only information accessible being the Communist press. . . . Anxiously the people looked forward to the announced session of the Petrograd Soviet which was to take action in the Kronstadt matter.

The Petro-Soviet met on March 4. . . . As Chairman [of] the Petrograd Soviet, Zinoviev [spoke on] the Kronstadt situation. I . . . came to the meeting disposed . . . in favor of the Zinoviev viewpoint: I was on my guard against the vague possibility of counter-revolutionary influence in Kronstadt. But Zinoviev's speech . . . convinced me that the Communist accusations against the sailors were pure fabrication . . . , his . . . manner . . . gave the lie to his words. I could sense his own conscience protesting. . . . The resolution against Kronstadt was passed by the delegates wrought up to a high pitch of intolerance . . . amid a tumult of protest from . . . delegates of Petrograd factories and . . . the sailors. The resolution declared Kronstadt guilty of a counter-revolutionary uprising . . . and demanded its immediate surrender. . . .

. . . Many Communists refused to believe that the resolution would be carried out. . . . In the circle of their friends many sober-minded Communists threatened to resign from the Party should such a bloody deed come to pass.

Trotsky on . . . March 5, . . . issued his ultimatum:

The Workers' and Peasants' Government has decreed that Kronstadt authority and the rebellious ships must immediately submit to the . . . Soviet Republic. . . . Only those surrendering unconditionally may count on the mercy of the Soviet Republic.

Simultaneously I am issuing orders to prepare to . . . subdue the mutineers by force of arms. . . .

This warning is final.

TROTSKY
Chairman, Revolutionary
Military Soviet of the Republic
KAMENEV
Commander-in-Chief

* * *

Kronstadt, heroic and generous, was dreaming of liberating Russia by the Third Revolution which it felt proud to have initiated. It formulated no definite program. Liberty and universal brotherhood were its slogans. It thought of the Third Revolution as a gradual process of emancipation, the first step . . . being the free election of independent Soviets, uncontrolled by any political party and [expressing] the will . . . of the people. The . . . unsophisticated sailors were . . . confident that . . . the workers of Petrograd . . . would hasten to their aid.

Meanwhile Trotsky had collected his forces. . . . Tcheka detachments, and . . . units consisting exclusively of Communists were now gathered. . . . The greatest military experts were rushed to the scene to [plan] the blockade and attack. . . .

The . . . bombardment of Kronstadt . . . began on March 7. . . .

On . . . March 17 . . . the Bolsheviki broke into the city, and then there began the most brutal slaughter. The Communists spared by the sailors now betrayed them, attacking from the rear. . . . The city which for fifteen days had not harmed a single Communist, now ran red with the blood of Kronstadt men, women and even children.

For several weeks the Petrograd jails were filled with hundreds of Kronstadt prisoners. Every night small groups of them were taken out by order of the Tcheka and disappeared. . . .

The prisons and concentration camps in the frozen district of Archangel and the dungeons of far Turkestan are slowly doing to death the Kronstadt men who rose against the Bolshevik bureaucracy and proclaimed in March, 1921, the slogan of the Revolution of October, 1917: "All Power to the Soviets."

A Step Backward*

. . . For Lenin [the Kronstadt revolt] was the Writing on the Wall. [Soon after a] more dangerous outbreak occurred in . . . Tambov, where the peasants began forcibly to resist the food requisitions. . . . Troops sent to suppress [the rebellion] made common cause with the rebels. Lenin [swiftly] ordered the requisitions . . . stopped, and rushed into the affected area . . . kerosene, salt, tools, clothing . . . , and had them sold in the village markets, which had almost ceased to exist during . . . Military Communism. By sheer force of personality Lenin forced the Communist Party Congress, then in session, to a tacit acceptance of the reopening of markets on a "free trade" basis elsewhere, and informed it that the unpopular requisitions would . . . be replaced by a tax in kind, "the single food tax," [averaging] ten to fifteen per cent of the total annual crop. When the Congress ended, it was committed to a new economic program that would sweep away much of the artificial Communism of the past three years.

During the [following] years . . . Lenin held [firmly] to his new line . . . and it is significant in the light of future events that Stalin followed him implicitly, whereas

Trotzky, Bukharin and other leaders who had hitherto overshadowed Stalin in popular esteem, voiced theoretical, ideological, . . . almost . . . theological, objections. . . . "Facts are stubborn things," Lenin told them. ". . . The cities and towns are starving and the peasants refuse to produce more food than they need. For the time being the peasants have beaten us; we have [to] retreat. One day we shall resume the advance. . . . The time element is against us. We cannot yet give the peasants what they want in our way, so we must give it them in their way." Stalin echoed his words, as . . . in 1926, he echoed them again when he refused to admit that the time was ripe for the expropriation of the *kulaks* . . . , advocated by Trotzky and the "ultra-Lefts." Stalin had played an important rôle in the Civil War, although Trotzky won greater glory . . . , but his support of Lenin in the N.E.P. controversy marked him . . . a coming man and did much to secure for him the appointment as General Secretary of the . . . Party, . . . the foundation of his subsequent success.

The essential feature of N.E.P. was that it allowed the free buying and selling of goods . . . , that is . . . private trade, which had been almost wholly suppressed during the Communist period. [Thus it greatly stimulated] production. It brought other important changes such as the introduction of piece-work, a scaled system of wages, income and other taxes, and of course payment of public services like street-

* SOURCE: W. Duranty, *I Write As I Please,* New York, Simon & Schuster, 1935, pp. 119-121. From 1921 to 1934, when he served as resident correspondent for *The New York Times* in Moscow, Walter Duranty was largely responsible for the image of the Soviet Union held by the intelligent public of the United States.

cars, trains, theaters, [etc.], which had been nominally free before. Finally it allowed a limited traffic in money by individual groups, and unlimited individual production of goods, even small-scale factory production. N.E.P. was thus . . . a reversion to . . . at least . . . the outward forms of Capitalism. Nevertheless, Lenin from the outset intended it to be only a temporary reversion and, what is more, it was only a partial reversion. . . . The main sources of production and means of production, transportation, big finance and big industry, . . . mines and . . . natural resources [remained] in the hands of the State. . . . [N.E.P. also had] important social effects in restoring the influence and power of money for the benefit of private managers, traders, middle-men and producers to the detriment of Communist officials, soldiers, policemen and the working masses.

A Famine-Stricken Village*

I [ask] about the famine. . . . The men are . . . reticent . . . as if . . . the failure of the harvest is a reflection upon themselves. [Many associate] the present drought [with] the plundering of their landlords' estates . . . four years ago. . . . One of the peasants . . . murmurs . . . : "We are suffering for our sins. . . ."

. . . The . . . children . . . are not playing; they are walking about slowly . . . like old people. . . . We hardly meet half a dozen pigs in the whole village. All have been eaten . . . or sold to the towns for flour. . . .

They showed me many [empty] houses. . . . In some cases . . . the owners went away with their families . . . in the hope of getting work in Siberia in some Government factory or mine. . . . Other . . . men have gone but left their families in the village, hoping that their wages will supplement the scanty harvest. . . . Some have sold their houses for fuel, and we see empty places where some unfortunate has "eaten his house," as the peasants say. . . .

I [walk] off with an old peasant away from the others, in order that the presence of the two Soviet officials . . . may not embarrass us, although I am bound to say . . . that I have not yet noticed anything

* SOURCE: C. E. Bechhofer, *Through Starving Russia . . . A Journey to Moscow and the Volga Provinces in August and September, 1921*, London, Methuen & Co., 1921, pp. 84-95.

intimidating about [their] behaviour. My guide points out [the hut] of a man who has just died.

"What did he die of?" I ask. ". . . of hunger?"

"He died of eating too much," replies the old man. . . .

"[He] had not eaten . . . for a long time; and then his wheat ripened, and he was so hungry that he ate it as he plucked it, husks and all. . . . He ate so much that his stomach swelled up . . ."—he describes a huge arc in front of him,—"and then he got very ill and died . . . ."

I ask why . . . his neighbors [hadn't helped him. Could they not] have given him a little food . . . until his harvest was ripe?

"Ah, in the old days everybody helped his neighbour. . . . But nowadays . . . [?] Just look at the bread I am eating."

He takes [a piece] out of his pocket. . . . It is a loathly greenish-purply mess. . . . Traces of flour embedded in patches of clay, and held together by . . . fibres of grass and weeds. . . . I try to eat a little . . . but I cannot swallow it. My gorge revolts. . . .

The peasant looks at me as I hand it back to him.

"Is that bread? . . . Ah, we shall all die from hunger."

He leads me to a heap of pigweed. . . . "This is what we eat. . . ," he says. . . .

". . . Cattle do not like it, but we eat it gladly now." . . .

. . . I notice a woman and her [fourteen year old pregnant] daughter. . . . They are so thin as almost to be transparent. . . . Reduced by want, [they are] the slaves of the village, doing whatever work [there is for] a little of that "bread." In the towns it would mean prostitution and the filthier . . . domestic work. Here in the village it means, in addition to this, the incessant carrying of water and heavy burdens. . . . Mother and daughter have become like ani-mals. . . . [Clearly] they are marked out to be the next victims of the famine. One could foretell almost to a day . . . when they must crawl away to die.

I ask Matvey Ivanich how the present famine compares with others he has been through. [He remembers] the famine of 1891, . . . until now . . . regarded as the worst ever suffered by the Russian people. "Yes," he says, "that was a terrible year. . . . The cholera killed thousands. But [then] we had potatoes. This year even they are lost."

The March of the Starving Millions*

When I came to Samara the first thing I saw, and smelt, was a refugee camp of about 15,000 peasants . . . outside the rail-road station. . . . The adults were . . . haggard but far less dreadful than the chil-dren . . . with . . . bloated bellies and . . . shriveled limbs . . . That came from eating [indigestible] clay and bark and refuse. . . .

. . . Like cattle in a drought they waited . . . for death. . . . The only movement among them was the . . . stretcher-bearers carrying off the dead. . . . Few died of ac-tual hunger, but typhus, cholera, . . . the diseases of malnutrition, took their . . . toll. Right across [the road] from this herd of moribund humanity . . . was a food mar-ket [guarded by] one policeman. . . . It was only a little market, the firstfruits of N.E.P.'s new private enterprise, but there was fish . . . for those who had money . . . , even roasted meat, whose savory smell . . . carried . . . to the starving peasants, who neither moved nor seemed to care. . . . They lacked strength . . . to cross that narrow road or face the sentry's rifle and seize [some food]. The local au-thorities gave them . . . black bread, two ounces daily, and hot water in which bones . . . of animals had boiled. . . . No medi-cal attendance . . . and for each one that died there came five more, trudging slowly . . . from the country-side. . . .

. . . When they see that the crops have failed, they drift away from their villages, not ravenous like locusts, but helpless like sheep. . . . All along the Volga [hundreds of thousands] were moving through the dust. . . . [It was the same] across the steppes of the North Caucasus and the rich black earth of the Ukraine. . . . [Thus] 5,000,000 souls took part in that dreadful ex-odus. . . . The Soviet authorities reckoned . . . that upwards of 30,000,000 . . . were made destitute by the Great Famine of 1921 [and] would have died without relief. The Soviet . . . fed 13,000,000 . . . at the peak of its relief work, and the A.R.A.[1] peak was 11,500,000. Nansen and the Quakers and the other aids fed 2,500,000 more, a total of 27,000,000. . . .

. . . The Soviet authorities . . . were overwhelmed by this invasion, which might well have taxed the resources of a prosper-ous and efficient administration. . . . The most striking characteristic of all Russia at that period was exhaustion. The whole country was on the verge of succumbing to the triple strain of Civil War, Military Communism, and the attempt at manage-ment by people who lacked . . . training,

* SOURCE: W. Duranty, *I Write As I Please,* New York, Simon & Schuster, 1935, pp. 128-133.

[1] American Relief Administration.

ability and experience. The spur of war and the fanatic belief in the rightness of the Communist Cause had kept them going before, . . . but once the pressure was relaxed it seemed as if the whole country was paralyzed by nervous reaction. It must not be forgotten, too, that N.E.P. was bewildering . . . to the best . . . Communists, especially in the provinces, where their intellectual level was often not high enough for them to understand . . . Lenin's motives in introducing it. They felt, as one of them told me, like officers of a vessel whose compass had ceased to function. "Has all this bitter struggle been in vain?" he asked me sadly, "that now when the victory seems won we are ordered to retreat and abandon what we fought for?" He did not know, as Lenin knew, what price the "victory" had cost. . . .

It was therefore unfair of me to be shocked . . . by the apathy . . . of the local authorities at Samara and the other Volga cities . . . in face of the famine-refugee problem. In Samara . . . , I went to a . . . "children's home," which was more like a "pound" for . . . dogs. They picked up the [lost or abandoned] children by hundreds off the streets, and parked them in these "homes." At the place I

visited an attempt had been made to segregate those who were obviously sick or dying from their "healthier" fellows. The latter sat listlessly, 300 or 400 of them in a dusty court-yard, too weak and lost and sad to move or care. Most . . . were past hunger; one child of seven with fingers no thicker than matches refused the chocolate . . . I offered him and just turned his head away. . . . Inside . . . the house . . . children in all stages of . . . different diseases huddled together . . . in the most noxious atmosphere I have ever known. A matron and three girls were "in charge" of this pest-house. There was nothing they could do, they said wearily; they had no food or money or soap or medicine. . . .

"At least you could . . . heat some water and . . . wash them, even without soap," I said indignantly, "and surely you can get some rations from the city Soviet to make soup . . . for some of them."

The matron shrugged her shoulders, "What is the use?" she said. "They would die anyway."

I went away . . . hating myself for being healthy and well fed. [All] I could do [was] write the story in its naked ugliness and hope that it would move [Americans] and hurry their . . . aid. . . .

Death and Madness*

I awoke suddenly one midnight. A voice in the next room was saying: "The ARA[1] man went crazy. He tried to count the corpses in the barn but he couldn't get beyond forty-eight. There were hundreds of corpses but he kept saying 'forty-eight, forty-eight' the rest of the day. . . .'"

* SOURCE: Anna Louise Strong, I Change Worlds, New York, Henry Holt, 1935, p. 123. The author, originally a Socialist from Seattle and a friend of Lincoln Steffens, was, when she published this book, a fanatical devotee of the Communist party and of Stalin. In 1949 she was arrested in the Soviet Union for alleged espionage and expelled from the country. She was publicly rehabilitated in 1955.

[1] American Relief Administration.

. . . I went into the next room. Hecker, one of our workers, had left us three weeks before to get news of the famine; he had been behind the storm and returned. When I saw his face, I cried: "Are you ill?" He laughed. . . .

He told of dead bodies piled in warehouses, stripped of clothes which were needed by the living. . . . He told of wailing children who fought with dogs for crusts of bread. "I saw starving men with exasperated nerves strike children, and they fell down spiritless, just moaning. The dogs also, if struck, crawled off and made no resistance. If there was food for which to fight, the dogs and children would struggle a little."

He had passed through many villages; the only signs of life were around the relief stations. He had seen men arrested for can-nibalism; they had killed and eaten a young boy. Other cannibals did not kill, but stole corpses. Someone asked the prisoners how human flesh tastes, and they said: "Quite well; you don't need much salt." . . .

Boomtown Moscow (1921-1923)*

Moscow had changed during my three weeks' absence. . . . Dilapidated . . . buildings were being refurbished. . . . Shops, cafés and restaurants were being opened. . . . Shabby one-horse victorias . . . had appeared and traffic on the streets had increased tenfold. The city was full of peasants selling fruit, vegetables [etc.], or transporting building materials in their clumsy . . . carts. Suddenly [hidden or hoarded] goods began to appear. . . .

For . . . former aristocrats and rentiers N.E.P. was a respite from pressure, to restore perhaps a semblance of the . . . position they had lost, and . . . a [possible] chance to escape abroad. To the Communists and to the small group of proletarian leaders who had benefited by the Military Communist period N.E.P. was . . . repugnant, but to the mass of the workers it brought jobs that would henceforth be paid in money instead of valueless paper or moldy rations, and the certainty that with money they could buy the food and necessities . . . previously . . . lacking. To the traders N.E.P. meant . . . better days. Until August 9th it was technically a crime to possess goods of value, gold or silver or jewels or foreign currency, and a crime to buy and sell anything. It is true that many people continued to own valuables and that buying and selling was practiced more or less overtly, even in public markets, but the latter were continually raided to "suppress speculation" and any owner of valuables might [be] arrested, and [have] his property confiscated. The N.E.P. decree changed

all that, and the people of Moscow, after a pause of bewilderment, seemed to realize N.E.P.'s possibilities simultaneously, and rushed at them like famished swine to a feeding trough.

The most striking features of N.E.P. in this early stage were its rapid acceleration, its confusion, its opportunities for quick . . . profit, and the immense stimulus it gave to employment of all kinds. Not to mention its growing contempt for the rules and restrictions . . . previously enforced by the Bolsheviks. The first twelve months of N.E.P. were like the old Roman Saturnalia, when for three days each year slaves . . . might usurp . . . the pleasures . . . of their masters. Its waves, thick with greed and eagerness to tear from life the joys . . . denied so long, swept over Moscow and the rest of Russia like a flood which the Bolsheviks were powerless to check. They stood aghast before [their] Frankenstein which was changing with startling velocity laws and values they had accepted as immutable. Their leaders watched the flood and let it roll, . . . conscious that it was bringing a new silt of energy and growth to Russia's frozen soil. . . .

Ill-informed foreigners . . . naturally saw first the superficial phases of N.E.P., its reckless gambling and easy money, its corruption . . . but . . . the years of N.E.P.'s flourishing, the last quarter of 1921 until the end of 1923, were also years of national recovery and development. . . .

. . . The authorities . . . for a time . . . deliberately "took the lid off." . . . Gambling halls and night clubs [got] licenses from the municipality on condition that part of the receipts was reserved for the

* SOURCE: W. Duranty, *I Write As I Please,* New York, Simon & Schuster, 1935, pp. 138-150.

State. . . . It was estimated that the receipts of the Moscow Soviet from this source were 4,000,000 gold roubles in . . . 1922, which was used for . . . repairs to the streets, sidewalks, drainage and lighting systems.

The biggest gambling [den] was [the] Praga. . . .

It was a strange sight, this Praga, in the center of the world's first Proletarian Republic. Most of the men looked like . . . the low-class jackals . . . of any boom, . . . but there were [also] former nobles in faded broadcloth and Red Army soldiers in uniform, back from fighting Moslem rebels in Central Asia or from "liquidating" Makhno's anarchist movement in the Ukraine, eager for Moscow's fleshpots and a flutter at the tables. A smattering, too, of foreigners, fixers, agents and the commercial vanguard of a dozen big firms attracted by Lenin's new policy of Concessions, hurrying to find if [it] was true that Russia might again become a honey-pot for alien wasps. And . . . daughters of joy whom N.E.P. had hatched in flocks, noisy . . . as sparrows. Later in increasing numbers the wives and families of N.E.P.-men, the new profiteers, with jewels on their stumpy fingers. . . .

Then there was a restaurant called "Bar." . . . In the winter of 1921-22 it sold good, simple meals in one large dining-room [with] music in the evenings. . . . By the fall of 1922 "Bar" was doing a roaring trade as a snappy restaurant, night club and brothel. . . . The sale of wine and beer became legal that year, but at "Bar" there were vodka and liquors as well. In the winter of 1922-23 . . . cocaine and heroin were to be had. . . . A merry little hell it was in the spring of 1923, although the American colony tended to boycott it because one of our number had been robbed there in a . . . way, which indicated . . . police . . . "protection."

In the end the game was spoilt, not by police interference, but by a tax collector.

. . . The gang had been paying taxes on a declared profit of $1,000 a week, but the probe revealed that . . . profits from . . . dope . . . girls and . . . blackmail, were upwards of $10,000. . . .

. . . Less flagrant and luxurious . . . was the Red Light district . . . near the Trubny Square. . . . In the . . . big tenement houses . . . were corridors . . . where . . . beside the name and number of the small . . . rooms was tacked a photograph of its fair occupant in the scantiest of costume. . . .

One morning [in October] I saw a man sitting on the sidewalk selling flour, sugar, and rice . . . His stock was part of an A.R.A. food-packet . . . received from his Finnish relatives in Helsingfors. These food-packets contained ten dollars' worth of flour, sugar, cocoa, rice and tea at American wholesale prices, which the A.R.A. delivered in Russia on order and payment abroad. In 1921 they were worth from thirty to forty dollars in Russian values, sometimes far more than that in the famine areas, and they formed the foundation of many small businesses, especially amongst the Jewish population of the southwest, where many people had relatives in America.

. . . By . . . May [the Finn] had . . . a fair-sized store, to which peasants brought their produce fresh each morning. As his own middle-man he paid them more than they could get at the market, which he continued to undersell. In July he opened a dry-goods section, then added hardware. . . . After a year's trading he sold out. . . . He had made $20,000 or $30,000 clear profit, but the point is that his enterprise stimulated . . . peasants to fatten chickens . . . plant vegetables, or fashion wooden bowls. . . . The same thing was being done all over Russia. . . . In a single year the supply of food and goods jumped from starvation point to something nearly adequate, and prices fell accordingly. . . .

The Commanding Heights*

In my few short trips into Moscow streets during the winter [of 1921-22], I had been disturbed by the growing speculation and private trade. I [went] to Krasnoschekoff [assistant commissar of finance in Moscow].

"Tell me," I asked, "how I am supposed to regard all these shops that are opening? The other correspondents . . . rejoice; they measure Moscow's progress by the number of stores and the things you can get. To me each seems a step of defeat. . . . There's a horrible new-rich set growing and the opera audiences have changed from workers to petty traders showing off their women. . . . Must one be glad of this?"

"Would you be glad," asked Krasnoschekoff, "if you saw a starving man and tried to feed him and all your good food gave out, and the man turned to crusts of bread in a garbage wagon . . . ? This private trading is food in a garbage wagon, filthy with . . . all the diseases of capitalism. But it is better than letting men starve.

"If our government could say to the workers: 'Here is food for six months,' it could also say: 'Produce for us.' If we could say to the peasants: 'Here are implements and clothes and salt,' we could demand the peasants' harvest. But never yet have we had even the beginnings of a surplus on which alone communism can be built. We began with ruin and were forced into civil war; we encountered blockade and pestilence.

"When by extreme revolutionary spirit, workers managed to produce without first being fed, in the hope of giving goods to the peasant and getting bread, their goods went not to the peasant but to the war. If, under interest or compulsion the peasants gave us food and trusted to later returns, that food went not into production but into the army. Then we had two years of drought ending in famine.

* SOURCE: Anna Louise Strong, *I Change Worlds,* New York, Henry Holt, 1935, pp. 127-139.

"So now we must say frankly to the people: 'Your government cannot feed all and produce goods for all. We shall run the most necessary industries and feed the workers in those industries. The rest of you must feed yourselves in any way you can. This means we must allow private trade and private workshops; it is well if they succeed enough to feed those people who work in them, since no one else can feed them. Later, as state industries produce a surplus, these will expand and drive out private trade.'

Slowly he added: "It was not only goods of which the intervention robbed us. It robbed us of our comrades. Whenever we Bolsheviks planned the revolution we always thought that we should be there afterwards to run things. But now we know that most of us do not survive the revolution; the communists were first to be slaughtered on every front. Ah, if we had all those good comrades now. . . . Our men and means are exhausted; we must train up new forces and create a new surplus."

His words reassured me for the time. But the Moscow to which I returned as Hearst correspondent in the late spring of 1922 seemed to have changed in my three months' absence from a city of comrades living on rations to a city of profiteers charging fantastic prices. . . .

One could see at least that the country was becoming better organized. One by one the railroads opened for general passenger service. . . . The regions where one could not go without being inoculated against cholera were cleared up. . . . There was a struggling attempt to furnish blankets on the express trains, but not yet sheets. . . .

A fury of repair-work was sweeping over Moscow. On every block I had to turn aside for sidewalk repair or the whitewashing of buildings. . . . Color and life came back in

. . . flower-beds in the city's squares . . . , children began to play and young men and girls to stroll gayly in the evenings.

The aftermath of famine still gripped the Volga, but elsewhere everyone rejoiced in the new harvest and the increasing food. . . . But "enough to eat" still meant one meal a day. . . . Not for another year did eggs or butter . . . appear for breakfast. . . .

Outside [the] charmed circles of comrades there raged a . . . hunger for money . . . more unashamed than anything I had ever seen in America. American business men came to negotiate for concessions. They were . . . a flashy type, . . . in hope of quick gain. They declared that all the recovery was due to private trade. Russia had learned her lesson; she was going back to . . . capitalism. . . .

The communists knew, what nobody else believed, that the life of private capital would be as short and as circumscribed as they could make it. They knew the plan they had for eliminating private capital; but they did not know how rapidly it could work.

Their plan was to hold the "commanding heights" of industry, on which all lesser enterprises depend. They had studied capitalism far better than most capitalists; they knew its sources of power. They retained ownership of land and natural resources, banks and foreign trade, railways, all heavy industries and all large industrial enterprises generally. The state itself operated four thousand large industrial enterprises, employing a million workers; they were ready to lease to coöperatives or to private capital four thousand small enterprises, employing eighty thousand workers. City lands and buildings were the property of the municipalities, which ran the city budgets from their rents. Retail trade and numberless incidental enterprises fell into the hands of any person who would run them, but the government callously used its licensing power and discriminatory regulations to force the direction of private investment or to crush it altogether.

"We keep the commanding heights." Thus said the communists. To me, and to many of us in 1922, the state seemed to have chosen all the worst enterprises on which nobody could make money. The State Bank's only capital was rapidly depreciating paper rubles; the state railroads were utterly demoralized; the coal mines of the Donetz were ruined by long invasion and the miners fled to the farms for food. Steel production was five per cent of normal; the oil of Baku was flooded deep in water. All the commanding heights were ruined hills. But the lighter industries and retail trade could make money rapidly, and these were permitted to capitalists. . . .

Such state industries as were able to do so profiteered shamelessly, even more shamelessly than the private capitalists, since they had less to fear. Were such state trusts, I wondered, really socialistic? Apparently it didn't worry the workers; they not only exulted in each new accumulation of profit in state-owned enterprises but made incredible sacrifices to attain it. They gave their holidays to making street cars or locomotives as presents in a May-Day celebration. . . .

It was the president of the State Bank who gave me my first lesson in economics. I went to him to ask by what alchemy he turned ten million dollars' worth of rapidly depreciating paper rubles into twenty million good gold dollars in a single year. . . . He [gave me] an answer I shall never forget.

"You see, comrade, I'm not a banker. My chief training was ten years in a tsarist jail. Now it seems we need a state bank to establish a gold reserve. We can take our choice between two kinds of presidents: expert bankers who want to see our state bank fail, or a man like myself who would give his life to make this bank succeed, but who knows nothing about banking. So they put me in charge and give me the expert bankers as assistants, and I have to make them work and keep them from cheating." It was a perfect picture of the whole of Russia's economic life.

Months later I saw him again; he showed me bars of gold and high piles of British and American currency. . . . The ten million dollars' worth of paper with which he had opened his bank had depreciated to one-third of its value in the first three months. Yet he had twenty million dollars in gold. "How did you make this from paper?" I asked in amazement. "As the money-maker of a government which doesn't believe in money, tell me."

"No governments believe in money," he smiled swiftly. "They make their people believe in it. Rulers believe in coal and oil and natural resources—the real wealth of the world."

Then he explained. "We loaned money to the State Timber Trust—paper rubles with which they paid their bills in Russia. They exported timber to England and paid us in English pounds. Not only the loan with interest but also a share in their profits; sometimes we took half they made! The fur industry is also very profitable, making two and three hundred per cent in the export trade; on this we demanded a good share. We also charge ten per cent in gold on all remittances received from abroad."

"No wonder the state industries call you a robber," I gasped. This callous banker smiled. "The party permits this robber policy," he said, "till we get our gold reserve."

The State Bank shamelessly showed me that when a currency is dropping in value, those who pay workers and creditors in depreciating paper and sell abroad for sound values can make millions. . . . Thus the State Bank . . . was allowed to "rob" the struggling industries to make a gold reserve which later served to build up these same industries.

The state industries were called "trusts,"

a capitalist word which perplexed me. . . . Then I saw that their form was really that of the capitalist trust, but the shares were held by the state. They were made by combining groups of factories under boards of directors, who were partly engineers and partly communists, and who were charged to make the properties self-supporting and self-expanding or face removal after their first report.

They began their struggle . . . with ruined equipment and without money for wages. Coal miners from Donetz sent delegates to Moscow, saying: "We work waist-deep in water on a scanty diet. . . . Give food and means to repair the mines." But Moscow answered: "Not yet! Give coal for famine transport, . . . for steel. Here's what bread we can spare for you in a year of famine. Next year, perhaps, you'll get some wages."

The miners gave coal till their food was exhausted and then fled to the farms for bread. The union halls all over the Donetz posted lists of "deserters" who stopped giving coal because they wanted to eat. They posted also lists of "heroes" who collapsed at their work but returned as soon as they could stand. Thus they mined coal on the Donetz through the civil war and the first year of peace. Yet by 1922 the Donetz miners put the railroads and industries back on mineral fuel instead of the wood fuel of the civil war. Only then did they begin to get paid for their coal. . . .

Painfully and slowly, ignoring the wild clamor of speculation that filled the market places, they organized and strengthened the jointly owned "commanding heights" of their economic life.

The Worker Rulers*

How are we going to make our steel mills go? And our coal mines? And our oil wells? These questions were on everyone's lips in the Soviet Russia of early 1923.

* SOURCE: *Ibid.*, pp. 165-173.

Workers discussed them in union meetings; administrators of industry conferred with trade union representatives in public conferences to work out joint programs. People who had grown used to the terminology of war and beaten the enemy on many fronts, and who recently had fought on the "famine front," now spoke of the "battle-front of industry."

The *Pravda* . . . ran a contest to determine the "best directors in our enterprises." Imagine an American newspaper holding a contest to decide whether . . . some factory manager in Pittsburgh is the best director! Even more amazing than the contest itself, from my American point of view, was the standard set and the way decision was reached.

Letters came to the paper from workers, bragging about [or] denouncing [their] bosses. . . . The twelve best candidates, set up by their own workers and then checked by investigating committees from other factories, were . . . decorated with . . . highest honors. . . .

The standards of judgment set by the workers surprised . . . me. They wrote: "Our factory was working part-time. Then Archangelsk came. . . . He enthused . . . us. . . . He rapidly brought production to 120 per cent of prewar. Comrade Archangelsk spends all his . . . strength for his . . . workers. He repaired housing and the workers' dormitories. He arranged courses of technical instruction for factory youth. . . ."

Of a bad director they wrote: ". . . 2,500 more tons of oil were used than were needed; . . . accidents increased. . . . He took no interest in education. . . ."

. . . These workers . . . were not asking if the manager piled up profits. They were not even discussing hours and wages. . . . They asked: "Can he . . . set our factory in order, to produce a good life for all of us?"

. . . These workers spoke as owners. . . . Rakovsky, president of the Ukraine, was going to the Donetz [Basin] to attend local party congresses and prepare a report on coal and steel. [I went] with him. . . .

Half a day south of Kharkov in Rakovsky's private car we plunged into the [Donetz] valley of coal and steel, the proletarian heart of the Ukraine. You could tell you were among . . . ruler-workers, by the blasts of criticism that began. "Hallo,

there, Comrade Rakovsky, when are we going to get those working-clothes they promised? When are we going to get those safety-lamps for the mines?" . . .

. . . Newspapers were full of workers' correspondence, most of it devoted to attacks. "Comrade Stepansky had a big opening celebration for his power station last December, but the station isn't delivering power yet!" . . . "The milk from the municipal farm that should go to tubercular workers goes to friends of the administration while the workers stand in line and find it gone." . . . "Our mine has fine equipment . . . but it's under the care of 'specialists' for two years with no results but trouble. Give us honest workers' management; these 'specialists'[1] sabotage!" . . .

Down in one of the mines I met some American miners. . . . They told [me] what they thought of Russia.

"Pretty awful last year. Conditions upset by the famine. . . . But now . . . we live about as well as we did in the States. The mines aren't well organized and it takes a week to earn what we made there in two days, but over there we couldn't count on more than two days' work a week. . . . We'd rather have it regular. It's more peaceful here."

"Peaceful," I exclaimed, remembering the civil war and famine barely over. But they gave me the workers' idea of peace.

"Yep. No strikes nor lockouts. You can go to bed . . . feeling sure of work in the morning, which we never could do in the States. No rows with your boss at all. You've your union and your mine committee and you're insured against sickness and accident. . . . We don't get on with the older peasant-workers; they call us bourgeois when we go to town in decent clothes. Those fellows have got to be educated before they'll get coal here. They're so shiftless that they won't learn reading and writing when the union organizes classes at the mine entrance after work. This government gives them every chance but they don't take it. But we wish this government could af-

[1] The term "specialists" refers to former factory managers or owners who were being used to direct production.

ford to buy good machinery. They've good intentions but no machines. But we don't want to go back. . . . In five or ten years this will be a first class country for a worker."

It was . . . the typical attitude of American workers in their first experience of Soviet industry. They believed in the country's policy; they wanted to do good work; they were annoyed when backwardness of Russian workers or lack of machines injured their own efficiency. Not for years did I understand why the leading Russian workers called the Americans "too passive."

In spite of their energy in production they were socially passive, waiting for machines to come, waiting for lazy men to die, waiting for inevitable progress to save them. The Russians said it was because they were accustomed to bosses, whom they had never overthrown by revolution. Certainly they lacked that intimate sense of ownership and responsibility which I found in the more advanced of the Russian workers who had seized these mines by bloody struggle and who knew that under any and all conditions they must somehow bring "their mines" to production.

Intraparty Strife: Trotsky Versus Stalin*

Towards the end of 1923 I began to get wind . . . about grave disagreements in high places. . . . I was told . . . that Trotzky had walked out of a Plenary session of the Central Committee of the Party . . . after delivering a furious attack upon the organizational methods of the Secretariat, that is . . . Stalin, and that he had later presented a statement to the Politburo criticizing the Party leadership and declaring that it was ruining the country—that was the period of the alarming "Scissors" crisis to which I referred. . . . Trotzky's salvos had been followed by a . . . broadside known as the "Statement of the Forty-Six," signed by forty-six prominent members of the Party, most of whom had taken part in former opposition movements. The forty-six made a direct attack upon Stalin and claimed that he was abusing [his] powers as General Secretary of the Central Committee. . . .

During the long intra-Party controversy there was never any great disagreement about the goal at which all were aiming; the struggle was to decide who should determine the policies of the Soviet State,

what those policies should be, and how they should be carried out. It is easy . . . to dramatize the situation . . . , to make it simply a struggle for power, . . . between Stalin and Trotsky. . . . The personal conflict motive fails to take into account the fanatical devotion of all the Bolsheviks, including Trotzky and the other oppositionists of one category or another, to their Cause. Everyone . . . from Stalin downward, was so devoted to the success of Bolshevism that he could not believe that any policy that he himself considered wrong could be other than . . . heresy, to be . . . extirpated, at all costs. . . .

. . . Not long before Christmas it was announced that the Thirteenth Party Conference had decided that 100,000 "workers from the bench" should be invited to join the Party without delay. The inference was obvious that this new membership . . . would be hand-picked by the Secretariat, through its subordinate personnel in Moscow and the provinces. When it subsequently became known that the new members would have a right to vote for delegates to the next Party Congress (in May, 1924), [it] became clear [that] the Secretariat had boldly added twenty per cent of the total electorate to its own supporters

* SOURCE: W. Duranty, *I Write As I Please,* New York, Simon & Schuster, 1935, pp. 212-216, 259-267.

in what bade fair to be an [even] contest. . . . Years later a veteran Communist told me that he thought this to have been the turning-point in the struggle between Stalin and Trotsky. "Prior to that . . . the odds were in Trotsky's favor. He was popular with the Army . . . and his prestige at home and abroad was indubitably greater than that of Stalin."

*   *   *

In August, 1925, I returned to Moscow and found the country in a state of bewildering confusion. . . . I sat down to think things out . . . and reached four . . . conclusions, which I have never had reason to change as follows:

1. That inside the Bolshevik Party there was a hard central core which had never wavered from the intention to create and develop a successful proletarian State upon Socialist foundations;
2. That the Party controversy did not affect this determination, but was concerned with three points: by whom, how, and at what speed the socialization process should be conducted . . . ;
3. That N.E.P. . . . was no more than a temporary measure, the ostensible purpose of which was to give the whole country a breathing space, but whose real purpose was to enable the Bolsheviks to build up enough industry and commerce, and store up enough reserve to . . . tackle the work of building a Socialist State with greater success than in 1918-21;
4. That a new reckoning with the peasants was inevitable and not far distant.

. . . The peasant question was not, I could see, yet acute, but, I told myself, I must keep it . . . in mind as a big future issue and more immediately as a key pawn in the merciless chess game . . . between Stalin and Trotsky. . . . There was no reason for me to change my opinion that Stalin would beat Trotsky in the long run

—had not the latter been removed from the Commissariat of War a few months earlier and replaced by Frunze?—although I had read and admired Trotsky's pamphlet called *The Lessons of October* . . . published in the previous fall. It was a strong and subtle piece of work, which the Stalinists . . . found . . . difficult to answer. . . .

In this pamphlet Trotsky called for a return to the [fundamentals] of Marxism, of which he said the Bolsheviks were losing sight. His main thesis was that the Revolution must be dynamic, not static, that it could not mark time, but must always, everywhere, push forward. Trotsky utilized this [argument] for a telling attack upon the home and foreign policies of the Stalinists and more particularly upon the theory, which they had not yet fully adopted, although it was in process of formation, that it was possible to "build Socialism in a single country." This theory, be it said, Marx had once described as rank heresy, although Stalin's apologists later argued with evident justice that in speaking of "a country" Marx had in mind the comparatively small States of Europe rather than such vast and economically self-sufficient . . . units as . . . the U.S.S.R. Trotsky thus appealed to Marxist internationalism and the ideal of World Revolution against Stalin's policy as ruler of Russia; he was trying to drive a wedge between the Bolshevik as . . . Marxist revolutionary, and the Bolshevik as statesman directing the destinies of a nation. To this apple of discord flung into the midst of his victorious opponents in the Central Committee, Trotsky added a grain of mustard seed, which later . . . flourished exceedingly, in the shape of a question about class differentiation in the villages and the right course to be adopted towards the kulaks and middle peasants.

I thought about the pamphlet for a long time, and [decided] that the Party controversy was big news. The next day I went out to gather information. . . . I had guessed right. . . . I heard that the Kamenev-Zinoviev group in the Stalin *bloc* were showing signs of restiveness, partly because they saw that Stalinism was progressing from Leninism (as Leninism had progressed from Marxism) towards a form . . . of its own, partly because they were jealous and alarmed by Stalin's growing predominance. All my informants agreed that the Party fight would be the news center for the coming winter.

Sure enough . . . Zinoviev and Kamenev spent the autumn in creating inside the majority *bloc* a new opposition movement and . . . concealed their doings so dexterously that it was not until the delegates to the December Party Congress had been elected that Stalin perceived how the wind was blowing. Kamenev's case was relatively unimportant; he had a fair measure of support in the Moscow delegation but nothing like a majority. Zinoviev, however, had long been undisputed boss of Leningrad and had packed the delegation . . . with his own henchmen. It was too late to change the delegations, but the Party Secretariat (*i.e.,* Stalin) lost not a moment in cutting the ground from under Zinoviev's feet. There was a radical change in personnel amongst the permanent officials of the Leningrad Party machine, particularly in the Communist Youth organization, where pro-Zinoviev tendencies were most marked. The editorial staff of the two Party organs, the *Leningrad Pravda* and the *Leningrad Communist Youth Pravda,* were sweepingly reformed; and a vigorous "educational campaign" (*i.e.,* propaganda drive) was begun in every factory and office in the city. . . .

At the December Congress Zinoviev and Kamenev played possum, but in the following spring they joined Trotzky to form a united opposition *bloc* which concentrated its assault upon Stalin's agrarian policy,

demanding that the kulaks be expropriated immediately. Stalin refused to yield; he . . . used all the weapons in his armory, from control of the Party machine and the Press to police regulations about public meetings. It availed his opponents little to say that he forced them into a position of illegality, into holding secret conclaves or using "underground" printing-presses to disseminate their views. The news of a secret meeting which they held in the woods near Moscow in the autumn of 1926 produced such a furore that Trotzky, Zinoviev and Kamenev were expelled from the Politburo without a voice being raised to defend them. The six chief opposition leaders yielded to public indignation and issued a formal disavowal of "underground tactics" and "illegal factional meetings," but in the following spring and summer they returned to the charge in the belief, which perhaps was justified, that the Party masses were really stirred by the kulak danger. Again Stalin muffled the attack by control of the Press and public meetings. The opposition leaders lost their heads; on November 7th, anniversary of the Revolution, they "came out into the streets" in Moscow and Leningrad and appealed to the people from balconies or in the public squares. The attempt was a fiasco; the public was indifferent. . . . But in Soviet law this was counter-revolution. For the last time Trotzky had played . . . into Stalin's hand; this error was fatal—political suicide. On December 18th the Fifteenth Party Congress expelled the seventy-five leading members of the opposition from the Communist Party; its adherents followed, neck and crop. In January, 1928, the oppositionists great and small were scattered in exile across Siberia and Central Asia.

Terror as a Political Weapon*

. . . Rumors about new tension in high quarters began to spread. It could be heard in the growing queues of people [outside the] food stores. It was common gossip . . . in restaurants, . . . at intimate parties. . . . The Black Marias were again heard screeching their way up Lubianka at all hours. . . . Obviously the tide of persecution in the countryside was finally reaching the capital. Again, as in 1924, the victims of the terror were not as yet the Trotskyists, but the so-called *Lishentsi,* a newly coined name for Nepmen. The exact meaning of the word—"deprived ones"— made it a fitting term for men and women torn from their homes and shorn of all human rights.

A new feature in this wave of horror was railway terminals crowded with Lishentsi. . . . Hungry, and in rags, thousands of men, women, and children sat or stood around waiting for freight trains to carry them [away]. . . . At the October terminal I stood for hours watching Chekists load victims on a freight train. . . .

As the . . . terror mounted, Muscovites became aware of a new breed of sadists, worse even than the professional Chekists. They were the communist youth shock brigadiers mobilized by the Apparat[1] to help the GPU. . . . On instructions from Stalin's headquarters these brigadiers went through Moscow's homes in search of suspects. . . .

Personal grievances and old scores were being settled by arrest. The refusal of women to submit to the advances of . . . shock brigadiers was known to result in

the . . . exile of entire families. There were no legal safeguards. . . . Not a word had as yet been published about the new split in the party, but Stalin had prepared the way for it by putting the whole country into a state of panic.

Mass terror . . . soon reaches a point where most people feel physically and mentally paralyzed. . . . Worst of all, they begin to suspect one another of being spies and *provocateurs.* . . . Panic often destroys even the devotion of home and family. In such an atmosphere conspiratorial underground resistance becomes ever more difficult. The dictator can then proceed in the manner of a surgeon in the operating room. His patient is prostrate, his staff awed by his presence and submissive. He may do what he will . . . for he has succeeded in engineering a mass resignation to fate.

Long before he is ready to strike down a foe, Stalin takes pains to isolate him in a spiritual vacuum. The victim, with few exceptions, eagerly grasps at mere life, oblivious of ideals, honor, or chivalry. There is little room for lofty principles in a land lorded over by a gang of assassins whose chief operational slogan is "the end justifies all means."

[Thus] Stalin paved the way for his final onslaught on Trotsky. In doing this he was again trampling down the helpless, inarticulate, disorganized masses. It was they who paid with their life's blood for every move of the ideological gangster on his way to absolute power.

During this period of panic I, like other foreigners in Moscow, went about in a widening vacuum of social isolation. Some friends vanished; others, though still in Moscow, kept away. . . .

Still, there were Russians who continued to visit me unmolested. Many of them were Rights; others, Trotskyists like Sasha. The feeling of security among the Rights was

* SOURCE: W. Reswick, *I Dreamt Revolution,* Chicago, Regnery, 1952, pp. 166-173. William Reswick emigrated from Russia to America in 1904. In 1922 he joined the American Relief Administration in the Ukraine. In 1923 he was sent back to Russia to serve as special correspondent for the Hearst newspapers.

[1] Stalin's political machine.

understandable—they were still in charge of the government. But how was one to explain the almost total, if only temporary, immunity of Trotskyists? Beginning in winter, and throughout the spring and early summer of 1926, they were busily engaged in printing and distributing illegal leaflets. In some they called Stalin the "Tsar of the kulaks." In others they accused the Rights of hatching a "counterrevolutionary conspiracy." Unable to hire halls, they would hold clandestine meetings in one-room apartments. . . . But the GPU did not seem to mind. . . .

About the same time there came persistent reports of unsuppressed strikes. What was behind this laxity of the police . . . ? Some believed that [Stalin] was determined not to violate a deathbed promise to Lenin to safeguard life within the party. Others explained it by Stalin's fear of a Red Army still devoted to Trotsky. People more realistic [believed] that Stalin was deliberately provoking his foes in order to expose their clandestine activities and thus prove to the men in the government that the Trotskyist movement had reached the proportions of an actual counterrevolutionary menace and must be dealt with summarily.

Those advancing this view pointed to the utter impossibility of clandestine printing in a country where all machinery and paper were in the hands of the Apparat. They pointed out that in a capital honeycombed with spies and *provocateurs* there could be no secret meetings without the active participation of undercover men from the Apparat, . . . assigned to draw out the foe in order to destroy him.

As yet, Stalin was still far from being undisputed master of Russia. He still had to justify his every major move in face of growing resistance from the Right. He knew too well that further progress towards a one-man dictatorship depended on his ability to keep his actual and potential foes separated until he could face them all with a special armed force at his command. At the moment, his newly organized military police amounted to no more than a few widely scattered regiments, but he was working fast. . . . Few people realize when they speak of Russia's enormous police army that it was this army which enabled Stalin to head off any effort of his opponents to save Russia from his despotic rule. Only military force could settle this issue, and Stalin had the advantage of always thinking in terms of force. At the time I speak of he was proceeding cautiously, always on the alert against . . . an understanding between Lefts and Rights. They were both doomed, he knew, if they persisted in going separate ways until he had his . . . police army ready.

Trotsky Outwitted *

Stalin had good reason for delaying the public announcement of his new feud with Trotsky. He was waiting for the outcome of Trotsky's negotiations with Zinoviev and Kamenev, their widely rumored attempt to unite in an anti-Stalinist block.

Stalin was aware that he could not liquidate the Trotskyists along with the "deprived" Nepmen so long as Trotsky was still the living symbol of military victory. . . . The thing to do was to drag the hero

* SOURCE: *Ibid.*, pp. 175-183.

off his pedestal. This difficult task would be made easy if Trotsky were to unite with these two widely discredited leaders, who in 1924 had demanded his arrest and expulsion from the party.

A Trotsky-Zinoviev-Kamenev bloc seemed . . . unthinkable to the millions of devoted Trotskyists. But Stalin, an acute observer of men, had reason to believe that this supposedly uncompromising leader was capable of unprincipled maneuvers. He had evidence of it in Trotsky's disavowal of

Max Eastman's book *Since Lenin Died,* with its revelation that Lenin's last letter to the party had demanded the removal of Stalin as General Secretary. . . . Stalin demanded, on pain of disciplinary action by the party, that Trotsky disavow the author and deny that such a document as Lenin's Testament existed. For some time the matter hung fire, and everybody assumed that Trotsky must be grateful to Eastman for revealing not only the testament but the conspiracy of the troika—Stalin, Kamenev, and Zinoviev—against him after Lenin's death. Trotsky's disavowal of Eastman's book shocked those who looked to him for leadership. . . . Trotsky in exile "disavowed his disavowal" and published a letter . . . praising Max Eastman. . . . But that was long after. At the time, I remember a conversation with Yenukidze about this act of weakness.

"Trotsky was not alone," he said, "in telling this lie as a matter of party discipline. Lenin's wife Krupskaya joined him in it. But Krupskaya is not an idol as Trotsky is. An idol must never step down from his pedestal. If he does, his glory may be dimmed forever."

. . . Trotsky committed this grave error in April 1926; and Stalin was not slow to exploit it. Through his controlled media of press and platform, he informed the public that Trotsky was again on the warpath against Lenin's party, bolstered now by a formidable "cabal of anti-Leninists." This demanded a campaign of "enlightenment," which consisted of the publication of old compromising truths, half-truths, and newly invented . . . lies. Apparat columnists recalled Trotsky's quarrels with Lenin. They brought up Kamenev's telegram to the Grand Duke Michael congratulating the late Tsar's brother on his accession to the throne. Again and again Stalin's feature writers reminded Kamenev and Zinoviev of their crime of opposing the insurrection in October 1917. There followed a flood of quotations from speeches and writings in which the rebels had at one time or another abused Lenin or ridiculed his theories. The quotes were taken at random and out of context. The rebels countered with underground pamphlets in which they were soon demanding the publication of Lenin's suppressed testament—so recently declared to be nonexistent. The net result of this combat of quotations was to befog the plain truth that the factions were fighting for control of the party machine unconcerned by the growing plight of the people.

*   *   *

In the spring of 1926 the Rights gained unexpected strength. It came from the countryside, where millions of peasants went on strike in retaliation for the ravages of GPU execution squads. As if by tacit agreement they refused to go into the fields unless the government called a halt to repression and supplied them with rural essentials. At the same time the peasants overwhelmed their sons in the Red Army with letters of woe. . . .

More than ever now the Rights were concerned not only with freedom within the . . . party but also with basic human rights for the whole country. They renewed their demand that Stalin put an end to this new wave of terror and were successful in compelling it sooner than he wished. Moreover, at both the April and July meetings of the Central Committee they demanded and secured a . . . frank debate on all the issues then facing the country. Of still greater importance was Stalin's yielding to a demand by Rykov to publicize the proceedings. Thus everybody knew that at both meetings delegates from industrial districts reminded the leaders that while Russia was preparing to celebrate the tenth anniversary of the Revolution, many Soviet workers were still living in vermin-infested barracks where the allotted living space for each worker was "about the size of a coffin."

At the April session of the Central Committee, Health Commissar Semashko told the delegates that Russia's nine million shelterless children were a "living reproach to its conscience." At the same conference Lenin's widow Krupskaya revealed that most of these children were no longer the heritage of the civil war but came from homes ravaged by the GPU. . . .

Dzerzhinsky, founder of the GPU, told

the delegates: "When I look at our Apparat, as well as at our incredible bureaucracy, I am literally horrified." But he also denounced the Trotskyists, saying that their chief concern in the midst of this widespread misery was to intrigue for power. He bitterly attacked Trotsky's demand for a higher tax levy on the peasants.

"True," he said, "our hundred million peasants have saved four hundred million rubles—four rubles apiece—and with this Comrade Trotsky proposes to build a Soviet industry!" . . .

[Stalin] kept his peace for the rest of that summer. But early in the autumn he hit on a clever diversion. . . . He announced a "popular proletarian debate on Trotskyism." By way of refuting the charge of a one-man dictatorship, he let it be known that the Soviet workers would actually decide the issue in their resolutions to be adopted at each meeting. It was a clever move, one to which the Rights, as champions of Soviet democracy, could take no exception.

The announcement of the debate was followed up with a campaign of renewed slander in the press, calculated to goad the rebels into appearing before hostile, indifferent, or terrorized crowds to answer the charges.

Many of Trotsky's friends advised him to stay away from these meetings. But *provocateurs* were on hand to urge him to lay his case before the "proletarian tribunal of last resort." . . . Trotsky and his followers walked into the trap. They found that the "tribunal of last resort" was a gang of Stalin's roughnecks. . . . Everywhere their appearance on platforms was greeted with yells, catcalls, and riots . . . engineered by men from the Apparat who, under instructions from the Secretary, raced from hall to hall and from factory to factory.

After a week of this "proletarian debate," all Moscow knew that the Trotskyists were near the end of their rope. Nowhere had any of them got a chance to speak his mind. Everywhere they had been yelled at, yanked, and pushed off the platform. Everywhere flying wedges from the Apparat had been busy breaking up meetings.

The majority of workers, having lived through years of terror, were in no mood to defend the rebels. A temporary increase in rations coupled with a promise of better living quarters lulled most of them into a state of apathy. The Trotskyists' long-winded Marxian arguments fell on deaf ears.

At a [factory] meeting . . . I saw Trotsky hissed, spat at, and all but kicked off the . . . platform. . . . In less than a year the hero of the people had become an object of pity. Thanks to his errors and to the astuteness of his enemy, his prestige was destroyed.

The riots in Soviet factories, though provoked by Stalinist gangsters, were used as a pretext to suppress the opposition. Larin, one of Stalin's chief spokesmen, openly warned them that unless they submitted to party discipline the issue would be settled with machine guns. The Rights were worried. In an effort to prevent bloodshed, Yenukidze, Rykov, Bukharin, Tomsky, and others made desperate efforts to arrive at an understanding with Trotsky, but for ethical reasons they were unwilling to deal with Zinoviev and Kamenev. Resentful of this insult to his unprincipled friends, Trotsky took another long step on the road to ruin. He decided to negotiate directly with Stalin, whose emissaries assured him that he and the other leaders of the opposition would be dealth with "humanely." The first seeds of an intrigue against the Rights were planted at these unholy peace talks between the blind fanatics and the unprincipled schemers.

As a consequence, in the beginning of 1927 it began to look as though strife within the party was a thing of the past. Officially there was peace on Soviet earth and contentment in the Apparat. But as the year advanced, it became increasingly evident that this hastily patched up *mariage de convenance* was no cure for Russia's desperately sick economy. In the tenth year of the Revolution, Russia's prerevolutionary reserves were almost gone and its industry was reaching the point of exhaustion. The situation in the countryside was going from bad to worse. After a brief lull in the terror, there was renewed agitation against the "murderous kulaks," who as if by common agreement resumed the massacre of village correspondents—also of officials sent to the country to "buy" grain at arbitrary prices for the army and for industrial workers. It was a repetition of the previous year's troubles, but on a much larger scale. Soon the shortage of food was felt in Moscow's barracks and factories. Again, as in every crisis, the city seethed with rumors of strikes and riots.

In these circumstances the Rights renewed their agitation for wider economic and political concessions at home and abroad. The Trotskyists, after months of adherence to their agreement to "behave," became restive again. Always on the alert for some weak spot in Stalin's armor, they were quick to exploit his high-handed policy in China which resulted in the massacre of many Chinese Communists. On that occasion they succeeded in circulating an anti-Stalinist protest signed by eighty-three leading Bolsheviks. It began to look again as though they might reach out for power. Their steadily mounting volume of illegal printing, coupled with a temporary silence of the Apparat, gave rise to rumors of a newly forged anti-Stalinist bloc which included the Rights. . . . It looked as though Stalin, blinded by an excess of power, had made some fatal mistake. . . .

At that time two events put an abrupt end to all such hopes. In May 1927 the British Government, after raiding the Soviet Trade Delegation in London, broke off diplomatic relations with the Soviet Union. Shortly thereafter Warsaw flashed the news of the assassination of the Soviet Ambassador Voykov. Within a day the Apparat was hard at work whipping up a war scare. With his inborn taste for terror, Stalin began by executing twenty former aristocrats. . . . Few Muscovites had any doubt about their innocence. But their execution touched off one of those chain reactions to which Russia had become accustomed under Stalin. The capital rocked with rumors of . . . arrests and . . . executions. At the same time there was persistent talk that the murder in Warsaw had been planned in Moscow. It

was the timing of it that gave rise to these rumors. The killing of the ambassador came just in time to prevent a showdown with Stalin. For weeks preceding Voykov's death Stalin had been on the defensive, but the next day he had the Soviet capital in a state of total panic and was loudly accusing Trotsky and his followers of treason. Whatever progress may have been made in forging an anti-Stalinist front was thus wiped out overnight.

During the preceding lull in party strife I had discussed the situation with Yagoda. Like others at the top, he believed that "radical adjustments" in the Apparat were imminent. But the day after the murder of Voykov he was a changed man. He drank heavily and seemed anxious to avoid all talk about the event. Earlier in the evening I had visited the Literary Club where pro-Trotskyist sentiment ran high at the time. It was there that rumors of the Apparat's connection with the Voykov murder first reached me. I told Yagoda what I had heard and saw his face tighten. He leaned close saying: ". . . As a friend I must advise you to avoid all such talk. The way things look to me, we are on the verge of war." This was the new line, then: WAR! What could be more timely than a wave of terror based on the assassination of a Soviet ambassador and the threat of foreign attack.

Now Stalin devised new methods to convince the country of its imminent peril. One of them was Cheka raids on trains, boats, and other means of conveyance. On my way to Leningrad one night I was witness to what the chief conductor called a "routine checkup." . . . An hour out of Moscow the train was stopped and boarded by a detachment of officers, soldiers, and armed civilians. They went through the coaches . . . subjecting everyone to a search. . . . Many of the passengers had no identity papers. They were removed from the train and placed under arrest in a roped-off space on the platform.

. . . Children were in terror, their mothers hysterical. Men pleaded in vain. . . . There was no violence; just machinelike obedience of soldiers to their commander.

Stalin at the Helm*

On September 9, 1927, Stalin answered a number of questions directed at him by a delegation of American trade unionists:

Question 8. Is the opposition in the Russian Party strong and on what circles does it rest?

Answer: I think that it is very weak. . . . Today's [paper] contains a survey of the last few days' discussions. [More than] 135,000 members of the Party voted for the Central Committee and its theses, and only 1,200 voted for the opposition. . . . I think that the future votes will be even more disastrous for the opposition. Our discussion will last up to the Congress. . . . We will canvass the whole Party and you will see that the relative strength of the opposition . . . will be even more insignificant. . . . It is quite possible that at our Fifteenth Party Congress the opposition will not have a single . . . delegate. . . .

On what circles does the opposition rest? I think that the opposition is supported primarily by non-proletarian circles. . . . Why? Because . . . the opposition [struggles] essentially . . . against the Party, . . . against the regime of the proletarian dictatorship, with which certain non-proletarian sections cannot but be dissatisfied. . . .

Question 9. Is [the] contention, now circulated in Germany, that the present leaders of the Comintern and the Russian Party are betraying the workers to the counter-revolution, correct?

Answer: We must assume that it is correct. There is also reason to think that the Comintern and the C.P.S.U.[1] are betraying

the working classes of the U.S.S.R. to the counter-revolutionaries of the world. Moreover, I can inform you that the Comintern and the C.P.S.U. recently decided to bring back all landlords and capitalists who have been driven out of the country, to restore their factories to them. . . . The Comintern and the C.P.S.U. have [further] decided that the time has come for Bolsheviks to become cannibals. Finally, we have decided to nationalize all women and to make it a practice to violate our own sisters. [General laughter. Several delegates: "Who could have asked such a question?"] I can see that you are all laughing. Perhaps some of you will think that I am not serious on the question. Of course, comrades, a question like this cannot be treated seriously. I think that such questions can be answered only by ridicule. [Loud applause.]

Question 12. Can you outline briefly the characteristics of the Society of the future which communism is trying to create?

Answer: . . . Briefly, . . . it is a society in which (a) there will be no private ownership of the means of production but social, collective ownership; (b) there will be no classes or state, but workers in industry and agriculture managing their economic affairs as a free association of toilers; (c) national economy, organized according to plan, will be based on the highest technique in both industry and agriculture; (d) there will be no antithesis between town and country, between industry and agriculture; (e) the products will be distributed according to the principle . . . "from each according to his abilities, to each according to his needs." (f) science and art will enjoy conditions conducive to their highest development; (g) the individual, freed from bread and butter cares, and of the necessity of cringing to the "powers that be" will become really free, etc., etc. Clearly we are still remote from such a society.

* SOURCE: J. Stalin, *Interviews with Foreign Workers' Delegation*, New York, International Publishers, 1927, pp. 50-51; and J. V. Stalin, *Works*, Moscow, 1954, X, pp. 139-141.

[1] Communist Party of the Soviet Union.

With regard to the international conditions necessary for the complete triumph of communist society, these will develop and grow in proportion as revolutionary crises and revolutionary outbreaks of the working class in capitalist countries grow. It must not be imagined that the working class in one country, or in several countries, will march toward socialism, and still more to communism, and that the capitalists of other countries will sit still with folded arms. . . . Still less it must be imagined that the working class in capitalist countries will agree to be mere spectators of the [victory] of socialism in one or another country. As a matter of fact, the capitalists will do all in their power to crush such countries. [But] every important step taken towards socialism and still more towards communism in any country will be inevitably accompanied by the unrestrained efforts of the working class in capitalist countries to achieve . . . socialism. . . . Thus in the . . . progress . . . of the international revolution, two world centers will be formed, the Socialist center, attracting to itself all the countries gravitating towards socialism, and the capitalist center, attracting to itself all the countries gravitating towards capitalism. The fight between these two centers . . . will decide the fate of capitalism and communism throughout the . . . world, for the final defeat of world capitalism means the victory of socialism in the arena of world economy.

Problems of Urban Life*

"Do you live like this in America?" Marfousha asked. . . . "In this apartment there are six families. . . . The Bogolubovs, . . . the Krassovs. . . . He's a former 'White' officer—the scamp! Then the Blitzmans. . . . There's . . . a Jew in every apartment. And their dirty children! But he's rich. . . . Next to them . . . Adamov . . . a railroad conductor. . . . What his wife does when he's away is a shame! Then . . . the Laptevs—factory workers. . . . Four children and the worst room—it stinks."

"That's about twenty-five people in this seven room apartment?" I asked.

"[Plus] servants. Three . . . families . . . have one. . . . You must have a servant if you have a family—to look out for the children, to stand in line at the stores. . . ."

All this because the impoverished government could not build fast enough to offset the rush to the Centre. A city with less than a million people grew to two millions when it became the political and economic capital of the land. . . .

"Is your husband a Party member?"

* SOURCE: W. C. White, *These Russians*, New York, Scribner's, 1931, pp. 2-14, 157.

"No, he's too lazy. He works in an office and earns only a hundred rubles a month. He's a good husband, but he drinks too much. . . ."

So lives most of Moscow—a family to a room; two thousand people . . . in a house which formerly held five hundred. . . . "What is your conception of an ideal home?" was the theme . . . assigned to a class in Moscow. One answer said: "A room through which strangers do not have to pass to get to their room."

*   *   *

[A typist told me about a Communist in her office whose wife was offered a two-year job in Siberia as an agronomist.] ". . . Her husband couldn't leave his work and she couldn't let this chance go by. Of course they divorced before she went away; what sense . . . staying married at that distance? We Russians are not hypocrites! After a year the husband married a girl in our office. Now his former wife has come back to Moscow for further study—"

"Where does she live?"

"With her former husband and his wife

of course. What other room could she find? . . ."

*   *   *

. . . Side by side . . . live professors, policemen, clerks . . . actors. . . . Strangers to one another, . . . their lives are intimately bound together. At four [P.M.] seven housewives or their servants crowd in each kitchen, preparing seven kinds of soup with seven conflicting odors. . . . In one apartment seven families . . . fight over their turn at the bath. [They also argue about cleaning the corridor and about telephone and electric bills.]

Moscow usually buys its food at the [inadequately supplied] corner stores, . . . operated by the government. . . . Before 1929 there was no rationing. . . . With poor distribution, stores received limited amounts—and lines formed. Now, with ration cards, lines [are shorter] but rations seem severe—three quarters of a pound of meat . . . several times a week. . . . The factory-working class receives double . . . rations. . . . Within the limits of the rations the prices are low. A few private stores exist where one can buy to any amount, but . . . the average Muscovite cannot pay [their prices].

"The worst thing [said Marfousha] is standing in line. . . . Sometimes I and my sister and my husband [Andrei] are standing at three different stores at the same time. . . ."

. . . Rents are low. The house is managed by a committee made up of one member from each apartment. In addition there are two or three salaried members who devote all their time to finances, to arranging for repairs, to registering passports and personal papers. They set the rents, which depend on the amount of space occupied, the number in the family, and the salary and profession of the tenant. There is nothing to bar you from all the space you want if you can pay the increased rent—and if you can find the space. A factory worker with a large family will have a big room for a few rubles a month; a doctor will pay more; and a private merchant, if he is allowed to have a room at all, will pay even ten times as much as the factory hand. If the tenant is unemployed and in good standing, the rent is almost nothing. The committee collects the money and apportions it for repairs; for major repairs they can borrow money from the government.

Andrei came in one evening to collect the rent. He is a messenger boy in a government office. . . . In addition he is the member of the house committee from the apartment.

"This committee work keeps me busy, as if six hours each day in my office wasn't enough. . . . Meetings, . . . nothing but meetings. . . . And the house committee must campaign for government bonds, for the Red Cross; it conducts a day nursery for children while their mothers go to work, and a school to 'liquidate illiteracy' in the evenings. . . . They blame the committee . . . for everything, just as if we were paid for our services. . . ." He changed the subject abruptly. "Is it true you have prohibition in America? Life must be awfully lonesome there without Vodka. . . ."

*   *   *

Marfousha came the next morning, looking a few years older.

". . . How old do I look—thirty-five?"

My embarrassed silence was a positive answer.

"I am twenty-six, but I have had nine abortions. . . . The doctor said . . . I must never have another one. But I can't have any more children, on a hundred rubles a month. . . . Abortions are free. . . . The hospital [does] them without asking any questions, but they give you nothing to stop the pain. Often the clinic is crowded. I [stood] in line [seven hours]. . . ."

The Government has instituted free abortions, for ignorance, superstition and religion act as barriers to the spread of birth control information.

"You can get medical attention free, can't you?" I asked.

"Yes, if you belong to the trade union. And everybody does, except the 'former people.' . . ."

Fathers and Children: Old and Young*

Abram Mosevitch: The Merchant

"The government is content to let us private merchants exist because they need us," he began. "We do bring certain supplies onto the market which perhaps would not reach there otherwise. . . . Yet to-day I saw clearly their policy. They permit us to exist but tax us almost . . . to that point at which we must close up shop. The . . . tax commissioner came to-day to my stand. 'How much was your income during the past six months?' he asked. I told him, 'About eighteen hundred rubles.' '[If true], your tax will be eight hundred rubles.' Just like that. . . . And mind you, being 'deprived' means I have to pay more for everything. Where can I find eight hundred rubles? . . .

"Then the [commissioner] went to the neighbors. . . . He asked them 'Has Silverson's wife had a new coat? . . . New furniture? . . . That's the way this . . . financial ministry [checks] on incomes. . . . If only I could find something else to do I should give up my stand, but, as one 'deprived,' I am barred forever from any government work. So they force us to continue private trading by closing everything else to us—and then try to stop us by preposterous taxes. . . . Trade was possible for a few years after . . . 1922, but now it is getting worse and worse. . . ."

"I don't see how you do any business at all with the prices you charge," I said.

"They call it speculating here," he replied bitterly. ". . . The peasants would rather sell [butter and eggs] to us, for we pay higher prices than the government. We bring the goods to Moscow. Our taxes, our higher costs [force us to ask] almost three times as much as the government stores. And our profits are small. But we have one advantage. The government sells everything

by rations. . . . [But], we can sell as much as the purchaser wishes. The government collects its butter and eggs in the villages. Then it figures out a minimum ration—and exports the 'surplus' to Europe to secure precious *valuta*.[1]

". . . I hear people [say], 'Food is scarce because the peasant keeps it and eats it himself.' . . . What rot! I [was] in villages last winter where the horses were killed for food. . . . How rapidly life changes! Twenty years ago in our little village there was quiet. . . . Almost all the people in our village were Jewish; we never mixed with the few Russians. . . . I feel more anti-semitism after this great revolution, than I ever felt before. Particularly . . . in the villages.

"The peasants blame the revolution on the Jew. Stupid . . . Russians. Would there have been a successful Communist party without the support of the peasantry? . . . Now the Communists say that peoples must mix, that Jew and Russian must intermarry,"—he paused—"they must not. We Jews are not like these lazy, vodka-swilling . . . Russians. . . ."

He called me one evening. . . . "Can you come to my room about ten? My son will be there. . . . He is very much interested in America. . . ."

. . . Abram Mosevitch explained. ". . . He works in Turkestan, he is an important Communist down there—he's in Moscow now for some conference. [By working in Turkestan] he avoids any of the disadvantages of his father's deprivation—as it were, disowns me. That is the revolution!"

The son came late. . . . "I am glad to meet an American," he said. . . .

". . . We buy eighteen million dollars worth of cotton each year from America; now we are trying to raise our own in

---

* SOURCE: *Ibid.*, pp. 20-79, 129-131.

[1] Foreign currency; it was used to buy machines abroad.

Turkestan and make ourselves independent of the West. We shall save that much *valuta* for other things. . . . We work with people who ten years ago were in the middle ages. . . . Now we are tugging . . . them into the twentieth century; that is what the revolution means for them. Of course, we have a lot of backward customs to fight. . . . We are moving so rapidly that everything in Europe must seem staid, flat."

"You are moving but none of you know in which direction," said Abram Mosevitch. . . .

"You haven't changed much since I saw you last," said the son.

"How can I change? I am still 'deprived,' still a private merchant, overtaxed and kicked about. . . ."

"I have never known which you can least forgive—my being a Communist, or the fact that I married [a Christian girl]."

". . . Why should they be severe with anyone trying to earn an honest living?" Abram Mosevitch demanded.

"Because the principle of trading for private profit is wrong, because one must work for the State, for the common good."

". . . Being 'deprived' I can find no other work—"

". . . Papasha, there is a movement to get the Jewish traders out of the city and back on the land. . . . Once you work on the land the 'deprived' brand is removed."

"But I am too old to go to farming. And on what will your mother live while I wait for harvests? Anti-semitism is strongest . . . among the peasants."

*　　*　　*

A long time passed before I saw [Abram] again. . . .

He came . . . one night with a burlap bag. . . . "Do you want to buy any oriental rugs?" he asked. . . . "This is illegal. Rug selling has been made a State monopoly. . . ."

"What happened to the butter business?" I asked.

"I had to stop—the government . . . now taxes us out of business. It wants to control all the food supply. . . . What are we [private traders] to do? There are [dishonest] ways to get a living. . . . Samuels, the butcher, you remember him? He is in jail for [peddling illegally acquired cotton cloth]." . . .

He came again in November. . . .

"I had to stop the carpet business—I could sell nothing. . . . I am penniless. . . . They have begun to sell machines here to weave stockings. Anybody can use them at home. The government counts such work 'honest labor' and perhaps I can have the 'deprived' mark taken off. Then my wife could go to the State hospital—she is sick.

"Earlier, when I had money, . . . we could go to private doctors. . . . If I had two of those machines my wife and I could operate them at home and earn . . . a living. . . . But those [imported] machines cost a hundred and fifty rubles each. . . . Yet where can I find three hundred rubles? I cannot borrow it as I have no security. . . ."

Then, with the appearance of a man grasping at a last hope, he asked, "Can you lend me three hundred rubles?"

Pavel Nestorovich: The Village Priest

He is nearing seventy. . . . He is a priest at the church in the Spassky convent, the last of fifty who once attended there. The convent . . . has been closed, but the white-walled church is open on Sundays for service and its bell tower . . . still marks the hours for the little village. Eight years ago the . . . nuns were dispersed. . . . They live as . . . women of all work, in the villages round about. On Sundays . . . they return to the church to sing in the choir, or to [pray]. . . .

. . . There are five other [closed] churches within the [convent] walls. . . . "One [church] is enough," the workers living in the former convent decided. One has [become] a day nursery. . . . Another is a "club." . . . [Two others house firewood], and the fifth is a storeroom for the community store.

The factory workers decided long ago that the old priest should not be allowed to live within the convent. He has a little two-room house half a mile away. His family is scattered. . . . There is left only a daughter, Sophie . . . , and a son, Dmitri. . . . Dmitri . . . is a Communist. . . . He is an active member of the Atheists' Society and is . . . ashamed that he still feels drawn to his father. . . . He [conceals] the fact that he is a priest's son . . . , it might mean no job. . . . Yet every week he travels forty miles to see his father and sister and . . . gives them part of his salary. . . .

[Pavel Nestorovich] is, of course, one of the "deprived." . . .

Vladimir Alexeitch: The Professor

[The physics professor] Vladimir Alexeitch took me into his study. ". . . I should like to see you frequently—I must have contacts abroad. . . . But [I] must be careful. . . . We [of the intelligentsia] are not against the proletariat, but because we are not of it the Communists regard us . . . as potential enemies. So, seeing foreigners too often gets some of us in jail. . . . Yet I must keep in touch with more than merely the scientific developments in the world outside. Have you any magazines or new books . . . ?"

The revolution came early to the universities; some . . . professors went abroad. Those who remained were divided into two classes: the group whose subjects [had no] political bearing and that group whose subjects—history, politics, economics—had to be taught on the basis of the new philosophy of class. The first group continued to teach; the most famous of the second group were pensioned, the others dismissed, and a new set, the "Red professors," arose. These were chiefly younger men, members of the Party or [sympathizers].

At the same time "class consciousness" was applied in admitting students. . . .

"Every year," said Vladimir Alexeitch, "our work becomes more difficult. . . . Every year the Communist Party reaches out for greater control. . . ."

He questioned me about the professors I had met. Most of them, teaching politics and law, were . . . Red professors.

"[They are] loudspeakers for the Communists, [not scholars. They] cull anthol-ogies from Lenin and Marx . . . rewrite each others' books. . . . 'The Peasant on the Way to Socialism,' . . . 'Lenin on Disarmament,' 'Lenin on Community Kitchens.' . . . They say some medical student wanted to offer a thesis—'Lenin on Appendicitis.'

"The title 'professor' . . . still means [something] in science and medicine. But in other fields—! . . . [We] who aren't 'Red' are watched closely for any 'counterrevolutionary' manifestations. They haven't troubled me much; I have my teaching and the government is helping me build a laboratory. With its limited means the government does its best for science. Besides, it is difficult to be counter-revolutionary in physics. . . .

". . . Some of my colleagues have done great research—all the greater if you consider the atmosphere we work in. And we work loyally—those of us whom they allow to work. . . . [We] believe Communism is a passing phase. Russia will find herself. They need us here—we are few. We have our work . . . it is the one firm rock left for us. . . ."

*   *   *

"My wife is very religious," Vladimir Alexeitch [said].

"Lord," [she broke in], "all this propaganda against the church? . . . Who runs the Atheists' Society? Jews, Jews, Jews! . . ."

[Natalya Ivanovna] shuddered. "To think that Russia should be fought for between a Jew [Trotsky] and a Georgian (Stalin)! . . . Scoundrels! . . . Wait, wait. There will be a pogrom. . . . When this damned system breaks [you] will be able to row [through Moscow] on Jewish blood. . . ."

"Before the revolution there were very few Jews in Moscow . . . ," Vladimir Alexeitch explained. . . . "They were . . . terribly persecuted. . . . Many times we helped them—. . . students, intelligentsia, you know. . . ."

"And what have we got for it? Now they are . . . running everything. It is all Jewish."

"Comrade Stalin isn't, my dear."

"What difference . . . between a Georgian and a Jew? Wait . . . until trouble begins. . . . Before the revolution the Jews lived in one section. Now they are everywhere, a family in each apartment. And each apartment will have its own little pogrom."

"My dear, the great Russian fault has always been not blaming things on defects in our own character but on the Jew. They are our great national excuse."

"But now everything is the fault of the Communists and they are all Jews."

"My dear, not ten per cent are Jews. . . . [You] remind me of the sign in the kosher butcher shop [on] the anniversary of Lenin's death. . . . It read 'Lenin is Dead But His Work Goes On.' It fell down and partly covered another sign already there. From the street, the sign in the window . . . read, 'Lenin Is Dead But His Work Goes On . . . Under the Supervision of Rabbi Cohen.' Dear, please get us some more tea."

*   *   *

Adamova: The Student

The professor [was lecturing at] the First Moscow University. . . .

"Comrades, to-day we take up the subject . . ." he began. . . .

A girl in a black leather coat, . . . a bulging briefcase under her arm, rushed to the platform.

["Comrades," she cried], turning to the students, "this lecture cannot be held to-day. The meeting of the *Comsomoltsi* scheduled for this evening has been moved to this hour." . . . The Class broke up.

"That was Adamova," said my friend Voronov, another student. "She's a peasant, the secretary of the *Comsomoltsi*—the Young Communist's League. They have as much power in this university as the professors. . . . Another meeting, the Devil, always meetings. . . . She's in everything. . . . Why is it . . . always the unattractive women who go into politics? . . . Is it the same in America? . . . Now that little *blondinka* down there"—pointing to a student below—"she's non-Party. But she's just as busy as Adamova . . . with other things," and he winked.

The First Moscow University specializes in politics, economics, law, languages, and literature; the Second University teaches the sciences. . . . Side by side sit boys and girls of eighteen, just in from provincial cities, with policemen, detailed by their superiors for college education; factory workers of forty on leave of absence for a few years; the brighter pupils from Moscow's secondary schools. Russians and swarthy Uzbek from Turkestan, Jew and Georgian, . . . Mongol and . . . Ukrainian are students together beneath the slogan "Science belongs to the workers." They are lucky. . . . Ten times their number have been refused admission.

Admission depends on the entrance examination . . . and on . . . the applicant's "social origin." . . . There is no room for the children of the "former people," [or] of priests, private merchants, or other classes. . . . "Science belongs to the workers"—and the children of the factory worker or of the peasant . . . claim their right. No wonder one embarrassed applicant filled in the answer to the question "What is your social origin?" with "Father, —two workmen; Mother,—one peasant."

Each student receives a "stipend"— twenty-seven rubles a month. . . . This is the sole income for most of them. [Some] find space in the inexpensive dormitories. . . . Others room wherever they can. . . . The students eat at restaurants run for them and share in . . . theatre tickets now and then, medical attention, cheap transportation home. But twenty-seven rubles a month presents problems even to the most economical. . . .

[In the students' club] I sat with Voronov one evening. Adamova was the centre of a little group near by.

". . . It is hard," her voice topped the others, "but . . . student marriages turn out badly and interfere with our work."

Someone mentioned the need for higher stipends.

"Comrades. . . . Is our government a millionaire . . . ? We must make sacrifices too. No marriage . . . it is unnecessary."

Another student spoke of a secretary of a Young Communist League group who had been . . . dismissed for using his position to force favors from the girls in his unit.

"And rightly so," said Adamova. "We must have . . . high standards. . . . If that gets abroad the capitalist press will say, 'See, that's what all Communists do.' . . ."

"From women such as Adamova, deliver us, oh God," Voronov whispered to me. "She's like the woman in the play. Two chemists discover a new brand of soap. What shall they call it? One suggests . . . , 'Karl Marx's first kiss.' The other vetoes that and they agree to name it 'Soviet Woman.' But then, how shall they advertise it? They draw a big picture of a fat cow, with a red bandana tied around its head. And underneath they write—'Soviet Woman.'"

* * *

". . . Tell me, [Adamova asked me], why did such a cultured country as America kill Sacco and Vanzetti? . . . And why does . . . America treat the Negroes as inferiors? Don't you realize that all race hatreds are fostered by the capitalists; they direct the discontent of the oppressed workers against the Negro peoples. It is the same as the Tsarist autocracy did here with the Jews. . . .

". . . Look at us in the University . . . Russian, Chuvash, Jew. . . . Under socialism there is no race hatred. . . . You see we know more of America here than you know of us. We want to learn—we are a backward country and you can teach us much. But in America you think 'Pff, what can we learn from Russia?' . . . I know America—I have read Upton Sinclair, Jack London. We shall learn all we can from you, . . . and overtake you. We are a young people. We are building. . . ."

Adamova [went on]. "You think this is a bad way to live? Crowded . . . but we are used to that in our [village huts]. . . .

"The worst thing here is our health. . . .

"Tuberculosis . . . and in winter every-

body gets tonsilitis. But look at how many want to get in the University. Here education is free, for everybody. . . ."

"But supposing your social origin is unfavorable?"

". . . We have no room to educate our enemies. Your American universities keep out certain classes, and so do we; only here education is for the majority, not for the pampered minority. . . . Look at me, before the revolution should I have come into Moscow University? I grew up in a village in Karelia. . . . There were eleven in our family and my father had three acres of land. . . . When I was thirteen I ran away —there was no food in our village. . . . What about women in your universities? Are they interested in labor problems, [in politics] . . . ? [I represent] our University in the Moscow Soviet. . . . I teach a [factory group] to read and write. . . ."

"But what about studying?"

"I do that of course. But our universities are not only for studying. All our social work is part of our education." . . .

* * *

. . . In the main university building . . . months later . . . hung a red banner with the wording: "Any student who knows reasons why another student should be deprived of his right to vote [must] report to the Students' Committee." . . . A bulletin board [listed those] barred from the right to vote [citing] after each name "daughter of a priest," "son of a factory owner. . . ." This was the *chistka* (cleanout) before the annual elections; the right to vote, too, depends on social origin, so the *chistka* is an opportunity to discover which members of the disenfranchised classes were in the University under false colors.

I found Adamova . . . , a crowd around her . . . , talking about the *chistka*.

"How those students slip in, I don't know."

"Oh, they falsify their identity cards."

"They come from far away and think we shan't find out. . . ."

"There is no room in the university"— Adamova was speaking—"for these 'former people.' There are too many workers trying to get in."

The group broke up and Adamova said, ". . . I am so busy with this *chistka*. . . . One of the girls whom we 'cleaned out' yesterday committed suicide last night. . . .

"The 'former people' had their chance to run Russia; we have abolished them and there is no longer a Russia. It is our Soviet Republic . . . *ours*. . . . And now, building the Soviet Union and Communism all the world over has become our life.

"Do you know many 'former people' here? . . . You don't take your opinion of Soviet Russia from them, I hope. . . . Their desire that . . . we shall fail keeps them from [noticing] how we are succeeding. We have some . . . in the University— professors whom for the moment we must use. . . . They work, but only half loyally. . . . We watch them and in the meantime we are training our own intelligentsia; peasant boys . . . will be doctors, engineers. . . . Peasant girls too. . . .

"Never forget . . . that the revolution is continuing. We have enemies. . . . Against those who . . . creep into our institutions . . . we have the *chistka;* against those in our institutions who misuse [our] trust . . . we have the GPU. . . . Last week

. . . three former mine owners . . . working as engineers were shot by the GPU. . . . There was no need to publish details about [their crimes]. Their background is conviction enough. . . . What if a thousand, what if a million perish . . . if we shall be able to build socialism in our country for the remainder? We make mistakes —of course. . . . We . . . criticize ourselves . . . when we are wrong. But it is better that a hundred innocent perish than that one guilty conspirator against our class escape."

. . . About this time [newspapers] were prophesying . . . an attack on Soviet Russia by some alliance of European powers. There were endless . . . mass meetings. At one . . . Adamova [spoke].

"We must always be ready, comrades. The capitalist West grows more jealous every day as . . . our Soviet power [grows]. . . . We are a menace . . . to their blood sucking system. Here the working class moves forward. . . . [Over there] are . . . strikes, unemployment, exploitation of man by man. . . .

. . . "She's a good speaker, . . ." [Voronov whispered]. "But she sounds just like the newspapers. . . ."

New Ways in the Village*

At one o'clock the last [of sixty-five patients] had been interviewed. . . . "An easy day," she said, ". . . I have three operations this afternoon. . . ."

Fifty to a hundred patients, from thirty miles around, come to her hospital every day. Those from . . . near by come for the slightest cause. "They like having someone look after them," she explained. "But those from a distance wait too long. They try their own remedies first. . . . That's where the local charlatans have their hold. And what they do!—put the baby in the

hot oven for five minutes to cure rickets!

"And abortions. [More every] week. The women . . . will not bear twelve and fifteen children. . . . The government says we must do them on request, but I only do them when they already have three children."

The hospital, run by the local Soviet, has a yearly budget of sixteen thousand rubles. It has a ward of twelve beds, an operating room, and supplies a limited stock of medicines. . . . Everything is free. . . . The clinic is open six days a week, from eight until one. "If anyone comes after that time I have the right to charge him, but what

* SOURCE: *Ibid.,* pp. 262-264, 358-362.

can these people pay? . . . The twelve beds in the ward were filled and another dozen beds in the corridor also. "What can I do? This is pneumonia weather and the village Soviet is so poor." . . .

"Why not charge the patients a small sum?"

"It must all be free; they complain of taxes enough as it is. If they had to pay they wouldn't come here."

I declined an invitation to the afternoon's operations and went to the school. It was like all village schools: . . . the science laboratory with a half dozen pieces of pre-revolutionary apparatus; the museum with a few stuffed birds, some of the local rocks. . . .

"They all want to learn so badly," said [the doctor's husband], as he took me around the village, "but the village is so poor. . . . Yet we sent six from here to universities last year. . . . All from . . . [illiterate] parents. About seventy per cent of the population is illiterate. We can't bother to teach them for we are too busy with the younger generation. There is . . . a peasant reading room, in the village, but no one goes there except the children. The parents are supposed to go and someone reads to them; they say it's too boresome, always propaganda."

* * *

The trial began when Gavril Borisovitch came from a side door and walked to the platform. . . . A woman . . . and a man . . . followed and sat with him. The room quieted. . . . [The case involved a peasant girl, pregnant out of wedlock, who had been shamed by her step-mother and step-sister into killing her new-born child.] . . . Gavril frequently interrupted the testi-

mony . . . to ask questions. . . . He did most of the cross examining, in the absence of lawyers. . . . Sometimes his two assistants helped. The step-mother and her daughter were self-confident until Gavril asked . . . : "Did you know she was going to have a child?" "Did you suspect that she might kill it?" "Why didn't you do everything possible to help her have the baby in comfort?"

* * *

Gavril came to the postmaster's that evening. He said . . . , "[We decided] that case in half an hour. [The girl] killed the child. She will be sentenced to seven years but, since she did it because . . . of the cruelty of relatives, the sentence will be commuted to six months. And she has already served four months while waiting for trial. . . . There is a law that says a family must look out for the health of a child in it. We are going to try [the girl's] step-mother and step-sister for breaking that law. . . . The peasants must learn that the revolution removed all shame from the birth of any child. Why should a woman be punished by her family for having a baby?"

I told him of the part that lawyers play in [America] and he laughed. "We don't need them here except in important cases. There is a College of Defense in the district town whose members are assigned to defend cases. But why have lawyers here? They only complicate things. . . . A lawyer is a poor profession [since] the revolution. We don't use precedents and forms. . . . In most of my cases I hear the evidence, ask questions, and give a decision. If you know the customs of a place and the people in it you can always give a fair decision. Our People's courts work rapidly and honestly."

The Engineer*

[Andrei Georgievitch showed me his comfortable four room apartment.] "It is very expensive, but we engineers are well paid. . . ."

"Will [the five-year plan] work?" I asked. . . .

"The first year looks good," Andrei Georgevitch explained, "although the cost of some of our achievements must be paid for by later generations. We go short on food now to build up . . . surplus for export [to] get foreign capital to buy . . . machinery.

". . . We are putting what little money we have into electric stations, mines . . . cement works—primary undertakings that will provide the material to build . . . shirt and shoe factories. . . . [Our biggest problem is to] raise the quality of our labour. . . .

"You might think . . . that, in our Socialist state, you could tell [workers]; 'Men, take pride in your work, these things are yours.' To the Communists and skilled workers that does means something. The others only answer, 'How about [higher] wages?' . . .

"There is always trouble with our superiors. . . . In a private firm you are responsible to one head. Here you take orders from a half dozen . . . bureaus, [each contradicting the other].

". . . A factory building . . . stood idle. . . . Some department . . . decided it would be . . . suitable for refining . . . metals. Another department got the machinery, it was too large to go in the doorway, so the front of the building was removed. After the mill was rebuilt another department found that the machines were too heavy for the foundations. . . . The front was again torn down and the machinery taken out. It lay there to rust. Another department decided to use the plant

* SOURCE: *Ibid.*, pp. 80-97.

to clean wool. Then it was found to be too far from the source of supply; so the mill stands idle to-day, the result of . . . red tape.

". . . At the head of every industry there is a trust which determines how much each of its factories shall produce and how they shall operate. Nothing is more important here than costs of production. Although our industries are government owned, no . . . stockholders, no . . . dividends, no banks to worry them—yet it is always a fight to bring down our production costs. We are not efficient . . . and our costs stay high [often] higher than in your capitalist world. The trust tells a mill, 'Your production costs must be cut twelve per cent.' . . . If the director of the factory doesn't succeed, he and his staff will be replaced. So the easiest way to cut costs is to reduce quality. . . .

"[See] today's *Pravda*. . . . The Tomsky laboratory found cans of fish that contained . . . sand, . . . entrails, even eyes. . . ."

"But how do such things cut costs?" I asked.

"They don't. . . . But a factory is ordered to produce so much and it does [and does it fast]. Director, Communist leaders, foremen—all combine . . . to make a good showing. Just so they can say, 'We have produced more yet our costs are lower.' How to decrease costs, increase quantity yet still maintain quality is the problem which must be solved before the Plan can be realized. If we can't produce cheaper than [capitalism] . . . what is the use of Socialism?

". . . But I can never decide whether it is Socialism or Russia that causes the faults in our system. . . .

"The whole thing goes back to that fear of taking responsibility. . . . The Communist group . . . gives the orders and each man strives to put them through . . . assuming as little responsibility . . . as he can. . . . Every paper . . . must wait for the signatures of four or five men—anything to avoid . . . blame for mistakes. . . . [So] tractors go out without carburetors. . . . The Clothing Trust sent out trousers with one leg shorter than the other. . . .

"No factory director cares to take any responsibility. He always goes to the trust. . . . One director wrote to his trust to ask if the families of [his] workmen [might] use the factory baths. . . ."

"Why don't the well paid engineers take responsibility?" I asked.

"Because, unless they are Communists, they are afraid. . . . In this country, where factories are everything, the engineers have the power that will determine whether or not the scheme succeeds. Most of us are not Communists, but . . . most of us are loyal. Yet, when the situation forces the Communists to give control of . . . their factories . . . to a group outside their 'Workers of the World,' . . . they [suspect] that group.

". . . A little sabotage in one of our big power houses [can destroy] thousands of dollars worth of government property. . . . Such a thing . . . is a crime against the State. . . . No engineer wants any responsibility. . . ."

"But what about the new engineers, educated from proletarian stock?"

"The government does all it can to [rush] them through the schools. . . . But one is not a master engineer after four years in technical school. They cannot replace us —yet. And there is little proof that when these proletarian lads are engineers they will still be proletarians: we get good salaries. . . ."

The Worker*

Georgei Lukitch came [in]. . . . [He] began to talk with Pavel about the factory.

"We are up to our throats in work," he began. "Moscow orders us to increase production twelve per cent before October. . . . We have about six hundred workmen, . . . only a hundred and twenty-five are Communists. . . ."

"Georgei is chairman of the factory workmen's committee," Pavel interrupted. "He controls everything connected with the interests of the workmen. And he heads the Party group at the mill. So he is responsible for having all Party orders carried out, he's the most important man in the factory."

"You forget there is also the technical director," Georgei continued for my benefit. "Our problem now is to make non-Party workmen take the interest they should. Some . . . foremen are no better. . . . There is no discipline. . . . We had a

* SOURCE: *Ibid.*, pp. 111-126.

frightful accident last week, just from carelessness. . . .

". . . We must make our workmen realize that it is their factory. The amount we spend replacing mislaid tools and parts broken [carelessly]! The director of the factory is non-Party of course and he doesn't want any responsibility. He does little to lower the percentage of cloth spoiled. So long as the plant runs he is content. But he'd better remember that the director of a mill in Shermetovka was dismissed for continually falling below the required production figures!"

"Have you carried on a campaign of 'self criticism' here?" I asked. "Self criticism" was adopted all over the Union [to encourage] workmen to [expose] flaws in the industrial mechanism.

"Yes," said Georgei sadly, "but it's not very successful. We arranged that workmen could hand in any criticisms. . . . We printed some in the factory paper but many were anonymous and . . . personal: 'Antonov drinks himself out of his mind,' or 'Why didn't Vanyetov appear at work Monday? Find out the girl he had in the woods Sunday night.' Those comments don't help us. . . . Besides, the non-Party workers are afraid to criticize us Communists.

"We organized 'shock brigades' . . . among the workers, mostly the Communists, and, especially, the Young Communists. They worked hard to find ways to cut costs and to improve conditions. Thanks to their work the factory director had to order Platonov to clean up the factory restaurant. . . . Everybody complained but no one did anything until the 'shock brigade' went into action. Yet 'self criticism' should have remedied this long ago."

"Self criticism?" Alexei Mikhailovitch came in. . . . "You [can't] expect that to [help]. . . . No matter what . . . they do [the workers] hold their jobs because . . . this is the Workmen's Paradise. Your . . . Party can't afford not to pamper the workmen; its power rests on them. . . ."

"Sometimes you seem like a plain counter-revolutionary type," said Georgei. "Why I haven't had you dismissed long ago—"

"Have some more beer, Georgei," Alexei laughed. . . . "But if you want concrete suggestions—let them send better shoes to our store. [A friend of mine] asked for shoes and tried one on. . . . Nails went into his foot. . . ."

"You boast about America, old man. Don't mistakes ever happen there?"

"You know as little about America as the peasants that Kalinin was addressing in a village one day. 'How are things?' Kalinin asked. 'Rotten,' some peasant called out. 'Look at our clothes, . . . rags for stockings, . . . flour bags for shirts.' 'Yes,' said Kalinin, 'but think of the American Indians. They have no clothes at all to wear.' One old peasant . . . said, 'Very likely true, Comrade Kalinin, but perhaps they've had the Soviet system longer over there.'" . . .

Georgei asked with some heat, "See here, Alexei, would you like to have the Tsar back?"

"What?" Alexei asked. . . . "Of course not! But I should like to reach the levels which I have seen in other countries where there are also no Tsars. In the meantime your . . . Party talks about what a paradise it will be in the future—and food supplies diminish steadily! . . ."

"He's the best mechanic we have," said Georgei as he saw Alexei go out. ". . . but if he talked like that around the mill I'd . . . have him fired."

"Where did he find all the stories he tells?" I asked.

"Those anecdotes? They go from mouth to mouth. . . ."

*   *   *

The first year of the [five-year] plan . . . was nearly finished. . . . Newspapers were publishing reports of *chistki,* the periodical "cleanouts" of "social-dangerous elements" from factories offices and Party. . . . To see a *chistka* in operation, I went out to the [factory]. . . .

. . . From all walls hung slogans about "Socialist Competition." In the vestibule was a . . . "wall paper," with . . . typewritten [columns]. . . . One was labeled "Self Criticism." It contained [such items as]:

"An anti-alcohol club was organized a few months ago and nothing has been heard of it since. Is the director, Comrade Loshadyenko, spending too much time in the [tavern]?"

"The autobus . . . has no stop before the cooperative store. This is very inconvenient for housewives with heavy bundles."

"Why can't the cross be taken down from the former . . . Church [now] a children's nursery . . . ?"

"The washroom . . . is . . . dirty. Why can't it be cleaned?"

"Some people are taking the empty spools out of their machines and throwing them on the floor. Bad accidents can result. . . . Let baskets be provided for these spools."

The factory meeting [began]. . . . Georgei presided. . . . He . . . announced the names of . . . irresponsible workmen [and those of] "social-hostile groups" [who had been fired]. . . .

"I want also to tell you about the first

results of our . . . 'socialist competition' . . . with the Red Textile Mill in Ivanovo-Vosnesensk. We promised to cut down damaged goods by seven per cent. Comrades, we have reduced it by eight per cent." There was great applause. "We agreed to cut down . . . days lost . . . by drunkenness . . . by fifty per cent. . . . In September, we lost forty-four . . . days. . . . [Last] month we . . . lost but thirty, and four-fifths of them were due to Bubnov, whom we have just 'cleaned out of the mill.' " The applause was even louder.

"We promised to increase our production by eleven per cent. We shall increase it by fifteen per cent before November, when the new English machinery is put in place." The applause was terrific.

Endless speeches followed. . . . Alexei . . . spoke briefly: "You know, comrades, I have been in America. [What] makes life go forward there is competition. Now [with] 'socialist competition' between factory and factory and shift and shift, we too shall go forward. My shift hereby challenges shift number three to increase . . . production . . . by fourteen per cent. . . ."

[Georgei] met me after the meeting. . . . "What a change I found in Alexei this evening!" I said.

"Yes, he has a different viewpoint now. Our plant was running poorly until a few months ago. Discipline was bad and the factory director, a non-Party engineer, fought with me. Then from . . . Moscow came orders to introduce 'socialist competition'. . . . At first it was hard to arouse enthusiasm; there was no extra pay [for] harder work. [But] Alexei and others became enthusiastic. In other places it has not been so successful."

"Are you going to introduce the 'five day week' also?" I asked. Plans were being made . . . so that everybody might have five consecutive days' work and one holiday, one group being free on Monday, the next on Tuesday, thus arranging that work goes on seven days a week . . . except on legal holidays.

"We are [starting] it next month," he replied. "It may be confusing at first, but we [will do our best] to fulfill . . . the . . . Plan."

*   *   *

"I was surprised at your speech to-night," I [said, when I saw Alexei].

He smiled. . . . "I laughed at the idea of 'socialist competition' [at] first. . . . It seemed like another way to trick the workmen . . . , like these 'voluntary labor Sundays' when, if you don't load bricks, you may find your name on the 'black list' at the factory. Then Georgei . . . appointed me head of my shift, and set another shift to compete with us. They were more experienced workers and beat us the first week. . . . Now we work like horses and have the best shift. . . . Besides, I have just finished a little invention for changing spools on the machines and the factory gave me a premium of five hundred rubles. In America the workman could patent it and make much more. But I am satisfied.

"I am convinced now that whatever the Communists may be doing they are at least building up Russia. We shall be a great industrial nation when our Plan is completed and I have always longed to see it. What's that slogan? 'Equal and surpass America!' Perhaps—I at least know what they have to catch up with and most of our Communists don't. But we are beginning—and I may join the . . . Party myself."

A Visit to Moscow *

[In June 1931, Stalin ordered the elimination of relative wage equality in the factories, introducing a piece-work speed-up system that was eventually to lead to the super speed-up device of Stakhanovism. Shortly thereafter, Kravchenko, then an engineer undergoing specialized training at the Metallurgy Institute of Dniepropetrovsk, was designated a member of a commission to investigate why production was going badly at nearby Nikopol, the site of a large metallurgical *combinat*. There he found gross inefficiency due to central planning, and continuous prying and spying by bureaucrats and police officials. He also found the workers to be living in barracks, that were rat- and bedbug-infested, beflooded when it rained, and improperly heated in cold weather. Sheets and pillowcases were seldom changed, and if workers complained they were taken away by the G.P.U., never to return. Kravchenko decided to go to Moscow to direct attention to these evils to Commissar of Heavy Industry, Sergo Ordzhonikidze, whom he had befriended on an earlier occasion.]

On [my] previous visits [to Moscow] I had not been so conscious of the contrast between the capital and the rest of the country. [The contrast was] due in part to improvement in the appearance of the capital, but even more so to the rapid deterioration of the provincial cities. I was driven to the Metropole Hotel in a big Lincoln. Towards evening I went to the [elegant and crowded] hotel restaurant. A big jazz band was playing. Couples were dancing.

Could this really be part of our Soviet Union? Had I blundered into a cinema

set? I saw men in European clothes, wearing neckties. Some of the women were in low-cut gowns. One group was in dinner jackets.

The thought of the barracks in Nikopol intruded. "Welcome to our palace. What will you have, rats or bedbugs?" But I pushed the thought aside. Soon I would be "conferring" with one of the most powerful leaders.

*   *   *

"Well, comrade, I congratulate you" [said Ordzhonikidze's secretary, as I left the office]. "Here are tickets for the Bolshoi Theatre. And here's a thousand rubles. A gift from Comrade Ordzhonikidze. Have a good time."

Again I was conveyed to the hotel in a big motorcar. A Gypsy chorus was singing when I went into the restaurant for supper. [Having] just been closeted with Ordzhonikidze and Bukharin made me feel at home here, like one of the elect. How easy it was to yield to the fleshpots of power and luxury! How long would the verminous workers weigh on my conscience if I [lived] in Moscow, with plenty of money, [had] an automobile and [danced to] jazz bands?

Recalling that Comrade Lazarev, the lecturer who had drawn me [into] the Party many years ago, was in Moscow, I decided to look him up.

"A thousand rubles, theatre tickets, Lincolns, the Metropole," he said, a little sadly. "Yes, that's how the granddukes of the old regime treated their favorite retainers."

"You're not being quite fair, Comrade Lazarev," I retorted [heatedly]. "The commissar understands the plight of our common people. And if he does, I must assume that Stalin does too. That's why I feel encouraged."

Lazarev served on powerful committees of the Party. Yet, as we talked that afternoon, our rôles seemed strangely reversed.

* SOURCE: V. Kravchenko, *I Chose Freedom*, New York, Scribner's, 1946, pp. 75, 77-83, 85-86. (Adapted and abridged.) On April 4, 1944, Victor Kravchenko walked out of his job in Washington with the Soviet Purchasing Commission in the United States and severed his connection with the Communist party.

His ardor had ebbed. Now it was I who apologized for the Party.

"Have you been to the villages recently?" he asked me suddenly.

"No, but I know a good deal about what's happening."

"Knowing is one thing, seeing is another. You see, I've just returned from the Ukraine. My job was to put through collectivization in one region."

Lazarev covered his face with both hands, as if to shut out the memory.

The Agony of Collectivization*

[Kravchenko, was deeply moved by the story of Katya, a peasant child, who had managed to escape from the freight train transporting her family into exile after their property and cattle had been expropriated by the village Soviet.]

The ordeal of one child shocked me into facing the ordeal of all peasant Russia. I was determined to accept the first chance to go deep into the collectivization regions. The chance came sooner than I had hoped. Through the Party office at the Institute I was instructed to report at the Regional Committee. The purpose: mobilization of Party brigades for work in the villages.

About eighty of us were in the conference hall, mostly younger men. A member of the Central Committee of the Party made a speech.

"Comrades," he said, "you are going into the country. The local village authorities need an injection of Bolshevik iron. Throw your bourgeois humanitarianism out of the window and act like Bolsheviks worthy of Comrade Stalin. Beat down the kulak agent wherever he raises his head. The last remnant of capitalist farming must be wiped out.

"Secondly, it is absolutely necessary to fulfill the government's plan for grain delivery. The kulaks, and even some middle and 'poor' peasants, are not giving up their grain. And the local authorities sometimes show weakness. Your job is to get the grain at any price. Pump it out of them, wherever it's hidden.

"Your third task is to complete the threshing of the grain, to repair the tools, plows, tractors and other equipment.

"The class struggle in the village has taken the sharpest forms. Kulak agents are getting into the collective farms where they sabotage the work and kill the livestock. I am sure you will carry out the directives of our beloved Leader."

The final words, conveying a threat, were drowned in obedient applause.

I was summoned to the office of Comrade Brodsky. He pressed a bell and two other men were led into the office. One was the student [Seryozha] Tsvetkov. The other was a man about forty.

"Shake hands all around," Comrade Brodsky said. "You three will go to the village of Podgorodnoye. Kravchenko will be in charge of completing the threshing [and] be responsible for putting tools and machinery in order. Tsvetkov, together with Arshinov, will wind up the collectivization and grain collection. Arshinov [is] in charge. He's an old Party worker."

* * *

[Arriving in the village, Kravchenko spoke to the representatives of the village peasants.]

"I've come from the Regional Committee of the Party to help you [put] things in order. Just look around. Dirty cattle. Unprotected grain ricks. Valuable tools rotting. I know how you feel. But why should the cows and horses be punished. I want to appeal to your pride as farmers."

"Right! This comrade makes sense," someone exclaimed.

* Source: *Ibid.*, pp. 87-93, 100-104, 111-112, 118-122. (Adapted and abridged.)

"Then let's get down to business."

We talked for hours. In the end each board member agreed to a specific duty—to organize the threshing, to clean up the animal houses and so on.

At supper time, my host told me that he had seen some of the board members after the meeting. "They say you started things right. They're pleased, especially because you don't swear or threaten. [The peasants] are bitter about having lost their land and cattle and machines. All the same, [life] must go on."

After the meal, I saw Seryozha. He looked unhappy.

"Well, how are things with you?"

"I called delinquents on the grain collection one after another. It was always the same story. The peasant takes off his hat and sits down respectfully. We argue back and forth. The government needs the grain, I insist, and the peasant says, 'And how about my wife and children? The harvest was bad. Who's going to feed us all year after you've robbed us?'"

"I collected fifty-two *poods* today but that isn't a fraction of what Arshinov expected. These people are tired and frightened. Maybe some of them have more grain than they admit, but they don't dare give it up, with the winter coming on."

The following morning I went to the collective farm. Work was in full swing. The place began to look almost normal. The collectivized farmers were in better spirits. The women were even singing Ukrainian work songs. These simple people, at bottom, loved their work. The weather was good and they understood the value of every rainless day. [Days later] I called on Arshinov. He was aware that my work was proceeding well and seemed jealous. He worked off his irritation in a tirade against [Seryozha] Tsvetkov.

"Yesterday I searched some houses," he said. "People whom our softie let off easy. In every case I found grain hidden away. I confiscated every bit of it. Lying to the Soviet power, the dirty kulaks! I'll teach them. I was at the District Committee today and they're behind me. On Tuesday things will happen."

"What will happen?"

"That's my business."

Threshing went on all day Sunday. Even the most religious [peasants] understood that time was short.

[Late that night] I asked Tsvetkov how he was getting along with Arshinov.

"He's a son of a bitch and a sadist. The beast drags the peasants from their homes [at] night. He beats them up."

"Why in hell didn't you tell me? Get dressed, let's go!"

In the Soviet building we found peasants squatting on the floor. A constable with a revolver was sitting inside. I heard the cries of a peasant and the swearing of Arshinov behind the closed office door. "As usual," said [the constable], "Comrade Arshinov is pumping grain and having a little talk with those who won't join the collective farm."

Suddenly Arshinov's voice rose. We could hear the peasant groaning: "Why are you beating me?" [I entered the office.] Arshinov was startled. On the floor was an old man, his face bloody.

"Let the peasants go!" I shouted. "Look here Arshinov. You have a right to demand grain and to search premises. But you have no right to use violence and carry on nocturnal inquisitions." I turned and [went]. In about half an hour [Tsvetkov] arrived.

"I've been at the hut of the peasant who was beaten up," he told me. "He has a sick wife, five children and not a crumb of bread in the house. The old man has given me a declaration of his willingness to enter the *kolkhoz*. I begged him to stop being bullheaded, to take pity on his family."

*   *   *

At the collective farm things were going well. Threshing was in full swing, the cattle and horses were being cared for, the farm implements were almost in order. On Tuesday afternoon I went into the fields where the women were husking the corn. I joined in the work. Evening was falling when I drove into the village. Agitated groups stood around. Women were weeping. I hurried to the Soviet building.

"What's happening?" I asked the constable.

"Another round-up of kulaks," he replied. "The G.P.U. and District Committee people came this morning."

A large crowd was outside the building. Policemen tried to scatter them. Women and children were weeping hysterically and calling the names of their husbands and fathers.

Inside the Soviet building, Arshinov was talking to a G.P.U. official. In the back yard, guarded by G.P.U. soldiers, stood about twenty peasants, young and old, with bundles on their backs. A few [wept]. The others stood sullen, resigned.

So this was "liquidation of the kulaks as a class"! Simple peasants stripped of all their worldly goods, and shipped to lumber camps or irrigation works. On this occasion most of the families were being left behind. Their outcries filled the air. As I came out of the Soviet house again, I saw two militiamen leading a middle aged peasant. His face was black and blue and his clothes were ripped. I heard a woman shouting. A couple of G.P.U. men started running towards her. The woman held a flaming sheaf of grain in her hands. She tossed the burning sheaf onto the thatched roof of the house, which burst into flame.

"Infidels! murderers!" the woman was shrieking. "We worked all our lives for our house. You won't have it!"

A Summing Up in 1930*

Has Soviet Russia actually contributed . . . to the sum total of human experience in an economic and social sense? Everyone knows that there has never been an economic and social experiment on a scale to compare with it.

In terms of present human well-being it would, no doubt, have been better for the generation of the Russian people who witnessed the Revolution if the experiment with Socialism had been abandoned at the time of the New Economic Policy. The benefits which will accrue to the Russian people during the next decade, even if the grandiose plans of the Party are realized, can hardly compensate for the years since the Revolution.

Living conditions in Russia have been worse during the present year than at any time since [1921]. Millions are seriously undernourished and in some parts of the Soviet Union actual famine conditions have been approximated. Faced by this situation, the Government has not hesitated to safeguard the standard of living of the workers

* SOURCE: C. B. Hoover, *The Economic Life of Soviet Russia,* New York, Macmillan, 1931, pp. 334-343. (Adapted and abridged.)

in the largest cities at the expense of [the rest] of the population. The supply of almost all commodities is better in Moscow than in any other part of the country. Every available pound of food-stuffs is swept up from the country side. A nominal subsistence minimum is supposedly left to the peasants, but in many cases they are left practically without grain or flour. The Party is determined that the Revolution shall not perish, even if a few peasants starve. Some foreign observer who was in the Soviet Union in 1925 visits the country now and is shocked to find food conditions much worse. It appears that the Soviet regime is about to collapse.

On the other hand, American engineers and capitalists are shown the great new factories and plants which are being built. They report that Soviet Russia is making gigantic [progress]. The capitalistic world is puzzled. Certainly both types of story cannot be true.

The extraordinary thing is that both are true. The hard conditions of life are due to the unsatisfactory agricultural situation during the past several years, and to the determination to industrialize the country at the earliest possible moment. These conditions, however, must not be taken to prove that the Soviet economic system has been a failure. On the industrial front impressive successes have been scored.

At present the standard of living of the labourer is in some respects worse than during Tsarist times in terms of food, clothing and shelter. But when the advantages of the shorter working day, vacations and social insurance are considered, it must be recognized that the labourer has gained from the Revolution. The standard of living of the individual peasant is distinctly worse than before, and this is true to an even greater extent of the old intelligentsia, office workers, school teachers, and the "white collar" workers in general. Certainly if the *average* standard of living of Tsarist times be compared with [that of] the present, conditions must be said to be much inferior. The income which was taken from the "exploiting classes" has not as yet fully accrued to the exploited classes who despoiled them.

Nevertheless, the standard of life is so low now, largely because of the determination of the Party to make it much higher in the future.

It is probable that the standard of living in Russia will never reach a level of comparative luxury such as that attained by the bourgeoisie in capitalistic countries. Simple food, communal housing, proletarian club houses, plain clothing, motor transport, short hours of labor, vacations at state recreation houses may be taken to represent the final goal of Communist effort. Such a goal is, no doubt, wholly unacceptable to the bourgeoisie, the intelligentsia, the greater part of the agricultural population and even the upper strata of the working classes of the capitalistic world. It is probable, however, that it would have a wonderful appeal to the most poorly paid and most unintelligent fifty per cent of the population of the capitalistic world.

If the Soviet system has greater possibilities in respect to productivity than is usually realized, in respect to the psychological and intangible possibilities of the system the record is not an encouraging one. In Utopia, meanness, pettiness, greed, envy, and bitterness were to disappear. But Soviet Russia is further removed from Utopia than is capitalistic civilization. In Soviet Russia there is not less bitterness but more. The struggle for power has replaced the struggle for wealth. Within the state Trusts and Commissariats, within the Party, the struggle for power is sharper than within the institutions of Capitalism. The orthodox Party member of today finds tomorrow that his orthodoxy has been successfully attacked by a fellow Party member who hates or fears him and he is ruthlessly expelled from the Party. The institution of the chistka or "cleaning" is used in every institution in Russia to give full rein to suspicion, envy and sadism.

Has the new order of life in Russia resulted in a new brotherliness of man to man? The attitude of those in power toward their subordinates is [no] improvement over the attitude of persons similarly placed in the capitalistic world. True, workers themselves are pampered *as a class*. But "white collar" workers are only one degree better off than the "deprived" classes who are branded as enemies of Soviet Power. The same is true of the old intelligentsia who took service under the Bolsheviki. The number who hold positions in the political and economic apparatus is being constantly reduced by "cleanings" and by the G.P.U.

Nor [is] there evidence of increased brotherliness among the industrial workers. The form of address "Comrade," has [no] real significance. One [is] struck by the general air of irritation and ill-feeling. One rarely sees a smile or hears a laugh. Partly this is due to the food shortage. But the sense of repressed anger seems due to other causes also.

Never in history have the mind and spirit been so robbed of freedom and dignity. It is not merely that academic freedom, freedom of speech, press, thought are forbidden. The Party is not content with mere abstention from unauthorized action. Men must publicly deny their real thoughts and feelings. Nor is the matter so simple that it is possible to embrace a set of beliefs and feel safe within the precincts of orthodoxy.

When Stalin was fighting the Trotskyist Left it was the orthodox thing to belittle the kulak danger and to favour conciliation toward him. Two years later the kulak is branded by Stalin as the primary danger. The writer once attended a Party chistka in which a woman . . . who was being "cleaned" cried out, "One day I am told that the views of Bukharin are right. Now I am told that they are all wrong. How am I to know?"

An engineer is arrested, charged with [sabotage] and is shot. His son is a Party member. He is ordered to sign a statement that he approves of the execution of his father. He refuses, and is expelled from the Party. Never has the human soul been so placed in bondage.

The Soviet regime is founded upon force and fear. The Communist declares that the present policy of violence has been necessary to preserve the socialistic character of the Revolution. Without the activities of the G.P.U., the former bourgeoisie, with the aid of foreign capitalists, might have re-established the old regime. Unrelenting warfare on economic heresy has been necessary to preserve the Revolution from internal decay.

Russian Communism has attacked head-on some of the most difficult problems of modern economic and social life. It has had the courage to try out radical solutions for agricultural and unemployment problems and the status of women.

If the desirability of achieving a really socialistic order is taken for granted, then considerable credit must be given to the Russian Communist Party for having preserved the dynamic character of the Revolution and for having developed a truly socialistic system. The contribution to human experience and knowledge for which the Soviet system is responsible cannot be denied. It has been proved that a socialistic state can exist and carry on the functions necessary for survival.

It is possible, then, to find some justification for the violence and force of the Revolution, the Civil War and for a reasonable period thereafter. However, thirteen years since the [November] Revolution [vio-lence] still continues. It appears that violence has come to be inseparable from Communism.

It has been no small triumph of Communism that it has, partially, at least, substituted interest in the success of the Five Year Plan for interest in the economic success of the individual.

It must be admitted that the foreign observer feels that life has become a dreary thing, indeed, when placed on such a level. The Communist retorts that this is bourgeois prejudice. The economic struggle may give zest to life for those who are successful, but it offers no compensation to the vast majority who fail in the struggle to "get ahead" and who are always confronted by the threat of economic disaster.

The creation of a system of life which has displaced the money standard of measurement for even the moral and subjective values which exist in bourgeois civilization must be registered as a distinct contribution to human welfare. While it is true that the struggle for power has in many ways replaced the struggle for money, this fact does not entirely destroy the value of this element of the Soviet system. In Soviet Russia men do not devote their time to money-making activities in order to ape the standards of a leisure class. The state employee in a retail shop is not particularly interested in whether the customer makes a purchase or not. He does not, therefore, either fawn on [him], or subject him to high-powered salesmanship. He does not address the customer as "Sir." The spiritual advance which is registered cannot be gainsaid. Waiters in restaurants [and] household servants, have also lost both the servility and the false "Happy-to-serve-you-Sir!" attitude so characteristic of similar workers in the capitalistic world.

There is no class which has a special position on account of wealth ownership. Power, influence, and authority are not accorded to fools, incompetents, and mediocrities simply on account of wealth. Toadies, bullies [and particularly fanatics] do attain to power much more frequently than in the capitalistic world. One cannot but hail, therefore, the destruction of wealth as the universal standard of all values, while recognizing that the transfer of power to the dominant group of leaders in the Communist Party from the owners of wealth has not yet been shown to be a change for the better.

What is the attitude of the population as a whole toward the Soviet regime? In spite of the food shortage of the last several years, many of the workers are still positively loyal. Most of the remainder are at least passively loyal. The Soviet Government has always favoured the proletariat. The workman knows that any change would almost certainly make his lot worse. Nevertheless, even among the urban workers there is bitterness. In Moscow, during March 1930, the writer accompanied by two other foreigners was returning home late at night. We were all better dressed than most Russians. A man passed us. He had been drinking. He hurled a curse at us and said, "You Party people! We will cut you to pieces!" The proletarian assumed that anyone who was warmly dressed must be one of the Party leaders. Two years earlier he would have cursed us as Nepmen, but now that the Nepmen were gone his anger turned toward the only class better off than he.

On account of the grain requisitions and the enforced nationalization of the land, the peasants are bitterly hostile. Most of the poorest peasants are loyal, for the same reason that the urban proletariat is loyal. They have been favoured at the expense of the other peasants. [Perhaps] twenty per cent of the peasant population are active supporters of the Soviet regime.

If it were possible to put the matter to a free vote the majority would vote [for] a return of the old Tsarist regime in preference to the present one. [But this] is [not] a fair statement of the case. The present moment is critical. Living conditions are worse now than they were two years ago and worse than they probably will be two years from today. Furthermore, the majority against the present system would come from the peasants. The peasant is being torn up by the roots and transplanted into strange soil. In ten years the peasant may have forgotten his present grievances and may be an enthusiastic supporter of collectivized agriculture.

The significance to the capitalistic world of developments in the Soviet Union cannot be exaggerated. If the present crisis is passed, the Soviet Union, within a decade, will be in a position to offer a standard of living [superior to] that of the more poorly paid workers in capitalistic countries. Unless in the meantime capitalism has notably improved its technique of marketing and distribution, so that underconsumption and unemployment can be prevented, and unless the standard of living of such workers in the capitalistic world shall have been materially raised, the World Revolution will begin to make rapid strides.

Man-Made Famine*

The first dividends of collectivization were death. Not a word appeared in the newspapers, [but] the famine throughout southern Russia and Central Asia was common knowledge. Despite harsh police measures to keep the victims at home, Dniepro-

* SOURCE: V. Kravchenko, *I Chose Freedom*, New York, Scribner's, 1946, pp. 111-117, 118-122. (Adapted and abridged.)

petrovsk was overrun with starving peasants.

Because the famine coincided with the triumphant finish of the first *Piatiletka* in four years, the press was hysterical with boasts. The shouting about the new "happy life" seemed ghoulish, more terrifying even than the famine itself.

Everything depended on the new harvest.

Would the starving peasantry have the strength and the will to reap and to thresh in the midst of millionfold death? To make sure that the crops would be harvested, to prevent the farmers from eating the green shoots, to save the kolkhozes from breaking down under mismanagement, to fight against enemies of collectivization, special Political Departments were set up in the villages, manned by trusted Communists—military men, officials, professionals, N.K.V.D. men, students. An army of more than a hundred thousand stalwarts, selected by the Central Committee of the Party, was charged with safeguarding the new harvest.

Armed with a mandate from the Regional Committee, I set out for the Piatikhatsky district. The local officials were unnerved. Questioned about the new crops, they could talk only of the mass hunger, the epidemics [and] cannibalism.

Yes, they agreed, we must prepare to reap and to thresh the new grain; but how to get started seemed beyond their paralyzed wills. The jails were jammed with peasants arrested for unauthorized reaping of grain —"sabotage" and "theft of state property."

What I saw making the rounds of houses with [kolkhoz chairman] Chadai, was inexpressibly horrible. People dying in solitude by slow degrees. They had been trapped and left to starve by a political decision made in a far off capital. Most terrifying were the little children with skeleton limbs dangling from balloon-like abdomens. Everywhere [were] men and women lying prone, their faces and bellies bloated.

A gaunt woman was busy at the stove. "What are you cooking, Natalka?" Chadai asked her.

"You know what I'm cooking," she answered [furiously].

Chadai pulled me by the sleeve and we went out.

"Why did she get so angry?" I asked.

"Because—well, I'm ashamed to tell you. She's cooking horse manure and weeds."

My first impulse was to return and stop her, but Chadai [said]: "Don't do it. She might kill you if you take away the contents of her pot."

My course seemed clear. I would ignore

orders. Unless I restored the strength of these peasants, everything would be lost. I told [Makarenko, the manager of the cooperative store] about my decision to feed the children of the village and asked him to help.

The little man was alarmed. He was torn between orders from headquarters and his fear of offending me as the Party Representative.

"Yes, comrade, I have some salt, candy, groats, and a little soap. If the kolkhozes will sign a promise to pay in grain and hay, I'll agree. But first I must obtain permission of the district office. I'll give you my answer tomorrow. But I also want to give you a little advice. Why not tap the butter station?"

"What do you mean?"

"He means the place where we deliver all our milk," Demchenko explained. "It's processed into butter for export."

The butter plant was some distance outside the village. Butter was being wrapped in paper which bore the imprint, in English, USSR BUTTER EXPORT.

"I know that the peasants are starving," the [plant] manager said. "The idea of this butter going to foreigners cuts me like a knife. But I have my orders. I'm far behind my plan and no doubt will be punished. The peasants steal the milk; they're hungry. And the cows don't produce because there's not enough fodder."

"All the same," I said, "I must have your help. The children must be fed. Surely there are by-products of the butter making that we can use."

"That's easy for you to say. But like Makarenko, I not only have to fulfill plans from the center but I have to feed local officials. All of them take my butter and milk."

"Well, from today all buttermilk must be turned over to the new children's project," I declared.

"That's all right with me, provided I obtain the approval of my superiors." Then he paused as if gathering his courage. "Tell your people to come for the buttermilk tomorrow. I, too, have children."

Anger lashed my mind as I drove back

to the village. Butter being sent abroad in the midst of the famine!

In bed that night I thought of the new privileged class in the village—the Party and Soviet functionaries who were receiving supplies from the cooperative shop while everyone else starved. Slavishly they obeyed orders from the center, indifferent to the suffering people. The corruption of character by privilege was fearsome to behold; these men who only a few years ago were poor peasants had already lost the last trace of identification with their neighbors.

Art in the Service of the State*

In 1932 a slight relaxation in Soviet life began. . . . [It] was heralded by a . . . decree [suspending] the activities of RAPP, the Association of Proletarian Writers. For years the RAPP and its affiliates in other artistic fields dominated Soviet literature, . . . painting, music, . . . etc. Marxist theories, political slogans, and statistics of the Five Year Plan had taken the place of beauty . . . and genius in art. . . .

. . . The decree was followed immediately by vigorous attacks on [the] leaders [and] active members of the RAPP. They were accused of having ignored non-Communist and non-proletarian writers, of having judged writers by their political ideology rather than by their talents. . . . They had done all [this] on . . . instructions from the party. Now they were punished for having . . . obeyed those instructions. Later, during the purge, many RAPP members were arrested; some were shot.

Among the victims of the RAPP regime [were] folk songs. They were supplanted by songs on the Five Year Plan made to order by composers and poets. In the summer of 1930 the Park of Culture announced a concert by a Ukrainian peasant chorus. The big hall was jammed because Ukrainian folk songs were . . . great favorites. . . . [To our great disappointment, the chorus] sang translations of new Soviet industrial

songs. Between the songs a commentator, representing the RAPM, the equivalent of RAPP in music, analyzed each song . . . stressing its political significance. Then he said:

"Now that you have heard the beautiful songs of the new free Ukraine, you will be able to judge how . . . poisonous were their old folk songs, . . . created . . . to lull the poor peasants into obedience so that the landlord could the better exploit them. . . ."

When he finished, . . . the chorus began singing our favorite Ukrainian folk songs. . . . The audience went berserk. They . . . stamped their feet, and demanded endless encores. The embarrassed commentator permitted no encores.

After the abolition of the RAPP, the authorities not only brought back folk songs and all other folk arts; they began to stress their importance. At an official opening of an art exhibit . . . Commissar of Education Kerzhentsev tried to impress on foreign newspapermen the greatness of Russian folk art and how important it was for the people to know and love it. . . . Kerzhentsev . . . used words and ideas which we had defended all along against the party liners who condemned folk art. Once again I marveled at the swift clicking of a Communist brain to a party-line zigzag.

At [a RAPP literary meeting] Boris Pilniak, the well-known Soviet author, was [denounced as "bourgeois" and "counter-revolutionary"]. He sat there . . . without saying a word. What was the use? Nothing he said could win the audience. No one

* Source: Markoosha Fischer, *My Lives in Russia,* New York, Harper and Brothers, 1944, pp. 91-97. Markoosha Fischer, wife of Louis Fischer, noted writer on Soviet affairs, was born in Russia and attended school there around 1900. During the years 1927-1939, she lived in Soviet Russia.

dared oppose the RAPP . . . , the mouth-piece of the Communist party. [But] V. Polonsky, a civilized Russian, the most prominent Soviet literary critic, stood up to defend Pilniak. He said that whatever Pilniak's background and political opinions might be, he was a writer of talent and friendly guidance instead of vituperation might help him change his attitude; Soviet literature would greatly gain. He had hardly finished . . . when up jumped Peluso, an Italian . . . Comintern official. . . . He shouted that Polonsky had finally revealed his real face . . . and did not deserve to be a critic of . . . Soviet literature. The audience knew [him] as a representative of the Comintern and dutifully greeted his words with applause. Polonsky did not finish his defense of Pilniak. He stood there . . . his face gradually turning . . . gray. . . . He knew what Peluso's words and the audience's applause meant. He had tried to save a good Soviet writer. He thus ended his own brilliant career. Next day brought [a vicious] attack on him in the press. . . .

Another storm center was Boris Pasternak, [perhaps] the greatest Russian poet since Pushkin. . . . He . . . could only write about [matters] close to his heart. The political and economic developments around him were not the subjects of his poems. He was . . . loved . . . by many thousands. During the supremacy of the RAPP, and to a slighter degree before and after too, he was frequently attacked as an enemy of the revolution who refused to write on current themes. . . .

. . . I once attended a literary "trial" where Pasternak was to explain why he wrote about nature [and] human emotions . . . instead of . . . economic and political problems. . . . After several . . . literary pigmies, had [defamed] the character and work of the [great] poet, Pasternak was called upon to answer the accusations. His big blue-gray eyes were wide open but he hardly saw anyone. . . . Several times his lips . . . opened. . . . Finally, he [stammered]:

"I cannot write to order. I can only write what I want to write about. I can try to write differently but I don't think I will succeed."

His complete honesty was obvious. . . . A girl . . . with a Komsomol pin, whispered excitedly to her friend . . . :

"Look at his eyes! A real poet by the grace of God!"

In her excitement the young Communist forgot herself and slipped into the old-fashioned Russian definition of a true poet. . . . The rest of the audience booed. . . . Pasternak was declared beyond the pale of Soviet poetry.

. . . The poet was near suicide that night. . . . His numerous friends . . . were unable to fight for him as long as the RAPP had official party backing. Only after the government condemned the RAPP [could] they show their true feelings. [When], after a long absence, Pasternak appeared again in public to read his poems, the large hall . . . was jammed full. For . . . minutes the . . . cheers prevented him from starting. For four hours he recited . . . and [the] audience . . . only let him go after all lights were put out in the hall. . . .

[With the end of RAPP] it was [again] possible to paint a still life without the figure of a worker in it. Lyrical music, love poems, . . . were no longer regarded as caresses for the ears of the decaying bourgeoisie. Tchaikovsky was rehabilitated [from the charge of having written] decadent music. . . . Beethoven's symphonies on the radio were no longer interrupted by a lecture on the importance of manure. . . .

Art and literature were encouraged by the government. Talented children and adults were given every opportunity to develop their . . . gifts. [Official] talent scouts combed the country. . . . There were free scholarships for all who showed ability. . . .

But Soviet art has never . . . regained the free expression it enjoyed during the first years of the revolution. It remained under the firm hold of the party and changed . . . with every twist of the party line. Writers and artists often rose and fell according to their ability to quickly adapt . . . to political changes.

The First Five-Year Plan: Stalin's Report*

From the report delivered on January 7, 1933 to the Joint Plenum of the Central Committee and the Central Control Commission of the Communist Party:

What was the fundamental task of the five-year plan?

The fundamental task of the five-year plan was to transfer our country, with its backward technology, on to the lines of modern technology.

The fundamental task was to convert the U.S.S.R. from an agrarian and weak country, dependent upon the caprices of the capitalist countries, into an industrial and powerful country, fully self-reliant and independent of the caprices of world capitalism.

The fundamental task was, in converting the U.S.S.R. into an industrial country, to completely oust the capitalist elements, to widen the front of socialist forms of economy, and to create the economic basis for the abolition of classes in the U.S.S.R., for the building of a socialist society.

The fundamenetal task was to create in our country an industry that would be capable of re-equipping and reorganising, not only industry as a whole, but also transport and agriculture—on the basis of socialism.

The fundamental task was to transfer small and scattered agriculture on to the lines of large-scale collective farming, so as to ensure the economic basis of socialism in the countryside and thus to eliminate the possibility of the restoration of capitalism in the U.S.S.R.

Finally, the task of the five-year plan was to create all the technical and economic prerequisites for organising determined resistance to any attempt at military attack from abroad.

What dictated this fundamental task of the five-year plan?

* Source: J. V. Stalin, *Works,* Vol. XIII, Moscow, 1955, pp. 174-185. (Adapted and abridged.)

The necessity of putting an end to the technical and economic backwardness of the Soviet Union, which doomed it to an unenviable existence; the necessity of creating in the country the prerequisites that would enable it not only to overtake but in time to outstrip the advanced capitalist countries.

Consideration of the fact that the Soviet regime could not maintain itself for long on the basis of a backward industry; that only a modern large-scale industry, one not merely not inferior to but capable in time of surpassing the industries of the capitalist countries, can serve as a real and reliable foundation for the Soviet regime.

Consideration of the fact that the Soviet regime could not for long rest upon two opposite foundations: on large-scale socialist industry, which *destroys* the capitalist elements, and on small, individual peasant farming, which *engenders* capitalist elements.

Consideration of the fact that until agriculture was placed on the basis of large-scale production, until the small peasant farms were united into large collective farms, the danger of the restoration of capitalism in the U.S.S.R. was the most real of all possible dangers.

But the restoration and development of heavy industry, particularly in such a backward and poor country as ours was at the beginning of the five-year plan period, is an extremely difficult task; for, as is well known, heavy industry calls for enormous financial expenditure and the existence of a certain minimum of experienced technical forces, without which, generally speaking, the restoration of heavy industry is impossible. Did the Party take this into account? Yes. The Party knew how heavy industry had been built in Britain, Germany and America. It knew that in those countries heavy industry had been built either with the aid of big loans, or by plundering other countries, or by both methods simultaneously. The Party knew that those paths were closed to our country. What, then, did it count on? It counted on our country's own resources. It counted on the fact that, with a Soviet government at the helm, and the land, industry, transport, the banks and trade nationalised, we could pursue a regime of the strictest economy in order to accumulate sufficient resources for the restoration and development of heavy industry. The Party declared frankly that this would call for serious sacrifices, and that it was our duty to make these sacrifices. The Party counted on carrying through this task with the aid of the internal resources of our country—without enslaving credits and loans from abroad.

A bold task? A difficult path? But our Party is called a Leninist Party precisely because it fears no difficulties.

The Party's confidence in the feasibility of the five-year plan and its faith in the working class was so strong that the Party undertook the fulfilment of this task not in five years, but in four years.

What are the results of the five-year plan in four years in the sphere of *industry*? We have accomplished more than we ourselves expected, more than the ardent minds in our Party could have expected. That is not denied now even by our enemies.

We did not have an iron and steel industry, the basis for the industrialisation of the country. Now we have one.

We did not have a tractor industry. Now we have one.

We did not have an automobile industry. Now we have one.

We did not have a machine-tool industry. Now we have one.

We did not have a big modern chemical industry. Now we have one.

We did not have a real and big industry for the production of modern agricultural machinery. Now we have one.

We did not have an aircraft industry. Now we have one.

In output of electric power we were last on the list. Now we rank among the first.

In output of oil products and coal we were last on the list. Now we rank among the first.

We had only one coal and metallurgical base—in the Ukraine—and it was with difficulty that we made do with that. We have not only succeeded in improving this base, but have created a new coal and metallurgical base—in the East—which is the pride of our country.

We had only one centre of the textile industry—in the North of our country. We shall have in the very near future two new centres of the textile industry—in Central Asia and Western Siberia.

And we have created these new industries, on a scale and in dimensions that eclipse the scale and dimensions of European industry.

And as a result of all this the capitalist elements have been irrevocably ousted from industry, and socialist industry has become the sole form of industry in the U.S.S.R.

And as a result of all this our country has been converted from an agrarian into an industrial country; for the proportion of industrial output, as compared with agricultural output, has risen from 48 per cent of the total in the beginning of the five-year plan period (1928) to 70 per cent by 1932.

And as a result of all this we have succeeded by the end of the fourth year of the five-year plan period in fulfilling the total programme of industrial output to the extent of 93.7 per cent, thereby raising the volume of industrial output to more than *three times* the pre-war output, and to more than *double* the level of 1928. As for the programme of output for heavy industry, we have fulfilled the five-year plan by 108 per cent.

It is true that we are 6 per cent short of fulfilling the total programme of the five-year plan. But that is due to the refusal of neighbouring countries to sign pacts of non-aggression with us and due to the complications that arose in the Far East.[1] We were obliged, for the purpose of strengthening our defence, hastily to switch a number of factories to the production of modern defensive means. This switch resulted in these factories suspending production for four

[1] The Japanese threat rising out of Japan's occupation of Manchuria in 1931.

months. As a result of this operation we have completely filled the gaps with regard to the defence. But this was bound to affect adversely the fulfilment of the programme. But for this circumstance, we would almost certainly have overfulfilled the total production figures of the five-year plan.

Finally, as a result of all this the Soviet Union has been converted from a weak country, into a country capable of producing on a mass scale all modern means of defence in the event of an attack from abroad.

Now, after all this, judge for yourselves what worth there is in the talk in the bourgeois press about the "failure" of the five-year plan in the sphere of industry.

And what is the position in regard to growth of industrial output in the *capitalist* countries, which are now passing through a severe crisis?

Here are the official figures.

Whereas by the end of 1932 the volume of industrial output in the U.S.S.R. *rose* to 334 per cent of the *pre-war* output, the volume of industrial output in the U.S.A. *dropped* during this same period to 84 per cent of the pre-war level, in Britain to 75 per cent, in Germany to 62 per cent.

Whereas by the end of 1932 the volume of industrial output in the U.S.S.R. *rose* to 219 per cent of the *1928 output,* the volume of industrial output in the U.S.A. *dropped* during this same period to 56 per cent, in Britain to 80 per cent, in Germany to 55 per cent.

These figures show that the capitalist system of industry has failed to stand the test in competition with the Soviet system.

We are told: This is all very well; but it would have been far better to have renounced the policy of expanding the production of means of production, or at least to have relegated it to the background, so as to produce more goods for mass consumption.

It is true that the output of goods for mass consumption was less than the amount required. But, then, we must take into account where such a policy of relegating the task of industrialisation to the background would have led us. Of course, out of the 1,500 million rubles in foreign currency that was spent during this period on equipment for our heavy industries, we could have set aside a half for importing cotton, hides, wool, rubber, etc. Then we would now have more cotton fabrics, shoes and clothing. But we would not have a tractor or an automobile or a big iron and steel industry; we would not have metal for the manufacture of machinery—and we would remain unarmed while encircled by capitalist countries.

We would have deprived ourselves of the possibility of supplying agriculture with tractors and agricultural machinery—consequently, we would be without bread.

We would have deprived ourselves of the possibility of achieving victory over the capitalist elements in our country—consequently, we would have raised immeasurably the chances of the restoration of capitalism.

We would not have all the modern means of defence without which it is impossible for a country to be politically independent, without which a country becomes a target for military attacks of foreign enemies. Our position would be more or less analogous to the present position of China, which has no heavy industry and no war industry of its own and which is being molested by anyone who cares to do so.

In short, in that case we would have military intervention; not pacts of non-aggression, but war, fatal war, for in such a war we would be almost unarmed in the face of an enemy having all the modern means of attack.

This is how it works out, comrades.

An Outsider's View of Plans and Purges *

. . . In 1933 . . . Stalin announced the successful end of the first Five Year Plan and the beginning of a new, . . . joyous era. The first Five Year Plan concentrated on . . . heavy machinery. . . . The second . . . promised . . . everyday needs. . . .

The production of women's clothes . . . and accessories assumed uppermost importance. . . .

Press photographers went to dances in factories and schools and took pictures of dancing couples. The captions mentioned what dresses the girls were wearing. This was new in Russia and very exciting to those photographed. . . . The authorities regularly reminded the public how . . . prosperous life had become . . . and encouraged people to be gay and dress well. Zealous officials soon overdid this. . . . A silk dress, a manicure, or patent leather shoes almost became earmarks of good Soviet citizenship. . . .

I had a friend, a beautician. . . . Among her clients were several elderly Communists. . . . According to the old party line, their drab appearance had to demonstrate . . . contempt for the bourgeois world. The new party line [required] these elderly women to reflect the country's prosperity by acquiring a permanent wave and a facial.

The new plenty was comparative. . . . Supply [never] equalled the demand. Even during the "fat" years [1933 to 1936] one had to stand in line [for] hours. . . . [But Russians] found it easy compared to the years before. [Goods] were being turned out in quantities . . . unknown in Russia's history. But neither had Russia ever known [so many] buyers. . . . Millions of peasants had for generations satisfied themselves with [crudely-made] shoes, . . . textiles [and] furniture. [They] now wanted and could afford . . . manufactured shoes, ready-made clothing, victrolas, . . . silk stockings, [etc.].

* SOURCE: M. Fischer, *My Lives in Russia,* New York, Harper and Brothers, 1944, pp. 98-211.

New dances were regarded for years as highly bourgeois, . . . unworthy of a . . . Soviet citizen. . . . In 1933, . . . dancing . . . became an approved part of Soviet life. . . .

. . . Factories, . . . schools, and government offices ran classes in "Western Dances." . . . Our American friends . . . were fascinated by the seriousness with which teachers and pupils clapped their hands to mark time and wrinkled their brows [so as] not to miss the subtle distinctions between American, French . . . , Hungarian . . . fox trots. . . .

. . . To watch Russians dance in those years seemed funny. . . . Their deadly serious approach [looked odd]. But [it] moved me deeply. Only a short while ago all these . . . dancers . . . had not known a moment of relaxation. . . . They had worked beyond their strength, and eaten below their needs. Today they still worked hard, though less hard, but they ate well now—and they danced. This latter was to them . . . proof that the hardships of the first Five Year Plan had not been in vain.

The improvement . . . showed itself predominantly in food. . . . Rationing was abolished. . . .

The food stores . . . improved their service. They introduced home delivery [and] accepted orders by telephone. . . . [Imagine] what this meant to a Russian housewife who had never . . . seen any service to the public. . . .

. . . Sausage factories turned out dozens of different types of sausage; the dairies experimented with new kinds of cheese. . . .

. . . Everything which appeared after years of absence delighted the Russians. When . . . dyes were sold again, we [dyed] everything from dish rags to overcoats. When . . . paints . . . and wallpaper [became available] Moscovites . . . indulged in . . . fantastic color schemes. It meant [much] to . . . women when . . . yarn of different shades reappeared . . . in 1934, and they no longer [had] to mend flesh colored stockings with coarse white or black thread.

Being better fed, people were now more fit to stand evening courses after hard working hours. Those who earned little . . . knew that [greater] skill and knowledge [meant] a higher-paid job in the future. To the innumerable schools, colleges, *technicums,* study groups in factories and offices were added radio courses in science, . . . languages, economics [and others]. Millions of [adults] studied one subject or another. Foreign languages, accessible before the revolution only to the highest classes, were studied in towns and villages. English was in greatest demand. . . . The government encouraged language studies.

In 1934 the first open-air café, . . . decorated with colorful parasols, drew huge crowds. . . . Russians quickly adapted themselves to . . . spending a leisurely evening with friends over tea, coffee, or a drink. [Often] I heard Russians say:

"If we can have this, why can't we have everything else they have in Paris, New York, and London?" . . .

Quick-service shops were opened where . . . suits [were] pressed, . . . shoes shined. They were called "Amerikanka" to suggest American speed. Barber shops and beauty parlors were opened in large buildings and railroad stations. The latter were modernized and [had] gorgeous rest rooms. . . .

. . . Cosmetics and perfumes were packed in fancy boxes and bottles. . . . They were given romantic or revolutionary names: . . . "Red Moscow," . . . "To My Beloved." . . .

. . . "Keep Smiling" became the motto of the day. Government leaders, actresses, . . . tractor drivers . . . , all showed their teeth in newsreels and . . . magazines.

The fact that not all this brightness was spontaneous and that much of it was ordered from above disturbed only a few. . . . The great majority had gradually been trained to accept obediently anything which came from higher quarters. [And] life had become so good . . . that questions of free thought or free art bothered only a [few].

The young, [having] hardly any recollection of freedom, [did] not [miss] it.

*   *   *

. . . When I [became] a council member we, the non-Communist parents, were urged by the authorities to take an active part in school work. . . .

Members of the Parents' Council visited classes and later reported to the parents. When I sat in a class I [saw most clearly] what the revolution had done. . . . I thought of my own school days . . . the divisions between poor and rich, educated and uneducated, nationalities and creeds. [Soviet children] were all equal. . . . The children of Bolshevik leaders, . . . writers, scientists, . . . had no greater opportunities for education than the children of . . . laborers or peasants. . . . This part of school life made me happy. But the spiritual regimentation disturbed me.

In the winter of 1933-1934 I once sat in [a] class while the teacher discussed the old and the new Russian village. A ten-year-old girl showed an excellent understanding of the advantages of the new collective farm over the old individualistic peasant farm. Yet none of her answers satisfied the teacher. She made the child change her answers so that at the end they showed no trace of a bright childish mind but sounded like a *Pravda* editorial. When I talked to the teacher, . . . an intelligent person, she tried to justify her attitude but finally admitted the truth. She showed me a list of answers, issued by the Commissariat of Education, which were to be accepted. It was the teacher's duty to insist that the children answer in the official language.

The activities of our Parents' Council were manifold. But I never dreamt that we would have to light Christmas trees in Soviet schools. The Christmas tree had been frowned upon after the revolution. But in 1929, when everything connected with bourgeois life had to disappear, the Christmas tree became a leading taboo [like] Trotskyism, capitalism, . . . etc.

. . . Late in December, 1935, a letter signed by Postyshev, the popular Soviet leader in the Ukraine, appeared in the Soviet press. In it he wondered why Soviet children were deprived of one of the greatest joys of bourgeois children, the Christmas tree. . . . Of course, Postyshev said, Soviet children would not dream of celebrating Christmas, but why not . . . have a New Year's tree. . . . We knew immediately that the Christmas tree under a new name had been sanctioned by the Kremlin.

That same day the Moscow evening paper . . . accused the market managers for neglecting . . . Soviet children and not providing New Year's trees. . . .

The very next morning the markets were full of trees. All night long, axes had been busy in the suburban forests of Moscow. . . .

*　*　*

. . . The government's control over spirit and mind constantly grew tighter. Many executions and arrests had occurred in 1935 as a result of the assassination in December, 1934, of . . . the very popular Soviet leader, Sergei Kirov. The dark spots, however, still seemed small compared with the light which pervaded life. . . .

. . . The new Soviet Constitution was in the making. When the draft was first broadcast . . . in 1936, many Soviet citizens wept. It was . . . magnificent compensation for all their past suffering. The Constitution pledged freedom and happiness to all. The draft was given to the country for discussion and the population indulged in an orgy of debates.

Interesting . . . as this discussion was, another absorbed my interest. For some time there had been rumors about a change in the abortion law. There were too many abortions, and . . . women's health suffered from them. . . . Men felt little responsibility toward women because there was always the possibility of an abortion. We all hoped for a change . . . and expected . . . a gigantic campaign, the kind of thing the Soviet government had so well mastered, to teach people that abortion was a poor form of birth control. This could have been accompanied by an increase in the output of . . . contraceptives. . . .

But . . . the . . . published . . . draft

of the new anti-abortion law . . . disappointed . . . everybody I knew. It flatly prohibited abortions, except in cases of severe illness. It did not mention birth control. . . . People were stunned. But the draft was open for [public] discussion. . . .

. . . Editor's desks . . . were heaped high with . . . letters criticizing the draft of the new law. Scientists, . . . ballerinas, . . . housewives, . . . poured out their hearts. [The letters] all had the same burden:

"We want . . . children . . . but we do not want to [become] child-bearing machines. We want the right to have as many or as few children as we please. Give us more housing space and build more nurseries, and you will not have to resort to drastic measures to raise the population. Let us not give up . . . being the only country in the world [having] the legal right to abortion." . . .

. . . The whole country watched this war of letters, which raged for weeks. For the first time the Soviet public was asked to voice its opinion in the press on a vital problem and it made clear its violent objection to the proposed law. Much zest . . . was added to the . . . discussion because it came at the time of the new Constitution and . . . seemed to be the beginning of a new era fulfilling Lenin's promise [of government] by the people.

*　*　*

[On] August 15, 1936, thunder struck from a clear sky. Headlines read: Zinoviev and Kamenev on Trial for Treason. . . . Two of the most prominent . . . leaders only a few years ago, to be shot! . . .

For the solace of my soul I tried to justify the . . . trial and the death sentences. The . . . government accused the defendants of plotting against it and the party leaders. Like most Russians, since 1927 I had been inclined to believe that any opposition to the Soviet government was treason. But everything in me rebelled against the execution of men who had helped to make the revolution— . . . intimate friends of Lenin. I was at a . . . loss to understand the eager competition of the accused to blacken themselves and their past. . . .

. . . By spring of 1937, though continuing to lead normal lives outwardly, larger groups of the population were gradually being disturbed by the purge. One heard of innumerable arrests and executions. . . .

. . . Familiar faces disappeared and others took their places in . . . offices, factories, universities. The new appointees were heralded as saviors after the "wrecking" committed by their predecessors. But soon many of them were in turn called wreckers and purged.

We tried to [carry on] as if nothing were happening. . . . People tried to escape by listening to old operas . . . , reading . . . , visiting museums. But . . . it soon became impossible to think about anything else but executions, arrests, and exiles. Our boys [told us] about the purged parents of their schoolmates. A neighbor would drop in. Niura would rush in with the latest news. . . .

"Did you hear that so-and-so was shot, exiled, arrested, committed suicide?" . . .

. . . [One day she pointed] to a middle-aged man in the street, [and] said:

"Look, there goes . . . an old Bolshevik but he is not arrested yet."

"But why should an old Bolshevik be arrested?" I asked.

"Why, don't you know? Every one of them is a traitor. They want to kill Stalin and bring back the landowners."

. . . Stalin had succeeded in convincing the masses that the old Bolsheviks, those who had made the revolution with him, those whom the public had been taught to worship . . . , had gradually, for different reasons—jealousy of Stalin, desire for power, loss of "revolutionary vigilance" (the favorite slogan of 1937), and what not—turned against the revolution and its prophet, Stalin. Niura . . . represented the [popular] mentality. . . . She felt sorry for purge victims and helped them in secret if she could. But she [had no] doubts and accepted every official utterance as gospel. . . .

On a December morning in 1937 [our neighbor] Natasha rang the bell and asked for our morning paper. Grigori, [her husband], suffered from diabetes. He was not well that morning and had not gone to the office where he got his newspaper. Natasha promised to bring the paper back soon. But she did not [return] till late that night. All day long the GPU had been searching their apartment and now Grigori had been taken away. While he was still home, Natasha had controlled herself. She had even tried to keep him in good humor. But now it was over. The anguish of . . . months of waiting exploded.

"What shall I live for now? I will never see Grigori alive again. . . . He can't live [without] his medicines. I begged them to permit him to take his pills along. They refused. And I begged them on my knees not to take Lenin's letters and picture away. You know what they said? 'A traitor's house is not the place for it!' Well, if Grigori can be called a traitor . . . life is worthless for me!"

. . . She . . . joined the army of thousands of fathers, mothers, husbands, wives, children [seeking] to locate their loved ones . . . at the GPU information windows, and at prison entrances [only] to learn, after hours of waiting . . . in bitter cold . . . "He is not in this prison." "We have no record of him." . . .

Six weeks after Grigori's arrest, a GPU agent came and told Natasha to prepare some clothing . . . for her husband for the next day at a certain hour. . . . The following day a big GPU truck stopped in front of the house. . . . Uniformed men [ran] back and forth into the nine entrances of our house carrying bundles and throwing them into the truck. We knew that many people had been arrested in our house but had never realized that the number was so great. The truck moved half a block and stopped in front of another large apartment house. From our windows we could see the . . . same procedure. . . .

. . . Days later, [after Natasha's arrest], GPU men came again . . . , this time to empty Natasha's apartment and to throw . . . into the truck all the furniture, clothing, [etc.].

There were special stores where . . . belongings of purge victims were sold. . . .

They were . . . in obscure neighborhoods which few foreigners . . . visited. I once walked into such a store. . . . Piles of ill-assorted objects: . . . oriental rugs, worn-out shoes, . . . an evening gown, a broken mirror, . . . photographs . . . ; all that had meant a home. . . .

. . . A GPU man and his wife moved into [Natasha's] apartment. . . .

Among our . . . friends was a couple, Andrei and Liza. . . . He had been a rev-olutionist from early youth. . . . He was . . . devoted to his work and to the Soviet Union. . . . But [he was arrested]. . . .

. . . Liza . . . had a good job but [a few days later she was discharged]. She could get no other work. . . . She had to provide for herself and her two daughters. She also had to face a serious problem with her older daughter, Valya. . . . [That problem] many mothers had . . . during these years. . . . The children either had to be told that their fathers were enemies of the revolution . . . or that their fathers were loyal citizens—which meant that the Soviet government was wrong in arresting them. This for a Soviet child is just as heartbreaking as to discover that the adored father is a counter-revolutionary. Most of the mothers [tried not to hurt] the child too deeply. . . . Liza told Valya that her father remained [a] good revolutionary. . . . But through some old friends, Liza said, he might have known of the existence of an opposition to the . . . government. It was his duty to report this. [But] he could not . . . inform on friends. But "at this serious moment in Soviet history" (this phrase has often misled not only little Soviet girls) it was not proper to suppress such information.

After having been refused work for a long time, Liza went to the Soviet Control Commission where every Soviet citizen can go with a complaint against a government office. She demanded her right as a Soviet citizen to work and support her family. . . . The . . . Commission . . . made it clear that as long as she remained the wife of . . . an enemy of the people, she iden-tified herself with his ideas and . . . could not be helped. In other words. . . : Divorce

your husband or starve. . . . Liza rejected the idea of a divorce. How could she desert Andrei? He had always dearly loved his family, and now they were all that re-mained to him in this world. A letter or a snapshot from them which took at least three months to reach him by train and reindeer, and a package which reached him . . . after seven or eight months were like a ray of sun in the far-away Polar wilder-ness. How could she inflict the pain of divorce on him? But after [further] un-successful job-seeking . . . , Liza saw no other way out. . . . [The children] had be-come anemic. . . . So she divorced Andrei and promised never to write to him. . . .

There were many such tragedies among our friends. . . . [But there were plenty of] people who were untouched by the purge and who had reason to be happy. . . .

There was Pasha, . . . a . . . woman in her fifties. . . . She grew up in fear of God, of the landlord, of rich people, . . . and of the czarist police. When I met her in 1932, she still lived in the world of her old fears. She had little contact with Soviet life. Communism to her was something like the Antichrist. I saw her gradually los-ing one fear after another until they were all gone except her fear of God. . . . She went to [an] evening school and learned to read and to write. She saw her . . . daughters changing from . . . clumsy village girls into . . . city girls who dressed well, talked an educated language, . . . and re-ceived salaries which Pasha had never heard of before. . . . They lived like the rich . . . of Pasha's youth.

Pasha spent the summer of 1936 in her village and there she found dozens of stu-dents, aviators, . . . a professor, a ballerina . . . whom she had known as unwashed . . . peasant youngsters . . . who came to spend their vacations in their own village and help with the harvesting. . . . Her life was full and rich. . . . If one was critical in her presence, she would say:

"Now, don't you say anything against the Soviets. Where would I and my daughters be today if not for the revolution?"

During the purge, she would, like a good old-fashioned Russian, sigh over the misery

. . . and even cross herself . . . when told of an execution, but nothing could shake her confidence in the government.

[Another neighbor] was an old railroad worker [on] old-age pension, [living] with three of his five sons. Two . . . were engineers, one was an actor, one an aviator, one an agricultural expert. Their wives were all professional women and the many grandchildren were in high schools, colleges, and factory schools. . . . Even if the purge had lasted ten years longer and a hundred times as many people had been executed, it would have made no difference to this old man.

"Lenin," he once said, "put the keys to happiness into my hands. . . . The least I can do . . . is to be a good servant of the Soviet government."

Many people were . . . deeply grateful to the government. . . . The purge had not directly touched them and they believed the newspapers which said that those [purged had] wanted to destroy the gains of the revolution. . . .

* * *

. . . The confessions were obtained in prisons. Some of the accused confessed [in] three months . . . , some eight months after their arrest. But if the entire . . . case rested on these confessions . . . , on what grounds were the men arrested in the first place? . . .

. . . A foreigner . . . was even more at a loss than the Russians to understand. . . . The foreigner's own experience led him to assume that when a government arrests or shoots a person, he must have committed a crime. But it does not work [that] way in dictatorship. Soviet citizens have been "liquidated" because the government thought they knew too much, or were too popular, or might some day oppose a change in policy, or had been friendly with a victim of the purge. . . . There are no free newspapers or political independents in Russia and it is . . . [easy] to kill or banish a citizen who is not guilty. . . . He has

no redress. The . . . government [need not fear] that the press or radio or . . . Congress will criticize it. . . .

. . . Questions which disturbed our small circle . . . bothered only [few] Russians. The [people have] been taught to accept the following formula. There are two possible rulers in the Soviet Union—the Soviet government, alias the Communist party, alias the Politbureau, alias Stalin—or landlords, . . . capitalist exploiters, German Fascists, and Japanese generals. There is nothing in between. Any attempt to oppose the Soviet government, which doubtlessly had the support of the population, was therefore . . . an attempt to restore the landowners. . . .

* * *

I began to suffocate . . . from lack of freedom. . . . I simply wanted to say aloud the thoughts I had in my head, to be able to say what play, book, movie, person I liked or disliked. It depressed me, after having seen a [poor] play to read in the *Pravda* that this was the greatest play ever produced in the Soviet Union, after which I had to keep my own opinion . . . to myself. Yura and I once read a book which we both thought excellent. . . . One morning . . . we read in the *Pravda* how full of political mistakes the book was and how harmful for Soviet readers. . . .

I resented the mental insecurity and confusion. . . . Once I was in a friend's house when she was tearing up Marshal Yegorov's picture after his execution. Her eight-year-old son, who was devoted to the Red Army leaders, walked into the room.

"What are you doing?" he cried.

She explained to him that Yegorov had been shot as a traitor. With . . . a gesture of despair, the boy said:

"Now I don't understand anything any more," and left the room with tears in his eyes.

"I know exactly how he feels," said his mother sadly.

Plans and Purges Seen from the Inside*

The village horrors left psychological lesions which never healed; however, [I] reached out desperately for compromises with conscience. After all, one could not simply "leave" the Party. One could not even slacken his activities or betray symptoms of fading faith. It would have meant removal from school, disgrace and persecution. [I had] to squelch those emotions, [especially] with the purge in the offing.

Soon [Purge Commissions] would [hold] public sessions in factories, offices, institutions, schools. Every Communist in the land would run the gantlet of public inquisition. A Purge Commission usually consisted of two or three members and a chairman; Party men of unblemished loyalty. Comrade Galembo was chairman of the Commission at the Institute.

Those found wanting would be deprived of their Party cards. They would become *ex*-Party people, quite different from *non*-Party people. The ex-Party citizen is one who has been rejected; forever distrusted, barred from promotion, a political leper. Towards the end of 1933 [the] press published lists of who was to be purged and where. The all-too-human relish for tearing down successful neighbors was artfully inflamed.

The first condition for retaining membership, of course, was unwavering allegiance to the General Line of the Party; above all, spotless loyalty to Stalin. Even the hint of "deviation" was fatal. But the purgee's intimate life and thoughts were also fair targets for public attack. The proceedings combined the worst features of third-degree interrogation and bear-baiting, with the Communist in the role of bear. For the audience it was a circus. Attendance throughout the weeks of purge was obligatory for all Party people, and the "non-

Party masses" were encouraged to be present.

No Communist was ever informed in advance of the charges [to] be brought against him. Uncertainty was the most upsetting element. You reviewed your past, over and over again, wondering whence the danger might come.

Didn't you talk too much one night three years ago under the influence of good fellowship? One of your uncles had been an officer under the Tsars. True, you had never met him. But what if someone has dug up that ghost? A woman who was your lover was later arrested as a Right deviationist. What if this relationship were suddenly thrown up to you? Pavlov is likely to be expelled—how shall I disassociate myself from him before he drags me to ruin? Save your own skin—somehow.

The purge at our Institute opened with a speech by Chairman Galembo. He told us that our beloved Party was honeycombed with enemies. They must be rooted out for the health of the Party and our Beloved Comrade Stalin!

Thundering applause greeted every mention of the Leader's name.

Finally the purge got under way. The Commission members sat behind a red-draped table on a platform decorated with portraits of Politburo members and a bust of Stalin. The Communist to be examined was called to the platform. He handed over his Party card to the chairman and began a recital of his life history, his origins, his career, his interests, with confession of sins, near-sins and mistakes. It was always better to bring up errors yourself, if you suspected that they were known to the Commission; "concealing" anything from the Party compounded the gravity of the crime concealed.

After the confessional, the purgee was questioned by members of the Commission and by the audience. He was reminded of omissions and tricked into contradictions.

* SOURCE: V. Kravchenko, *I Chose Freedom*, New York, Scribner's, 1946, pp. 132-134, 187-190, 192, 198-199, 213-218, 302-306. (Adapted and abridged.)

Comrades spoke up in his favor or against him. If the Commission seemed friendly to the victim, the process was brief and routine. But once the audience sensed that the purgee was in disfavor it trampled him without pity; especially his frightened friends and associates hastened to join in the verbal lynching to protect themselves. The ordeal might last a half hour or an entire evening. The purgee might fight back, offer proofs of innocence, weep—or he might be crushed into confusion and silence.

Those who passed the purge were handed their Party cards. Friends congratulated them, relieved for their own sakes. The rejected were ignored and avoided. Suicide among expelled members was [common].

* * *

In September, 1935, a "miracle" occurred in the Donetz Basin. A worker named Stakhanov mined 102 tons of coal in one shift—fourteen times the normal output. To a practical engineer the deceit [was] transparent. Special conditions and special tools and assistance had been provided. It was a miracle made to order for the Kremlin in launching a new religion—the religion of speed-up.

What Stakhanov had done, all miners could do! What miners could do, all other industries could do! Doubters were damned. Technicians who raised practical objections were defeatists. Workers who could not toe the mark were slackers!

Moscow screamed the new Stakhanovite slogans. Telegraphic orders began to pour into Nikopol from Kharkov and Moscow headquarters. We must instantly create Stakhanovite brigades, as pace-setters for the slowpokes.

Our plants had been operating less than six months. They worked on three shifts under many handicaps. Neither the amount nor the quality of the steel and other raw stuffs was adequate. The workers were mostly green, the staff mostly inexperienced. Because of undernourishment and bad living conditions, the physical vitality of the personnel was low. What we needed most was smoother integration of the productive process. This seemed the worst possible moment for overloading either the men or the machines. Rhythmic teamwork, rather than spurts of record-breaking, was the key to steady output. More than fifteen hundred workers engaged on a common task, in which every operation meshed into the next, couldn't speed up arbitrarily without throwing the whole effort into chaotic imbalance. But orders were orders.

In my own sub-plant, I was obliged to resort to artificial speed-up, a crime against the machines and the workers alike. I regrouped my labor, putting the best workers, foremen and engineers into one shift. Then we selected the best tools and materials for the special shift. Having thus stacked the cards, we gave the signal for the specious game to start.

One evening, with reporters and photographers present, the "Stakhanovite" shift got under way. As expected, it "overfulfilled" the normal quota by 8 per cent. There were flaming headlines. Congratulations arrived from officials in the capitals.

But this "victory" on the industrial front left me heartsick. The other two shifts, deprived of their best personnel and their best tools, lost more than the favored group had won. By contrast they seemed ineffective if not "lazy." They naturally resented being made the scapegoats. They cursed the lucky ones and the officials.

Throughout the Soviet land the speed-up drive turned into a furious campaign. Thousands of administrators were dismissed, many were arrested, for sabotage of the new "socialist production" and for "failure to provide the proper Stakhanovite conditions." Every lag in output was blamed upon the engineers and technicians. The picture created in the public mind was that of workers eager to step up production but "held back" by scheming managers.

A wedge was thus driven between workers and technical staffs.

Even to the simplest-minded factory hand or miner it was apparent that the new records set by forced speed-up would soon be set up as "norms" for everybody.

When the drive was at its height, in November, a national convention of leading

Stakhanovites was called in Moscow. It was addressed by Stalin [who contrasted] their zeal with the backwardness of other workers. From that time forward, the Stakhanovites became an *élite* of labor, earning a lot more than their fellows and enjoying all sorts of privileges.

And thus the Kremlin drove a wedge also between various categories of workers. The ancient technique of dividing to rule was being applied to a whole nation under the banner of "building socialism."

It was not long before the worst misgivings of the workers came true. Peremptory orders arrived to revise the "norms" of production, on which wages were based, upward by 10 to 20 per cent. It was a roundabout order to exact 10 to 20 per cent more work for the same wage. In my plant, of fifteen hundred men, perhaps two hundred qualified as speed-kings. For the others the revision of norm meant simply a serious cut in earning power. The general resentment was unmistakable.

To add insult to injury, the new norms had to be presented and accepted by the workers "themselves," not only "voluntarily" but enthusiastically.

Separate meetings were called of the various sub-plants, where all workers were present. Technical and political leaders, assisted by "activists," proclaimed the rehearsed slogans and proposals. At the meeting of my sub-plant, the workers sat glumly. Automatically they applauded every mention of Stalin's name. The perspiring Party cheer leaders scattered through the hall could not pump up the desired enthusiasm. Most of the men and women had just finished eight hours of hard labor. They were tired, bored, eager only to have the comedy over with and go home. A report on the glorious achievements of Stakhanovites was read; newly proposed quotas were announced. Then some rank-and-file trade-union members, previously prepared for this role, took the floor and urged the adoption of the new quotas. Voting began.

"Comrades, I propose that the resolution be adopted unanimously," the trade-union chairman shouted, as he had been instructed to do.

Who is in favor? A forest of listless hands. Who is opposed? Silence. Suddenly a woman's voice exclaimed:

"Comrade chairman, Kiryushkin here didn't vote."

For the first time the meeting came to life. Some obscure Kiryushkin had dared not to raise his hand.

"Comrade Kiryushkin, aren't you voting?" the chairman asked, in a peeved voice.

A thin, meek-looking man stood up. His face, stained with oil, was calm.

"Why should I vote?" he shrugged his shoulders in a pathetic way. "One way or the other the norms will be passed. It's my job to work and I work. What else do you want? My wife and children expect me to make some more money and this means that I'll make even less."

"Comrades, Kiryushkin is throwing mud on the great Stakhanovite movement!" someone yelled. "He's not class-conscious."

"Class-conscious?" Kiryushkin, still on his feet, again shrugged his shoulders. "I don't know what you mean. Yes, I'm conscious that I make only 140 rubles a month and have three children and a wife to feed."

"Enough of this comedy! Let's accept the resolution!" the chairman interrupted. But the meek workman seemed overcome by his own daring.

"What do you mean, comedy?" he raised his voice unexpectedly. "Look at me: This one working suit is the only one I have. My family goes hungry. If this is a comedy, then what's a tragedy?"

*   *   *

Politics, flying the banners of efficiency, had the right of way. Communist and police officials often had the final word as against the engineer and manager, even on purely technical problems. We were in the midst of an era of anarchy and civil strife in industry. I was caught between instructions from Moscow and suspicion from below, between tougher tasks and declining discipline. Nervousness became almost my normal condition.

One night I was awakened by the telephone [and called to the factory]. One of the machines had suddenly broken down, leaving half my sub-plant idle. Engineers ran around in circles, while in my office police specialists questioned suspects.

What had happened was instantly clear to me. Stakhanovite enthusiasts had decided arbitrarily to increase the rotating speed of a roller. As the pipe had not been imbued with Stalinist faith, a large segment of it burst on the main belt and one of the machines was put out of commission.

The police-minded swarm of officials, however, was less concerned with restoring operations than with finding culprits. The investigators buzzed through the plant. Interrogations went on at N.K.V.D. headquarters. Several times I was called out and questioned; after a night of it I was hardly much good at the factory. Obvious explanations made no appeal to [NKVD official] Gershgorn's devious mind. He demanded "evidence" against this or that person. Each time he mentioned a name, out came a *dossier*. Not only officials but simple factory workers were under surveillance.

"Kravchenko, you're not cooperating with us," Gershgorn screamed. "You may pay for this, believe me!"

*   *   *

The temporary easing of police pressure [in 1936] gave me a short lived illusion of personal independence. That, in turn, predisposed me to a hopeful view of the newly announced Stalin Constitution. [It contained] explicit guarantees of civil rights and limitations on the forms of seizure and arrest. Assuredly the worst of the terror was over. An occasional revival of hope was almost a condition for remaining alive. Europe seemed headed for war. Perhaps our masters had decided to unite the masses behind them by [granting] a few crumbs of freedom?

The Nikopol *combinat* was being enlarged. Hordes of new construction workers strained our food supplies and housing. One day, in the midst of the inflated hopes for better [times], I noticed N.K.V.D. soldiers around the new building area. Forced labor had been brought in. Four or five hundred

haggard men and women were working under armed guard. They went about their work like people doomed, too apathetic to commune with the free workers near them.

At the end of each day the prisoners were marched off to prison barracks. This labor had been "contracted" for by the construction officials. A flat sum per prisoner, about equal to the amount paid free workers, was paid to the N.K.V.D. Besides using millions of political prisoners directly, in mining salt or felling forests, the N.K.V.D. farmed out its surplus slaves.

One weekend, that summer, I went down the Dniepr in a motorboat with a friend. Along a marshy stretch [of shore] hundreds of men and women were working under military guard. The ragged workers, knee-deep in mud, seemed scarcely human. Clouds of mosquitoes hovered over them. The guards had built bonfires to drive off the insects, but the prisoners seemed inured to the pest. My eyes rested on a young woman. Her hands and face were black with mosquitoes but she plied her shovel, as if unaware that she was being eaten alive.

An officer approached us.

"Why don't you go about your business, citizens?" he said. "This isn't a show."

"I'm a Party man and the head of a plant," I said. "This interests me, purely technically. What are they doing?"

"We're clearing the swamp."

"An N.K.V.D. project?" I asked.

"No, the Nikopol Soviet is doing the job, with 'contracted' N.K.V.D. labor."

We steered for home. To continue the outing seemed indecent. All morning we had talked of the Constitution and the possibility that its promises might be real.

*   *   *

The fall of any leader or official meant that all his appointees and cronies would be purged. After the arrest of Brodsky, the N.K.V.D. motorcars picked up his assistants, his friends, the men and women whom he had put into jobs anywhere in Nikopol. The Commandant of the Nikopol Garrison went into the hunters' bag, then the local Prosecutor and all his legal staff;

finally the chairman of the Nikopol Soviet himself. The local bank, the newspaper, all commercial institutions were "cleaned." Everywhere new people assumed authority, and often within a week or a month these were, in turn, picked off.

In whispers people told of the arrest of the chairman of the Soviet, the highest civil official in the city. He was a former miner, with a proud civil war record. He was awakened in the middle of the night.

"I am the representative of the Soviet power in Nikopol," the chairman shouted at the uniformed men. "You have no right to arrest me!"

"Step along, you dirty dog! We'll show you who has what rights," the arresting officer growled and shoved him out of the door.

A new man, a stranger to our factory, came to take Kozlov's post. His name was Los. He was a dull-witted, fanatic. The last drops of comradely feeling evaporated in the heat of Los's zealous hunt for culprits. Meeting on the grounds, we technical and Party officials looked at one another in surprise. "What! Are you still among the living?" our looks said.

The headquarters of the N.K.V.D. on one of the main streets was working twenty-four hours a day. The arrested people were not held long. Nikopol was, after all, only a minor branch office of the business. They were packed off to Dniepropetrovsk, from Dniepropetrovsk to Kharkov, to other centers, to make room for more and still more.

And Nikopol was only one tiny segment in the widening swath being cut by the super-purge. Instructions from our trust, Trubostal, and from the Commissariat in Moscow, were increasingly signed with unfamiliar names, so many of the old officials had been cut down.

The outside world watched the several blood-purge trials staged in Moscow. The Moscow trials were just a façade behind which the real horrors were being piled mountain high. The public trials involved a few dozen carefully selected and rehearsed victims. The purge involved hundreds of thousands, ultimately around ten millions who were sorted and disposed of rapidly: these to prison, these into exile, these for the forced labor battalions, these to die.

Crowds of women and children swarmed around the N.K.V.D. building in Nikopol at all hours despite the bitter cold. The N.K.V.D. men would disperse them, but soon they were back again, weeping, screaming, calling the names of fathers, husbands, brothers. And through the howling of the stricken, press and radio announced the adoption of "the world's most democratic Constitution" in November, 1936.

The hysteria reached a point where jittery Party men went to bed in their clothes, "just in case." Every day cattle-cars hauled their human freight out of Dniepropetrovsk. Four years ago the freight had consisted of peasants; now the quality was better: Communists, government leaders, Army men, technicians, non-Party officials. "What can Stalin and the Politburo have in mind? The whole thing seems unrelieved madness," Brachko said, then regretted having said it, as I could see from his alarmed look.

My turn came in November, 1936. I had the psychological advantage of having expected the blow and of having sat through many rehearsals with other comrades in the leading roles. The chief thing, I told myself, was not to lose control of my senses. Through sleepless nights I had tried to imagine what could be charged against me. Would it be something I had said or done five years ago? Would it have reference to the work in my plant?

We were having a Party meeting in the factory club. Several members had been brought up on charges. Local Communist sections now demonstrated their "Bolshevik vigilance" by acting against their members even before the police got around to it. In three cases the meeting had recommended expulsion. Now the meeting seemed nearly ended.

But suddenly Los rose to speak. I was thinking of something far removed from this ugly gathering when the purport of his words went through me like an electric shock. *This was the moment!*

"Comrades," Los began, "I suggest that we discuss the case of the director of the pipe-rolling sub-plant, the Communist member Victor Kravchenko. We have reports containing very serious accusations."

"Let the accusers speak up!" someone shouted.

"Quite right," Los said. "Engineer Makarov may now have the floor."

As Makarov walked to the platform, the comrade sitting at my right [muttered] something about "going for a smoke." The man at my left also moved away. I had been turned into a leper. Makarov was one of those incompetent people who survive by exploiting one's sympathy. I had gotten him his job at Nikopol, had found him an apartment, and had always taken it for granted, naively, that he was grateful to me.

"I've known Kravchenko for many years," he was saying now. "He was a member of the Bureau of the Party Committee at the Metallurgical Institute. Most of his colleagues on that Committee have been arrested. I wonder whether this is accidental, comrades! This Kravchenko has many friends and 'connections' in Moscow. Let me say in passing that some of [his] Moscow 'connections' have been exposed as enemies of the people.

"But that's all by the way, comrades. What I want to say is that in all these years as a Party member Kravchenko has lied to the Party. He has concealed *the political past of his father!* Why hasn't he admitted to the Party that his father had been an active Menshevik before the revolution?"

"Talk about Kravchenko, not about his father!" someone interjected.

"The apple doesn't roll far from the apple tree," Comrade Los shouted back. "Go ahead, Comrade Makarov."

"That's right," Makarov proceeded, "Kravchenko is no better than his father. He has surrounded himself with 'alien elements.' Is it accidental, do you think, that he has gathered so many non-Party people in his department? Who are his assistants? Who are his foremen? Who is the arrested Menshevik Dubinsky? Who is the arrested German fascist, Zelman? I could mention many others. All non-Party people or actual

enemies whose wrecking has been exposed by the N.K.V.D."

In the midst of my distress I thought: *So that's what's biting him; the fact that I did not raise him to full assistant!*

"Comrades, Zelman is a Jew and a German Communist. How can you call him a fascist?" It was a worker interrupting the speaker.

"Very well, you say he is a Jew and a Communist," Makarov argued. "Hasn't Hitler sent thousands of spies over here? What better disguise than a Jew and a Communist? What better protection for such filth than under the wing of a Kravchenko with his important connections?"

"Comrade Los," Director Brachko now spoke up, "I suggest the speaker stick to facts and stop messing around in nonsense."

"I'll give you facts, Comrade Brachko. Think back to the time when the new norms were voted in line with our glorious Stakhanovite movement. Wasn't it clear to all of us that Kravchenko opposed the change? Only one worker [attacked] the norms, a man named Kiryushkin. What did Kravchenko do, this big-hearted humanitarian? Why, he rewarded Kiryushkin with a better job! Yes, I accuse him of protecting all the anti-Soviet elements in our midst, and I accuse him, above all, of hiding his father's Menshevism."

As he left the platform there were cries of "Right! Well done!" and also cries of "Lies! All lies! Absurd!"

"Member of the Party engineer Shaikevich has the floor," Los announced.

Shaikevich was an undersized man, with tiny cruel eyes.

"Comrades, I also sent in a denunciation of Comrade Kravchenko," he said in a falsetto voice. "I have watched him for a long time. It's true that the newspapers and radio have praised him to the skies. But what if all these services to the country were just a smokescreen, behind which [he] carried on his dastardly work?"

"Facts, not rhetoric!" Brachko called out.

"Kravchenko is a doubter!" the orator, angered by the interruption, struck an even shriller note. "At the Institute he criticized collectivization. Everyone knows that. And in the factory—always a long face, nothing to his grand taste! Why has he such a high position at all? Because he has friends in Moscow and in Kharkov! Not ability but connections!"

"That's a lie, comrades!" Brachko again called out. "Kravchenko [is] one of the best engineers in Trubostal."

"But you can't deny, Comrade Brachko, that he's the son of an anti-Soviet father and has concealed this from us!" the falsetto rang out in triumph. "He deprived all of Stalin's loyal, devoted Communists in his sub-plant of promotion."

And now I recalled. I had been sorry for the frustrated little Shaikevich, and had tried to cover up his blunders. But in the end, after discussing the problem with Brachko, I had transferred him to a department where less demand would be made on his limited knowledge.

After Shaikevich, Yudavin rose to round out the accusations. His was the authentic voice of the N.K.V.D. Knowing this Yudavin as a police agent, I had avoided him. Now he was ready to pay me back with interest.

"Comrades," he said, "I not only support the conclusions of the other speakers but I want to come to the most serious point. Kravchenko is a saboteur!"

The dreaded word exploded like a canon.

* * *

The publication in 1938 of a new official *History of the Communist Party* marked the tapering off of the super-purge.

I do not mean that the terror was stopped. "Normal" arrests by the thousand, executions without trial, arbitrary exile of "undesirable elements" whose labor was desirable in forsaken regions, tortures and inquisitions continued. Already whispered estimates placed the slave labor forces at more than fifteen millions.

I mean only that the specific campaign to cleanse the Party and the bureaucracy, planned after the assassination of Kirov, was now almost completed. There was not an office or an enterprise, an economic or cultural body, a government or a Party or military bureau, which was not largely in

new hands. Had a foreign conqueror taken over the machinery of Soviet life and put new people in control, the change could hardly have been more thorough or more cruel.

The magnitude of the horror has never been grasped by the outside world. Perhaps it is too vast ever to be grasped. Russia was a battlefield strewn with corpses, blotched with gigantic enclosures where millions of "war prisoners" toiled, suffered and died. But how can the mind's eye take in anything so vast?

In the Council of People's Commissars, only Molotov remained. The Central Committee of the Party, in theory the heart and mind of the ruling group, counts 138 members and alternates; only about a score of them remained. Of the 757 members of *Tzik,* the Central Executive Committee, sometimes described abroad as Russia's "Parliament," only a few dozen survived.

The ruin was even bloodier in the so-called autonomous "republics" and regions. Without exception the commanding staffs of their governments and their Party organizations were wiped out by orders from Moscow—a sufficient commentary on their supposed autonomy. Industry and technology, the arts and education, the press and the armed forces—all were turned upside down, their leaders and most gifted personalities being shot, imprisoned, exiled or at best, stripped of influence.

The temptation in looking at the piled-up horrors is to concentrate on the famous and important victims, whereas the *pogrom* extended to the whole population. In the ruling Party, 1,800,000 members and candidates were expelled, which was more than half the total in these classifications; and in most cases expulsion meant concentration camp or worse. At least eight million more, Comsomol members and non-Party people, were liquidated—meaning anything from execution to exile or removal from their jobs.

But even these colossal figures don't sum up the tragedy. Their very immensity makes them a bit unreal. One must think of the victims not in such impersonal terms, but as individuals, [having] relatives, friends, dependents who shared their sufferings. To the historian of tomorrow, to the sociologist of today, these are statistics. But to me, who lived through it, the digits have bodies and minds and souls, all of which were hurt, outraged and humiliated. Moreover, millions who escaped the purge were maimed in their minds and wounded in their spirits by the fears and the brutalities amidst which they lived. For sheer scale, I know of nothing in all human history to compare with this merciless persecution.

It was the wind-up of this long war that was signalized by the appearance of a new history. It proved to be a document probably without precedent. Shamelessly it revised half a century of Russian history. I don't mean simply that it falsified some facts or gave a new interpretation of events. It deliberately stood history on its head, expunging events and inventing facts. It twisted the recent past—a past still fresh in millions of memories—into bizarre shapes, to conform with the version of affairs presented by the blood-purge trials and the accompanying propaganda.

It was conscienceless fiction. There was a certain magnificence in its unabridged cynicism, its defiance of the common sense of the Russian people. The roles of leading historical figures were perverted or erased. New roles were invented for others. Trotsky was represented as a fiendish agent of foreign capitalists who had sought to sell out his country, in collusion with virtually all the other Fathers of the Bolshevik Revolution. Stalin, of course, emerged as the sole leader inside Russia before the revolution, and as Lenin's one intimate and trusted associate thereafter. All books, articles, documents, museum materials which contradicted this fantasy parading as history—and that means nearly all historical and political writings and documentation—disappeared throughout the country!

More than that, living witnesses, as far as possible, were removed.

The directing staff of the Institute of Marx, Engels and Lenin in Moscow, repository of ideological truth, were removed. The same thing happened in branches of the Institute in various parts of the country.

The story of one of the outstanding figures in the Institute, Professor Sorin, [sums] up the whole shabby era.

Sorin at one time had been publicly denounced by Stalin. Then the culprit "confessed his errors" and emerged as one of Stalin's mentors in Marxist theory, fabricating speeches and articles to which Stalin attached his name. He was made assistant director of the Marx-Engels-Lenin Institute, dug diligently for documents and quotations to support any policy Stalin wished to foist on the country, and seemed happily adjusted.

But a point seemed to have been reached at which the meek Sorin balked. He was willing to find and quote texts as required —but he drew the line at *inventing* texts and *falsifying* quotations. And so in the middle of one winter night the N.K.V.D. wagon came to Professor Sorin's fine apartment and took him away. His wife and child were evicted from their home. All of the professor's books, documents and notes were carted off to the N.K.V.D.

Other Institute people who knew too much about Communist history and theory to accept the faked version were similarly shut up, among them the chief director, Adoratsky. The head of the Party's propaganda division, Stetsky, was arrested. Thousands of others from the historical, political and literary "fronts" were sent on the one-way road to oblivion. The path was thus cleared for falsification without limit. The new "history" became possible.

To brand the shame more deeply on our minds, "study" of the new version was made obligatory for all responsible Party people. History classes met nearly every night in this period and lecturers from Sverdlovsk came to our town to help hammer home the lies. Whatever human dignity remained in our character was humiliated. But even the most gigantic lie, by dint of infinite repetition, takes root. I could see terrible falsehoods, at first accepted under pressure, become established as unquestioned "facts," particularly among younger people without personal experience to the contrary to bother them.

It fell to me to deliver a "lecture" on one

phase of this Party history to Party members of the Pervouralsk district. My subject was "The Communist Party in the Struggle for Collectivization of Agriculture." I crammed my mind with the appropriate passages from the official history, read up Stalin's speeches on the subject, then stood in an auditorium filled with people and lied for more than an hour.

Every falsehood tore open the half-healed wounds of my own shattering experiences in the collectivization drive. I felt as if I were mocking the children with bloated bellies and violating the corpses I had seen piled up in the villages. My listeners, too, knew I was lying. My words and their applause were equally spurious; we were so many actors going through our prescribed parts.

Why did I, why did the audience, submit to the indignity? For the same reason that you hand over your wallet to a footpad who points a gun at you.

Another result of the big purge deserves mention. Every Communist carries a Party card. It is his personal passport, his political patent. The booklet, besides personal data, has on it the signatures of the local Party officials who issued it. Because most of the leading Party officials had been purged, it transpired that most Communists had their blessed status affirmed by enemies of the people. The Kremlin could not tolerate this ironical touch. With a view to erasing the handwriting and the memory of the dead and the imprisoned, a new registration of Communists was ordered in this fall of 1938. Where cards had been signed by liquidated "enemies of the people," new ones were issued.

The process was turned into a new, though minor, purge. Every Communist again appeared before three-man commissions and submitted himself to elaborate questioning. The new cards, besides, were no longer the simple affair they used to be. They now included a photograph. Besides, a special booklet was now compiled for every Communist, in two copies, containing detailed biographical data, a record of activities, rewards, punishments; one copy was deposited at his City Committee, the other at the Central Committee in Moscow. The whole procedure looked like a police documentation rather than a record of members of a political organization. The last pretense that we were participants in a voluntary association of comrades was dropped.

That there might be no illusions in this respect, a new rule was put into effect: Thereafter a Communist wishing to leave one city or region to settle in another—even if the change were on orders from above—had first to wait for a formal decision by the City Committee authorizing his departure. The ruling Party became, in effect, another prison—fitted out with comforts and privileges not enjoyed by the inmates of the larger prison called Russia, but still a place of confinement.

Stalin in a Soviet Novel*

The conference of foremost flax and hemp growers with Party and government leaders was to open at the offices of the Central Committee of the Party. Anna and her roommate went there right after breakfast. . . .

. . . All of a sudden . . . [a] burst of clapping . . . and the people in the hall

* SOURCE: V. A. Smirnov, Sons, Garden City, N.Y., Doubleday, 1947, pp. 274-284. Trans. by Naomi Y. Yohel.

rose. . . . Anna saw a group making for the presidium table. And in that group her eyes found Stalin. . . .

"Our own father—our own," she whispered.

Stalin, Molotov, Kalinin, Kaganovich, Ordzhonikidze, and Andreyev took their seats. . . . Anna gazed at Stalin with wet, feverish eyes. [From far] he looked . . . just like his picture.

It was a long time before the chairman

could restore silence and get everyone to sit down. But [then] Anna heard Stalin say, looking keenly at the collective farmers in the hall:

"Not many women."

The conference started. People mounted the platform and told quite informally, as they might in their own *kolkhoz,* about their Stakhanovite work. They spoke to Stalin, Kalinin, and Molotov, who asked detailed questions and took an interest in every little point. . . . Anna conjectured at first that the Party and government leaders wanted to learn the secrets of flax growing. But by the thoroughness with which Stalin . . . talked about the . . . processing of flax, she realized with surprise that he probably knew as much about it as any of the Stakhanovites. . . . Now and then he would . . . make notes on some sheets of paper.

Anna saw with envy how the delegates who rose to speak walked up to the presidium when they had finished and shook hands with Stalin and all who were there with him. How badly she wanted to shake his hand! But she dared not ask for the floor, though she would have liked very much to tell him about her *kolkhoz* flax. . . .

During the intermissions the delegates clustered about Stalin. . . . Anna went up close and had a good look at him. He was older than in the picture, and not so tall and stocky. He was on the thin side, if anything, and probably not much taller than herself. She liked everything about him: his calm gait and the trick of occasionally fingering his mustache; the friendly smile of his big, kindly lips; his quiet, even voice and his way of stressing the main point of what he said. And above all, she liked his simple manner. . . .

"Are all great men as simple as that?" she wondered, and replied, "Yes, I suppose so. . . ."

An old man in big horn-rimmed spectacles was stopping Stalin now. . . . The delegates around Stalin . . . stood [aside]. Blinking shortsightedly . . . , the old man was asking questions, . . . and seemed to be flurried. Stalin listened and explained in calm, quiet tones.

"Who's that?" Anna asked in a whisper.

"A member of the Academy. . . . A world-famous scientist," came the whispered reply.

She moved up closer to listen. But they were talking about something complicated, and she could not follow. She only saw that the old man had stopped blinking and was smiling and nodding. . . . [He] . . . gripped Stalin's hand, thanking him.

And everything that Anna had perceived before in looking at Stalin was now illumined for her with a new light.

"So that's what he is like—our great man, our father," she thought, without taking her burning eyes from his face.

*   *   *

On [the] second . . . day of the conference Anna saw how Stalin sized people up. The manager of the hemp trust was on the speaker's platform; he was a . . . corpulent fellow. . . . Things were evidently not going . . . well in his trust, but he would not admit it and spouted an endless stream of words. . . .

"This reception is a momentous event for us," the . . . manager babbled. . . . "It is a tremendous stimulus for us. It will stimulate us for years. . . ."

"Lots of stimulus, but not much hemp," Stalin put in. Laughter burst out all over the hall, and it was a long time before it died down.

The manager . . . launched into a confused explanation of why his trust was doing badly. He, the manager, had taken steps, had given warning in time, but—

"It was awkward to go over the head— of the Commissariat of Agriculture," he stammered.

Stalin turned quickly to face the platform and took the pipe out of his mouth.

"Since when has it been awkward to go to the Central Committee?" he asked searchingly.

"That's right," Anna thought with approval. "If things aren't working out, go and say frankly whose fault it is. . . . Maybe it's your own fault." . . .

The conference was drawing to a close. An intermission was called, and Anna . . . again saw Stalin surrounded by delegates. Her roommate . . . elbowed her way through to him. . . .

"Comrade Stalin," she said loudly . . . "Here's a friend of mine who would like to talk to you but feels bashful."

Stalin smiled, everyone made way, and he walked up to Anna and shook hands.

She was confused at the feel of his warm palm in her own trembling hand. . . . He asked her where she came from, what her name was, what she did in the *kolkhoz*, and went strolling with her down the lobby.

As she faltered out her replies Anna stole a look at him, and . . . noticed . . . the silver threads at his temples. "He's got gray hair, like mine," she thought. . . . Yes, . . . he was only a little taller than herself, thinnish, and looked a good deal older than in the picture. "He ought to drink milk fresh from the cow," she thought, and recalled how fond her husband had been of fresh milk with rye-flour pancakes. . . .

"The folk in our *kolkhoz* told me to say that they think well of you. . . ."

"Thank you," Stalin said simply. . . .

. . . Anna . . . started saying how badly she felt that she had not brought him a present as others had done. . . .

"A present?" Stalin stopped her. "From you, Anna Mikhailovna? Why, you've brought me the best present. . . . Your sons are my present." He . . . said nothing for a few moments. . . .

"About the flax, it's good, very good," he said. . . . "But what is flax, after all? . . . The children are the main thing. They are our future, our hope. . . ."

That evening the conference closed, but the delegates were asked to stay in [Moscow]. . . .

[They] visited . . . the museums; went to the theater and, needless to say, took a ride on the subway. . . . But nothing moved Anna so much as Lenin's tomb.

When she saw the stately marble structure . . . and the silent queue of visitors, tears welled to her eyes. . . .

Lenin lay in a coffin of glass. . . . He might have been asleep. . . .

Anna walked slowly round without taking her eyes off Lenin's face. . . .

On leaving the tomb she noticed that some of the visitors queued up again at the entrance, and she did the same. . . .

. . . She . . . went to bed early. She dreamed that she visited Lenin a third time. . . . She kissed him on the forehead, and he opened his eyes and got up. For a long time they walked about the lobby talking pleasantly. . . .

Two days later, at a meeting of the Presidium of the Central Executive Committee in the Kremlin, Kalinin presented Anna with an order . . . and congratulated her. . . . Shining in relief on the order . . . was the image [of Lenin].

Toward the end of the meeting, . . . Stalin came into the hall. . . .

He . . . greeted her like an old friend.

"Here they've given me this decoration," Anna said quietly. "I don't know myself what for." . . .

"For your flax," he said, then . . . added with a smile: "And for your sons, Anna Mikhailovna."

Anna gave a little sob; she made as if to embrace him but did not dare.

Then a photographer came. Anna found a place in the fourth row; she stood up on tiptoe and raised her head. . . . The photographer got ready to snap.

"Just a moment," Stalin said. He sought Anna out and sat her down at the table with the most celebrated of the collective-farm women, while he himself stood behind.

Section 5

World War II and After

A HARD-WON VICTORY

URING the initial phases of World War II, Soviet forces overran eastern Poland, some Finnish territory, the Baltic States, and Bessarabia. Stalin's new domains were quickly subjected to large-scale purgings of those most likely to prove resistant to sovietization. The Soviet State police efficiently removed hundreds of thousands of Polish and Baltic political and intellectual leaders from their homelands and sent them to prison camps or resettled them in remote regions of the U.S.S.R. "A nation thus deprived of her backbone and nervous centres," writes Arthur Koestler, "becomes a kind of amorphous jelly, reduced to the degree of malleability necessary to adapt herself to [Soviet] conditions. . . . These millions of new citizens of the U.S.S.R. [had] to learn to live without parliament, without public criticism, under new laws [restricting] their personal liberty of movement, of speech, of reading, of work, and confine their whole range of existence between narrow limits undreamt-of even under the semi-dictatorial Polish or Lithuanian regimes. The greater the difference between the cultural levels (and standards of living), the more radical this softening process [had] to be, to make the conquered nation digestible by the Russian regime."[1] After June, 1941, when the Germans invaded the U.S.S.R. via the newly added buffer areas, thousands of Poles were released from Soviet camps so that they might join in the struggle against the Nazis. From these former prisoners have come many accounts of life in the forced-labor camps.

The German panzers moved swiftly forward along an 1,800-mile front. By the winter of 1941-1942, they had almost encircled Leningrad[2] and stood at the gates of Moscow; in the South, they had penetrated the Russian lines as far as Rostov-on-the-Don. In the course of the spring and summer of 1942, while battlelines along the Leningrad-Moscow sector remained relatively stabilized, the Nazis launched a major drive in the South that carried them to the lower Volga (Stalingrad) and to the eastern coast of the Black Sea. The battle for Stalingrad went on from September,

[1] A. Koestler, *The Yogi and the Commissar*, New York, 1946, p. 200.
[2] The Germans' two-and-one-half-year blockade and bombardment cost Leningrad about 1 million lives.

1942, to January, 1943, and was the turning point of the war. After Stalingrad, the Red army remained on the offensive until the Germans were defeated.

How, aside from matters of military judgment, strategy, and peripheral aid—such as American lend-lease given the U.S.S.R.—is the Soviet victory to be explained? What was it that enabled the people of the U.S.S.R. to withstand the shock of the *Blitzkrieg* that had caused Polish and French resistance to crumble within days? What made it possible for them to endure and adjust to the rapid loss of much of their best food-producing and industrial regions, the immense number of soldier and civilian casualties, and the deliberate ruthlessness of the German conquerors?

Soviet resistance is best described as a "communal effort." The German generals soon discovered that their soldiers were fighting not only the Red army but virtually the entire population as well. Unquestionably, the Germans themselves did much to bring that about. They introduced so monstrous a terror in towns and villages and made so plain their design to slaughter or enslave all the people, that even such elements as the Ukrainian peasants and the Baltic peoples, who at first believed that the Germans had come as liberators, found themselves compelled to resist the invaders in every possible way. The people of Russia, ever famous for valiancy in defense of their country, demonstrated a capacity for sacrifice such as the world has seldom witnessed. Their hatred for the Germans turned them into tigers. The soldiers at the front refused to surrender. Young women by the thousands served as flyers and tank drivers. Others eagerly joined the partisan bands that sprang up everywhere to engage in sniping, spying, raiding German sentries and quarters, and dynamiting roads, bridges, munitions dumps, and so on. Even the children understood the menace of the German, and many fantastic exploits were achieved by ten-year-olds.

In industry, too, the effort was immense. All considerations of personal comfort seemed put aside for the war's duration. With factories, dismantled for shipment eastward, went all their skilled help. Women and children, in replacement of recruited men, worked at their machines for interminable hours, often amid direct bombardment, to turn out weapons and other military needs.

German brutality certainly heightened Soviet morale, but it did not account for the basic feeling of popular unity that evinced itself in a variety of ways. Contact, usually at great personal risk, was maintained between occupied villages and partisan groups in the vicinity. Workers from factories visited the front lines to bring gifts and to see for themselves how much the fighting men suffered. At the same time the soldiers became aware of the heroism in the cities, what with hardships caused by constant bombings and shortages of food. Besieged Leningrad produced its own million-souled army to build fortifications, to join the front-liners and, although death through starvation was common, to keep grenades and bayonets flowing to the soldiers. An affectionate glow was in constant play between soldiers and civilians, and each side wanted to do the utmost for the other.

Much has been written about the government's wartime relaxation of attacks upon religion and the propagandistic tribute paid Tsarist Russia's heroic past. These clever devices served to appease many who were secretly hostile to the regime, so that they could unleash their full hatred against the invaders. But most important as a force that rallied the people behind the war was probably the idea of the struggle for the *Socialist* fatherland. The people, by and large, felt that they were fighting for their own land, their own industry, and the Soviet promises for the future—all those things for which they had given so much. They were fiercely proud of what had been accomplished. In a sense, the war was the supreme test of whether it had really been done, and there was a strong feeling of outrage regarding the Nazi pigs, who, in Stalin's words, had stuck "their snouts into the Soviet garden."

Other elements conducive to high Soviet morale were the ubiquitous party and Komsomol members, ready in many a critical situation to take charge among a people well disciplined to take orders from such leaders. It should also be mentioned that each individual felt secure in the thought that whatever happened he was not alone; that the State would do its best to provide for him and his children.

A negative interpretation of the popular fury against the foe is given in *Dr. Zhivago*, the famed novel by Boris Pasternak. The Soviet people, he suggests, were releasing the savage hatreds built up in them during the repressions of the 1930's which had left them uncertain about whom to strike out against. The war finally gave them a situation clearly black and white. They knew beyond doubt what side they were on and could let go with all their strength in killing Germans. Thus they were able to rid themselves of long suppressed feelings of resentment against Stalinism and of guilt for having permitted the mass murders to run their course. An almost identical view was later expressed in Evtushenko's *Precocious Autobiography*: "The war lifted a weight from the soul of the Russians. No longer did they have to be insincere."

STALIN'S LAST YEARS

Emerging from the war, the authority of the Soviet regime extended westward into Germany, eastward into Manchuria and Korea, and southward almost to the Aegean Sea. The military might of Germany and Japan had been destroyed, and the Red army was an enormous force consisting of about 400 battle-tried divisions. But within the U.S.S.R. proper the war had wrought incredible destruction. Some 30 millions had perished; the cities of European Russia were rubble; and the farm land, whether destroyed by retreating natives or stripped of crops and animals by the Germans, lay virtually waste. Heartbreaking sorrow had been caused among the populace. Few families had not lost some loved ones, and the brutalities of the German occupation had left the minds of countless infants paralyzed with fear.

In some ways the situation was like that of 1920 and might logically have called for a policy similar to that of the N.E.P., instituted in 1921. The people would have welcomed a chance to restore their lives to a semblance of order free from omnipresent governmental controls and pressures. But such was not to be the case. Stalin, unlike Lenin in 1920-1921, refused to relax his iron grip. He had little need to fear revolt.

Why, in view of the circumstances, he proceeded as early as 1946 to order a resumption of the drive for rebuilding and advancing heavy industry and for developing the most modern of military equipment is still uncertain. But reasonably safe assumptions can be made about his motives. To the aged leader of world communism and the greatest of Russian Tsars, the postwar international situation posed both a great temptation and a grave threat. The temptation lay in the possibility, before he died, of extending communism to war-ruined western Europe, to Asia, and to the rest of the world and of winning Russian outlets to the Mediterranean Sea and perhaps even warm water ports in the Pacific. The threat lay in the postwar positions held by the atom-armed military forces of the United States, which were based in Japan and Germany. The "dying beast" of capitalism, as Lenin had warned, would one day attempt to crush the world's socialist center. Stalin, it seems, intended to be prepared for that day.

The danger of invasion, so often used by him to justify his calls for sacrifice, again became the theme of Stalin's demands for unflagging and unrewarded labor by the Soviet people. The last years of the great pharaoh's life amounted to an immense whipping on of his grim and weary subjects, with the purpose, perhaps, solely of constructing the greatest pyramid of all time to commemmorate their oppressor's eternal glory. The overseers of this vast undertaking were the Security Police, recruiters of prison camp labor, and the Komsomol members, who, themselves largely cynical about the doctrine, carefully watched the younger elements, particularly students, for signs of heresy. In 1946, a high-ranking Politburo member, Andrei Zhdanov, assumed the role of chief censor. He imposed severe restrictions upon all manner of artistic expression to make sure that writers, critics, and so forth demonstrated complete adherence to Stalin's views, unconfused by any wartime contacts of Soviet citizens with Western or other ideas that might pervert the literary norm known as "socialist realism." In the meantime, the cold war propaganda of the single-station radio and the single-party press stabbed incessantly at the nerves of a people who had lived through one or two devastating invasions (depending on age), who had been raised on the teachings of Lenin, and who, in the last analysis, had no way of verifying that which they heard or read. In September, 1952, en route to England, United States Ambassador George F. Kennan told the press of the "icy cold" atmosphere in which he lived in Moscow. He said it had become impossible for an American to engage a Russian even "in simple conversation," and he deplored the Communist "hate campaign" against America.

The above-mentioned measures of compulsion, coupled with a merciless drain upon the Communist-dominated countries of east-central Europe, brought remarkably swift improvement to the war-devastated economy of the Soviet Union. This was done while arms were being produced at a higher rate than ever before; while labor was drawn from farms to factories to meet higher production norms; and while millions of tons of grain were sent abroad, on the one hand, to help embattled Communist China and, on the other, to obtain rubber and machines from Britain. The Fifth Five-Year Plan, introduced in 1951, called for production goals of 1955 to be more than double the Soviet production of 1940, the year before the invasion. The plan promised a 60 per cent increase in consumer goods.

In 1952 there were still no big department stores in Russia. Shop windows contained little that was eye-catching. Consumer goods, by U.S. standards, were still painfully skimpy. However, nylon stockings, evening gowns, refrigerators, and washing machines were appearing. In Moscow alone, there were 10,000 TV sets. Perfumes and lipsticks were cheap and beauty parlors, run by the State, were available. Housing was insufficient, but there were no serious food shortages. Though still lacking in many rudimentary comforts, the Soviet citizen knew that conditions were slowly improving. A clear sign of progress came on April 1—large-scale price reductions, the fifth since the end of the war. However, the pace of industrial progress sapped the vitality of the people who had known nothing but extreme pressure for more than two decades. An overwhelming sense of futility set in, and it was coupled inevitably with large-scale moral laxity.

The newspapers reported numberless accounts of racketeering and theft in high bureaucratic places and among lesser Party figures, while periodical cartoons mercilessly lashed at corpulent collective farm directors and the like. Letters to editors carried complaints about heads of trusts, mine managers, and so on; most of them named names. In this way, it seems, Stalin was, as ever, finding prominent scapegoats whom he could blame for the brutal impositions forced upon the workers by the impossible production quotas.

Stalin died in March, 1953. This may have saved the lives of thousands. There were indications that dissatisfaction was rising to the level of rebellion and that Stalin, knowing this to be the case, was about to let loose a reign of terror, based on fraudulent charges, such as had once before wiped out or silenced all his opponents.

THE THAW AND DE-STALINIZATION

The death of Stalin was bound first to produce an initial shock, followed by a movement toward freedom from the iron grip which Big Brother had maintained on the behavior of the low- as well as the high-placed in the Soviet Union and its satellites. Aside from the normal yearnings for freedom in the hearts of all concerned, the Stalinist bonds needed loosening if only because of the almost universal stagnation that had begun to set in. The fields of pure science were, since they represented no ideological trend, little subject to conflict with Stalin's dogmas. In physics and mathematics, for instance, the freedom of thinking permitted the scientists would soon pay great dividends in progress. But all other spheres of intellectual life showed signs of cynicism and rigor mortis. The peasants, ever the stepping-stones for Stalin's goals, were apathetic. Bureaucracy, which lorded over industry and was in turn commandeered by the party, had, out of inability to dispute orders from above, become heavy at the top and corrupt throughout. It was better to arrange to meet schedules of production through fixers than try to argue with an officialdom that feared to make decisions. Such decisions might contradict the wishes of the boss or the demands of a mystical party line that no one really understood. The party functionaries themselves—even many in the higher councils of the party—had lost whatever sense of initiative they might once have had.

In the two or three years immediately following the master's demise, the heirs of Stalin moved gingerly forward. The so-called Collective Leadership—including Malenkov, Beria, Mikoyan, Molotov, Khrushchev, Kaganovich, Bulganin, and others—was hamstrung by not knowing yet how to act on its own, either with respect to internal or foreign affairs. Also, being so accustomed to treachery and spying and being as yet conditioned to thinking of Stalin as still present and watching—as indeed he was in the persons of Beria, Molotov, and Kaganovich—the Collective Leadership did not dare to take really decisive steps in the direction of freeing the country from its fetters. The most immediate menace to those who desired progress was Beria, Chief of the Security Police, the man most likely to reimpose Stalin's system. He was, therefore, rapidly gotten rid of, apparently assassinated by his erstwhile colleagues, whereupon Malenkov, the first post-Stalin Premier, proceeded to call for better conditions of life for peasants and workers.

The "butter instead of guns" policy seemed to forestall an immediate return to Stalin's program of aggression. But as the year went on the official attitude of the U.S.S.R. became suspicious, quarrelsome, and contradictory. Hopes for Big Four talks on the German question were deflated and then inflated again. The Korean truce became an endless source of irritation. Soviet delegate Andrei Y. Vishinsky, addressing the United Nations General Assembly in November, sounded Stalin's old theme of "capitalist encirclement" of the Soviet Union. He declared that West Germany was being prepared as a "springboard for attack on the U.S.S.R."

Yet the few Americans allowed to visit the Soviet Union found its people sometimes friendly and always curious about Americans.

In 1954 the Soviet government did much to give Russia a brighter appearance.

A housing program went into high gear. Big metropolitan hotels were refurbished. For the ladies, the cosmetics trust marketed dozens of new creams. For the gentlemen, there were brightly colored neckties.

In a break with the grim past, the Kremlin, ancient stronghold and symbol of Russian autocracy, was abandoned by high government officials, and during the year served largely as the setting for holiday parties and balls for children and for almost daily public functions attended by thousands of common Soviet citizens. Forced-labor camp inmates were released in droves, and those remaining in the camps were accorded legal rights and the privileges of corresponding with relatives and receiving parcels of food, and so on.

To the intelligentsia the new policy, or "thaw," [3] brought exhibits of Western art, long taboo, and, in general, an atmosphere more conducive to expression of opinion. Writers experimented with new forms and musicians dared openly to talk about jazz. High level work in psychology and psychiatry, a sure sign of concern for the welfare of individuals, also was making significant progress.[4]

But the road was tortuous and soon the Collective Leadership split into factions, one insisting that Stalinism not be abandoned (Molotov, Kaganovich, and allies), another, centering about Khrushchev, considering it necessary to kick over the old traces. As Khrushchev gained strength, possibly because of his growing appeal to the broad masses, particularly the peasants, the younger and the more dynamic elements within the party, and the large group of specialists that had been created to head the great technological-industrial system that Stalin had built, he found himself ever more isolated within the summit of the party. However, his opponents could not prevent him from dominating the Twentieth Party Congress of February, 1956, on which occasion Khrushchev, abbetted by Mikoyan, pronounced Stalinism an anathema, in the famous secret speech that was leaked to the West, and charged Stalin with crimes against loyal Bolsheviks and even with bungling the war against Hitler. Needless to say, this called for the immediate preparation of a new official history of the Communist party to downgrade Stalin and his closest associates. The "history," however, left intact the image of the one-party system under which so much evil had flourished. Khrushchev, himself a one-time disciple of Stalin, emerged from its pages as a man of clean conscience.

The denunciation of Stalin opened the gates to widespread expressions of hostility to all that Stalin had stood for. In the U.S.S.R. proper, as well as in the satellite countries, a veritable tide of long-pent desires for freedom of thought and of criticism found vent in novels, plays, and poems. Some remained in the desk drawers of writers and poets, but many were printed and exposed to the light of day. In 1956,

[3] The term became popular as a result of Ehrenburg's novel by that name published in 1954.
[4] A. Mintz, "Further Developments in Psychology in the U.S.S.R.," *Annual Review of Psychology,* Vol. 10, 1959.

Vladimir Dudintsev published his novel *Not By Bread Alone* exposing the hypocrisy of the Communist bureaucracy. Boris Pasternak's *Dr. Zhivago,* also completed in 1956, was in July of that year submitted to the magazine *Novi Mir* for publication in serial form. Turned down there, it was smuggled out of the U.S.S.R. to create a world-wide sensation upon its publication in Italy.

De-Stalinization brought forth rude questions by young people about events of the recent past. Many lost all faith in what they had been taught in their history classes and began to regard all government pronouncements with cynicism. There was unrest in some parts of the U.S.S.R. But the ferment reached its greatest heights in Poland and Hungary where the grievance of national oppression was added to all the other bitterness. The Hungarian revolution of October, 1956, cost the Soviet regime a tremendous loss of prestige.

The following year, Khrushchev had to fight his battle for survival against the Stalinist elements, now joined by all the rest of Khrushchev's rivals in the party presidium. Khrushchev was charged with errors of softness that had endangered the nation as well as the victory of world communism. Aided by war-hero Marshal Zhukov, whom he later purged, and the relatively youthful Central Committee, Khrushchev withstood the challenge of the summer of 1957. His opponents, including Kaganovich, Molotov, Malenkov, Shepilov, and Bulganin, were denounced as the "anti-party" group and relegated to minor posts in the government, if not imprisoned or executed. Khrushchev had triumphed—but by the narrowest of margins.

KHRUSHCHEV'S LINE

From 1957 through mid-1964, Khrushchev's program fluctuated quite wildly, because he was caught between the "dogmatism" of his die-hard Stalinist and Chinese critics and his own "revisionistic" aim of ending the cold war. Khrushchev revealed himself to be a man of folksy wisdom and Russian proverbs, who saw in Marxism a call for raising the living standards of the average citizen. Having destroyed the Stalinist "cult of personality," Khrushchev replaced it with a less blatant cult of his own leadership capacities.[5]

The Khrushchev line manifested itself on all levels of foreign and domestic policy.

While constantly advertising Soviet military might along with the dangers of imperialist plots against the Soviet bloc and giving moral or military support to the Communist movement the world over, the Soviet regime also stressed the need for competitive coexistence, for disarmament, and for doing away with war altogether.

Despite the drive for increased efficiency in the production of food and of con-

[5] The front page of *Pravda* of June 8, 1961, has a photograph of a florid-faced, white-suited Khrushchev against a background of dark-suited men and some women, who applaud the party leader as he greets the delegates of youth who had recently been sent to schools for training as industrial specialists.

sumer goods,[6] the State budget for heavy industry and military needs remained unduly high. Thus, in May, 1962, the price of butter and meat rose 25 and 30 per cent, respectively.

The general trend toward economic and social liberty went together with greater freedom to criticize. Writers and poets, momentarily silenced in 1958 as a result of the old guard's bitter reactions to the explosive results of de-Stalinization, again were permitted considerable leeway. However, they were told specifically to stop short of attacking the foundations of the existing order.[7]

Religion remained under attack, but the propagandists of atheism were instructed to refrain from heaping personal abuse upon the character of citizens who happened to be religious. Such instructions were even supposed to apply to the sectarians who had lived in constant fear under the Tsars.[8] Beginning in 1961, religious and Zionistic Jews were subjected to a campaign of virulent persecution. However, the regime revealed marked sensitivity to foreign criticism of its anti-Jewish activities.[9]

Among other signs of ambivalence in Khrushchev's "New Deal" was the relaxation of travel to and from the Soviet Union, while now and then Americans or other foreigners were arrested under charges of espionage. Scientific, technical, and agricultural experts, artists and athletes, and students and professors were exchanged with their counterparts from abroad—notably with the United States.

A Soviet exhibit in New York was matched by a United States exhibit in Moscow. At the New York exhibit in 1959, the Soviet guides, surrounded by curious and skeptical Americans, held firmly to the party line of the moment. The United States and other foreign exhibits in the U.S.S.R. drew vast throngs. Among these were numerous Komsomolists loudly explaining that one or another eye-opening display of a home, a modern kitchen, or other luxury item was not in truth the kind of thing the working people of the West enjoyed.

Perhaps the chief exhibit to leave the U.S.S.R. was Khrushchev himself. His epoch-making trip through the United States in September, 1959,[10] was a sensation in

[6] Khrushchev himself never tired of traveling about the country, personally instructing peasants in improving their agricultural techniques. State planning was decentralized to allow for more realistic apportioning of production norms in terms of the productive capacities of the separate regions.

[7] The popular young Evgeny Evtushenko was, for a while, a kind of court poet. He preached the need for uncompromising criticism directed against the corrupters of Communist ideals, past and present, coupled with an equally basic need to support the ideals themselves and the way in which the regime of Khrushchev was carrying them out.

[8] In 1957 a group of Dukhobors, considering themselves persecuted in Canada, sought asylum in the Soviet Union. At the beginning of 1963, on the other hand, 32 Baptist peasants arrived in Moscow from Siberia, hoping to find, in the United States embassy, protection from persecution.

[9] See M. Decter, "The Status of the Jews in the Soviet Union," Foreign Affairs, January, 1963.

[10] Speaking to a crowd at Vladivostok about the cannon salvos that greeted his arrival in the United States, Khrushchev said: "After the first salvo, I thought: This is to . . . Marx! A second salvo to . . . Engels! A third . . . to . . . Lenin, a fourth . . . to its majesty, the working class! That was not bad, comrades, not bad at all."

California, Iowa, and Pennsylvania. The people of the United States hung on Khrushchev's statements as his every public move was captured on the television screen. Though visibly enjoying his trip, Khrushchev availed himself of every opportunity in the United States to voice his conviction that the capitalist system would be replaced by socialism.

Intended perhaps as an old party leader's crowning glory[11] was the announcement on July 30, 1961, of a new party draft program, the third in the history of bolshevism, reflecting the advances made to date and proposing such immense economic progress within 20 years that the United States and all of capitalism would soon be overtaken. Beginning on October 17, 1961, the Twenty-second Party Congress sat for two weeks and adopted the proposals of the new party draft. Khrushchev, having previously announced the end of the H-Bomb test moratorium, exploded the biggest H-Bomb to date (October 30, 1961). At the Party Congress itself, Khrushchev, this time openly, exposed Stalin to the Soviet people as a sadistic torturer.[12]

The coupling of these events indicated Khrushchev's wish to prove that the Soviet Union intended to remain militarily mighty, that, indeed, nuclear war against her was futile, while denying that the achievement of immense military power was inextricably bound to doctrinaire attitudes and to government by terror over the Soviet people.

[11] Khrushchev was almost seventy at the time.

[12] On November 1, the people of the U.S.S.R. learned that Stalin's body had been removed from its enshrinement in Lenin's mausoleum and that it had been reburied in an ordinary grave within the Kremlin walls, marked by a small black marble slab inscribed "J. V. Stalin, 1879-1953."

Hunger*

Whenever [Russians] hear . . . the words "lend-lease" they think of cans piled up like mountains. . . . From 1942 to 1945 [we] lived . . . on American products. . . . We could have held out without American planes and tanks, but we would have [died] without American food. . . . [Early in] 1943 . . . all the shops in . . . large Soviet cities were stocked to the ceiling with sacks of coffee beans. Before the war coffee in the bean had been a luxury. . . .

[But now] people began to buy coffee by

* SOURCE: G. Klimov, *The Terror Machine*, London, Faber & Faber, 1953, pp. 355-366, 363-368.

the sack. [Not] that the Russians [liked coffee]. They cooked the beans, threw the . . . liquor away, then dried the beans, pounded them in a mortar . . . and made bread of the flour. . . .

During the war all the metal utensils in the U.S.S.R. were made from American cans [labeled] "pork meat."

. . . To diminish the effect of this propaganda by food conserves, the N.K.V.D. spread stories that the Americans [canned] the flesh of South American monkeys to send to the Soviet Union. . . .

While working in . . . Gorky I was crossing Sverdlov Square one day in March. There were puddles of snow and mud. . . .

Two young girls, probably students . . . , were trudging through the water. Suddenly one . . . dropped her case. . . . Books . . . scattered in the mud. The girl took a few staggering steps [and fainted].

. . . An elderly woman . . . began to lament . . . : "Poor kids! You're hungry, hardly able to stand on your feet, yet you're giving your last drop of blood. . . ."

[Many at] the blood-transfusion centres [were] girl students and mothers with little children. In exchange for . . . blood they received 125 roubles, which would buy not quite a kilo of black bread. After each transfusion they received an extra ration card entitling them to [additional food]. These mothers and girls knew their patriotic duty . . . ; knew the blood was for their husbands and brothers at the front. But it was chiefly hunger that drove them to the centres. The mothers tried to feed their hungry children at the price of their own blood. . . .

One evening I stood with a group of comrades in the foyer [of the Sverdlov Municipal Opera] during an [intermission]. Dancing was going on in the hall to the music of an orchestra. A slim, good-looking girl dancing with an officer attracted my notice. . . .

"Who is that girl?" I asked a comrade. . . .

"A student; she's in the last year of the medical faculty," he answered curtly. . . .

[Another said], "If you're interested in knowing her for a night, . . . one can of conserves or a loaf of bread."

I stared at him incredulously. . . . In pre-war days the students had been the [most moral] group in society. Could one year of war have [made] such a change?

"Don't talk bosh!" I retorted.

"It's . . . the . . . truth. She lives in . . . one room with five . . . friends. They have two or three visitors every night. Chiefly officers. Who [else] has anything to spare these days . . . ?"

Before the war there was practically no prostitution in the Soviet Union. The average . . . man's budget did not include this item. . . . There was only prostitution for political purposes, under N.K.V.D. protection, in the neighborhood of the Intourist hotels . . . and wherever foreigners congregated. And some commerce in human bodies went on, to a small extent, among the higher circles of the new ruling class, who had the means to buy such articles.

But now, . . . hunger was driving women on to the street.

*　*　*

Shortly before the end of the war I traveled back to Moscow . . . by train. At every station . . . [stood] ragged women . . . with children in their arms. The infants' . . . eyes [shone] with hunger. . . . Other children stretched out . . . thin hands and asked for "Bread, bread!"

The soldiers . . . silently handed their rations . . . through the windows. Each . . . was oppressed by thoughts of his own wife and children. . . .

Moscow. The last days of the war. A lively trade was going on in the city markets. Pale . . . women huddling in corners, a few knobs of sugar or one or two herrings in their extended hands. They were selling their meagre ration . . . to get milk or bread for their children. . . .

. . . The markets swarmed with war-wounded, without legs, without arms. . . . The militiamen turned a blind eye to these violators of the Soviet trade monopoly.

If any of them did try to take away one of the war-wounded, the air rang with indignant shouts: . . . "What did he shed his blood for?" His comrades came hurrying up, waving crutches and sticks.

Defeatist Attitudes*

I recall three women in a store quite openly saying such things as: "What of Hitler? Things can't be worse and perhaps he will allow us to have our church and pray to God." A skilled worker, who lived in the same house with me, said openly: "In the end deliverance will come and the scoundrels will be thrown out." He expected nothing good of the Germans but considered it of primary importance that an end should be made of the Bolsheviks. Similar feelings characterized whole layers of the population from workers to highly classified specialists.

The failure against little Finland in the "Winter War" of 1940, to which the people of Leningrad had borne direct witness, convinced them that, however strong the government might be in terrorizing the people, it was weak against foes from the outside. The people believed that any state that did not have the Soviet system was, by that fact alone, militarily powerful. Such a state, they also thought, was likely to act justly and humanely. At first they did not even

expect the Germans to bombard an open city like Leningrad.

Where was the effect of the mighty apparatus of Soviet propaganda, which was announcing that fascist Germany was some kind of hellish thing that aimed at enslaving and even wiping out the Russian people? The people didn't believe it. Nobody believed it. I was literally surprised when I saw that a significant number of Jews also refused to believe in the "bestiality of fascism." They believed and expected that the Germans would impose some restrictions upon them, but did not think it was better, therefore, to flee to safety into the further depths of the socialist fatherland. Later I was able to ascertain that this was not merely a Leningrad phenomenon but that similar feelings among Jews had existed in the Caucasus as well.

Thus it was that various Leningraders tried to get out into the suburban areas to meet the Germans, thinking that their wartime hardships might better be endured under the Germans than under the Soviets. From where I was working—digging trenches—I could not help noticing the times when quite ordinary women with their children were sitting under trees waiting for the Germans.

* SOURCE: K. Kripton, *Osada Leningrada* (The Siege of Leningrad), New York, Chekhov Publishing House, 1952, pp. 65-69. (Adapted and abridged.)

Women and Children: Workers and Fighters

The Boys and Girls of Leningrad[1]
. . . [Catherine Borschenko, a teacher, spoke of] rest homes for adolescent workers [as] something to which the Leningrad Soviet attached the greatest importance. . . . The physical and nervous strain of working in Leningrad, for instance in a

[1] SOURCE: A. Werth, *Leningrad*, New York, Knopf, 1944, pp. 54-56.

place like the Putilov works which was almost in the front line, was very considerable, and it was essential to give these young people [an occasional] break from [a grim routine].

"We have fifteen villas here . . . for girls [and] boys of . . . fourteen to eighteen. . . . We give them plenty of recreation and extra-good food. . . ."

Comrade Borschenko . . . conducted us [to] beautifully tidy dormitories. . . . I remembered . . . Tamara and . . . Tanya. Tamara was a little girl of fifteen, very . . . run-down. . . . On her little black frock was pinned the . . . medal of Leningrad. "Where did you get that?" I asked. A faint smile appeared on her pale little face. . . . "An uncle with spectacles came to the works one day and gave me this medal." "What works?" "The Kirov works, of course," she said. "Does your father work there too?" "No," she said, "father died in the hungry year, died on the 7th of January. I've worked in the Kirov works since I was fourteen, so I suppose that's why they gave me the medal. We're not far away from the front." "Doesn't it frighten you to work there?" She screwed up her little face. "No, not really. One gets used to it. . . . Only last week . . . a shell landed in my workshop and many were wounded, and two Stakhanov girls were burned to death." She said it with terrible simplicity and almost with the suggestion that it wouldn't have been such a serious matter if two valuable Stakhanovite girls hadn't lost their lives. . . .

[Tanya was] bright and talkative, and said that everybody at her shell factory was sure that the Germans would [soon] be chased away from Leningrad. "Have you ever seen any Germans?" I asked. . . . She told . . . how she had taken part in the capture of German parachutists in the summer of 1941. "We were staying in the country . . . and there were lots of Leningrad kids—forty of us—and we hunted parachutists. We caught three. . . . The girls were very frightened, for all the Germans had tommy-guns. There was one hiding behind a bush . . . firing all the time. . . . Several of the boys crawled up to him from behind, pounced on him, bit him and took away his tommy-gun. But he had time to kill one of the boys. This one they handed over alive to our troops, the other two they killed. They would have run away—there was nothing else to be done." . . .

. . . These boys who were hunting and disarming parachutists . . . were children of ten, eleven and twelve. . . . [They were daredevils like] the Moscow boys who, during the first raids on Moscow in the summer of 1941, [grabbed] incendiaries with their bare hands until they were taught a safer method.

Katia and Katiusha[2]

At the factory airport, they taught young pilots to fly. Katia never stopped badgering the officials . . . to give her a chance and finally . . . they . . . allowed her to enroll in the school.

. . . [At] Stalingrad . . . fighter pilots were urgently needed. . . . Katia, wearing her new . . . uniform . . . , was sent to the Stalingrad squadron.

"Men laughed at first," she said. "They thought it a joke. . . . We usually fly in pairs, with each pilot looking after his partner. None of the men wanted to fly with me."

But discipline is discipline, and one of them had to accept her as a flying mate. They took off on a reconnaissance flight, and when they returned an hour later, her partner smiled and cried out, *"Khorosho,"* which meant, "Okay." She had been accepted. . . .

She had her miraculous escapes as all pilots do. [Once] she was attacked by two Messerschmitt 109Fs. . . . She got one of them . . . and then she and the remaining Messerschmitt . . . fought for twenty-five minutes—a long time for a dogfight. Each tried to maneuver into good positions. . . .

Finally Katia got him in her sights. She pressed the button—and nothing happened. She was out of ammunition. Well, she would try to make him think she still had ammunition. She circled and climbed and dived, and then he managed to get behind her, and she had a horrible moment when she realized that he was in a beautiful position. She dived. He followed, but the expected fusillade didn't come. Then she realized that he, too, had run out of ammunition.

"It was very silly," Katia says gravely. "There we were flying close to each other and neither of us could do anything about it."

[2] SOURCE: Q. Reynolds, *The Curtain Rises*, New York, Random House, 1944, pp. 126-132.

Katia laughed. She had to go, really she did. She had an appointment—at the Kremlin. Rather shyly she confessed. . . . [She] was going to receive the second Order of the Red Star, and then she would be off to the front again.

*   *   *

When war came, sixteen-year-old Katiusha tried hard to enlist. . . .

"We have plenty of machine gunners," the commandant told her, "but we do need nurses. Will you join us as a nurse?"

To get to the front, Katiusha would have joined anything. Luckily, she had studied nursing at school. A group of infantrymen were just leaving for the front. Katiusha went with them. . . .

She was often sent on reconnaissance because she knew the section so well. On one of these long forays she found a cool swimming hole. . . . One day she found a soldier preparing for a swim. She cried out, "Zdorovya, tovarisch," or "Hello, pal," but his answer was in . . . German, and he went for his gun.

"I had dropped my gun," Katiusha says, frowning as though reproaching herself for her carelessness, "so I reached into my boot and pulled out my knife. I threw myself at him, and just before he got his gun, I stabbed him. . . ."

"Was he the first German you ever killed?" I asked the child.

"Oh, no," Katiusha said. ". . . He was the sixty-seventh. . . ."

. . . Katiusha and her group were given orders to capture a village. They . . . had to capture house after house. Katiusha, . . . with a Tommy gun in her hands, crashed into one house. She swept the room with her gun, killing two out of three Germans. The third, an officer, held up his hands.

"I walked close to him to get his gun," Katiusha says, "and then he noticed that I was a woman. He was enraged and he hit me on the side of my head. I went sprawling. Well, I was pretty mad, too, so I emptied a whole drum of bullets into him before he could raise his gun. . . . Have you seen Lady Hamilton?"

At the moment, the film Lady Hamilton

was the most popular picture in Russia. Katiusha had just seen it. She would really rather talk of how . . . handsome Laurence Olivier was, than . . . of the Germans she had killed. That was the commonplace part of everyday existence.

"I have seen Lady Hamilton three times," she said, and she looked like any schoolgirl now (except for her wound stripes and her decorations and her uniform). "And now I'm going to see it again. Then tomorrow" —she smiled happily—"I'm going back to the front."

"How Dare We Be Tired?" [3]

I asked the women [in the factory]: "Where did you seek shelter when Moscow was bombed?" They looked surprised. They said: "Shelter? We were not supposed to seek shelter. We were supposed to keep the machine tools at work, bombing or no bombing." (The manager, at this point, interrupted to say that twelve bombs had fallen in the vast factory grounds, doing little damage except breaking windows, and that the work had not been interrupted "even for two minutes." The women thanked him with a smile for the compliment.) I asked them: "Eleven hours a day, making grenades and mines, munitions, mine throwers . . . are you tired?" I shall never forget the way those Russian women and girls proudly shook their heads—the way they almost shrieked in protest and repeated several times, to make sure I understood them: "No, no, we are not tired— not tired." One of the women put forward the argument, to which I was getting used now because it was the motto of all Russian civilians at work: "Our men, the soldiers in the Red Army, fight night and day in the snow, at the front, at forty below zero, and they are not tired. How should we dare be tired?" Another very young, . . . girl made a step toward me. . . . Looking at me straight in the eyes, she said . . . : "We like it. We like working eleven hours." I feel unable to convey with words the cheerful courage, and also the defiance, there was in her voice. I think that the . . . girl

[3] SOURCE: E. Curie, Journey Among Warriors, Garden City, N.Y., Doubleday, 1943, pp. 191-192.

meant something like this: "Perhaps in *your* countries, in the West, women cannot work eleven hours. Perhaps *you* who are here cannot work eleven hours. But we in Russia can do anything in the world."

. . . Several times since my arrival in the USSR, I had [seen] young girls perched on . . . powerful machines and doing men's jobs. I had seen women on cranes and women mechanics on the wings of aircraft, toiling in the cold wind. On the road to Volokolamsk I had seen girls in uniform sitting in the open, on gun carriages coming back from the front. I knew that there were still other women in Russia—famous ones —leading a real warrior's life, such as Major Valentina Grisodobova, a well-known flier whose job was to take bombers over the enemy lines, to wound and to kill Germans. On such war aces Stalin was bestowing the title of "Heroines of the Soviet Union."

Communal Effort

Patterns of War Production[1]

. . . The factory . . . in Kuybyshev was by no means a "model" factory. The only amazing thing about it was that it should be there at all and that a section of the great Kaganovich plant in Moscow should now be making . . . ball bearings here in Kuybyshev. . . .

The "secretary" . . . took [the] press correspondents to visit the plant. . . . He . . . told us about the . . . evacuation of the . . . plant . . . in mid-October 1941. . . .

". . . We tried to make a systematic [and speedy] job of the transportation of our equipment. The Kaganovich factory was to be divided into sections and sheltered in scattered buildings, these buildings being scattered themselves in different cities such as Kuybyshev, Saratov, . . . , etc. We took with us most of our qualified workers, and often had to take care of the evacuation of their families. Our success in the transportation of machine tools and men was, first of all, due to the way our railway system 'held' under the terrific pressure. . . . Some engineers and railway workers . . . drove trains for twenty-four hours without . . . a moment's rest.

"The evacuation . . . took place at the time of the first snowfalls. . . . We had to protect our equipment against . . . rust. We were not able to get covered freight carriages and had to load our tools on open wagons. Time was short. So we chose a simple way of protection. . . . We covered our machine tools with a thick coat of grease. The cold froze the grease, made it become hard—and off went our machines . . . under pouring snow. . . . [They] arrived in . . . good condition.

"Now about the timing of the evacuation: this particular section of the plant was still at work in Moscow on October 16th. We started putting the factory together in Kuybyshev on October 24th, and on December 1st we were able to begin our production here. For many of our workers this, of course, has meant, just as for the railway men, working two or sometimes three shifts running."

I had to examine, one by one, the samples of the Kuybyshev-made ball bearings that the little "secretary" handed to me with a delighted smile. He gave me . . . more details about the reorganization of the . . . factory:

"When the Government decided to move to the interior some of our key industries that had remained in the West, we tried to disrupt the production as little as possible. We moved first the plants producing tools or parts used by other plants—so that they should already be at work at the time of the transportation of these latter ones. It was an

[1] SOURCE: E. Curie, *Journey Among Warriors,* Garden City, N.Y., Doubleday, 1943, pp. 137-141, 188-189.

evacuation in a systematic series, with priorities given to certain sections of the industry. As soon as we got to Kuybyshev, we started to recruit young people as apprentices and to train them to become skilled workers—for we could not bring all our personnel from Moscow. Our factory here works now on a 24-hour-a-day basis. . . ."

[During] the interview one of the [American] correspondents . . . asked the secretary, "Where do your evacuated workers eat and sleep?" . . .

. . . The secretary of the plant, instead of answering the question, engaged in a lengthy discussion in Russian with the interpreter. The two men seemed puzzled as to what to say. . . .

The secretary was, without any doubt, quite worried at the idea that an American should get a "bad impression" of housing or food conditions for workers in Russia. . . . I wondered . . . why this . . . question had embarrassed the Russian at all, and why he had not given the American a direct answer—something like this:

"My dear fellow, we are struggling on a 2,000-mile front, and the Germans are eight hundred miles deep in our country. . . . While we were being attacked and bombed from every side, we have shifted our factory, under storms of snow, . . . to this small town on the Volga. We *don't* have proper accommodations for our workers. . . . Our workers eat what there is, they sleep wherever there is any room for them. . . ."

Had he said that, I think that the . . . American, . . . a fine boy and a good reporter, would have, the next day, cabled a stirring account of the sacrifices suffered voluntarily by Russian workers in order to win the war.

Again, I remembered the words of Anthony Eden: between Russia and her allies, there was "a legacy of suspicion on both sides." I could . . . see where the "suspicion" lay. . . . The visitors . . . from Allied countries were still thinking in terms of passing a final judgment on the Soviet way of life. The Russians knew that and skillfully played at the game of "Everything in the USSR is better than anywhere else." Neither had enough confidence in the other

to forget about boasting or pretense, and to say with simplicity: "We are allies. We both are men at war, meeting in a country desperately threatened by our common enemy. Let's just try to help each other, to work together." . . .

. . . On each floor of the building . . . men and women—more women than men —were busy near the greasy machines. . . . [These Russian women and girls] gave an impression of complete concentration on their job. . . .

The importance of speed . . . was . . . emphasized . . . in every way. One of the wall posters said: ACCOMPLISH ON THE 28TH WHAT YOU WERE SUPPOSED TO DO ON THE 30TH! . . . There were, of course, many portraits of Stalin and, on a red banderole, quotations of Stalin's words about the coming victory.

The machine tools came from different parts of the world—mostly from the United States. An automatic radius grinder was labeled "Springfield, Massachusetts." Several magnetic switches came from the General Electric Company. . . .

A very young worker . . . noticed that I was trying to decipher, on each tool, where it had been manufactured. As I approached one of the larger machines, he stopped me and made me understand that this one was of Russian make. He patted the tool of steel as if it were . . . his own beloved child. He repeated, *"Sovietskaya . . . Sovietskaya. . . ."* His face was beaming with pride.

*   *   *

. . . [Soviet newsreels had been] taken in Rostov on the day the Russians re-entered the town. . . . The camera [showed] close-ups of the victims of the retreating Nazis. There were . . . heaps of corpses in [the streets]. Some . . . people had been shot, some burned, some frozen. . . . The camera had followed the families of the victims as they wandered amidst the ruins, looking for their kin. It had filmed Russian women at the very second when they were recognizing their children or their old parents in a confused mass of corpses. . . . Day after day I was to think . . . of the last . . .

words of the Russian commentator . . . : "We will never forgive."

I saw other newsreels, less dramatic ones, [emphasizing] the solidarity between the soldiers at the front and the workers in the factories. The workers were always shown as they brought some unexpected help to the fighting men. A group of workers had been filmed while presenting to the Red Army [an] armored train—the result of the voluntary contributions . . . of men and women from several factories. Then there were reels showing the celebration of New Year's at the front [very near to the German lines].

The women, the girls, were seen as they jumped out of military trucks, all wrapped up in . . . warm coats. One woman, carrying a New Year present, would fight her way in the snow until she reached a lone, half-frozen sentry watching for the enemy. She would give him the package. Both would . . . rejoice. . . . Then . . . a scene in a wooden shelter where dozens of soldiers were having supper with the women workers. They would drink to the coming victory and sing patriotic songs. After a while some of the soldiers would leave and return to their post in the snow, and the women would kiss them good-by.

This was, of course, propaganda—but . . . showing, in a simple . . . way, a real "people's war." Whatever the purpose of the film . . . , the fact remained that men and women workers had actually gone to the front, had seen under what hard conditions the soldiers of the Red Army were fighting . . . , and had gathered first-hand reports from the peasants of the liberated zone about the persecutions inflicted on them by the invaders.

Life Amid Death[2]

I asked Semyonov to tell me . . . about life at the factory during the [Leningrad] blockade. . . . "Frankly," he said, "I don't like to talk about it. . . . [The] bombing, though it frightened people, also aroused their frantic anger against the Germans. When they started bombing us in a big

[2] SOURCE: A. Werth, *Leningrad*, New York, Knopf, 1944, pp. 66-68, 127-129.

way in October 1941 our workers fought for the factory more than they fought for their own houses. . . . One night . . . we had . . . three hundred incendiaries in the factory grounds alone. Our people were putting the fires out with a sort of concentrated . . . fury; like a thousand squirrels they rushed around, putting out the flames. They had realised by then that they were in the front line—and that was all. No more shelters. . . . And then, one day in December, in twenty degrees of frost, we had all our windows blown out by a bomb, and I thought to myself: 'No, we really can't go on. Not till the spring. We can't go on in this temperature, and without light, without water, and almost without food.' And yet, somehow—we didn't stop. A kind of instinct told us that . . . it would be worse than suicide. That it would be a little like treason. And sure enough, within thirty-six hours we were working again . . . with eight degrees of frost in the workships. . . .

. . . To this day I cannot quite understand it. I don't . . . understand . . . that will-power. . . . Many . . . , hardly able to walk with hunger, would drag themselves to the factory every day, eight, ten and even twelve kilometres. For there were no tramcars. We used all sorts of . . . expedients to keep the work going. When there were no batteries, we used pedals from a bicycle to keep the lathes turning. Somehow, people knew when they were going to die. [They] thought of their families. . . . I remember [an] older [workman] staggering into this office one day and saying to me, ['Comrade Chief], I know that to-day or to-morrow I shall die. My family [is] very weak. They won't have the strength to manage the funeral. Will you be a friend and have a coffin made for me, and have it sent to my family, so they don't have the extra worry of trying to get a coffin? You know how difficult it is to get one.' That happened during the blackest days in December or January. . . . All that was possible and impossible to eat, people ate. They ate . . . carpenter's glue. People tried to sustain themselves on hot water and yeast. Out of the 5,000 people we had here, several hundred died. [Many] died right here. The factory was the thing that mattered most to them. It looked as if they wanted to die here rather than at home. Many a man would drag himself to the factory, stagger in and die. It was like a call of duty to come here.

*   *   *

"The Leningrad Public Library was of great help," [said Vishnevsky]. "People went there at first—actually before the blockade began—and studied every conceivable book on . . . sieges. . . . Then during the blockade there were no matches. . . . Scientists and others . . . looked up books, 100 and 150 years old . . . on all the primitive methods of making matches. [There is an eighty-five year old curator in the library.] He refused to be evacuated. He said, 'Leningrad won't be taken—to hell with you! . . .'

". . . We were all very hungry. To walk up to the third floor was agony. You'd stop a dozen times. . . . But people didn't complain. They never looted bakeries. Many thousands died quietly every week. The Komsomol did all it could to keep people's morale up. They would drop in on people who were . . . going to pieces and say, 'Look here, old man, it wouldn't be a bad thing if you had a wash and a shave.' . . ."

"The Komsomol and the Pioneers," somebody said, "did a lot to help. . . . They'd go to the houses of older people and would help them to change their ration cards which were about to expire. An enormous number of letters kept coming to Leningrad, especially from our own Leningrad front. The children did the work of postmen. They whistled outside houses till the people came down to fetch the letters addressed to them. With food rations what they were, you naturally couldn't expect the children to run up and down hundreds of stairs.

"There was a terrible fuel shortage. . . . In the Port of Leningrad . . . the coal ships from Cardiff used to be unloaded. . . . When coal is unloaded [some of it] drops into the water. Well, large holes were cut in the ice, and divers went down and worked for many days in the icy waters;

and they brought to the surface 4,000 or 5,000 tons of coal! . . .

"One of the greatest examples of how Leningrad fought for its life was when in the spring 300,000 or 400,000 people came out into the street with shovels—people who were scarcely standing on their feet, so weak and hungry were they—and proceeded to clean up the town. All winter the drains and sewers had been out of action; there was a great danger of epidemics spreading with the coming of the warm weather. And in a few days these . . . weak, hungry people—many of them . . . old people who had never handled a shovel . . . —had shovelled away and dumped into the river and the canals all those mountains of snow and filth which . . . would have poisoned Leningrad. And it was a joy to see the city streets . . . all clean and tidy. It had a great moral effect."

The Discharged Veterans[3]

Looking after the discharged veteran was not a matter for the State alone, though the Departments of Social Welfare had a complete system of "after-care" till he should be absorbed in a job. It was everybody's business.

Before a wounded soldier left the hospital he had to go through two commissions: one determined whether he returned to the army; if not, the other settled to which of three invalid groups he belonged—the first and second groups did not have to work immediately, the third must. The Medical Work Commission decided what medical care should be continued, and recommended work, but the soldier himself had the final voice in deciding his job.

The veteran then received from the district department for social security his pension, a job, and orders for further medical care and training. Pensions started a month before the soldier left the hospital; the amount depended on what work he did before the war, and to which invalid group

---

[3] Source: E. Winter, *I Saw the Russian People*, Boston, Little, Brown, 1945, pp. 144-146. The author, a Fabian Socialist, and second wife of Lincoln Steffens, was a frequent and sympathetic observer of Soviet life from 1936 through World War II.

he belonged. He received a two months' vacation at home before he started working. Disabled students were taken back without entrance examinations into institutions where they had studied previously. War invalids could not be made to work overtime.

In addition to State help for invalided veterans, assistance was organized by trade unions and Party organizations. Rooms were found for them, apartments repaired, fuel provided, their allotments rushed. Special orders were issued by the Moscow Soviet and by Party committees to supply servicemen with goods, and all bodies insisted that "the families of troops must be cared for by the whole people." Children's camps, victory gardens, industrial training for mothers, the right job, were all part of the common task of rehabilitation.

The Secretary of the All-Union Central Council of Trade Unions reported that in 1943 the Central Committee of the Unions had spent about . . . [14,000,000 dollars] on families of fighting men. . . . The total sum called for in 1944 was to be increased to 80,000,000 dollars. . . .

[The] apparent lack of emphasis on psychiatric war casualties was so remarkable, I consulted several Moscow psychiatrists. They answered by telling of the treatment of brain injuries, but they could say little about mental breakdown. One physician said every Soviet soldier knew why he was fighting, every soldier knew what was being done for the disabled, every soldier knew he would have a job when the war was over. There was little use to press the point—indeed, these answers seem to be correct, for most visiting American psychiatrists corroborated the apparent lack of psychiatric cases. . . .

Wehrmacht Atrocity and Russian Courage

Germans and Guerillas[1]

The guerillas had a world, a whole segment of life of their own. Because of its dense woods, and because the Germans set up permanent housekeeping there first, White Russia was one of the main partisan areas. Whole sections of it behind the German lines . . . never submitted to Nazi rule. Villages kept their own Soviet schools and hospitals; ran their own newspapers, distributing them by pony express; celebrated Soviet holidays, flew red banners in the streets. There was a complete guerilla medical organization, with . . . ambulances, doctors, drug supplies, distribution centers for patients.

The Germans were maddened by this; they organized punitive expeditions . . . , deported whole village populations. They tortured, froze, beat, hanged, gouged out eyes, drove men and women—and young girls—naked through the snow. . . . I saw a

[1] SOURCE: E. Winter, *I Saw the Russian People,* Boston, Little, Brown, 1945, pp. 144-146.

child whose tongue they had cut out for refusing to reveal her father's whereabouts.

The answer of the villagers was to take away their children in the night, their cattle, goats, food, utensils; and to melt into the forests, where they hid in little islands in the marshes and buried their possessions in dugouts. The women washed clothes with ashes instead of soap. They operated on their wounded in tents by candlelight, with primitive instruments. They slept in trenches on pine boughs. They taught school, had concerts and plays, in dugouts. . . . The Nazis combed and raked the forests. They were so scared they put signs on tree-trunks: ACHTUNG—PARTISANEN! (Look out—Partisans!) All in vain. The Germans never destroyed the guerillas or broke their resistance. In fact, the Nazi brutalities nourished and strengthened the movement. . . .

[Saveli Lescheniya] was a brigade commissar in the guerilla army.

"When the Nazis first overran Byelo-Russia, it was a great surprise to us," he said. "The war caught us unawares. But our people went to work quickly. Even as the Panzer troops were advancing, we organized. . . . Villages were being wiped out. . . . The Germans would call men, women and children together in a barn, and set fire to the barn. This made many partisans.

"When the Germans heard of one Communist, or one guerilla, in a village, they would send a punitive expedition and detroy that village, burn every house. . . . They thought they could break our guerilla movement that way. But it had the opposite effect."

We heard an isolated shot outside. A German in the woods. . . .

"We were not sure at first that we had the right to destroy Soviet property," Saveli was saying. "Then came Stalin's speech [of July 3, 1941] saying it was the duty of every man to do all he could behind the lines. That reassured us. And later, when the Nazis were at the Volga, there was great tension. . . . People flooded our movement then."

Guerillas were divided into detachments. Saveli's detachment started with ninety-five men. "The bravest and most authoritative were always chosen as commanders, and their orders were regarded as law. Each village was ruled by a . . . village elder, and each district by a guerilla commandant who never lost touch with the Soviet State." The main jobs were to blow up trains, dynamite bridges, harass supply lines, attack German individuals in their headquarters. . . . Saveli explained how they got their weapons.

"Some we picked up after battle," he said. "Others we could buy. They had a regular price. A rifle would be so many dozen eggs or three hens; a tommy gun could be had for a kilo of butter. The Germans were very venal." He smiled with quiet contempt.

Little bands of guerillas went on missions in the night, killing sentries. . . . They hid till German scouting parties were deep in the forests, then fell upon them. . . .

"Our main help, though, came from the villagers," Saveli said. "They gave us food, information, scouts, advance notice of Nazi movements, showed us where arms were hidden. They knew where the enemy had sowed mines. We could count on our villagers, their loyalty and support. Every peasant was a guerilla assistant."

Sitting next to Saveli was a blond woman. . . .

"I was earning 1,500 rubles a month," she said. "When the Germans came, life became impossible. I am Jewish. The Germans burned nearly all of Minsk, including my house. I had no clothes, nowhere to go, nowhere to work. The Germans built . . . concentration camps near the city, and drove into them most of our men, all our war prisoners. Sometimes they gave them no food for . . . nine days; they did not permit them to lie down, nor did they give they give them water even in the greatest heat. They beat them and shot them; many perished.

"The Germans carried through a registration in the town, Jews and Russians separately. Jewish intellectuals in the camps were shot first, then Russians, then White Russians. Workers were released for work in the factories. . . .

"November 7 and 8 was the first pogrom. . . . There were 80,000 Jews in the ghetto. In two days, they killed 18,000. They had kept them completely without food for three days, then they beat or shot them. But they shot them so carelessly that three quarters remained alive, and when they buried them the whole earth moved.

"November 1943 was the last pogrom. . . . This time they did not kill only Jews. Jews were only an excuse.

"They killed people in the Gestapo jails, secretly. They organized public hangings to terrorize people. . . . They left the bodies hanging so that we should all see them. They maltreated Soviet war prisoners worst of all. They gave them no food, no water— once I saw them throw rotten potato peelings out of a trough over the barbed wire, and shoot the prisoners as they scrambled for them. . . .

"On the twentieth of October"—the dates had etched themselves into her mind— "there was a very cold rain which froze as it fell. They brought many exhausted Soviet prisoners that day on to the cement bridge at Minsk. . . . They took off their uniforms and their boots, and made them stand in the sleet and snow. The men wanted water. They had had no water for days. A woman brought water—and was shot. The prisoners dipped their hands into the mud on the bridge and sucked it. Passers-by wept as they saw it. . . .

"When a soldier had worked all day long, and was dropping from weariness, they would tie bricks to his shoulders. I saw it," she said.

"In Polykharovka they brought very old people to the firehouse, locked it and burned it. . . . In Adamovo they knocked women and children on the head with hammer blows. . . .

"I and others took revenge," she said. ". . . We helped the partisans from within the town, in every little way we could— we sent them drugs and medicines and weapons. I had friends at the Medical Institute, so I could get some drugs. We got people to bury weapons and then let the partisans know where they were.

"After a while I couldn't work for the partisans from inside the city any more because the Germans were watching me. . . . Then I went into the forest; and since then I've lived with the guerillas."

Hitler: A Poor Prophet[2]

There was a lot of talk about the *levée en masse* and the *lutte à l'outrance* that had saved Leningrad.

"It's all very well," Vishnevsky exclaimed, "for the Germans now to say that the Leningrad line is much stronger than the Maginot line. At the beginning, when they were only approaching Leningrad, there was . . . not a damned thing. What made Leningrad impregnable was . . . a million people . . . working day and night on . . . fortifications. Our youth went into the army like one man. Our workers' divisions . . . played . . . a decisive part during those first stages. . . . An old . . . worker of 67, and all his six sons went off to the front.

[2] SOURCE: A. Werth, *Leningrad,* New York, Knopf, 1944, pp. 124-126.

The old man refused to be left behind. . . . Old veterans of the Putilov and Obukhov works went out to die. . . . [In August and September 1941, the Germans threw] forty-five divisions against Leningrad. . . . Approaching the city, they [set] fire to everything. There was a ring of fires round Leningrad—you could see them at night— it was the villages burning. But people here said, 'We're not going to budge.' Nasty things happened. There were Fifth Columnists in Leningrad; they would fire rockets at night to give guidance to the German guns and planes. Many Fifth Columnists had come in . . . with the refugees; some conscious, others unconscious—that is, stupid old peasants who were [spreading] rumours and enemy propaganda. . . ."

Somebody else said that the most critical day of all was the 14th of September. "That day our various high school students held together with the Komsomol an enormous meeting, as a result of which every single young man still in town volunteered for immediate service. Hundreds of thousands of young people volunteered that day and in the next day or two. . . .

"The people of Leningrad knew . . ." [Vishnevsky] said, "that they were fighting for their own skins. General Malwerstedt . . . made it . . . plain that the S.S. were going to undertake a gigantic purge of the city, that 400,000 people at least would be bumped off or tortured to death right away. He said that . . . unless you killed all the people in any way typical of the Revolution, you did not stamp it out at all. . . . I am glad to say that Malwerstedt was subsequently bumped off by the partisans. . . . They [dropped] leaflets calling upon us to declare Leningrad an open city. Our people laughed. . . . The Germans tried to frighten us out of our wits. They announced that Field-Marshal von Kuechler, who had smashed Warsaw to smithereens, would do the same to Leningrad. Hitler had already announced on [July 16] the imminent fall of Leningrad. Then on November 5th, when the town was already cut off, they dropped leaflets, saying, 'We shall do the bombing on the 6th, and *you* will do the burying on the 7th.'"

"How the Germans love sadistic jokes!"
I remarked. . . .

"Yes," said Vishnevsky, "they were going
to make it hot for us on the twenty-fourth
anniversary of the Revolution. On the night
of the 6th they dropped 65,000 bombs on
Leningrad—mostly incendiaries, but very
few started any fires. Our fire-fighting had
already been perfectly organised. Then on
the 8th Hitler announced that he would

starve us into surrender: 'That town will
raise its arms of its own accord.' The divine
Führer really didn't understand the first
thing about our people. . . . One of our
sailors had his foot blown off by a German
shell; he stuck the bleeding stump into a
large shell-case and carried on, . . . blood
pouring over the sides of the shell-case.
There was a sacred frenzy in these men
which . . . bewildered the Germans."

Heritage of Horror*

Nazi savagery fell with most shattering
effect on Russian children, who had known
only gentleness. . . . The kindness of
mother and teacher . . . the old familiar
life—were suddenly swallowed up. Unknown things took their place . . . the horror of having to . . . watch them do terrible things to your mother . . . , watch
fire . . . burning your home.

From this . . . nightmare millions of
children emerged fatherless, motherless,
homeless. From bombed-out houses in Stalingrad and Odessa they came, from cellars
and dugouts in Kalinin, Orel, . . . Kharkov. They emerged little old men and
women, pale, wan, bent. But Russia took
immediate . . . steps to save them by setting up clinics, hospitals, and homes.
. . . These children . . . are kept busy
all day, in groups as much as possible. . . .
The children stay in hospitals or sanatoria
as long as necessary; after they go home to
a parent or foster parent or an orphanage
they return periodically, for checking. The
Russians are training doctors and nurses to
understand war-disabled children; they are
trying to train surviving parents and foster
parents, too. Above all, they stress that these
children must have kindness, . . . love,
as much individual attention as they can
get. . . . Individual adoptions have been
widely encouraged. Thousands of mothers,

even those who had children of their own,
have adopted waifs. . . .

In Moscow the Institute of Mother and
Child has set up a new Psychiatric Division
to deal with . . . child rehabilitation. [Its]
head . . . psychiatrist, Professor Tatiana
Simson . . . took me through rooms full of
children playing games, . . . listening to
stories. . . .

"At first," said Professor Simson . . . ,
"we thought we'd never bring them back.
Some didn't speak for months. . . . Some
were so frightened they hid under chairs.
. . . They seemed not to understand . . .
what was being said to them. Some ran
around . . . crying over and over, 'I'm
afraid, Mama, a German is coming.' . . .
One little girl of four . . . kept repeating,
'. . . I will not lie down. The Germans are
sitting under our window.'

"One of the most tragic children," the
psychiatrist continued, "is a little girl who
had been with the partisans. The Germans
asked her where her father was. She would
not tell. They cut out her tongue and cut
off her ears. She tried to throw herself out
of the window. We stopped her, but she
. . . wrote us notes begging us to allow her
to kill herself. What use could she be in
life? We had to convince her of reasons to
live. . . . We had to give all the children
reason to live.

"It takes them a long time to learn that
not all human beings are going to . . .
torture them. And when they recover, they

* SOURCE: E. Winter, *I Saw the Russian People,*
Boston, Little, Brown, 1945, pp. 204-213.

. . . ask you to hold them in your arms. . . . They beg every adult they see, 'Please adopt me! Please be my mother!' . . .

"The younger the child the less he suffered. . . . For two- and three-year-olds, bombing was an adventure; they were more disturbed by the cries of adults than by the sirens and explosions. With these young children it was the little things that counted —having their toys taken away, a bicycle, a hat; or hearing angry words from frightened mothers or aunts. . . . Slightly older children have undergone serious personality changes. . . . When six-year-old Sergei heard his mother protest against the demands of Nazis quartered in her cottage, he cautioned her, 'Mama, we just have to remain alive.' And when she said he should beg food from them, he argued, 'Mama, the Germans won't give us anything and they'll beat me up into the bargain.' His mother insisted, and the Germans [threw] him head-first against the wall. 'He knew more than I,' wailed his mother. 'He is like a twenty-year-old.' Sergei comes here now. We have been trying for months to cure the tic in his face. When they could . . . fight back, they were generally better off. . . . Children who . . . fought with the partisans had an easier time, psychologically speaking. A child of nine who came to us had been a scout with the partisans. . . .

He slept badly and had headaches, but he was [soon] cured. . . . It is the children who had to endure their sufferings passively that were most gravely affected."

The . . . doctors have found war games and military toys to be excellent therapy. One four-year-old, Vassili R., who would talk gaily about anything, froze into silence when he was asked what had happened under the Germans. . . . "We asked him if he wanted a gun," Dr. Sucharevo said. "The moment his hands were around the toy he said, 'With this gun I'll shoot the Germans,' and his story came pouring out of him. We told him the Germans would never get into Russia again, the Red Army had driven them out. A few days later we heard Vassili say to his playmates, 'The Germans are bad. . . . But Papa at the front will kill them all.' And after that we could ask him anything about his life. . . ."

To make their child casualties "forget," the physicians must first make them remember. . . . The children must be prevented from driving underground emotions and recollections that may plague them through life in some other form. But with this accepted psychological treatment the Russians try to supply the simple security of a loving home and a natural family life. . . .

The Purge of Culture*

. . . The all-out campaign against the Leningrad Literary Group, [was] initiated in August, 1946, by the Politburo under the leadership of . . . Andrei A. Zhdanov, whom many regarded as Stalin's "heir apparent." This blast . . . was followed by attacks upon Soviet musicians, philosophers, scientists, . . . playwrights, critics, etc. . . . They were accused of being apolitical, non-Communist, formalistic, and of looking too

often to Western culture for their inspiration. The campaign has progressed with increasing intensity during the last three years.

Why such a herculean effort to curb intellectual thought and cut off all cultural pursuits from the outside world? . . .

. . . During the war, the Soviet leaders had been obliged to relax many of their ideological controls. It was inexpedient, for the time being, continually to attack the West and its accomplishments. Much greater latitude was permitted, and those

* SOURCE: W. B. Smith, My Three Years in Moscow, Philadelphia, Lippincott, 1950, pp. 284-299.

who had suffered under the stifling party controls of the thirties may have begun to believe that a new era of relative intellectual freedom had arrived. Very soon after the war it became apparent that this was not the case. The Government began an all-out effort to rekindle the fires of Stalinist ideology and to enforce blind acceptance of the promised glories of the regime.

Stalin and the other members of the Politburo knew all too well . . . that a totalitarian secret police state built on unfulfilled promises could not, for instance, tolerate the satire of the popular writer, Zoshchenko, . . . one of the principal targets of Zhdanov's blast against the Leningrad Literary Group. Zoshchenko had . . . satirically depicted an ape as the supreme judge of Soviet social order. Through the lips of Zoshchenko's ape came the impression that in the Soviet Union "it is better to live in a zoo than outside" and that "one breathes easier in a cage than among the Soviet people," Zhdanov said.

Such heretical thinking had to be stopped. And if the ideological machine were to be put back on the party main line, the intellectuals must cooperate loyally and obediently.

In the second place, since the theoretical basis of Soviet ideology is founded on the "scientific" theory of dialectical and historical materialism, all developments, facts and theories must be brought into conformity with this fundamental "truth." According to . . . Marx, all progress is brought about by . . . a struggle between . . . that which is dying away and that which is being born. . . .

. . . If, contrary to the claims of Soviet biologist Lysenko, man cannot inherit acquired characteristics, then one of the fundamental props of Soviet ideology falls to the ground. If the Soviet state, by environment and outside pressure cannot cause fundamental changes in man's character . . . the future of the whole Soviet system is questionable.

Soviet intellectuals must refrain, therefore, from exposing the shortcomings of the . . . regime. They must cooperate . . . in re-selling [its] ideology and glories . . . to the masses, even if they have to create new "proven" scientific theories . . . to do so.

The new party line on satire . . . was . . . stated in the . . . *Literary Gazette,* on December 11, 1948, when it demanded that Soviet motion picture comedies must satirize "everything that does not fit into a Soviet conception of morality and the Soviet way of life."

. . . Why were the Soviet authorities so apprehensive about the loyalty of the masses, particularly after the conclusion of a successful war?

. . . Until the Soviet Army advanced into Central Europe and the Balkans in 1944, the . . . Russian people had been . . . hermetically sealed from all . . . contact with the outside world. Soviet propaganda had painted a picture of abject misery as the normal condition of [the masses] in the capitalist world, and contrasted this with the better life of the Soviet people under . . . Stalin.

The authorities [feared] that their propaganda might boomerang [once] the Soviet troops found out . . . that Stalin's slogan . . . "Life is better, life is happier," applied to the outside world, not to . . . Russia.

Shortly after the Soviet Army entered Rumania, two well-publicized dispatches from a Soviet correspondent in Bucharest cautioned [the] Soviet troops . . . : "We will have to pass through many foreign countries. A lot of tawdry brilliance will blind your eyes, Red Army men. Do not believe these deceitful phantoms of pseudo-civilization."

He also warned them not to be taken in by the pretty . . . women, with . . . painted faces [and] short skirts. . . .

. . . Posters were put up warning the people at home: "Do not believe all returned soldiers." The posters [explained] that, after all the . . . hardship, [the soldiers'] judgments were lopsided. . . .

By August, 1945, the problem had reached such . . . proportions that . . . Kalinin, the nominal Chief of State of the U.S.S.R., found it necessary to [instruct] a large group of . . . agitators who were about to stump the country . . . to explain away the alleged attainments of foreign culture. This is a part of what he said: "There was talk here about people coming back . . . who have seen 'cultures' of German villages which made a certain impression on them. Our agitators must uncrown this German culture. . . ."

[A further problem rose from the fact that] the Soviet authorities during the war also had deliberately given the impression that a new era of ease and comfort would come with peace.

Thus Stalin's announcement in February, 1946, of at least three more five-year plans, primarily devoted to the production of capital instead of consumer goods, came as a shock to the . . . tired Soviet peoples.

All these considerations, together with fear of the possible disruptive force of a free intellectual movement, prompted the decision to launch the all-out campaign which began in 1946 to recall Communist ideology and to build up the ego of the Soviet people. [That is the] explanation of the long list of invention "firsts" which have flooded the press of the world during the past three years. Russians are now declared to have "invented" everything important from the steam engine to penicillin. . . .

When it was announced in the Soviet press a few years ago that a Russian had perfected the caterpillar tractor in the eighteen thirties, but that no one outside knew about it because it was not sent to a famous agricultural fair in Vienna, a foreigner in Moscow remarked that the only reason that they could not get the machine to Vienna, of course, was that the Russians had not yet invented the railroad.

As the Zhdanov ideological campaign progressed, its magnitude became more . . . apparent. . . .

"Not all of us," [Molotov said in 1947], "have yet rid ourselves of obsequious worship of the West, of capitalist culture. . . ."

This statement [confirms] the Kremlin's fear of a free-thinking intelligentsia, the existence of a train of Soviet thought about the glories of capitalism, as well as the tacit admission that there were many in the Soviet Union who would like to have an interchange of ideas with the West. . . .

How have the intellectuals been brought back into line and how effective has the campaign been? . . .

The "purge" of the intellectuals does not resemble in any way the . . . purge of 1935 to 1938. . . . The cost would be too high. And so the Kremlin apparently decided that a "horrible example purge," affecting a limited number of prominent individuals, coupled with an all-out ideological and publicity campaign, would . . . accomplish the desired results.

The method used was a highly organized campaign of criticism directed against individuals who had produced works or made statements which do not now conform to the party line. It made no difference if these writers and composers formerly had been praised . . . , honored officially and by the public, or were winners of the coveted Stalin Prize. . . . They were publicly chastised and humiliated. The party line had changed; therefore, facts, ideas and concepts must be changed to conform.

The music purge attacked such well known composers as Shostakovich and Prokofiev. . . . They [and others] were accused of following "bourgeois ideology fed by the influence of contemporary Western European and American music," of not making "use of the wealth of popular melodies . . . in which the creative work of the people of the U.S.S.R. is so rich," of "adhering to a formalist and anti-popular trend" and of having "anti-democratic tendencies in music." The composers, as well as all artists, were admonished by *Pravda* in January, 1948, "to play an outstanding part in Communist education; the party places before them the task of carrying Communist ideology to the masses." . . .

The musical critics fared no better. . . . [They] were charged . . . "with championing . . . 'degenerate, formalistic music,' . . . and showing subservience to this or that musical leader for reasons of personal friendship. . . ."

At the session where the matter was discussed, Prokofiev, I was told, kept his back turned while Shvernik and Zhdanov talked, and when reprimanded for his inattention said bitterly: "Oh, I know it already," adding in a loud aside to Shostakovich, "What do Ministers know of music? That is the business of composers." Prokofiev, Shostakovich and the others confessed their errors . . . to save their skins. . . .

Shostakovich's confession read in part: "I know that the party is right, . . . and that I must search for . . . creative paths which lead me to Soviet realistic popular art." . . .

Eugene Varga, the renowned Marxian economist, was humiliated several times because he gave too realistic an appraisal of developments abroad, based on facts which often conflicted with the need to support Communist morale, inside and outside the Soviet Union. He had asserted that the state could play a decisive role over the economy in a capitalist state. As the party doctrinaires saw it, he should have stated categorically that the state is under the complete control of the financiers—Wall Street. . . .

Perhaps the most humiliating and revealing confession was that made by the Mendelian biologist, Zhebrak. In his . . . recantation, he states: "As long as both trends in Soviet genetics were recognized by our party and the disputes between these . . . were regarded as creative discussions . . . , helping to find the truth, I persistently defended my views which differed from [those] of Academician Lysenko. But now that . . . the Michurin [Lysenko] trend in Soviet genetics [is] approved by the Central Committee, . . . I do not consider that I can adhere to the positions which have been acknowledged false by the . . . party."

Socialist Realism According to Alexander Fadayev*

Soviet literature has been created by the new, Soviet life. The new society is the air that fills our lungs. We ourselves are the makers of Soviet literature. . . .

We, Soviet writers, regard literature not as the coddled lady of an "ivory tower," but as the teacher of life, the educator of the people. Some assert that such a view of literature debases it as an art. . . .

Quite a few books have appeared in the postwar literature of Western Europe and America which are intent on proving that man is an anti-social creature, living a prey to elemental forces acting within and without him, that man is weak and despicable, and if he be strong it is with the wolfish strength of the brute. There are quite a few people among modern West-European and American authors who are chiefly absorbed in base sexual passions, devoid of all spirituality and even in the grossest physiological functions of human beings. These works show a marked preference for crimes and perversions of every kind. The authors of such books would seem to have conspired together in persuading millions of people that they are destitute of all great and noble strivings and hopes, that they lack human reason and volition and have nothing to hope for in the way of receiving a square deal from life.

This class of literature, both in Western Europe and in America, is opposed by a modern progressive and humanistic literature which we people in the Soviet Union are well acquainted with and highly appreciate. . . .

Soviet literature is striving to restore all true human values to their proper place of importance. It maintains that love of country, and friendship among the peoples are great human sentiments, that the love of man and woman is noble and beautiful,

* SOURCE: *Soviet Literature*, Moscow, 1949, No. 6, 1949, pp. 183-185. Fadayev was the Secretary General of the Union of Soviet Writers.

that true friendship is disinterested, that the name of mother is sacred and that man has been given life in order that he should work and create.

The old humanism, for all its greatness, . . . failed to understand that in order that good should triumph, evil had to be destroyed. . . .

Socialist humanism is able to celebrate its triumph in our country only because it has conquered social evil. Man, from the point of view of Socialist humanism, is not man if he does not work, do and create. One of the features of modern Soviet literature is that it shows the ordinary Soviet man as an active force, a fighter, a toiler, an innovator and transformer of nature and society. . . .

The heroes of these books and plays, while being perfectly real and living men, think in and live for the future. In their so ordinary yet creative workaday activities they do not drift with the stream, but anticipate the morrow and try to bring it nearer.

What is Socialist realism? Socialist realism is an ability to show life in the process of its development, an ability to perceive in today's life the germ of the future and to demonstrate it truthfully. . . .

In a review of my novel *The Young Guard* a French newspaper sounded a note of disapproval in that my portrayal of Soviet youth reveals no vices and meanness.

The reviewer was patently disappointed that Soviet youth lives according to human laws instead of the laws of existentialism. This is no fault of mine, however, and I am afraid I cannot help the gentleman.

It is sometimes said: Is it permissible that the Party and the state powers in the U.S.S.R. should express their attitude to facts of literature and, so to say, interfere in the process of literary development? Does not this trench upon the freedom of creative work? But the point is that literature in the Soviet Union expresses our present-day national, popular spirit, as do the Party and the State. The Party in our country represents the best and highest that our people have been able to produce from their midst during the last half-century of Russian history, during thirty odd years of the construction of Socialism. Both the Party and literature in our country have the same aim. Neither the Party nor the State interfere in the writer's individual creative work, has never dictated or attempted to dictate to him the subject and characters, still less the artistic forms in which he should write. . . .

Soviet literature creates with a sense of its great responsibility towards the people, the nation, the State and the whole of humanity. The Party fosters in writers this sense of responsibility. . . .

The Party, in particular, "interferes" in literary affairs when it sees literary tendencies arising that are alien to the spirit of the Soviet people. . . . At such times the Party truthfully and directly points to such tendencies and reminds the writers of their great duty towards the people. . . .

Only a little man, moving in the rut of his humdrum little world of individualistic feelings can regard such directions of the Party as interference in literary creation. . . .

Cold War Propaganda*

March 1, 1952

Here is what an anti-American play is like: The play . . . which I saw [in] Moscow

* SOURCE: F. Rounds, Jr., *A Window on Red Square*, Boston, Houghton Mifflin, 1953, pp. 139-147.

. . . is called *Under the Golden Eagle*. . . .

The action . . . takes place shortly after . . . World War II in [a] town in the Western occupation zone of Germany. The play [has] a dual theme of American efforts to prevent a group of Soviet prisoners of war (previously liberated by American forces) from returning to their homeland, and the countermoves of the internees to return to the "freedom of the East." Major Peterson and his adjutant, Lieutenant . . . Bentley, are the villains. . . . Leading the former Russian war prisoners in their attempts to communicate with the Soviet Repatriation Commission and thus return [home] is the Soviet sailor Makarov, who soon succeeds in enlisting the sympathy of the American foreign correspondent, Miss Fancy. . . .

. . . The scheme of the Americans is to make Makarov the victim of a frame-up, to charge him with murder, and then to offer him leniency in exchange for a switch of allegiance and his pledge to undermine the efforts of his fellow citizens to reach the Soviet . . . Commission.

In spite of the torture methods of Peterson and his M.P. henchmen, their plot is frustrated by Makarov's [valiance] and so the hero is marched off to his execution shouting, "It is better to die in honor than to live in disgrace." . . . In the beginning of the play Miss Fancy is in love with Lieutenant Bentley, but [discovering] that he also is an evil accomplice of American policy, she launches a campaign to expose the aims and methods of the U.S. authorities. It is during a conversation between these two that the audience learns [that] the goal of the United States is to use the Russians as conscripts in a huge army of mercenaries to implement the American design for world domination. . . .

. . . In the dark, I scribbled notes . . . on my program . . . which . . . give the tone of this . . . play, as well as . . . of the entire hate-America campaign now raging. . . .

One of the scenes in the major's quarters takes place at Christmas time. . . . The walls are decorated with . . . banners, one of which reads: "Marry Cristmas. . . ." Beside these decorations are pictures of pin-up girls and large photographs of lynchings. . . . The Christmas carol "Silent Night, Holy Night" (translated into Russian words) is played several times in this scene by means of a radio onstage, and in

subsequent scenes the carol becomes . . . the . . . pointed theme song of the play, with the . . . orchestra . . . taking up the melody as background music, and various characters—both Americans and Germans —humming and whistling the song . . . while engaging in murder and blackmail and lovemaking. . . . Also prominent in this scene is a Christmas tree, and the decorations . . . on the boughs [are] toy tanks and miniature bombs.

[Most of] the other . . . props contribute to the anti-American theme. . . . [In the tavern scene, next to] the bar . . . are Hollywood . . . posters (one reads: "American Film: Murder in the Jungle") and in one corner is [a] colorful advertisement: "Chew Gum—In America Everybody Chews Gum. . . ." In Major Peterson's office, is a . . . bust of a man who might be . . . Lincoln or Truman or Hitler; . . . in different lights, it resembles each, . . . and . . . the American M.P.'s use this bust as a . . . hatrack, sloppily tossing their white helmets on . . . the honored head.

In attitude and attire, the U.S. Army officers are . . . reminiscent of the worst type of . . . German storm troopers. . . .

A . . . showy crucifix, standing in the center of the major's desk . . . is the . . . focal point of much of Peterson's activities, a great deal of the play's action taking place within a few inches of Christ's outstretched arms. . . . In [one scene] the major menacingly leans over the crucifix as he argues about the list of Russian war prisoners, the cross-arms framing his angry face. . . . The business in [another scene] is over a string of black-market pearls, with Peterson making a deal with the German stooges. . . . In . . . this episode, the major dangles the jewelry over the arms of the Cross, fondling the pearls as he strings them around the head of Christ.

In . . . contrast to the American officers, Makarov is probably the most heroic hero ever to walk the stage. . . . By the time of the . . . investigation . . . his . . . jersey has become . . . shredded (an indication . . . that the Americans have tortured him), and the black ribbons of his Russian naval cap hang down over his bare and bloody shoulders. . . . Most important . . . are his noble speeches [one such made] to the major at the beginning of [the] investigation scene, his face glowing with glory: "Not before God, but as a citizen of the [USSR] I speak the truth, and nothing but the truth."

When this play first opened in Moscow, there were reports that one of the American M.P.'s wore a ring through his nose. . . . The sergeant looks and moves like a gorilla —and his crony, the second M.P., always enters a scene with a submachine gun on his hip, ready to fire; whether they are saying "Sir-r-r!" . . . to their senior officers, or mouthing "Merry Chreeeesmus" . . . to their German flunkies, or brusquely ordering the Russians to stand on their feet when Americans enter a room, the M.P.'s invariably behave as uncouthly as possible. The most maddening scene . . . takes place when the American sergeant rips the eyeglasses off the little blind boy . . . and then kicks him onto the floor.

And . . . how does the audience react to all of this? The villains were continuously . . . hissed. . . . The heroine was . . . warned of approaching danger by . . . the spectators. The hero was cheered and applauded . . . when he expressed brave, patriotic sentiments. . . . The Russian girl

. . . next to me quietly wept throughout the evening. . . .

March 5, 1952

An inspiriting time is what I had tonight [at a performance of Madame Butterfly]. I took along a biography of Puccini. . . .

At the first intermission I fell into conversation with the fellow who sat in the next seat. . . . He was a student in Leningrad, and was agog to ask me about American jazz. . . .

[We] got on to serious music. . . . At the end of the opera, I asked him if I might make him a present of my Puccini book, and when he protested, I said, "Oh, come on—accept it as a present from [an] American warmonger!" . . . He got very angry and asked if I thought for a moment that he was the sort of person to believe that all Americans were warmongers. He really was insulted. Finally, after I apologized, he accepted the book very gratefully, and autographed his program and gave it to me with apologies that it was the only thing he had to give me in return.

Well, if one educated Russian can not only fail to swallow . . . the picture of Americans his propaganda machine grinds out, but even gets angry at the suggestion that he might do so, there's . . . hope there are many thousands like him. . . .

The Impact of Stalin's Death*

An American scholar visiting Moscow during the "thaw" was able to unearth a number of poems written not to be published, but for the poet's "desk drawer." Following is one of them:

Contemporary Reflections

On that evening, in the mausoleum, Stalin was buried,
And the evening was ordinary—crystal

clear and limpid.
I walked quietly, tranquilly,
Alone with Moscow
And here is what I thought, verily,
Like a clever fellow:
The epoch of spectacles has ended,
The epoch of bread has arrived.
A smoking break has been declared
For those who have been storming the heavens.
The people, asleep in its shoes,
Not knowing the year,
Has sat down for an hour
To rewind its footcloths.

* SOURCE: A. Zr., "Poems Underground," *Harper's Magazine*, May, 1961.

No, I didn't think that,
I thought something else:
That here he was, and now he is not,
The giant and the hero.
Moscow is like
              a forsaken
                      deserted
                              house.
How will we live without Stalin?

I looked around:
Moscow did not lament, Moscow was
     vacant.
You cannot grieve unceasingly. All are tired
     to death.
Everyone was sleeping, only the janitors
Were furiously sweeping.
As if they were tearing at roots and

Raking from beneath the earth,
As if they were ripping from the frozen
     soil
The shriek of his orders, the handwriting
     of his decrees:
The traces of a three-day death
And old traces—
Of a thirty-year reign,
Of grandeur and calamity.
I walked on and on
And before me rose
His palaces, factories—
Everything that Stalin built:
The towers of his skyscrapers,
The quadrangles of his squares . . .

Socialism was constructed.
Settle people in it.

The Shock of De-Stalinization*

*Following is another poem written for
the "desk drawer":*

Propaganda
Today I don't believe anything—
My eyes—I don't believe.
My ears—I don't believe.
I'll feel it—then, perhaps, I'll believe.
When it can be touched—everything is
     without deception.

I recall the frowning Germans,
The sad prisoners of 1945,
Standing—hands at sides—at the
     interrogation.
I ask—they answer:

—Do you believe Hitler?—No, I don't
     believe.
—You believe Goering?—No, I don't
     believe.
—You believe Goebbels?—Oh, propaganda!
—And do you believe me?—A moment of
     silence.
—Mr. Commissar, I don't believe you.

Everything is propaganda. The whole
     world is propaganda.
A word of four syllables—propaganda—

Sounds in my ears to this day:
"Everything is propaganda. The whole
     world is propaganda."
If I were to turn into a child,
Studying again in an elementary school,
And it was said to me:
The Volga falls into the Caspian Sea!
I would, of course, believe it. But first
I'd find that Volga,
Follow its current down to the sea,
Wash myself in its turbid waters
And only then, perhaps, would I believe.

Horses eat oats and hay!
A lie! During the winter of 1933
I lived in the emaciated Ukraine.
At first the horses ate straw,
Then—the sparse straw from roofs,
Then they were driven to Kharkov to a
     dump.
I saw with my own eyes horses
Severe, serious, almost pompous
Bay ones and dun ones and dark-brown-
     colored horses

* SOURCE: *Ibid.*

Silently, unhurriedly wandering around the dump.
They walked, then stood
And fell and lay a long time.
They did not die quickly, the horses.

Horses eat oats and hay!
No. Not true. A lie. Propaganda.
Everything is propaganda. The whole world is propaganda.

The Thaw and the Intellectuals*

INTERVIEWER: How did you become aware of the "Thaw"? Did it follow close after Stalin's death?

BURG: Not immediately—there was a short period of groping confusion. Then in the winter of '55 all of a sudden people started to talk about things they would never have mentioned previously. About art for instance. Painters who had always hidden their work because it was abstract or unorthodox would hold semiprivate exhibitions. You would hear by word of mouth that they were showing in their studio, and you would go, and find others. I once went to such an exhibition and [saw] a student whom I'd always considered to be a straight Party-liner—he wasn't at all. And gradually there was more talk about politics, especially after the Twentieth Party Congress in 1956 when Khrushchev made his famous denunciation of Stalin. One heard names like Bukharin and Trotsky that had been unmentionable before. [At] the apartment of a good friend [I saw] a picture of Trotsky on the wall. I thought I was going mad. He said, ". . . I've been hiding this . . . long enough. Now I want to flaunt it, at least for a while."

INTERVIEWER: Did the students discuss the immediate struggle for power after Stalin died—Beria, Malenkov, Khrushchev, and so on?

BURG: That . . . remained confined to very close friends even after the Twentieth Party Congress. What we did talk about

* SOURCE: D. Burg, "The Voice of a Dissenter—An Interview with a Graduate of Moscow University," Harper's Magazine, May, 1961, pp. 127-131.

openly was the past of the Communist Party, especially the purges of the Party and intellectual leaders in the 'thirties. . . . One incident . . . [shocked] many of us. It involved Gronsky who had been a member of the Central Committee of the Party in the thirties and an editor of the literary magazine *Novy Mir*. In 1937 or 1938 he . . . disappeared along with many others. . . . In 1956 he was suddenly back in Moscow and was allowed to give a speech to a group of graduate students. . . . Gronsky . . . is quite a man—of peasant origin, . . . simple and straightforward . . . , cruel and dedicated and honest, typical of . . . the old unsophisticated Bolsheviks who were eliminated . . . in the 'thirties. It was an experience simply to see him speaking in Moscow.

But what he said was . . . astounding. He said that when Bukharin was arrested in 1937, he, Gronsky, had stood up in a meeting of the Central Committee and told Stalin that Bukharin may have had the wrong political view but he could *not* have been a traitor, because he had worked with him for twenty years and knew that Bukharin was a man of complete honesty. And Stalin looked at him and, in his heavy Georgian accent, had given orders that Gronsky be allowed to see Bukharin in Lefortovo prison, renowned as . . . the prison of torture.

And so Gronsky went and saw Bukharin and he challenged him to say that he was innocent but he found him terribly changed, completely broken. Bukharin looked at the ground—he had always looked people straight in the eye—and he said yes, yes, it was true, he was a traitor and an agent.

Now Gronsky still could not believe this, but after Bukharin was taken away, he was arrested himself, and they subjected him to week after week of awful torture and beating. But he would not sign a confession, he said, because: "How could I deceive the Party? I could not do it."

Later, Gronsky said, he was put in the same cell with one of the former chiefs of the Leningrad secret police who had confessed and Gronsky asked him if his confession was true. And the secret police chief had said: "You are probably the last man I'll talk to—they'll kill me soon. I tell you, there isn't a word of truth in the whole thing."

And then Gronsky said, "And what do you think, boys, what did I do? Do you think I took pity on him? No. I stood up and I socked him in the eye. I told him, 'What kind of a Bolshevik are you, deceiving the state in this way? The Party brought you so high and you are betraying the Party now'."

Gronsky was sent to Siberia for nineteen years, and now he was back. And by telling us experiences such as this he was trying to help the Party.

INTERVIEWER: How did the audience react to that speech?

BURG: The students . . . were deeply shaken. They'd never heard *anyone* speak like that. As we were filing out, a Komsomol secretary—the last man from whom one would have expected protest—pointed up at Stalin's statue which loomed very large on the staircase and he said, "Why don't we throw this bastard out the window, Comrades?" . . .

INTERVIEWER: You've said that various attitudes, formerly hidden, started to be expressed more openly. What were they?

BURG: . . . Among the intellectuals, there were four main dissenting attitudes. . . . The most widespread was [that] expressed by the popular young poet Evtushenko: "Comrades, let us give to the words their original meaning." That is, let us return to the original ideals of the Bolshevik revolution, let us go "back to Lenin," as some say. They hold that power should be re-

turned to the people who should be able to elect representatives to local governing authorities—the soviets; these soviets should in turn elect higher organs of government right on up to the Council of Ministers— a quite decentralized system you see. Of course soviets exist today but they have no power, and the Council of Ministers is in the hands of the Party apparatus. The Party, in the view of this group, should stay a leading force, but instead of suppressing opposition, it must constantly regain the confidence of the masses, winning its position democratically over and over again.

INTERVIEWER: Against the opposition of another party?

BURG: Well, that's it. These people talk only about inner Party democracy—genuine discussion *within* the Party on large political issues. Of course they believe in doing away with cultural regimentation—all the dissenting intellectuals are for that. But they are unequivocally for a centrally planned economy—they believe a market economy would lead to inequality. In short what you have here is a group that would like to revive the egalitarian spirit of the revolution and turn it against the present regime. . . . [Evtushenko's] work has had an enormous vogue—his verses were bought up as soon as they appeared. Every little high school student felt it his duty to quote him. . . .

INTERVIEWER: Did this neo-Bolshevism . . . remain on the level of parlor and dormitory discussion—or did it ever express itself in . . . action?

BURG: There have been a few incidents, most of them after I left the country. . . . During the anniversary celebration of the Revolution in 1958 there was an attempt by some students in Leningrad to organize a demonstration. Some of them—not completely sober . . . started shouting, "Long Live the Hungarian Revolution! Down with the Government of the Fatties! Long Live Inner Party Democracy!" That sort of thing.

And earlier, in the history faculty of the University of Moscow, a dozen or so students started distributing leaflets directly to the workers in the district, attacking Khrushchev personally and calling for inner-Party democracy. A direct appeal to the proletariat, you see, quite in keeping with neo-Bolshevik ideology. They were arrested in the summer of 1957 and given three to eight years in prison—relatively mild sentences, if one considers the past. And in the fall of 1959 *Izvestia* carried a report of the arrest of a similar group which was meeting often and preparing to distribute leaflets.

INTERVIEWER: In all this, Khrushchev appears as a villain?

BURG: Oh yes. For the young intelligentsia, Khrushchev is one of those people to whom Stalin offered one of half-a-million jobs—a residue from the previous era. He really doesn't communicate to the intellectuals, I think, except for the endless jokes about him. . . . That is true for all the dissenters of the intelligentsia, neo-Bolshevik or not.

INTERVIEWER: What are some of the others?

BURG: Exactly opposed to the neo-Bolsheviks, you find a cult of the West—a sort of Utopian vision of capitalism. . . . You find this among some of the *stilyagi*—the so-called zoot-suiters and teddy-boys in the cities. These [are] either the highly privileged sons of the very rich, or in contrast, the delinquent sons of poor urban workers. This sort of person isn't very political—he finds the regime dreary and oppressive and bad and simply assumes, or dreams, that what comes from the West must be good. Therefore he says he is anti-socialist and pro-capitalist.

You also find a kind of pro-capitalism among the students of the scientific technical colleges, at for instance the Moscow Institute of Aviation, an extremely well-regarded school whose standing might be compared to your M.I.T. Again the students aren't very sophisticated politically. Technological accomplishment, democracy, cultural freedom—all are lumped together for them in a Utopian picture of [the West]. But I never heard a concrete plan for converting Russia to a capitalistic economy.

Then there is a third attitude which might be called "liberal socialism." . . . The Bolshevik idea was wrong, they argue, but socialism in Russia is inevitable and desirable.

So they would like to reform the country on the basis of a democratically run multi-party system, a socialist market economy, and cultural freedom. One heard such ideas as this: Industries would be owned through stock companies in which the workers would hold shares, and a workers' council would actually run each industry. . . .

Finally, among the intellectuals, you find a fourth attitude which has an old history in Russia—and that is nihilism. . . . "We should try to destroy the regime in Russia," a nihilistic student once told me, "but we should be *very* reserved about any millennium, any suggestion of a better life to come."

INTERVIEWER: You've been talking about dissenting views among the students and intellectuals. Were you aware of such views among the rest of the population?

BURG: Outside the intelligentsia . . . the most definite feeling of resistance . . . is among the peasants. When I would visit the . . . countryside, I would meet hard resentment against city boys who are well fed and . . . wear a tie. In the countryside you sometimes encounter deep-seated hatred for the regime, . . . not a coherent plan but a sullen inchoate desire to throw over the whole social structure and [work] from scratch toward some vague . . . muzhik's paradise.

But . . . aside from the peasant hatreds, you do sense throughout Russia . . . the most . . . formidable kind of dissent—the . . . stolid refusal . . . of the people to let the political aims of the regime seize hold of their private lives. Many people would describe themselves as good . . . citizens [and] defend Soviet foreign policy. But they refuse to go to the virgin lands or to develop Siberia or to sacrifice their leisure for "social works"; they dodge the relocation of young specialists. In short, despite the regime's demand of absolute "sacrifice of the personal for the common goal," they refuse to think in political terms and . . . concentrate on . . . home life, . . . sports, on simply trying to enjoy themselves. . . .

INTERVIEWER: How widespread . . . is active political thinking among the students?

BURG: . . . About half the students in the universities are more or less nonpolitical. About 40 per cent . . . have consciously dissenting political views. . . . 10 [to] 15 per cent are Party activists—professional idealists, you might say.

INTERVIEWER: . . . You were in Russia while an atmosphere of conscious dissent was being created and you've described the excitement of the increased freedom at the beginning of the Thaw. How did you arrive at the decision to leave, and how did you . . . escape?

BURG: It is true I left at a most hopeful time—there was a general belief that things would get better. . . . I felt differently. I saw no chance for organized, effective political opposition. During the years of the Stalin terror the Party apparatus had become supremely strong, a centralized machine with fantastic power. . . . Elite groups, of managers and specialists and intellectuals, have emerged . . . but their power is atomized. They only have power over the specific work they do.

The Party, on the other hand, claims absolute political power and is able to exercise it whenever it wants—and I saw no reason why it would let that power slip away. That's not to say that I wasn't aware of real changes since the mass terror of Stalin's day. . . . His methods caused a crippling stagnation throughout Russian life—in industry, in culture, everywhere. The normal motives to work and create just didn't operate when life was completely insecure and people were arrested on the slightest suspicion. So, when the mass terror disappeared, not only did efficiency increase but people were far more willing to take the still [great] risks of free private discussion and even open publication—they felt they'd no longer have to pay . . . with their heads. In practice the Party had to allow some leeway in private life, although it was still striving to regain total control. But this was a far cry from genuine liberalization!

And I saw no chance of any group forcing the Party to make radical concessions.

. . . There was a more personal reason. [My] verses . . . had . . . circulated anonymously. . . . The secret police were making inquiries. . . . I suspected that they were close to finding [me] out. Finally, I didn't trust myself. . . . If something drastic . . . happened, like a student demonstration, I felt that I might foolishly plunge in. And I did not particularly fancy striking heroic poses in camps.

So, it was a combination of things. In any case, after graduating from the university I took a tourist trip to East Germany and took the subway to West Berlin. . . .

INTERVIEWER: Observing . . . the Khrushchev regime from the West, do you feel that decision has been confirmed?

BURG: Yes, particularly in the last year. But this business of the Thaw is very complex. It is a nice image but it involves many elements: the power struggle at the top, the intrigues within the Party, the pressure from the masses below for a better life, the craving of the intellectuals for more freedom. You have to take it all into account to understand any single policy.

As far as the condition of the masses is concerned, . . . one can . . . say that from 1953 to 1958, there was constant progress —more consumer goods, more housing, more food. . . . For the intellectuals, of course, 1956 and 1957 were the freest years.

INTERVIEWER: You mean particularly freedom to publish.

BURG: Yes, but not only that. Evtushenko's poetry was published and Dudintsev's novel, *Not by Bread Alone*. And Ehrenburg's *Thaw* even before that—all of them frankly implying criticism of the regime. But public discussions went further. Evtushenko got up at a meeting of the Writers' Union and said, "We are *not* going to let those who would return to old times have their way. We'll rap their knuckles." And this summed up the illusory confidence of the opposition. For in 1958, the screws were tightened. Khrushchev met with a group of writers at one of his dachas and said that the Hungarian revolution would have been avoided if some of the early trouble-makers had been shot. "*Our* hand is not going to tremble," he said. (At that point, I'm told, a woman writer fainted away.)

And after that, the liberal publishing policy stopped and instead of dealing with broad and burning social topics, literary discussion became much more technical and oblique—which kinds of artistic forms were "modern" and which were not, for example.

To be sure, there was still a spectrum of views: For instance, the magazine *Novy Mir* would take a more liberal line; the newspaper *Literature and Life,* a viciously reactionary one. It was nothing like the freedom of 1957 and 1958, but at least until 1960 hints of opposition were tolerated.

INTERVIEWER: And then?

BURG: And then came what has come to be called the U-turn in Soviet internal policy—although in fact it was taking place before the U-2 flight occurred. Suddenly the old Stalinist phrases reappeared: "the necessity for a new moral stimulus to labor," for example, which translated means that instead of stimulating productivity by making available more consumer goods, the administration would rely more . . . on coercion.

During 1960 and 1961 there have been crackdowns on private building—which grew considerably in the late 'fifties—and on private agriculture and private ownership of all sorts. There have been repressive measures against people doing work not deemed "socially useful"—for example, those who aren't employed by the state but make a living selling flowers or vegetables, from private plots, in the Moscow market. In short, the Party seems to have sensed a significant part of economic life slipping out of its control, and so it chose to tighten its grip, even though it meant slowing down the rise in living standards.

INTERVIEWER: What have been the effects on cultural life?

BURG: Curiously, the signs that a drastic suppression of cultural life may be on the way came after the economic measures I've mentioned—in fact, they are appearing right now, in the winter of 1960-61. One strong sign was the firing in December of Smirnov, the editor of the *Literary Gazette,* and his replacement by a downright Stalinist. I . . . fear that in the coming year we will see much more pressure on writers and artists and scholars generally to conform.

INTERVIEWER: You draw a dark picture.

BURG: Yes, but . . . I would end on an optimistic note. . . . Despite the immense power of the Party, strong currents of independent and dissident thought have continued to flow in Russia. . . . The intellectuals, the people, have not been able to break the power of the Party apparatus. . . . But neither has the Party been able to break all of them or their minds or their hopes.

Interviewed by R. B. Silvers

"The Man in the Street" in 1959*

Please note that the observations and opinions expressed in this report are those of recent visitors to the USSR and do not necessarily reflect the views of the American Committee for Liberation.

* SOURCE: *Soviet Attitudes; Report No. 3,* Information Center on Soviet Affairs, 1657 Broadway, New York City (a service of the American Committee for Liberation). (Adapted and abridged.)

This section of the report is based upon interviews of thirteen young American guides at the 1959 United States Exhibition in Moscow. Quite a few of them found time to visit other Soviet cities as well. One of the guides gives a good picture of the circumstances under which their impressions of the Soviet people were collected:

For the first time in the history of Soviet-American relations a sizable group of Russian-speaking Americans was to receive an opportunity to tell the U.S. story to the Soviet masses directly, without the distorting propaganda applied by the Soviet communication media. The significance of this fact was not lost upon the Soviet people themselves. The eagerness with which the Exhibition visitors overwhelmed us with questions suggested a pent up desire to learn about America from Americans. It was a new experience for most Soviet visitors to see, touch, taste and smell products of America. But more important was the opportunity afforded them to talk to the 75 guides.

As a result, visitors came in droves from all walks of life and from all parts of the Soviet Union. The Exhibition offered us one of the best opportunities to date to probe popular attitudes in depth.

Believability of Soviet Press and Radio

The American Exhibition guides' opinions were evenly divided about whether Soviet citizens believe their own press and radio reports, although not one felt that the Soviet people believe their media *fully*. Most agreed that, although they think there is some exaggeration in their press, they have no basis for comparison and tend to believe what they learn from their press and radio. At the same time, they read between the lines and are prone to believe rumors.

Students and intellectuals are generally far more sceptical of what they read in the Soviet press. One guide, however, reported encountering an interesting attitude in several Soviet citizens:

During my stay in the USSR, I didn't meet one Soviet citizen who really believed that everything he read in *Pravda* was the truth. Still, many intellectually justified propaganda because they felt that the press should lead the people and they didn't mind distorting the news as long as it was for the good of the people.

Lack of Foreign Reading Material

Seven guides reported hearing complaints about the lack of foreign reading material. As one of the guides remarked:

People seemed to be fairly adjusted to the lack of foreign reading material and don't think that anything can be done about it. But, at the reading exhibit I noticed that they literally devoured everything there was to read. They particularly sought the Russian History section and encyclopedias where they could actually check their own Soviet sources against foreign reading matter.

Many Soviet artists complain about the unavailability of art books in the Soviet Union. There is a mounting interest in Western art; the guides reported that American art books are very difficult to obtain and are passed from person to person. They can be obtained in the Soviet Union, but at very high prices.

The guides generally agreed that only those books which the Soviet government sanctions are easily available in the USSR. Thus, they read Jack London, John Steinbeck and some Ernest Hemingway. There is no access to Western political material.

Lack of Travel Opportunities

The guides were divided about the Soviet citizens' attitude toward travel restrictions. Five guides reported that they heard few, if any, complaints on this point; four said that many Russians, especially intellectuals, resent travel restrictions. All guides agreed, however, that Soviet people often ascribe the fact that so few Soviet citizens go abroad to a lack of funds.

A few Soviet citizens felt that were the people given the opportunity to travel freely, many would not return to the USSR. They were amazed to learn that any American could obtain a passport for foreign travel merely by paying a small fee and waiting a short time. Most were encouraged by the fact that they could visit the satellite countries and all felt that the desire to travel would eventually be fulfilled.

Rapport with Soviet Citizens

All the guides agreed that rapport was easily established when they found themselves with one, or a very few, Soviet citizens—especially outside the fairgrounds—by participating in conversations of a nonpolitical nature. Subjects of common interest such as sports, family life, accepted music, education, etc., helped to get friendly conversations going. The informal, candid approach was generally successful: "Russians don't like being talked down to. Therefore, I found that when I told them I knew little about a subject and that 'international problems are for the Eisenhowers and Khrushchevs, rather than for the little people like you and me,' I generally established good rapport."

Most of the guides agreed that it was best to admit real shortcomings in American life, particularly when pointing out the same in Soviet society. They also felt that specific examples which repudiated Soviet indoctrination are most effective. As one guide put it: "For example, I would say that in many parts of the United States we have done much to overcome problems of racial discrimination. This did not make much of an impression until I could point to the presence of two elected Negro councilmen on the Cincinnati City Council."

Open-Mindedness of Soviet Citizens

Although three of the guides felt that Soviet citizens are not at all open-minded, the rest (ten) agreed that most are always prepared to listen. But the guides always had to remain conscious of the Russians' peculiar way of reasoning. One guide reported:

Soviet citizens asked many questions which were based on the indoctrination they had received. However, many of my colleagues and I believed that some Soviet citizens asked these Party-line questions with the hope of hearing them refuted. When they wanted a negative answer to Soviet propaganda, it was much safer for them to phrase the question negatively rather than ask positively what they hoped to hear.

Patriotism

All the guides felt that patriotism, of both kinds—pride in recent Soviet accomplishments in science, and the traditional Russian feeling for country—plays an extremely large role in shaping the attitude of a Soviet citizen toward his country.

Many visitors to the Exhibition admitted some shortcomings in the present state of affairs in the USSR, but they always pointed out that the recent achievements in industrialization, science and education are signs of better things to come.

There is still a constant emphasis on the sufferings of the Russian people during WW II. The Soviet people are very proud of having accomplished so much despite the great destruction of the country twenty years ago.

Several guides pointed out that Soviet young people seem to be more devoted to the Soviet Union, whereas older people share the strong patriotic feelings of the young, but with the emphasis on allegiance to Russia. One guide said:

I spoke mainly to students and engineers, who were very sincere in the belief that their system, although it had many defects, would eventually prove to be the more efficient one. They truly believed in the Marxist concept of history and in the superiority of the socialist system. They felt the Soviet Union would eventually reach the ultimate level of Communism.

Another's comment reflected the consensus among the guides on the subject of Soviet patriotism: "In Soviet society, everyone is very patriotic, but this doesn't mean that they actively support the regime. One finds that, particularly, those who have complaints against the government tend to fall back on the traditional Russian patriotism which stems from their historical background."

The Soviet National Inferiority Complex

The Soviet inferiority complex is most frequently manifested in sensitivity to criticism from foreigners; any critical remark from an outsider leads to an immediately defensive reaction from the Soviet citizen. Soviet citizens realize that their standard of living is lower than that of the West and they attempt to compensate by attacking the West. However, one guide noted, "at the same time that they attempted to tear down the superior image of the West, one noticed their great desire to achieve that very same image."

Another guide said that they realize that they are behind, but are too proud to admit it. Here again, the Second World War affects Soviet attitudes: "Whenever I pointed out any shortcomings in the USSR, they were quick to explain that they underwent great hardships because of the war."

Fear

Fear still plays a prominent role in the life of the average Soviet citizen. First, there is the fear of the secret police, neighbors and spies. Most of the guides felt that people are still very cautious about openly expressing their attitudes. They did, however, feel that things are getting better. A typical comment was: "It's bad now, but it's no comparison to what it was under Stalin." One of the guides noted: "The higher the person's position, the less he was afraid. Editors of publishing houses, for instance, really believed that they could say anything they pleased. Conversely, someone in an insecure position, e.g., someone who had been expelled from the Komsomol, was afraid."

The other type of fear Soviet citizens display is the fear of the West and Germany. That people fear American bases and a rearmed West Germany was the consensus of many guides. Typical examples of guides' reactions are given in the two reports below:

A country that went through a war as devastating as World War II must be afraid of something. The people are still impressed by the regime's assertions that American monopolistic capitalism will force a war on the world. In general they manifest tremendous interest in the idea of peace and friendship among nations. As individual citizens, they are more afraid of Germany than any other nation.

* * *

The people's fear of war was made evident to me during a short walk in Brest-Litovsk. My companions and I were surrounded by farm people, who exclaimed, "Why do you want war? We want peace." When we tried to explain that we didn't want war, they replied,

"How can you say that? You don't know what war is." It was my feeling that many of the people believe that since we've never known war on our own soil there is a good possibility that we would start one. This belief is obviously exploited by the government which constantly emphasizes our military budget, our warlike preparations, etc. I found it impossible to counter these arguments. They believed none of my statements, approaching the whole matter quite emotionally.

Collectivity

Soviet citizens appear to be rather strongly motivated by the "collective" feeling. Following is a description of this phenomenon:

They possess a feeling of collectivity rather than of privacy. Travelling on a streetcar, a Soviet citizen will spontaneously begin a conversation with a total stranger. I got the feeling that they think of themselves as a unit. In fact, there is a certain pleasant informality of butting into other people's business. If you sit on the grass in Gorki Park, somebody is bound to approach you and tell you that you shouldn't sit on Socialist grass. Moreover, the young people are inspired by this concept of "our park," "our factory." Walking through Gorki Park, I often heard someone say, "Well, this is beautiful, and it is all ours."

Despite the complaints about crowded housing conditions, Soviet citizens seldom mentioned the lack of privacy. A Soviet friend of mine, who had lived in the United States for five years, but who now works for Radio Moscow, said that the Russians simply do not feel the need for privacy as much as a Westerner does. He also noticed that he himself felt a greater need for privacy than did the other members of his family who had never lived outside of the USSR.

The Communist Party

The average Soviet citizen said very little about the Communist Party, but the ones that did were quick to assert that it is leading the country toward a better society. One guide who had talked with many Party members had this to say:

Soviet citizens consider the Party the vanguard of the country. Although they don't criticize it *per se,* many intellectuals won't identify with it. They simply say that it is not for the elite because it is similar to the government. I talked to many Party members who, incidentally, are economically better off than the average person. For example, I visited a Soviet engineer in his apartment; it was in the only Moscow apartment house I considered livable. I established good *rapport* with him, for although he spouted a few Party doctrines about the United States, he certainly was open to ideas and did not criticize the United States too much. But he was an exception, for most of the other Party members whom I met, although they were better educated and intellectually responsive were less sympathetic, less open-minded and more dogmatic than the average Soviet citizen.

Other guides also reported Party members to be less open-minded, less willing to listen to opinions differing from their own, and more given to official platitudes.

However, the guides emphasized that Party members were more open-minded and candid in private and appeared to have a better grasp of the internal situation in the USSR, as well as its relationship to the rest of the world. Many young Party members are very idealistic and devoted to bettering the country. One guide met a Moscow student who, despite his rather liberal point of view, aspired to become a Party member. This young man can be considered to be a representative of the more idealistic Party youth:

He understood very well the problems which exist in the USSR, deprecated Stalin and claimed that one of his reasons for joining the Party was his desire to prevent the repetition of a Stalinist-type regime. He was confident that by becoming a Party member he could help build a new society that would benefit the greatest number of people. He conceded that an elite existed, but maintained that this was inevitable because of the essence of human nature. "Whenever you have a society," he said, "there are bound to be some people who are going to have more than others."

Most of the guides reported that Party members were in very obvious attendance at the Exhibition booths. They came to spy upon the crowd and heckle the Americans and were considered "very loud and not too bright."

Attitudes Toward Government Policy

Support for the Regime

Soviet citizens generally support the policies of the Soviet regime, at least in public. Although some express criticism of some internal situations, they appear to believe that the system is the best for them. Internal propaganda seems to have convinced them that they are not much worse off than the rest of the world. Most people approve of guaranteed employment, free medical care, free educational system, Soviet technological progress, etc., and the peace campaign is particularly attractive.

Criticism of the Regime

Several instances of disagreement with Soviet policies were reported by a number of guides. Most of the criticism was directed at restrictions on travel and inadequate living space.

Soviet youth is generally more critical of the present regime than older people are. Two guides commented on this:

One young Soviet citizen told me that there were too many people who had privileges. Others criticized other aspects of Soviet life— the lack of literature from the outside world, the limitation on travel, the small number of foreign films, the low standard of living and the discouragement of contacts with the West.

*   *   *

Although Soviet citizens support the regime, there is some criticism of it. The young students, for example, are impatient with the government for not constantly revising its policies in order to keep abreast of world developments. But they never question the form of government; rather they are impatient with the regime itself. According to the Soviet way of thinking, when a mistake is made it is not an ideological error, but a misunderstanding of the best method of executing the ideology.

Possible Alternatives to the Present System

Most Soviet citizens do not think in terms of alternatives to the system. They are rarely able to think even in terms of alternative leaders.

While Soviet attitudes toward the system itself are fairly constant, attitudes toward the leaders vary. If the leadership commits an error, it is considered to be not a fault of the system, but of the people at the top:

They find it difficult to conceive of freedom of political dissent. The average Soviet citizen cannot envisage a great change in the regime. Thus, while there are many who may feel that they are being frustrated by particular individuals—their immediate superiors—there are few who would do a great deal to change the regime or who think that there could be any benefit from a great change. Interestingly, many felt that any sort of freedom—as we in the West think of it—would necessitate a loss of employment and medical care. If they had to choose between freedom and employment, they would keep what they now have.

Main Goals of the Soviet People

All the guides agreed that the main goal of the Soviet people is to improve their over-all standard of living. One guide reported:

The main goals of the Soviet citizen are the development of an increasingly strong technological and industrial base which will make his nation more powerful and lead to the betterment of his living conditions. At present, it appears that the people are quite satisfied with their rate of progress toward these goals, for they have had noticeable additions to their individual prosperity. You don't see many queues of people shopping for the staples of life, although you occasionally see people standing in line for fresh cabbages. They also know from published reports that their industrial and technological rate of progress is extremely high.

Another said:

They want to surpass America. They constantly refer to what the Soviet Union accomplished in 40 years, as compared to America in 175 years. They do not consider the technological bases from which both started and sincerely believe that even though the previous 5-year plans were not fulfilled, the current 7-year plan will be and when that happens they will be living as well as, if not better than, the Americans.

Soviet Youth

As one guide put it:

As far as I could observe, the aspirations of Soviet youth were pretty bourgeois. Being very practical, they want to rise as high in the system as possible and they don't mind using the system for their advancement. Clearly, the old revolutionary spirit, if it ever existed to the extent that Soviet literature says it did, is lacking today. Soviet young people want quiet and comfortable lives, a car and the sort of life that is actually led in bourgeois society.

Many Soviet young people are reported to have contempt for labor. One guide reported:

I felt that the educated, well-off Soviet students have a feeling of contempt for the uneducated masses. They often made remarks about the poorer people who were passing us in the street. For example, one young engineer looked at a group of people composed of peasants or unskilled working men and complained that these people knew nothing of what a mid-twentieth century man should know. He was absolutely disgusted with them. Time and time again, I was struck by this snobbishness.

When one of the guides talked with Soviet young people about the "staunch" Soviet citizen, they would laugh and say: "These people are very stupid." The young people he met do not care whether they have capitalism or Marxism, so long as they have their fun and can look "sharper" than other people. They are most interested in Western dress, culture and jazz:

Typical of the new Soviet youth are the sons and daughters of high Party officials who are called the "golden youth." They aren't concerned with the Revolution or with building Communism. They are concerned, however, with going out for an evening of dancing and the Moscow night-spots are packed with these people. There is, of course, a good deal of resentment from the "non-golden youth" element.

Most of the guides found much less fear and caution among the young people. As one of the guides said:

Almost all the young people I met expressed a desire to travel and see things for themselves. This may or may not be true of the older generation, but it was particularly evident in the younger people and was reflected in the lengths to which they would go to establish contact with foreigners like ouselves, and the risks they would take despite their awareness of the possible consequences.

Religion

Most guides were asked questions about religion. The standard question from the young people was: "How can enlightened people living in this twentieth century with advanced technology still believe in God? Do you really have scientists who are religious?" The whole thing is quite incomprehensible to the Soviet citizen.

The American guides at the Exhibition reached more or less the same conclusions regarding religion in the USSR: most Soviet people attending church services are elderly, little children accompanied by their grandparents, or members of the lowest economic classes. Churches in rural areas are much better attended than in cities. Young people attend church very rarely, and when they do, it is simply out of curiosity. Many Soviet people feel that it is unwise to be seen attending church since that could result in losing one's job or getting into difficulties with the police or Komsomol officials.

The Status of the Soviet Jews

Most of the guides met Jews who, in private, complained about the different forms of persecution and discrimination to which they are subjected. One non-Jewish guide noted:

I met a Ukrainian Jew in his middle thirties who felt that the Russians and, even more so, the Ukrainians, were anti-Semitic. He said that

membership in the Party was almost out of the question for Ukrainian Jews. Although he had a good position as an engineer and appeared to be financially solvent, he felt that if he ever lost his job he would have great difficulty getting a new one, due to his religion. He added that he believed this would also be true in Russia, but to a lesser degree. Over and over again he said, "You have no idea. You simply can't understand. You don't know what it is like." I definitely got the impression from him that Jews are having a difficult time in the USSR. On the whole, Jewish life there is atomized. There is no Jewish group in Russia. There may be individual Jews, but there is no Jewish community.

Another guide, a Jew, said the following about job discrimination:

I am Jewish and I spoke to them in Yiddish. They complain about the fact that their passports are stamped "Jew" and that makes it hard for them to get jobs. I heard many, many stories about discrimination in getting jobs, advancing in jobs and admission to schools.

I met a Jewish engineer who told me, "I've never had any Jewish education, I don't speak Yiddish. I feel myself a Russian. I see no reason why 'Jew' should be stamped in my passport, but it is." He also told me he was offered a high position in the firm where he was working. When it came to filling out the final papers, he showed his passport. They looked at it and said, "No, I'm sorry, the position is not available."

Another Jewish guide said that the situation of the Jews in the USSR is much different from that of other minority groups there. Jews are much more hostile to the regime; almost all seem to be. They feel their affiliation with the West. Many Jews have relatives in Israel or in the United States or in both. There are reports of Jews having a very difficult time studying and obtaining positions in the physical sciences.

At the same time, many guides, especially the non-Jewish ones, found widespread resentment and dislike for the Jews. Some people said that Jews take all the good engineering jobs, and non-Jews are prevented from rising for this reason. A young Soviet girl said that "they were just being over-run and pushed about by the Jews."

There are synagogues open for worship in Moscow as well as in other cities in the USSR. However, the Jewish guides who attended services at these synagogues found that the congregation consisted largely of old people who appeared very fearful.

Talks with Kolkhozniki

The situation on Soviet Kolkhozes is best shown by the divergence between an official's statements and statements by kolkhozniki themselves:

One evening I met a man who was the head of a kolkhoz. He was congenial and, had he lived in the United States, would have been a member of the City Council, the Rotary Club and similar organizations. According to him, everything was great in the kolkhoz. People loved it, he said. I asked him if there were more women working there than men. "No, no," he answered. After pressing him, he admitted that there were a few more women than men, but that there were no problems. Everything was going along fine and the economic plan was being fulfilled, he said.

The other viewpoint was expressed by the workers themselves:

In a cafeteria, I talked with an old man who told me that he came from a kolkhoz. According to him, conditions there were so bad that they got only half a loaf of bread per working day. Therefore, he had come to Moscow to get a job. He added that none of us would ever see these kolkhozes because we wouldn't be permitted to go there. "And if you did visit a kolkhoz," he said, "you would be shown only the beautiful apples." He spoke in a harsh dialect and, after he told me this, refused to say anything more.

Another guide who talked to several kolkhozniki reported a conversation with a kolkhoznik who complained bitterly about the situation of his kolkhoz:

He claimed that since they are unable to save money he never had spare cash to spend on anything. He stated that he received all his payments in goods and saw a very, very small amount of hard cash in a year. He added that there was very little to do on the kolkhoz aside from reading in their small library and playing chess.

Kolkhozniki at the Exhibition were easily identified by their poor clothes, their mannerisms and their starry-eyed attitude toward all the Western things they had never seen or heard of before. A guide who took particular interest in the attitudes of the kolkhozniki at the Exhibition had this to report:

They were, of course, entranced with most of the things they saw at the Exhibit and particularly bedazzled by the colors and the general carnival atmosphere. Their comments seemed to be indicative of something which might be a problem with the younger people on the kolkhoz—that is, the lack of social activities or any kind of outside diversion.

They were extremely bored with their life on the kolkhoz.

One guide visited a kolkhoz in Siberia, obviously one of the "Pokazukha" establishments operated as a showplace for visiting foreigners:

I visited a kolkhoz in Siberia. Obviously, the government felt it was a good kolkhoz or they wouldn't have taken me there. However, I was not impressed with it, as it resembled a poor-grade farm. But the kolkhoz did appear to be well organized and I didn't observe anyone walking around in a state of depression.

As I was allowed to choose at random someone to talk to, I picked a Belorussian who was very satisfied in this kolkhoz. Because life had been hard in Belorussia where the land was poor and marshy, he felt that in this part of fertile Siberia he could better support his family.

The Komsomol

Soviet youth see the Komsomol as a means of getting ahead. Most guides encountered the official Party line first: "We are entering the Komsomol for ideological reasons." However, after talking for a while the majority of Komsomol members said they belong because "it is the thing to do," or because it furthers one's chances of obtaining a better job, a better apartment, etc.

This was pointed up by their lackadaisical and cynical attitude toward the Komsomol and its leaders, who are regarded as rather low types who spy on their classmates and make life miserable for non-members. Here are some representative comments:

Many Komsomol members feel that the Komsomol is a harmless organization. For example, I talked to a few people who had been kicked out of the Komsomol, yet they didn't seem to be particularly concerned about it. In fact, they considered it as only a little more severe than having been kicked out of the Boy Scouts.

Many students were cynical about the Komsomol. For example, four students I knew referred to their Komsomol leaders—in perfect English—as "the bosses." These students said that it was all right to have a few fanatics such as these people, but "it would be hell if everyone were that way."

Nevertheless, several guides found a somewhat different response:

I talked to a number of Komsomol members and found it quite easy to communicate with them since they are very often students in universities and thus have more knowledge of academic, social and political affairs and institutions. They also are more inclined than ordinary citizens to talk intelligently about Soviet literature and the arts. Despite this, they are more critical than the average Soviet citizen of Western life and conditions.

An Opinion of American Schools*

It was gratifying to observe the delight and interest with which the Soviet exhibit, "Technical and Artistic Creativity of Soviet Children," was received in the United States.

Americans went to the exhibit not just to see the displays. Many of them came in order to talk with Soviet people. Daily, from the pages of newspapers and television screens, Americans are deluged by a flow of fantasies, lies and distorted facts about the life of the Soviet people. Americans came to the exhibit to obtain, as they would say, information at first hand. Filled with all kinds of fantasies from newspapers and doubting them, they usually began their questions as follows: "Is it true that in Russia . . ." and then some cock-and-bull story would follow.

Now they want to know "everything—everything about Russia" (that is what they call the Soviet Union): "What is communism?" "If there is no private property,

what induces people to work?" Countless questions every day! And the most frequent one: "Do the Russians want war?"

At the Textbook Stand

There was a section at the exhibit called "Public Education in the USSR." Interest in it was not accidental. Since 1957, one of the most popular themes in the American press has been the "Challenge of Soviet Education." That is why every American, even though he was far removed from pedagogy and schools had heard something about the "challenge of the Soviet schools" and was interested in visiting the section to see personally what it was that helped the Soviet Union to catch up with the United States in the areas of science and technology.

Some of the people had heard of the book by Professor Trace entitled *What Ivan Knows That Johnny Doesn't*. The Cleveland professor of English makes a careful analysis of textbooks and curriculums in the humanities of Soviet and American schools. This is the conclusion he reaches (used as an advertisement on the book cover): "While American children climb the hill

* SOURCE: Z. Malkova, *Narodnoye obrazovaniye,* 1962, No. 11. (Adapted and abridged from the translation in *The Soviet Review,* Summer, 1963, pp. 71-87.) The author is a Soviet educator.

with Jack and Jill, Soviet children of the same age apparently study the height of this hill, its minerals, and its physico-political role in international affairs. . . . Our children are behind Soviet children not only in mathematics and natural science. By the time the American 4th-grader learns to read 1,500 words from the standard reader, the Soviet child in the 4th grade can read at least 10,000 words and is ready to dig into history, geography, and natural science. The fact is that when Ivan is reading Tolstoy, Pushkin and Gogol, Johnny is still reading the adventures of Jerry and the little rabbit who jumps about 'hop-hop-hop.' The Soviet schoolchild begins English as a foreign language in the 5th grade and studies it for six years. By the 10th grade he may, possibly, read more in English than the American child is required to do in the 12th grade."

Leafing through the Soviet textbooks, my schoolteacher friends say: "Yes, Trace does not exaggerate, Trace is right." Our conversation is interrupted suddenly by an angry man. A stack of algebra, trigonometry, and physics textbooks are in his hands.

"Are you going to maintain that all pupils in your schools study these subjects? Do you really think that all people are able to understand physics and solid geometry?"

The American is not pacified by my explanations.

"Do your schools include pupils who do not keep up?"

"Yes."

"What do you do with them?"

I tell him of the methods used by our teachers to encourage pupils, to evoke in them an interest for knowledge. Then I tell him of the system of mutual assistance, where the better pupils help the lagging ones.

"It is the state that forces them to help the lagging pupils," remarks the man. "As an individual I cannot understand why these talented children should waste their time on the lagging pupils when they could spend it on their own studies and achieve much better results."

Yes, it is difficult for us to understand one another. The American schools base their work on a completely different philosophy.

The Americans, particularly young people, always stopped at the stand with the sign: "All types of schools in the USSR, including the higher educational institutions, are free. Students at higher educational institutions receive government allowances." They would stop and sigh: "How lucky your students are."

A university education in the United States is an expensive thing and by no means can everyone afford it. The cost of instruction at good universities approaches 2,500 to 3,000 dollars a year. Many Americans who wish to educate their children at a university begin to save money for their studies as soon as the child is born. There are banks and companies that specialize in this type of savings. Here is an advertisement by one of these companies which we heard daily on television: "Are you preparing your son or daughter for college? In every family the cost of education is the largest expense after the purchase of a home. You can avoid worrying if you begin to put away money now and utilize the services of our company."

How many sweet and intelligent boys and girls came to the exhibit who spoke of their inability to go to college, or their having to drop out, because of the absence of funds.

Problem Number One

Meeting with American educators of various ranks, we would pose the following question: "What is the basic problem facing American schools?" To this question everybody would reply in the same way: "Money."

The lack of sufficient funds is really the number one problem of American schools. The United States has a so-called decentralized system of school administration. This means, first, that the selection of textbooks, the drawing up of curriculums and other factors in the work of the school are matters that are resolved by the local community in which the school is located. Second, schools exist on funds that are collected as a tax on the local population. The school budget is made up of the following parts: 55% from the tax on the population; 41% from the state; and 4% from the Federal Government.

Until recent times this system of decentralization was lauded in every way. It was said to be the most democratic system. Only recently has the opinion been expressed that this system is more suitable for the eighteenth century than for the twentieth.

The division of American cities into poor and rich areas is very clearly seen. When showing us a city the Americans would usually say, "The rich live here." And we would see splendid residences, far from the dust and smoke of the city, in the suburbs, and hidden by clumps of trees. "And this is where the poor live." This could be guessed without explanations: ramshackle houses squeezed against each other, garbage containers under windows, and children playing right on the streets.

It is quite obvious that if schools exist on the basis of local resources, then the schools in wealthy areas are in better material circumstances than in poor areas. Actually, in the suburbs, to which businessmen and the highly paid intelligentsia have moved, the yearly expenditure for each pupil is twice that of the expenditure in the poor areas. It was enough to look at the exteriors of schools to sense the difference.

We visited a seventy-five-year-old school in Minneapolis. Three classes study in one room at the same time; a library of 200 books is located in a small storeroom. In other schools we saw pupils studying on the stage and in the corridors because there were not enough classrooms. The situation is particularly bad in the southern states of the United States. We were shown a chart at the Ministry of Education that indicated the percentage of illiterate or partly literate in the adult population. The figure for the southern states is 20 to 25 per cent.

Money is needed to build schools. Local school communities cannot cope with this problem. That is why the American public is now demanding that the Federal Government increase its share in the financing of schools.

The Congress of the United States has more than once considered legislation for increasing school allocations. But it has been rejected every time: congressmen, half of whom are people with an income greater than fifty thousand dollars a year and a fifth of whom are millionaires, do not wish to spend money on public education.

In an Elementary School

The school is a one-storey brick building in a poor area. The people who live in this area are Negroes, Puerto Ricans, and whites, all of them at the lowest rungs of the social ladder. The school has a good library with a large reading room. But it does not have workshops, study halls, or laboratories. All study activity takes place in the classroom.

The 750 girls and boys in the school are assigned to classes according to a whole series of classifications. First of all, the school has a class for the mentally retarded children, a class for children with poor eyesight, two classes for the so-called emotionally disturbed children. The remaining children are assigned to classes in accordance with their "intelligence quotient."

More than a half-century ago American pedagogy came to believe that people are born with definite intellectual abilities and only one-fourth of the people can cope with intellectual activity. At that time, half a century ago, measurements were established —tests for measuring the intelligence quotient. Most American schools assign pupils to classes in accordance with the test results. Dozens of specialists, American and English, have proved that the tests measure not innate intelligence, but only the skills acquired by the child in classifying and systematizing, and his store of words.

Obviously, in taking these tests the best results are achieved by children from well-to-do families, where parents could afford to buy them toys and books. A low intelligence quotient is received, as a rule, by children from poor and, particularly, Negro families. Many progressive educators in the United States protest strongly against measuring the intelligence quotient of pupils, and consider this system faulty because it categorizes, without foundation, a large number of children as slow and deprives a great many children of an education.

Frankly, we Soviet educators were staggered by the harshness of this system. A youngster enters the 1st grade. But already in October he has been labeled "slow" and assigned to a specific class. The labels "able" and "slow" have a tremendous influence on the work of the teachers, even of those who are against the system. As a teacher said to us: "I am against testing. But knowing the intelligence quotients of the children in my class, I cannot force myself to be unbiased. I still look at them through the prism of this confounded quotient."

"Here Are the Slow Children"

We heard this phrase from a teacher every time we prepared to attend a class with an index of 4, 5, or lower. It is considered that the "slow" children are incapable of abstract thinking, that the teaching materials must be simplified for them, and that these materials must have a greater share of practical elements.

Reading in most American schools is taught with the method of "whole words." We were told that up to the 3rd grade pupils were not taught the alphabet and sounds. The problem of reading instruction is considered to be a most serious one. A large portion of children cannot read when they finish elementary school. This is a result, first of all, of the "whole word" method. This also implies, I think, that American schoolchildren write very little. As far as exercises and problems are concerned, the teacher mimeographs them beforehand. All the pupils have to do is to place the required number or word in the blank space provided.

Such mimeographed sheets save time. But the schoolchildren do little writing, and as a result, are slower in learning to read and spell. The inability to read handicaps the study of other subjects. We talked with a teacher in a 6th grade with an index of 5 about the teaching of social studies. She told us that the pupils learned all the material by listening to the teacher. "That's because they can't read the textbook," she explained.

An 8th-grade teacher of natural science told me the same thing. "My goodness!" he exclaimed when we asked whether pupils used their textbooks at home. "They can't read. All of the material is covered only in class."

Regarding the children as "slow," teachers in classes with an index of 4, 5 or lower teach arithmetic according to a reduced syllabus. The demands on the children's knowledge here are not great.

Upon hearing that we were going to a lesson in class 3-4, a young teacher warned us: "Bear in mind that these children are slow." We began to watch the "slow" ones. There are thirty-three pupils in the class; sixteen of them are Negroes. We noted an interesting pattern: the higher up the ladder of class "ability," the fewer Negroes.

The teacher distributes pieces of paper with a problem to solve: "One fishbowl contains three fish (a drawing of a fishbowl with the fish), and another has five (again a drawing of a fishbowl). If we remove the fish from the first bowl and place them in the second, how many fish will there be in the second bowl?" Amidst the noise, singing, and shouting the class solved the problem in twenty minutes.

The 6-4 class had a young man as a teacher. The teacher explains the division of a multi-digited number by a two-digit number, and divides 7,426 by 12. The pupils sit quietly but are indifferent to all that is taking place. Five or six of them listen and do the work.

Boys sit with their coats on at the back of the room, waiting for the bell. The girls, opening their handbags, look at themselves in their mirrors, file their nails, and comb their hair.

Having finished his explanation, the teacher gives the following problem to the class: "8,274 pieces of candy were divided among 42 classes. How much did each class get?" Another three pupils open their notebooks. The rest continue to occupy themselves with their own affairs. The teacher walks around the class and quietly passes by those who are not working. Not a single remark!

We were astounded by this neutral position of the teacher which we observed frequently. The teacher seldom uses methods to force the pupil to work or to stimulate him. Being under the influence of the theory of innate endowments, the teacher reasons: "What can you expect from this boy? He has an intelligence quotient of 75." The boy looks upon himself in the same way, since all of the children know whether they are "able" or "slow."

The teacher behaves differently in the schools of wealthy sections. He is active; he employs many methods to stimulate the pupil.

We observed the same kind of educational work in private schools. These are institutions where an education costs up to 2,000 dollars yearly. They are accessible only to children with very wealthy parents. There are no "slow" ones here either, and each child gets his needed share of attention from the teacher.

"Social Dynamite"

One of the most vulnerable spots in the American school is the absence of students' interest in knowledge. We saw students wearing buttons reading: "I hate school" and inscriptions on buttons and across the fronts of shirts and blouses, such as "I am an alcoholic"; "I like boys"; "Let's do the twist."

More than half of American students leave high school without having studied physics, chemistry, algebra, or a foreign language. Students select other subjects, often substituting chorus for physics. We must give American schools credit for the excellence of their choruses and orchestras.

Students in non-academic courses are not only deprived of a good education but are also deprived of the training necessary for getting a job. The school workshops do not to any degree provide the training which is demanded by modern industry. Trade union bosses object sharply to vocational training in schools, we were told by a school principal. They maintain that graduating students will compete with adults, thereby depriving the latter of their jobs.

One of the main reasons for the tremendous student drop-out rate after the 9th grade is the dissatisfaction with the school, which provides neither a good education nor vocational training. Barely half of those in the 9th grade eventually graduate from school. Boys and girls leave school and begin to look for work However, they are not met with open doors but with signs reading "No work." Where there is work there is a demand for people with good training.

Graduates completing the non-academic course also find themselves in a similar situation. They swell the ranks of those already unemployed. The percentage of unemployed among young people is twice [that of] adults. Among Negro and Puerto Rican youth the number of unemployed reaches 70 per cent. A condition has developed in the country which the well-known educator James Conant described as "the accumulation of social dynamite in cities and areas of poverty" which is ready to explode.

"Smile"

Student behavior in the American school appears to be rather strange to a Soviet teacher. They do not rise when the teacher enters or when reciting. Each one sits as pleases his fancy. Some put their feet on the desk. The lesson goes on, but the children stand up, walk about and leave the classroom. This type of discipline is supported by the theory that the child should not be repressed. In practice this simply leads to bad discipline. We saw classes where the teacher could not work because of the children's laxity. Teachers in New York experience tremendous difficulties. The matter has gotten to the point that legislation for corporal punishment has been introduced into the State Senate of New York. We noted that these punishments are not at all rare. While taking children on a tour around a museum, a teacher will take a misbehaving boy into a corner, slap his face and threaten: "And you'll get more!"

Student behavior in schools in smaller cities is better. Superficially, the children are courteous and one constantly hears them say: "Thank you," "Pardon me" and "Please." This surface propriety, we feel, is the result of the broadly disseminated theory in the United States that a man's success in life depends not on his knowledge or skills but on whether the man can get along with people.

"No matter how you feel, smile. A smile is success in life." Such posters hang in schools, in offices, in taxis and at railroad stations. However, the surface courtesy is deceptive.

Figures are incontrovertible. They show that crime among teenagers in the United States grows with each year. Practically every day newspapers report violence, killings, burglaries and other crimes committed by school-age children. When we became acquainted with the conditions in which American children grow up, we came to the conclusion that it would be difficult not to become a criminal under these conditions. The theme of violence resounds everywhere persistently—in books, the movies, television and in games.

The first thing you see in bookstores is a stand of books with colorful, glossy covers. There isn't a cover where someone isn't being stabbed, killed or shot. These are books about "strong" people who kill at every step. Alongside this stand, a prominent space near the entrance is taken up by a section with a notice reading "For Men Only." Here are books and magazines with the purest pornography. We have already written a good deal about American television. One must see these programs in order to understand how harmful any and the best of man's inventions can become when they become subservient to the dollar. From six in the morning to late at night, television screens show unceasing fights, killings, poisonings, thefts and arson. We sometimes joked, sitting before a television set at night: "We will count up to the twentieth

killing and then go to bed." In half an hour we could already go to bed.

We got into a conversation with an 8th grade supervisor. She complained about the lowering of morals, that children become interested in sexual matters too early.

"We saw several girls with painted lips in your class. Why do you allow this?" we asked.

"This is not my business," replied the teacher. "I have no right to interfere if the family does not object."

We became convinced that the viewpoint among American teachers is that the moral education of children is the business of the family and the church.

Meetings with American Colleagues

These meetings occurred often: at exhibits, in schools, in homes and at lectures. And no matter where we met, we always found a common language.

The majority of American teachers impressed us as being people dedicated to their cause and liking children. Many of them give all their strength to the school. But their work is poorly rewarded. American teachers became very surprised when they learned that the work of the teacher in the Soviet Union is remunerated in the same way as that of the doctor, the lawyer and the engineer. A teacher's salary in the USA is the lowest in comparison with other specializations that require higher education. Teachers, particularly men, are obliged to take supplementary jobs after school. We visited the family of a natural science teacher. He works in school during the day and in the evenings knocks at the doors of homes, publicizing the wares of an electric appliance company. According to official statistics, 72% of the teachers do this.

Anti-Semitism in the Provincial Press*

Under the Dark Vaults
of the Synagogue

As the Talmud says, fortune smiled on the lucky Rabbi Chonin Ben Dos: a golden plate from the Garden of Eden fell down for him out of the skies. But this happened to Rabbi Chonin and not to such as Chaim Fried, Bar Sokolovsky and Meir Soloveichik, the heads of the Minsk Jewish community. . . .

It is true that for them golden platters do not fall from heaven. Instead, tens of rubles (in new currency, of course) tinkle in their bottomless pockets. This money is brought to the synagogue by believers, and Chaim, Meir and Bar have indeed developed a good technique for extorting funds from their flock.

The most profitable days for them are those preceding the New Year, the Jewish holiday of Rosh HaShanah. At that time God determines "who will become rich and who turn poor." Places in the synagogue are also sold then. . . . Everybody knows that they cost no less than five rubles each. . . .

In order to attract more people to the synagogue, the community members sometimes organize drinking bouts on its premises. . . . Some believers subsequently walked home in "zigzags," shouting prayers at the top of their voices. Others just shouted words, the likes of which cannot be printed. . . .

The Minsk synagogue officials have yet other sources of income. Their synagogue is . . . visited by . . . tourists from Israel, who leave gifts in the form of *tallesim*

* SOURCE: *Minskaya Pravda* (Minsk Truth), April 4, 1961.

(prayer shawls—trans.) and prayer books. Fried, Sokolovsky and Soloveichik know how to turn these gifts into money: they sell them to the believers. . . .

While closing the cash-box, Fried, Sokolovsky and Soloveichik . . . put substantial sums into their pockets. Why do they need golden platters from the Garden of Eden . . . ? Besides this, they pay monthly visits, not to God, but to the district social insurance office, where they receive pensions for their families' subsistence. . . .

Who, then, are these men? Why have they, in the autumn of their lives, become so attracted to money? Because life failed to provide them with morality. Take, for instance, Chaim Fried, the community head. His father and he once owned a mill in Rogachev. Later he engaged in swindles while working as a purveyor. A similar path has been followed by his grandson, . . . who has now been convicted for robbery. . . .

Money! That is the God of the leaders of the Minsk Jewish religious community. . . . [A] Jewish believer is permitted [only] to eat meat [that] is *kosher*. This is [a] chicken or calf slaughtered "with a prayer" by a special slaughterer recognized by the synagogue. On this, Naftoli Kagan [speculates]. Slaughterer Naftoli lives at 10 Bersen Street and specializes in slaughtering [covertly] at home, taking 30 kopeks per chicken.

Thus, under the dark vaults of the synagogue, the crooks have feathered themselves a warm nest. . . . It is imperative to call to order all the ruffians of the Minsk Jewish religious community. . . . There must be a limit to everything.

Congratulations to a Spaceman*

KHRUSHCHEV—I am listening to you, comrade Gherman Stepanovich, and cordial congratulations.

TITOV—Comrade First Secretary of the Communist party of the Soviet Union Central Committee, I report that the task set by the party and the Government has been fulfilled. All the systems and equipment of the ship worked excellently. . . . I feel very well.

KHRUSHCHEV — Wonderful. You sound as if you had just returned from a wedding ball.

TITOV—You said it, Nikita Sergeyevich. It was a ball, but not a wedding. [Both laugh.]

KHRUSHCHEV—A ball, that is true, but not a wedding ball. For the newly married wedding ball is the happiest time. But what you have done, this is a happy time for the whole of mankind.

TITOV—Thank you, Nikita Sergeyevich.

KHRUSHCHEV—You have carried out an unprecedented cosmic voyage. How many circuits of the earth did you do?

TITOV—Seventeen and a half, Nikita Sergeyevich.

KHRUSHCHEV—In how many hours?

TITOV—In twenty-five hours and some minutes.

KHRUSHCHEV — Twenty-five hours and some minutes. This is a heroic deed. You have fulfilled mankind's dream. Not so long ago the dream of man's cosmic flight was considered not feasible. We are proud that you, a Soviet man, a Communist, have done it. You are now no longer a candidate member of the party. Reckon that your probationary period has already ended. Because every moment of your stay in space can be counted as years. You have already completed your candidate's proba-

tionary period for party membership and have shown that you are a real Communist and can hold high the banner of Lenin.[1]

TITOV—Many thanks, Nikita Sergeyevich. I shall try to justify the confidences of the party and promise to continue to fulfill the lofty duties of a party member as I have fulfilled them today.

KHRUSHCHEV—Very well. I congratulate you and your parents, your father and mother, for having brought you up as such a brave Soviet man.

TITOV—Thank you, Nikita Sergeyevich.

KHRUSHCHEV—We shall congratulate and thank your parents at a personal meeting in Moscow. We shall give you a . . . welcome . . . as a whole people, as a whole country.

TITOV—I sincerely thank you, Nikita Sergeyevich and I thank the party and the Government.

KHRUSHCHEV—How is your wife? She knew about your flight? I am asking you such questions because I have already asked such a question of the first cosmonaut, Yuri Gagarin.

TITOV—Yes, she knew.

KHRUSHCHEV—And did she approve of this flight?

TITOV—At first she did not quite approve and later she did.

KHRUSHCHEV—This is wholly understandable. She wanted her husband to perform such an exploit. This exploit was such that she might be deprived of her husband.

[1] Said Titov at a subsequent interview: "In his statement, Nikita Sergeyevich Khrushchev said that I . . . was worthy of being a member of the Party. I was very much moved and proud of that recommendation, but the next day, when I got home and opened the paper, and read the Central Committee Decision to admit me into the Party, my hands dropped with surprise and emotion. I had not expected that, nor even dreamt of it." (Gherman Titov, *First Man to Spend a Day in Space*, New York, 1962, p. 108.)

* SOURCE: Text of a telephone conversation as reported by Tass and transmitted by United Press International from its Moscow Bureau, August 7, 1961.

And therefore apparently she could have had some hesitation. This is a human hesitation and is understandable to all people. . . .

TITOV—Thank you, Nikita Sergeyevich.

KHRUSHCHEV—I kiss you and embrace you by telephone for the time being. But when we meet you at the airport I'll embrace you in a fatherly manner as the dearest and beloved son of our country.

TITOV—Thank you Nikita Sergeyevich, thank you very much.

Judgment Day for the Stalinists*

Many comrades who have spoken here have wrathfully condemned the subversive, anti-Party activities of the handful of factionalists headed by Molotov, Kaganovich and Malenkov. Our entire Party and the whole people have rejected these renegades who strove to re-establish the harmful methods prevailing at the time of the personality cult. They wanted matters to go back to those trying times for our Party and our country when nobody was safe from violence and repressions. We definitely reject such methods of so-called leadership.

Is it possible for different opinions to arise within the Party at various periods in its activities, especially at turning points? Yes, it is. What is to be done with those who express opinions differing from those of the others? We are against repressions; we stand for Leninist methods of persuasion and explanation. (*Applause.*)

In the years that followed Lenin's death, the Leninist standards of Party life were grossly distorted in the conditions of the cult of Stalin's person. He grossly violated the Leninist principles of leadership and permitted arbitrary methods and abuses of power.

Stalin could look at a comrade sitting at the same table and say: "There's something shifty about your eyes today." After that you could consider that the comrade whose

* SOURCE: N. S. Khrushchev, "Concluding Speech at the 22nd Congress of the C.P.S.U., October 27, 1961," *The Road To Communism, Documents of the 22nd Congress of the Communist Party of the Soviet Union, October 17-31, 1961*, Moscow, 1961, pp. 341-351. (Adapted and abridged.)

eyes had supposedly been shifty had become a suspect.

Comrade Delegates, I wish to inform the Congress of the reaction of the anti-Party group to the proposal to discuss at the Twentieth Congress the question of the abuses of power in the period of the personality cult.

Molotov, Kaganovich, Malenkov, Voroshilov and others raised categorical objections. In answer to their objections, they were told that if they opposed the raising of the question we would let the Congress delegates decide. We did not doubt that the Congress would be in favour of discussing the question. Only then did they agree, and the question of the personality cult was submitted to the Twentieth Party Congress. But the factionalists did not cease their struggle even after the Congress; they did their utmost to hamper an investigation of the abuses of power, fearing that their role as accomplices in mass repressions would be revealed.

Mass repressions began after the assassination of Kirov. Considerable effort will still be required to establish who was guilty of Kirov's death. The deeper we look into the records, the greater the number of questions that crop up. There is the fact that Kirov's assassin had on two previous occasions been detained by security people in the vicinity of Smolny and had been found to be carrying a weapon. But someone had ordered his release on both occasions. Then this armed man turned up in Smolny, in the very corridor along which Kirov usually passed. And it somehow happened that

at the moment of the assassination the chief
of Kirov's bodyguard was far behind him,
although, according to his instructions, he
had no right to lag so far behind the man
he was guarding.

There is another very strange fact. When
the chief of Kirov's bodyguard was being
taken for interrogation—he was to have
been interrogated by Stalin, Molotov and
Voroshilov—an accident was deliberately
staged on the way, as the driver of the car
afterwards said, by those who should have
taken the guard chief for interrogation.
They then reported that the chief of the
bodyguard had been killed in the accident,
although he was actually killed by those
escorting him.

That is how the man who guarded Kirov
was killed. Afterwards the people who had
killed him were shot. This was obviously
a deliberate crime. Who could have committed it?

Comrades, it is our duty to make a
thorough examination of cases of this sort
that are due to abuse of power. It is our
duty to establish the truth now, because the
longer the time that passes since those
events, the more difficult it will be to re-
establish the truth. You cannot bring back
the dead, but the facts must be faithfully
recorded in the history of the Party to prevent for ever the recurrence of similar cases.
(*Stormy, prolonged applause.*)

You may imagine how difficult it was to
solve such problems when there were people on the Presidium of the Central Committee who had themselves been guilty of
abusing power, of mass repressions. They
stubbornly opposed all measures for the exposure of the personality cult. Naturally,
they did not want to examine such matters.
Thousands of absolutely innocent people
perished. Many leading Party, government
and army people lost their lives.

Of course, those people on the Presidium
of the Central Committee who were responsible for breaches of legality, for mass repressions, tried hard to prevent the exposure
of the arbitrary acts perpetrated in the period of the cult of the individual. Then
they launched an anti-Party factional struggle against the Central Committee leader-

ship, concentrating their fire mainly against
me as First Secretary of the Central Committee, since I, by virtue of my duties, was
the one who had to raise those questions. I
had to take their blows and counter them.
(*Stormy, prolonged applause.*)

The members of an anti-Party factional
group wanted to seize the leadership in the
Party and the country and remove those
comrades who had made exposures of the
criminal acts. The anti-Party group wanted
to put Molotov in the leadership. If they
had done so, there would certainly have
been no exposures.

Even after the Twentieth Congress, which
condemned the cult of the individual, the
anti-Party group did everything it could
to prevent the exposures from going any
further. Molotov said that in big matters
good and bad things occur. He tried to
justify the acts that had taken place at the
time of the personality cult, and claimed
that such acts are possible and may yet re-
cur. Such was the line taken by the anti-
Party factional group. It was not just an
error. It was a calculated, criminal, ad-
venturous position.

Delegates have spoken here with pain in
their hearts of many innocent victims
among prominent Party officials and statesmen.

Such prominent army leaders as Tukhachevsky, Yakir, Uborevich, and others were
victims of the repressions. They were military men who had great services to their
credit.

Many splendid commanders and political
officers of the Red Army met their deaths.
Here among the delegates there are comrades—I withhold their names in order not
to cause them pain—who spent many years
in prison. They were "persuaded," persuaded by certain methods, that they were
either German, British, or some other spies.
Some of them "confessed." There were
even cases when some of those people, on
being told that the charge of espionage had
been withdrawn, themselves insisted on
their previous depositions; they thought it
better to stick to their false depositions in
order the sooner to put an end to their
torment, the sooner to go to their death.

That is what the personality cult means. That was the meaning of the actions of Molotov and the others who wanted to restore the evil practices of [that] period.

I knew Comrade Yakir very well. I also knew Tukhachevsky, but not as well as I knew Yakir. During a conference in Alma Ata this year his son, who is working in Kazakhstan, came to me. He asked me about his father. What could I say to him? When we were examining these cases in the Presidium of the Central Committee and were informed that neither Tukhachevsky, Yakir, nor Uborevich had committed any crimes against the Party and the state, we asked Molotov, Kaganovich and Voroshilov: "Are you in favour of their rehabilitation?"

"Yes, we are," they answered.

"But it was you who executed those people," we said indignantly. "When were you following the dictates of your conscience, then or now?"

They did not answer that question. And they never will. What can they say?

In his speech to this Congress, Comrade Shelepin told you how these fine representatives of the Communist Party in the Red Army were killed. He also quoted a letter from Comrade Yakir to Stalin. It should be said that at one time Stalin had a lot of respect for Yakir.

I can add that at the moment Yakir was shot he shouted, "Long live the Party, long live Stalin!"

He had so much faith in the Party, in Stalin, that it never occurred to him that the lawlessness was deliberate. He thought that enemies had infiltrated the organs of the People's Commissariat of the Interior. When Stalin was told how Yakir had behaved before his death, he cursed Yakir.[1]

The fate of the brother of Stalin's first wife, Alyosha Svanidze, who was less known to the bulk of our Party membership, was also a tragic one. He was a veteran Bolshevik, but Beria, by means of various machinations, made a case to the effect that Svanidze had been planted near

[1] About the time of the purges, Khrushchev described Yakir as "riff-raff." See *Pravda*, June 9, 1935.

Stalin by the German secret service, although he was Stalin's very close friend. And Svanidze was shot. Before he was shot, he was told that Stalin had said that if he asked forgiveness he would be pardoned. When Stalin's words were repeated to Svanidze, he asked: "Why should I ask forgiveness? I have not committed any crime." He was shot. After Svanidze's death Stalin said: "See how proud he is, he died but wouldn't ask forgiveness." It never occurred to Stalin that Svanidze was, above all, an honest man.

And that is how many absolutely innocent people died.

That is what the cult of the individual means. That is why we cannot show the slightest tolerance towards abuses of power.

Comrades, the presidium of this Congress has received letters from veteran Bolsheviks, who write that in the period of the personality cult outstanding Party leaders and statesmen, such true Leninists as Comrades Chubar, Kosior, Rudzutak, Postyshev, Eiche, Voznesensky, Kuznetsov and others, were done to death although they were innocent.

The comrades propose perpetuating the memory of those prominent Party and Government leaders who fell victim to the unwarranted repressions in the period of the personality cult.

We consider this a fit and proper proposal. (*Stormy, prolonged applause.*) It would be advisable to instruct the Central Committee that will be elected by the Twenty-Second Congress to take a positive decision on this question. Perhaps a monument should be erected in Moscow to perpetuate the memory of comrades who fell victim to arbitrary practices. (*Applause.*)

The Twentieth Congress of our Party condemned the cult of the individual, restored justice and demanded the elimination of the distortions that had taken place. The Central Committee adopted decisive measures to prevent a return to arbitrary and unlawful practices. The anti-Party group consisting of Molotov, Kaganovich, Malenkov and others tried hard to prevent the implementation of these measures.

The factionalists made an attempt to seize

the leadership and divert the Party from the Leninist path. They intended to deal harshly with those who upheld the policy mapped out by the Twentieth Congress. When the anti-Party group was defeated, its members thought they would be dealt with as they had dealt with people at the time of the personality cult, and as they would have liked to deal with those who approved of the restoration of Leninist standards in Party life.

A conversation I had with Kaganovich was typical. Kaganovich telephoned me and said:

"Comrade Khrushchev, I have known you for many years. Please do not let me be dealt with as people were dealt with under Stalin."

Kaganovich knew very well how people were dealt with at the time, because he himself had taken part in dealing with them.

I replied:

"Comrade Kaganovich, your words are further proof of the methods by which you intended to achieve your infamous aims. You wanted to turn the country back to the methods that prevailed at the time of the cult of the individual. You wanted to use violence against people. You measure others with your own yardstick. But you are making a mistake. We act, and shall continue to act, strictly in conformity with Leninist principles. You will be given a job," I said to Kaganovich, "and you will have the opportunity of working and living in peace if you work honestly as all Soviet people do."

That was the kind of conversation I had with Kaganovich. We Communists-Leninists must never allow ourselves to abuse power. We firmly adhere to Party-Leninist positions and believe in the strength and unity of our Party, and that the people are solid behind the Party. (*Stormy applause.*)

The Shape of Things to Come*

The Tasks of the Party in Improving the Living Standard of the People

The heroic labour of the Soviet people has produced a powerful and versatile economy. There is now every possibility to improve rapidly the living standard of the entire population—the workers, peasants, and intellectuals. The C.P.S.U. sets the historically important task of *achieving in the Soviet Union a living standard higher than that of any of the capitalist countries*.

This task will be effected by: (a) raising individual payment according to the quantity and quality of work done, coupled with reduction of retail prices and abolition of taxes paid by the population; (b) increase of the public consumption fund intended for the satisfaction of the requirements of members of society irrespective of the quan-

* SOURCE: *Programme of the Communist Party of the Soviet Union, Adopted by the 22nd Congress of the C.P.S.U. October 31, 1961*, Moscow, 1961, pp. 83-91.

tity and quality of their labour, that is, free of charge (education, medical treatment, pensions, maintenance of children at children's institutions, transition to cost-free use of public amenities, etc.).

The rise of the real incomes of the population will be outstripped by a rapid increase in the amount of commodities and services, and by extensive construction of dwellings and cultural and service buildings.

Soviet people will be more prosperous than working people in the developed capitalist countries even if average incomes will be equal, because in the Soviet Union the national income is distributed in the interests of all members of society and there are no parasitical classes as in the bourgeois countries who appropriate and squander immense wealth plundered from millions of working people.

The Party acts upon Lenin's thesis that communist construction must be based upon the principle of material incentive. In the coming twenty years payment according to one's work will remain the principal source for satisfying the material and cultural needs of the working people.

The disparity between high and comparatively low incomes must be steadily reduced. Increasingly greater numbers of unskilled personnel will become skilled, and the diminishing difference in proficiency and labour productivity will be accompanied by a steady reduction of disparities in the level of pay. As the living standard of the entire population rises, low income levels will approach the higher, and the disparity between the incomes of peasants and workers, low-paid and high-paid personnel and of the populations of different parts of the country, will gradually shrink.

At the same time, as the country advances towards communism, personal needs will be increasingly met out of public consumption funds, whose rate of growth will exceed the rate of growth of payments for labour. The transition to communist distribution will be completed after the principle of distribution according to one's work will outlive itself, that is, when there will be an abundance of material and cultural wealth and labour will become a prime necessity of life for all members of society.

* * *

Solution of the Housing Problem and Improvement of Living Conditions. . . . In the . . . the first decade an end will be put to the housing shortage in the country. Families that are still housed in overcrowded and substandard dwellings will get new flats. At the end of the second decade, every family . . . will have a comfortable flat. . . . Peasant houses . . . will . . . give place to new modern dwellings. . . . In the course of the second decade housing will gradually become rent-free. . . .

Reduction of Working Hours and the Further Improvement of Working Conditions. In the coming ten years the country will go over to a *six-hour working day* with one day off a week, or a *35-hour working week* with two days off, and on . . . enterprises with harmful working conditions to a five-hour working day. . . . A still shorter working week will be begun in the second decade.

The Soviet Union will thus have the world's shortest . . . working day. Working people will have much more leisure time, and this will add to their opportunities of improving their cultural and technical level. . . .

Health Services and Measures for Increased Longevity. The socialist state is the only state which undertakes to protect and . . . improve the health of the whole population. . . . The needs [for] all forms of . . . medical services will be met in full. . . . Special emphasis must be laid on . . . mother-and-child health institutions. . . .

Improvement of Family Living Conditions and of the Position of Women. Maintenance of Children and Incapacitated People at Public Expense. The remnants of the unequal position of women in domestic life must be totally eliminated. Social and living conditions must be provided to enable women to combine happy motherhood with increasingly active and creative participation in social labour and social activities, and in scientific and artistic pursuits. Women must be given relatively lighter and yet sufficiently well-paid jobs. Confinement leave will be extended.

It is essential to provide conditions to reduce and lighten the domestic work of women, and later to make possible the replacement of domestic work by public forms of satisfying the daily needs of the family. Up-to-date inexpensive domestic machinery, appliances, and electrical devices will be made extensively available for this purpose; the needs of the population in service establishments will be fully met in the next few years.

* * *

The set programme can be fulfilled with success under conditions of peace. Complications in the international situation and the resultant necessity to increase defence expenditures may hold up the fulfilment of the plans for raising the living standard of the people. An enduring normalisation of international relations, reduction of military expenditures and, in particular, the realisation of general and complete disarmament under an appropriate agreement between countries, would make it possible greatly to surpass the plans for raising the people's living standard.

New Mood in Moscow*

The City in the Morning

This poem by Evtushenko, appearing in the Moscow Literary Gazette, *gave literary expression to the growing spirit of freedom:*

All is as before . . . in this city
Stores, bathhouses, factories . . .
Fat, pompous pigeons,
Cycling . . . boys
And the special accent of Moscovites . . .
All is as before, and yet there
Is something new, whether in quiet or in
    conversation.
And some sort of great changes are
    occurring in this city.

Early in the morning . . .
On the trolley I climb with my uneaten loaf
    of bread
I see something new and decisive
Among the students with strained eyes.

Housepainters, doctors, and oily locksmiths
Go to their places of work as before,
But . . . they chat like people close to one
    another.
In that they argue heatedly over the
    newspaper;
In that, like a student whose forehead is
    pushed to the wall,
I understand that something is thoroughly
    finished.

It is clear that there is something new and
    great.
I notice that people have become more open;

* SOURCE: *Literaturnaya Gazeta,* Moscow, July 17, 1962.

People have become firmer with respect to
    baseness and falseness;
People have become more ironical, and more
    assured, and better, and more attentive
    than before.
I do not agree with such a designation as
    "The Thaw."
This is altogether springtime.
The way is very difficult.
And it's not without reason that some still
    have fear:
Those who grew accustomed only to
    hypocrisy and cowardice.
This city remembers "the black ravens."
It recalls the investigations, interrogations
    and the arrests. . . .
The city feels a responsibility for the future.
The city has reason to remember its past.

This city does not doubt itself.
It will not allow the dark shadows to rise
    again.
In it the memory of 1917 will be eternal.
In it there will never be another 1937.

Some say to me . . .
Why are you always so angry?
I was once good-natured,
But not for long.
Life smashed me and hit me in the teeth;
I was like a stupid puppy.
Struck, I offered my cheek again. . . .
And I now speak to you of evil.
When before a meeting, it was whispered
    to me: "Stop it!"
You are young, and you better just write,
And don't rush to thrust yourself into fights
    so soon."
But I refuse to retreat a single step:
To be bad for untruth—is to be good.
I am a communist in my very essence.

Communism commands me to become an-
    grier and angrier
With all that stands in its way.
And I will not be thrown off by advice.

There is no more of the former timidity in
    me.
It is interesting to be alive when you are
    angry.

Exit Khrushchev*

MOSCOW, Oct. 24—Of the many impressions a foreigner has had in Moscow
these last days none are more poignant than
these two:

—The eerie way in which Mr. Khrushchev, who was one of the most physical men
in world politics, became an "un-person"
overnight.

—The uncanny outward apathy with
which Muscovites have reacted to the news
that has shaken every other capital of the
world.

Mr. Khrushchev's last public appearance
was on a blurred television screen on Oct.
12, when he talked to the three cosmonauts
who had just gone into orbit. He bobbed up
and down in unashamed excitement and
pride. As usual, he was full of himself. He
was keeping in shape, he told the cosmonauts, because "we are planning a big home-
coming celebration for you."

Two days later Mr. Khrushchev had
ceased to be a party leader.

[His] removal was carried out smoothly
in the party Presidium and Central Committee. But in the streets the execution was
not quite as neat. There, the men in the
most exposed positions were those in charge
of hanging pictures of the leaders in all the
right places in preparation for the return
of the cosmonauts. The crucial hours found
these men almost literally half way up their
ladders with Mr. Khrushchev's pictures on
their shoulders and not knowing whether to
go up or down. In the end, of course, all the
pictures of the ousted Premier came down.

Were people afraid to talk? Soviet citizens
say no. Then they go on to give explanations. "Things are complicated, and one
wants to think them over before sounding
off. . . . The changes might affect one's
job. . . . There is a certain discipline that
we are used to. . . . About things like these
one talks to one's friends and certainly not
to foreigners."

When Mr. Khrushchev was still in power
one might have thought that he was gen-
uinely popular. The people waved at him on
parades even if they did not have to. He
made them smile with his homilies and
improvised speeches. A few days after his
political destruction the Moscow crowds
waved and smiled just as pleasantly at those
who had destroyed him.

The most precise formula of how he is
seen now by politically articulate Moscovites
perhaps is this:

He has done many good things; he has
been for peace; he has brought a new era to
the Soviet Union; but he has often been
vulgar and made a spectacle of himself and
of Russia; he has become a czar; he has put
his family members in high places; and he
was too fond of traveling abroad and being
feted by foreigners.

These are more or less the points on
which he is now being denounced by his
successors. But the same evaluation can be
heard so frequently also from plain citizens
that a foreigner may conclude that the official explanation does reflect the feelings of
the people.

* SOURCE: H. Tanner, "Khrushchev Ouster: Reaction in Moscow," *The New York Times*, October 25,
1964. (Adapted and abridged.)

Name Index